Matthew Brown Riddle

The Gospel according to Mark

Vol. 2

Matthew Brown Riddle

The Gospel according to Mark
Vol. 2

ISBN/EAN: 9783337714598

Printed in Europe, USA, Canada, Australia, Japan

Cover: Foto ©ninafisch / pixelio.de

More available books at **www.hansebooks.com**

THE
INTERNATIONAL REVISION COMMENTARY

ON THE

NEW TESTAMENT

BASED UPON THE REVISED VERSION OF 1881

BY

ENGLISH AND AMERICAN SCHOLARS

AND MEMBERS OF THE REVISION COMMITTEE

EDITED BY

PHILIP SCHAFF, D.D., LL.D.

*Professor of Sacred Literature in the Union Theological Seminary of New York,
President of the American Committee on Revision.*

VOL. II

THE GOSPEL ACCORDING TO MARK.

NEW YORK
CHARLES SCRIBNER'S SONS
743 & 745 BROADWAY
1881

COPYRIGHT 1881, BY
CHARLES SCRIBNER'S SONS
(*All Rights Reserved.*)

PREFACE.

This is the beginning of a series of popular commentaries on the New Testament, based upon the Revised Version of 1881, to be issued in small handy volumes. It is a cheap and abridged edition of the author's 'Illustrated Popular Commentary,' of which two large volumes have appeared, and two others are nearly completed. The large size and costly outfit of that book limits its circulation. By omitting the illustrations, the general introduction, the emendations of the Old Version, and the parallel passages, the price of the book has been reduced, in the hope of enlarging its field of usefulness. The text is, of course, that of the Revised Version, which hereafter must be the basis of every popular commentary. The American readings and renderings have been, for convenience sake, transferred to the foot of the page, with the exception of those changes which refer to classes of passages.

The new title which is to distinguish this edition from the 'Illustrated Commentary,' involves no pretension, but simply expresses a fact. It *is* an international and interdenominational work of British and American Scholars and Revisers. The majority of contributors were officially connected with one of the two Companies for the Revision of the New Testament, and the others were in full sympathy with the work. Moreover the aim of this commentary falls in with the International Sunday School Lesson system which has done so much in a short time to promote the popular study of the Bible throughout the English speaking world.

The plan of this commentary was conceived about thirty years ago. Its execution has occupied much of the time and strength of the contributors during the last twelve years. It was matured with the Revision in the Jerusalem Chamber and the Bible House. Its object is to make the results of the Revision available for the benefit of the rising generation of all denominations.

May the blessing of the God of the Bible rest upon this and upon every other effort to make its meaning clearer to the understanding and dearer to the heart of the reader.

PHILIP SCHAFF.

New York, October, 1881.

INTRODUCTION.

§ 1. *The Author of the Gospel according to Mark.*

This Gospel was written by MARK, or JOHN MARK, as he is also called (Acts 12: 12, 25; 15: 37). Its genuineness, attested by explicit testimony, has been little disputed; while its brevity and freshness have led to the opinion that it was the primitive Gospel. The theory that it once existed in briefer form and was enlarged to its present size by additions from various sources, is unsupported by evidence. (On the conclusion, see chap. 16: 9.)

MARK, or JOHN MARK, was a Jew, probably a native of Jerusalem, where his mother Mary resided (Acts 12: 12). She was a person of some repute among the early Christians, as Peter, when released from prison, naturally went to her house. Mark was probably converted by that Apostle (1 Pet. 5: 13), and the minute account of the young man who followed Jesus on the night of the betrayal (Mark 14: 51, 52), together with the omission of the name, points to the Evangelist as the person concerned. Going with Paul and Barnabas (his 'cousin,' Col. 4: 10), as their 'attendant' (Acts 13: 5), on their first missionary journey, he left them at Perga (13: 13), and in consequence became the occasion of 'sharp contention' between them (15: 36–40). Afterwards in Rome he appears as a companion of Paul (Col. 4: 10; Philem. 24). He was with Peter when that Apostle wrote his first Epistle (1 Pet. 5: 13), but was at Ephesus with Timothy at a date probably later (2 Tim. 4: 11).

Trustworthy details respecting his after life are wanting, but ancient writers agree in speaking of him as the 'interpreter' of Peter. This may mean that he translated for the Apostle, but more probably that he wrote his Gospel in close conformity to Peter's preaching.

§ 2. *The Character of the Gospel according to Mark.*

The close relation of the Evangelist to Peter is confirmed by the Gospel itself. Many events are recorded, as if from the lips of an eye-witness. Some suggest that the Gospel is based upon a diary of Peter. The style shows the influence of that Apostle. Peter's address to Cornelius (Acts 10) has been called the Gospel of Mark in a nutshell. A comparison of the accounts in Matt. 16: 13–23 and Mark 8: 27–33, indicates that Peter himself (or an enemy of his, which is impossible) occasioned the omission of the praise ('Thou art Peter,' etc.), and yet the insertion of the rebuke ('Get thee behind me, Satan,' etc.). Mark alone mentions the two cock-crowings, (chap. 14: 72), thus increasing the guilt of Peter's denial. Even if not submitted to the Apostle for approval (as Eusebius asserts on the authority of Clement of Alexandria), the faithfulness of the history may well be accepted.

The Gospel begins with the baptism of John, gives few discourses, dealing mainly with facts arranged in chronological order (see § 5), narrating these in brief, rapid sketches with graphic power. No subjective sentiments or reflections are interwoven (see, however, chap. 7: 19). Special prominence is given to the periods of rest and withdrawal on the part of our Lord, as if to prepare for fresh conflict and victory. Hence this Gospel is said to present the Messiah as the powerful King. Peculiar to this Evangelist are the repeated use of 'straightway,' and of the present tense in narratives, the prominence given to the power over evil spirits, such touches and incidents as the following: that Jesus was 'in the *hinder* part of the ship, *asleep on the boat cushion*') (4: 38); that 'He looked round about on them *with anger*' (3: 5); beholding the rich young man 'He loved him' (10: 21); the vivid details of the escape of the 'young man' (14: 51, 52). A few miracles and one parable also are found only here. These peculiarities serve to show both independence of the other Evangelists and the close relation to some eye-witness.

Although written in Greek, the Gospel was designed for Roman readers, and is especially adapted to their mind, so easily impressed by exhibitions of energy and power. It exhibits Christ as the spiritual conqueror and wonder-worker, the Lion of the tribe of Judah, filling the people with amazement and fear. Mark introduces several Latin terms; he even uses the Roman names of coins instead of the Greek for Greek (12 : 42), which Luke does not, and notices that Simon of Cyrene was 'the father of Alexander and Rufus' (15 : 21), who were probably Christians in Rome (Rom. 15 : 13). It is therefore most likely that the Gospel was written in that city, before the destruction of Jerusalem, whether before or after the Gospel of Luke, is uncertain (see § 3).

Mark may be said to form the connecting link between Matthew and Luke, Peter and Paul, the Jewish and the Gentile Christianity. But his Gospel is independent of the other two. Its similarity to Matthew has not only led the mass of readers to undervalue it, but exposed it to numerous slight alterations on the part of the early copyists. Precisely where Mark's peculiarities were most apparent, these attempts to produce literal correspondence with Matthew have been most frequent. Modern textual criticism has achieved here a proportionately greater work of restoration. Well nigh every verse of this Gospel as presented in the Revised Version contains some slight emendation which is due to a careful comparison with the earlier manuscripts and versions. In this commentary special attention will be called only to the more important corrections of the Greek text.

§ 3. *Time and Place of Writing.*

As already intimated, it is most likely that this Gospel was written at Rome. The date must be placed before the destruction of Jerusalem, an event which is only referred to as predicted. A more precise designation of the date involves protracted discussion in regard to the relation of the three earlier Gospels to each other. (These Gospels are usually termed 'Synoptical,' and their writers the Synoptists.)

Briefly stated, the case stands as follows:

According to the testimony of the earliest Christian fathers, Matthew wrote first, then Luke, and Mark third. This testimony is, of course, rejected by those who hold theories respecting the origin of these Gospels calling for another order. But even if we leave these theories out of the discussion, we cannot receive this testimony as conclusive.

If any Gospel shows internal evidence of priority, it is that of Mark. If it were a matter of importance to know what was the outline of the so-called traditional Gospel, we infer that it coincided in chronological order and salient features with the briefest, most vivacious Synoptical Gospel, which is most accurate in its order, and in its style shows most marks of originality. If, however, Matthew wrote in Hebrew, the priority must be conceded to his Gospel. The priority of Luke is inferred by many, from its relation to the book of Acts, which refers to it as a former treatise. The latter seems to have been penned shortly after the date when its narrative closes (A. D. 63). It is asserted that neither Matthew nor Mark could have written before this time, hence Luke wrote first.

It appears then, that patristic authority favors the priority of Matthew, internal evidence that of Mark, and the inference just suggested that of Luke. In other words, we are left in uncertainty on this point, which loses its importance, if we accept the view that the Synoptists wrote independently of each other. If a definite theory is necessary, it may be surmised that Luke wrote during the first imprisonment of Paul (A. D. 61–63), that Mark penned his Gospel immediately after Paul's temporary release, while Matthew prepared the Greek copy of his narrative about the same time, to meet the wants of Greek-speaking Christians, who had already become so numerous.

§ 4. *Chronology.*

In the Gospel according to Mark there are very few deviations from the chronological order. Hence it is the best Gospel to study for the purpose of fixing in the mind the outline of the history of our Lord's life on earth. The details peculiar to the other Gospels can then be readily fitted into their appropriate places in the narrative. The dates of our Lord's birth, baptism and death must first be fixed, and then a theory adopted in regard to the length of His ministry. With these points settled, the Gospel of Mark becomes an intelligible history in its chronological outline.

The theory adopted in this commentary places the date of the birth of Jesus at B. C. 5, year of Rome 749, probably in December; that of His baptism in A. D. 27, year of Rome 780, in January; that of His death on April 7, A. D. 30, year of Rome, 783; thus accepting a three years' ministry.

If the ministry were briefer, the probable dates would be: Birth, B. C. 4; Baptism, early in A. D. 28; Crucifixion, A. D. 30. See Lange on John. Other opinions are numerous.

It must be admitted that the data for a comparison with profane history are not sufficient to fix the dates with certainty, and the Gospels themselves do not seem to aim at chronological accuracy. The statements respecting the course of Abijah (Luke 1:5-8), the star of the Magi (Matt. 2: 2-7), the enrolment under Quirinius (Luke 2: 2), and the death of Herod (Matt. 2: 19), are of value in discussing the date of the birth of Jesus. The references to secular rulers in Luke 3: 1 give a clue to the time of His baptism, while the details respecting the last Passover, in all the Gospels, are used to fix the date of His death. The length of His ministry affects the order as well as the chronology, and the controversy turns on the view taken of John 5: 1. If the feast of the Jews there referred to was the Passover, then there were four Passovers during our Lord's ministry; if it was the feast of Purim, or some other feast, then there were but three Passovers, *i. e.*, the length of the ministry was only a fraction more than two years, and the events extended over two years by the other theory are to be compressed into one. The beginning of the last year is not in dispute.

The most important point is the date of our Lord's birth. This question is confused in many minds by the ever-present fact of computation from the so-called Christian era, which has only traditional authority and value, having been first used by Dionysius Exiguus, a learned monk, in the sixth century, who erroneously fixed the year of the incarnation as coincident with the year of Rome 754. In all discussions of Gospel chronology the year of Rome should be indicated to prevent further confusion from reckoning before and after Christ. (B. C. 1=753 of Rome; A. D. 1=754 of Rome.)

It is certain (from Matt. 2: 16) that Herod was still living when Christ was born. Nearly all chronologists agree in fixing the date of his death at (year of Rome) 750, just before the Passover, that is, four years before our Christian era. Our Lord's birth, therefore, could not have taken place later than the beginning of the winter of (year of Rome) 750. Chronologists differ as to the year: Bengel, Wieseler, Lange, Gresswell, Ellicott, Andrews, fix it at (year of Rome) 750; Petavius, Ussher, Browne, 749; Kepler, 748; Ideler, Wurm, Jarvis, Alford, and the French Benedictines, 747; Zumpt, 747 or 748, *i. e.*, 7 or 8 years before the common era. For particulars, see Wieseler (*Chronology of the Gospels*), Zumpt (*The Year of Christ's Birth*), Andrews (*Life of our Lord*), Robinson (*Harmony of the Gospels*), and Farrar (*Life of Christ*), and the Bible Dictionaries.

Since Jesus was 'about thirty years of age' (Luke 3: 23), when He began to teach, immediately after His baptism, the date of this introduction to the Jewish people may be fixed (as above) in A. D. 27 or 28. The date of the crucifixion is also variously assigned from 781 to 786, but the great majority of modern authors agree upon 783, A. D. 30.

The question respecting the length of the ministry is not a vital one, but derives some importance from its relation to questions of harmony. There is a general agreement as to the order of events up to the first Passover, and the return to Galilee through Samaria (in December after the first Passover; comp. John 4: 35). It is also clear that the feeding of the five thousand narrated by all the Evangelists (Matt. 14: 13–21; Mark 6: 30–44; Luke 9: 10–17; John 6: 1–14) occurred near the beginning of the last year of our Lord's ministry. The disputed order is therefore respecting the events recorded in Matt. 4: 13 to 14: 12; Mark 1: 14 to 6: 29; Luke 4: 14 to 9: 9; John 4: 1 to 5: 47. Some of the incidents mentioned by Luke (chaps. 11–13) are also in dispute.

The theory which accepts a two years' ministry compresses all the events in the passages above mentioned into one year, or more accurately into a few months (December A. D. 28 to April A. D. 29), usually regarding the feast mentioned in John 5: 1 as that of Purim, and not as the second Passover, agreeing, however, in general with the order advocated by Robinson and others. Lange, Ellicott, and many others, uphold this view.

The best known theory is that of Robinson, who accepts a three years' ministry, placing in the first year (between December and April), in addition to the events mentioned by John, those mentioned by Mark in chaps. 1 : 14–2 : 14. Matthew narrates the same occurrences without regard to chronological order; hence in this part of the history it is of great importance to follow Mark closely. The second year opens with John 5 : 1; Matt. 12 : 1; Mark 2 : 23; Luke 6 : 1.

There is still a third view, upheld by Lichtenstein and others, and fully detailed by Andrews. Accepting a three years' ministry, it places the whole of the Galilean ministry after the second Passover (John 5 : 1). This affects the position of Mark 1 : 14–2 : 14, placing this section a few months later. About the previous year the Synoptists are silent. The events of the second year are all those recorded in the passages in dispute. The order is much simplified by this theory. It avoids the great difficulty which has been felt in extending the Synoptical accounts over three years, and also the difficulty common to both the other theories, namely, inserting so important a visit to Jerusalem as that recorded in John v. at a point in the Synoptical narratives where there is nothing to indicate such a visit.

§ 5. *Plan of the Gospel.*

The Gospel follows the chronological order, with but two deviations. The section telling of the feast and discourse at the house of Levi (chap. 2 : 15–22) properly belongs after the return from Gadara (chap. 5 : 21). and the anointing at Bethany (chap. 14 : 3–9) would have its more exact position immediately before the entry into Jerusalem (chap. 11 : 1, etc.). The latter point is open to more serious doubt than the former.

In view of this straightforward narrative, presenting so few incidents peculiar to itself, it is difficult to arrange the contents on any other plan than the chronological one. Attempts have been made to analyze the whole with reference to the periods of withdrawal and rest before conflict and victory, which Mark emphasizes. But Lange well remarks: 'While it was the leading idea of Mark to indicate these contrasts, his Gospel was nevertheless not strictly and uniformly constructed or arranged upon such a plan.' The outline of the narrative may be better indicated as follows:

Year of Rome	A. D.		
780	27 January	I. Our Lord's introduction to His ministry . .	1: 1–13.
781	28 Spring	II. Beginning of the Galilean ministry [1] . . .	1: 14 to 2: 14.
781 782	28 Summer to 29 April	III. Early conflicts and triumphs in Galilee, culminating in the feeding of the five thousand, etc.	2: 15 to 6: 56.
782	29 Summer	IV. The closing of the ministry in Galilee [2] . .	7: 1 to 9: 50.
783	30 March	V. The journey from Perea to Jericho	10: 1–52.
783	30 April 1st	[VI. The anointing at Bethany [3]]	14: 3–9.
783	30 April 2–7	VII. From the entry to Jerusalem to the burial of Jesus	11: 1 to 15: 47.
783	30 April 19 to May 18	VIII. Resurrection and Ascension	16:

[1] This includes all that Robinson places before the second Passover, *i. e.*, from December, A. D. 27 to April, A. D. 28.

[2] The two years' theory places the entire narrative from chap. 1: 14 to 6: 56 between December, A. D. 28 and April, A. D. 29.

[3] This brief section, and chap. 2: 15–22, form the only deviations in this Gospel from the chronological order.

THE GOSPEL ACCORDING TO
S. MARK.

1:1   The beginning of the ¹gospel of Jesus Christ, ²the Son of God.
   2   Even as it is written in ³Isaiah the prophet,

¹ Or, *good tidings.*   ² Some ancient authorities omit *the Son of God.*   ³ Some ancient authorities read *in the prophets.*

Chap. I: 1. THE TITLE. The Evangelist, intending to narrate our Lord's ministry, without dwelling upon the earlier part of His life, prefaces the whole with a *title* (ver. 1), which is followed by a reference to the preaching of John the Baptist (vers. 2-8). This was necessary, since, in one sense, John's appearance was 'the beginning of the gospel of Jesus Christ.' A brief narration of the baptism of Jesus (vers. 10, 11) and of the temptation (vers. 12, 13) completes Mark's account of the preliminary events.

Ver. 1. **The beginning of the gospel.** This is regarded by some as the title of the whole book: here begins the Gospel. But the word 'gospel' in the New Testament is not applied to a book. It is used to translate a Greek word which at first signified a present in return for good tidings, or a sacrifice offered in thanksgiving for good news, then the good news itself. In the New Testament it always means *the glad tidings of salvation by Jesus Christ.* Others more properly refer the verse to this section alone, which gives the events forming the beginning of the gospel. A period has been placed at the close of the verse to indicate that it is a title. Some, however, connect it with ver. 2: The beginning, etc., as it is written. Others again, with ver. 4: The beginning of the gospel (was this), John did baptize, etc. Still another view puts a period at the close of this verse, but refers it to the ministry of John, taking vers. 2, 3, as a second confirmatory title.—**Of Jesus Christ**, *i. e.*, concerning Jesus Christ, who is the subject of the gospel.—**The Son of God.** Matthew (1:1), writing for the Jews, says: 'the Son of David, the Son of Abraham;' but Mark, writing for Gentile Christians, adds this title, the meaning of which is most fully brought out in the prologue to the Gospel according to John. The phrase 'Son of God' is omitted in the Sinaitic manuscript, but added by the first corrector; some fathers also favor the omission.

Vers. 2-8. THE PREACHING OF JOHN THE BAPTIST.—Parallel passages: Matt. 3: 1-11; Luke 3: 2-16; comp. also John 1: 6-18.

Ver. 2. **In Isaiah the prophet.** The common reading ('prophets') arose from the fact that only the second prophecy (ver. 3) is from Isaiah; the first is from Malachi (3: 1). Isaiah is named, be-

> Behold, I send my messenger before thy face,
> Who shall prepare thy way;
> 3 The voice of one crying in the wilderness,
> Make ye ready the way of the Lord,
> Make his paths straight;
> 4 John came, who baptized in the wilderness and preached the baptism of repentance unto remission

cause his prediction is the more important and striking, and the key-note of Malachi's prophecy. Matthew and Luke quote the latter in a different connection. Here, as in Matt. 11: 10 and Luke 7: 27, the form of the prophecy is changed from 'before my face' to **before thy face.** Our Lord, on His own authority, in the parallel passages, applies the phrase 'my messenger' to John, and 'thy face' to Himself, thus appropriating a pronoun which the Old Testament prophet applied to God. At the time Mark wrote, this application of the passage was well known and accepted by believers. The best authorities omit the phrase: 'before thee.'

Ver. 3. **The voice,** or, 'a voice.' Probably not without allusion to the four hundred years of silence in prophetic revelation since Malachi.—**In the wilderness.** John preached in the wilderness of Judæa (ver. 1); but both here and in the original prophecy there seems to be a thought of the desolate spiritual condition of the Jewish people.—**Make ye ready the way of the Lord,** etc. In Eastern countries roads were made for the approach of a monarch, obstacles were removed, and the paths straightened. The reference evidently is to the Messiah; and it is probable that the coming King is Himself meant by the word 'Lord,' which is Jehovah in the Hebrew. The prophecy could not have been fulfilled when the Jews returned from captivity, for no king was with them. The prophecy is cited by all the Evangelists, and is thus applied, but in John 1: 23 by the Baptist himself. The quotation is from the LXX.

Ver. 4. **John** (Greek, *Johannes;* Hebrew, *Johanan*), meaning, The Lord graciously gave. John was related to the holy family through his mother (Luke 1: 36), and was doubtless aware of the remarkable circumstances attending his own birth and that of Jesus.—**Came.** The connection is with what precedes, as is indicated by the emphatic position of the word translated 'came,' usually rendered: came to pass. 'As it was written,' so it was, so there appeared, or came, the one spoken of, John. The rendering of the A. V. obscures the emphatic word.—**Who baptized—and preached.** The correct reading makes this not so much a declaration of what John did, as an explanation of how he performed the duty of forerunner, according to the prophecy.—**In the wilderness** ('of Judæa,' Matthew). A rocky region east of the Dead Sea. It was not a desert in our sense, but a district little cultivated or inhabited. Compare the prophecy (ver. 3)

5 of sins. And there went out unto him all the country of Judæa, and all they of Jerusalem; and they were

thus literally fulfilled. The time when John began his ministry is stated in Luke 3: 1, 2; the same Evangelist having told of the remarkable circumstances connected with his birth (Luke 1: 5–25, 38–80), which occurred six months before that of our Lord. As the latter was about thirty years of age when he was baptized by John (Luke 3: 23), it is supposed that John made his public appearance at the same Levitical age (Num. 4: 3, 23). The year would then be A. D. 26, year of Rome 779, during the summer. John the Baptist here appears as the preacher of repentance, the connecting link between the old and the new dispensations, fulfilling the prophecies, and beginning the gospel. Contrast the abrupt introduction of John by Matthew and Mark with the full account of Luke (1: 5–80).— **The baptism of repentance.** Baptism was a religious rite, prescribed in the ceremonial law as a sign of moral renewal, and joined with sacrifice. It is said that John derived his baptism from the custom of baptizing proselytes; but it is not certain that this usage prevailed so early. Besides, this would indicate that he was the founder of a new sect, whereas he was the restorer of the ancient ways. By his preaching of repentance, he declared the moral impurity of the people in consequence of their sins; and his baptism of those who confessed their sins (ver. 5) was a sign of their purification. It was therefore a Jewish rite, the final one of the Old Testament economy, pointing to the new dispensation. Christ Himself received the rite (ver. 15) as a Jew, and some who had received John's baptism were re-baptized (Acts 19: 4), hence it was not strictly identical with Christian baptism. As regards the mode, John baptized by immersion in the river Jordan (comp. ver. 10), and this was and is still the custom in the Eastern and the orthodox Russian Church (where immersion is three times repeated), but in some cases affusion and sprinkling were used (certainly in the age of Cyprian, who defended the validity of this mode), and became by and by, in connection with infant baptism, the prevailing mode in the Western, (Latin and Protestant churches), except among the Baptists, who adhere to the original mode as essential. The word 'baptize' is derived from one, meaning 'to dip;' but in Hellenistic Greek it has a wider and more technical meaning of ceremonial purifications by the application of water—**unto remission of sins.** 'Repentance' was the prominent idea of John's baptism, while 'remission of sins' was to come from the Messiah, whose forerunner he was.

Ver. 5. **And all they of Jerusalem**, lit., 'the Jerusalemites.' This expression is peculiar to Mark. These are made prominent among the inhabitants of Judæa, since they lived in the capital city. Comp. Matt. 3: 5.—**Confessing their sins**; since 'repentance' was the main theme of this preparatory ministry.

baptized of him in the river Jordan, confessing their
6 sins. And John was clothed with camel's hair, and
had a leathern girdle about his loins, and did eat
7 locusts and wild honey. And he preached, saying,
There cometh after me he that is mightier than I, the
latchet of whose shoes I am not [1] worthy to stoop down

[1] Gr. *sufficient.*

Ver. 6. **And John was clothed**, etc. The dress and habits of John attest his prophetic character. His dress, like that of Elijah, corresponded with his preaching. The resemblance to Elijah was possibly in the mind of the Evangelist, since, as indicated above, the prophecy of Malachi (respecting Elijah) was accepted by Christians as referring to John.—**Camel's hair.** The coarse cloth woven of the hair shed each year. The fine cloth called camlet is made of the softer hairs. Zech. 14 : 3 suggests that this was the distinctive dress of the Old Testament prophets; but this is not certain. Elijah was thus distinguished (comp. 2 Kings 1 : 8).—**A leathern girdle**; of undressed leather. The austere preacher of repentance was clothed in a manner befitting his message.—**Locusts and wild honey.** The former are eaten by the poorer classes in the East, and the latter was abundant in Palestine. The literal meaning is therefore probable, although a number of fanciful interpretations have been given. John was a Nazarite, who came "neither eating nor drinking" (Matt. 11 : 18), in accordance with his message of repentance. Repentance precedes the sense of pardon; but the promise of a Saviour is the great motive to repentance, then as now (ver. 8).

Ver. 7. **And he preached.** Proclaimed, announced as a herald. All true preaching partakes of this character: it proclaims facts, announces a Person. John was therefore a prophet, announcing the Lord beforehand as well as speaking for God. Mark merely gives the sum of John's preaching as a forerunner of the Messiah.—**There cometh after me he that is,** etc. The A. V. does not give the definite idea of the original. The reference to the Messiah is unmistakable. — **The latchet of whose shoes.** The eastern sandals were fastened with a strap.—**I am not worthy.** The humility of this statement shows the greatness of John (comp. John 3: 30), and how fitted he was to be the forerunner of the meek and lowly Messiah.—**To stoop down**, etc. Matthew (3 : 11) speaks of bearing the shoes; Luke (3 : 16) and John (1 : 27) of unloosing them; but Mark only of stooping down. It is his peculiarity to mention gestures. The perfect independence of the Evangelists thus appears. Nothing could more vividly depict to an eastern audience the inferiority of John the Baptist to the Messiah, than these words. Here the *official* superiority of Christ is spoken of; the superiority of *nature* is declared in the Gospel according to John, chap. 1.

8 and unloose. I baptized you ¹with water; but he shall baptize you ¹with the ²Holy Ghost.
9 And it came to pass in those days, that Jesus came from Nazareth of Galilee, and was baptized of John
10 ³in the Jordan. And straightway coming up out of the water, he saw the heavens rent asunder, and the

¹ Or, *in*.   ² *Holy Spirit:* and so throughout this book.   ³ Gr. *into.*

Ver. 8. **I baptized you with water.** The weight of authority is against 'indeed,' and apparently against 'in' (in both clauses).—**He shall baptize you.** Christ Himself did not baptize (John 4: 2). The contrast is between John's baptism unto repentance, and the spiritual power which Christ would give (not the Christian rite), for full and entire salvation. The second baptism is figurative; hence nothing is suggested for or against the identity of John's baptism and the Christian rite.—**The Holy Ghost.** The third Person of the Trinity; not a contrast between external water and internal spirit. On the day of Pentecost, when the great fulfilment of this prophecy occurred (Acts 2: 3), the Apostles were baptized 'with,' not 'in' the Holy Ghost. 'With fire' is omitted here, because the Evangelist has not mentioned the severity of John's preaching. For fuller accounts of John's preaching, see the parallel passages.

Vers. 9–11. THE BAPTISM OF JESUS.—Parallel passages: Matt. 3: 13-17; Luke 3: 21, 22; comp. John 1: 31–34. The accompanying attestation: to John, a revelation that this was the Christ; to Jesus His Messianic inauguration. It therefore marks an epoch in the Gospel history, and doubtless in the consciousness of the God-Man Himself.

Ver. 9. **In those days.** Probably about six months after John began to preach; comp. ver. 4.—**Jesus came.** Notice this abrupt introduction of the principal Personage of the history (comp. ver. 1).—**From Nazareth of Galilee.** Mark assumes that Nazareth had been His home, and 'of Galilee' was added for the information of the special class of readers for whom he wrote.—**And was baptized of John in the Jordan**; lit., into the Jordan (comp. 'out of the water,' ver. 10), in allusion to the ancient mode of baptism. Jesus, who was sinless, came to a baptism 'unto repentance.' This condescension formed a part of the obedience to the Divine law (comp. Matt. 3: 15), rendered by Him as a member of the Jewish nation. The Jews were baptized in token of uncleanness, so He, 'numbered with the transgressors,' must needs go through the rites and purifications prescribed for them. This act closed the concealed life of quiet subjection and legal submission, opening the public life of mediatorial satisfaction. Hence He was baptized, both to fulfil all righteousness and to receive the Divine attestation; certainly not merely to honor John.

Ver. 10. **Straightway.** A favorite expression in this Gospel.—**He saw,** *i. e.,* Jesus Himself, though John also saw it (John 1: 32).—

11 Spirit as a dove descending upon him: and a voice came out of the heavens, Thou art my beloved Son, in thee I am well pleased.
12 And straightway the Spirit driveth him forth into
13 the wilderness. And he was in the wilderness forty

The heavens rent asunder.—A stronger expression than that used by Matthew and Luke. The original indicates that the process was seen. A miraculous phenomenon is plainly referred to.—**And the Spirit** (Matthew: 'the Spirit of God') **as a dove** (Luke: 'in a bodily form,' as 'a dove') **descending upon him.** All four Evangelists mention this appearance, which was a temporary embodiment of the Holy Ghost, publicly to inaugurate Jesus as the Messiah. The dove was the symbol of perfect gentleness, of purity, of fulness of life, and life-giving power. John (1: 32) says, 'it abode upon Him.' This was to John the sign that Jesus was the Messiah, the Lamb of God, the Son of God (John 1: 29–34). To Jesus it was the visible sign of a permanent anointing by the Holy Ghost, an induction into His public ministry. It is a divine mystery, revealed to us and to be accepted by faith; for we could not explain or prove how One conceived by the Holy Ghost can be anointed by the Holy Ghost. As the Anointed One, He is thus revealed as King and Priest; and with reverence we may suppose that with Him 'the Divine Spirit, though essentially one with Him, now entered into new relations, with a view to that mediatorial work in which they were to be respectively the Saviour and the Sanctifier of mankind' (J. A. Alexander).

Ver. 11. **A voice.** Doubtless heard by all present, as at the Transfiguration (comp. chap. 9: 7).—**Came out of the heavens.** The latter phrase is to be joined with 'came,' not with 'voice,' as in the A. V.—**Thou art.** Matthew: 'This is;' as a proof to John of the Messiahship of Jesus.—**My beloved Son,** lit., 'my Son the beloved.' This implies that no one else could be 'son' or 'beloved' in the sense here intended. Comp. the title already given in ver. 1.—**In thee.** So Luke; Matthew: 'in whom.'—**I am well pleased.** (Comp. Isa. 42: 1.) The original points to a past act, and more properly means, 'I fixed my delight.' So in the account of the Transfiguration (Matt. 17: 5). It therefore points, not to a good pleasure which begins at this time, but to the complacency of God the Father in His Son, when He assumed the office of Mediator. It is implied that the Godhead existed eternally as Father, Son, and Holy Ghost; but on this occasion the Three Persons are manifested and distinguished. This revelation of the Trinity at the baptism of Jesus agrees with the formula of Christian baptism. At such a time miraculous events might be expected. If Christ is what He claims, then the supernatural becomes natural in His life on earth.

Vers. 12, 13. THE TEMPTATION.—Parallel passages: Matt. 4: 1–11; Luke 4: 1–13. Mark gives only a brief outline.

days tempted of Satan; and he was with the wild beasts; and the angels ministered unto him.

14 Now after that John was delivered up, Jesus came into Galilee, preaching the gospel of God, and saying,

Ver. 12. **Straightway.** The same favorite word as in ver. 10. The A. V. uses seven different words to represent this one Greek word, which may always be rendered 'straightway.'—**The Spirit driveth him forth.** Comp. Matt. 4: 1. The expression here used is stronger than 'led up' (Matthew), 'led' (Luke).

Ver. 13. **Tempted.** It is implied here, as in Luke, that the temptation continued during the forty days, although the more personal assault was made at the close of the fast.—**Satan,** the prince of darkness, was personally engaged.—**With the wild beasts.** A graphic touch peculiar to Mark, enhancing the horror of the scene. Christ was probably threatened with physical danger from the wild beasts. Scarcely a figurative expression of His loneliness and helplessness. Possibly a hint of His lordship over animals, who could not hurt or flee from Him; or an allusion to the Second Adam as the restorer of Paradise.—**Ministered.** Probably with food (comp. Matt. 4: 11). The fasting, though not mentioned, is thus implied. That our Lord was actually tempted, His moral nature tested in many ways, but preeminently at this time, is plainly stated. Comp. Heb. 2: 13; 4: 15. How this could be, may be inexplicable; but the fact is revealed. The simple historical character of the Gospel narratives opposes the theories which make of the temptation a parable or myth; nor do the accounts point to a vision like that of Peter (Acts 10) or of Paul (2 Cor. 12). Some, objecting to the obvious and literal explanation of the story, find in it the record of an internal experience, a struggle in spirit with Satan. But such a theory fails to account for the numerous references to localities, to actions, and for the dialogues with the formulas of quotation from the Old Testament (found in Matthew and Luke). The narrative should rather be taken as literal history. Satan, the personal prince of darkness, whose subjects were unusually active during the ministry of our Lord, appeared in some bodily form to oppose and tempt the Prince of Life, who had appeared as a real man. This involves something supernatural; but what more natural under the circumstances, if there are any supernatural phenomena? That the literal explanation accepts the personality of Satan, is in its favor; for on this point the Bible is plain. Any theory of interpretation which denies the existence of such a being, admits of applications to the more blessed facts of the Gospel that rob them of all truth and power. The importance of the occurrence appears from the fact that three Evangelists tell of it; two of them (Matthew and Luke) in detail.

Vers. 14, 15. THE OPENING OF THE MINISTRY IN GALILEE.—Comp. Matt. 4: 12, 17, 23. This Gospel presents the fewest deviations from the chronological order. In the whole

15 The time is fulfilled, and the kingdom of God is at hand: repent ye, and believe in the gospel.

narrative of the ministry in Galilee, we find but one such: in the case of the feast at Levi's house; chap. 2: 15-22. The account begins at the close of the ministry of John the Baptist. On the intervening events, and the theories respecting our Lord's ministry, see below.

Ver. 14. **Now after John was delivered up,** *i. e.*, put in prison. On the reason of this imprisonment, see chap. 6: 17.—**Jesus came into Galilee.** Matthew and Luke, as well as Mark, begin their account of our Lord's ministry at this point. A number of events recorded by John (1: 19; 4: 54) certainly intervened; including the first passover at Jerusalem. Some place the second passover (John 5. 1) before this return to Galilee, which they fix at the beginning of the second year of our Lord's ministry. The difference of time between the two theories would be at most three months, since the return through Samaria (John 4:) must have occurred as late as December, and John may not have been imprisoned at that time. 'Galilee' was under the jurisdiction of Herod. It was the northernmost province of Palestine, the name being derived from one meaning a circle or ring. Samaria lay between Judæa and Galilee. Although the Galilæans were Jews by race and religion, they were regarded somewhat contemptuously by the inhabitants of Judæa, either because they were provincials, or because their closer contact with the Gentiles was held to degrade them. Not from fear of Herod, but on account of the opposition of the Pharisees, and also to reach the Galilean masses who had been impressed by the preaching of John.—**Preaching the gospel of God.** See below and comp. Matt. 4: 17, 23; from the latter passage the words: 'of the kingdom' have crept in here.

Ver. 15. **The time is fulfilled.** The right time, already predicted, has come in fulfilment of prophecy.—**The kingdom of God is at hand.** Matthew: 'the kingdom of heaven.' The reign of the Messiah, which is the kingdom of God, has approached. The Jews, however, thought it was to be a temporal kingdom. Hence they rejected an humble Saviour, and yet used this view against Him before Pilate (Luke 23: 2; John 19: 12). From this Jewish error the Apostles were not entirely freed until the day of Pentecost. It does not refer exclusively to a kingdom still future, but to the reign of the Messiah both in its inception and its consummation (at the future 'coming'). The former is the prominent thought here, in other cases the latter. In the widest sense it includes the Old Testament theocracy as a preparation.—**Repent.** Comp. the preaching of John the Baptist; Matt. 3: 2. The Greek word first meant, to change the mind, but 'mind' referred to the whole soul, and the term naturally passed into a specific sense, to turn from sin unto God. It suggests reformation rather than sorrow or remorse, and here implies that the people were corrupt and unmindful of God.—**Believe in the gospel.** Peculiar to Mark.

16 And passing along by the sea of Galilee, he saw Simon and Andrew the brother of Simon casting a net **17** in the sea: for they were fishers. And Jesus said unto them, Come ye after me, and I will make you to

The message of John the Baptist did not include this. As yet our Lord does not preach faith in Himself; that must come later. But even here is the germ of faith in a Personal Redeemer. The Jews all hoped for the kingdom of God. Jesus proclaims it, but adds something they do not seem to have expected; repentance and faith in order to enter it.

Vers. 16-20. THE CALL OF THE FOUR FISHERMEN.—Parallel passage: Matt. 4: 18-22; comp. Luke 5: 2-11. This occurrence seems to have followed closely upon the rejection at Nazareth narrated by Luke (4: 16-30), and to be immediately connected with the miraculous draught of fishes (Luke 5: 2-11). The order of Mark is more strictly chronological.

Ver. 16. **And passing along.** The form of the original shows entire independence of Matthew, and the more graphic style of Mark. —**The sea of Galilee.** More properly a lake; comp. Luke 5. 1: 'The lake of Gennesaret.' John twice (6: 1; 21: 1) gives a third name, 'the Sea of Tiberias,' from a celebrated city on its shore. The Old Testament name was Cinnereth (Deut. 3: 17), or Cinneroth (1 Kings 15: 20). The lake is of oval shape, from twelve to fourteen miles long, and about half as broad. It is formed by the river Jordan, and is 653 feet below the level of the Mediterranean; sudden storms of great violence descend upon it; compare chap. 4: 37, and parallel passages. 'The water is salubrious, fresh, and clear; it contains abundance of fish; the banks are picturesque, although at present bare; toward the west they are intersected by calcareous mountains; toward the east the lake is bounded by high mountains (800 to 1,000 feet high), partly of chalk and partly of basalt formation.' **Simon**; contracted from 'Simeon.' He was not yet called 'Peter;' hence Mark is historically more accurate.—**Andrew.** This Greek name shows how common that language was in the East. It is not known which was the elder brother; sometimes one and sometimes the other is named first. Their home was Bethsaida (John 1:44). Andrew and another disciple of John the Baptist, probably the Evangelist John, were the first followers of Jesus (John 1:35-40).—**In the sea**, not 'into;' the net was in the water, and they were moving it there.

Ver. 17. **Come ye after me.** The form of the command in Matthew is the same; but the A. V. there renders it: 'follow me.' This call to personal attendance is to be distinguished from the previous acquaintanceship and discipleship (John 1), and also from the later choice and call to the apostleship (chap. 3: 13-19)—All of the Twelve were in attendance upon our Lord before they were chosen to be Apostles. This training was the work of time.—**You to become.**

18 become fishers of men. And straightway they left
19 the nets, and followed him. And going on a little further, he saw James the *son* of Zebedee, and John his brother, who also were in the boat mending the
20 nets. And straightway he called them: and they left their father Zebedee in the boat with the hired servants, and went after him.
21 And they go into Capernaum; and straightway on the sabbath day he entered into the synagogue and

More strictly accurate than Matt. 4: 19, hence not copied nor condensed from that account.—**Fishers of men.** An apt and homely figure. 'The main points of resemblance cannot be mistaken, such as the value of the object, the necessity of skill as well as strength, of vigilance as well as labor, with an implication, if not and explicit promise, of abundance and success in their new fishery' (J. A. Alexander).

Ver. 18. **Straightway.** Mark's favorite word, but occurring in Matthew's account also. The obedience was prompt.

Ver. 19. **A litt e further.** An exact statement, peculiar to Mark. —**James**, *i. e.*, Jacob. He was probably the older brother, and the first Apostle to suffer martyrdom (Acts 12: 2).—**John**, the Apostle and Evangelist. Their mother's name was Salome (Matt. 27: 56; Mark 15: 40); and it is now regarded as highly probable that she was a sister of Mary, the mother of Jesus (John 19: 25). This relationship was doubtless not without its influence upon the two brothers. On their character, see chap. 3: 17.—**Mending the nets**; setting them in order after the previous night of toil. Matthew mentions in this connection that Zebedee was in the boat; Mark inserts that fact in the next verse.

Ver. 20. **With the hired servants.** Peculiar to Mark. Zebedee was not poor, and was not left helpless by this act of his sons. Nothing further is known of him.—**Went after him**; not simply, 'followed Him' (Matt. and Luke). The great particularity of the brief account suggests that Peter himself told Mark the story. Hence the order of Mark is probably the more exact, Peter being an eye-witness throughout.

Vers. 21-28. THE HEALING OF A DEMONIAC AT CAPERNAUM.—Parallel passage: Luke 4: 31-37. The order of Mark is more exact. It is significant that the beginning of our Lord's Galilean ministry was marked by such a miracle.

Ver. 21. **And they go into Capernaum**; 'His own city' (Matt. 9: 1). This was probably the beginning of our Lord's residence in that place, although He had previously healed the son of a nobleman who lived there (John 4: 46-54). Capernaum was a thriving commercial town on the north-western shore of the Sea of Galilee (Matt.

22 taught. And they were astonished at his teaching: for he taught them as having authority, and not as the
23 scribes. And straightway there was in their synagogue

4: 13). The exact site is in dispute. Robinson places it at Khan Minyeh, on account of a fountain in the neighborhood, of which Josephus speaks; Thomson, at Tell Hûm, from a resemblance to the ancient name. The latter view is confirmed by recent discoveries. The name means either, village of Nahum, or, village of consolation. The uncertainty as to the site and name fulfils our Lord's prediction (Matt. 11: 23).—**Synagogue.** 'During the Babylonish exile, when the Jews were shut out from the Holy Land, and from the appointed sanctuary, the want of places for religious meetings, in which the worship of God, without sacrifices, could be celebrated, must have been painfully felt. Thus synagogues may have originated at that ominous period. When the Jews returned from Babylon, synagogues were planted throughout the country for the purpose of affording opportunities for publicly reading the law, independently of the regular sacrificial services of the temple (Neh. 8: 1, *etc.*). At the time of Jesus there was at least one synagogue in every moderately sized town in Palestine (such as Nazareth, Capernaum, *etc.*), and in the cities of Syria, Asia Minor, and Greece, in which Jews resided (Acts 9: 2 sqq.). Larger towns possessed several synagogues; and it is said that there were no fewer than 460, or even 480, of them in Jerusalem itself' (Winer). —**And taught.** Our Lord was regarded as a Rabbi, and the simple synagogue service permitted Him to teach publicly in these places of worship.

Ver. 22. **Were astonished.** A strong word: 'driven from their customary state of mind by something new and strange.'—**Teaching,** rather than 'doctrine;' the former includes the manner as well as the matter of His instruction, both of which awakened astonishment.— **For he taught them.** This may refer to His habitual mode of teaching.—**As having authority.** 'One' is not only unnecessary, but incorrect. Christ is not 'one' among others 'having authority,' but the only one having authority in this highest sense, as the one coming directly from God, and Himself the personal embodiment of the Truth.—**And not as the scribes.** The scribes were expounders of the Old Testament. Their exposition, too, was in one sense authoritative, but they referred continually to the authority of learned Rabbis. Our Lord introduced His expositions thus: 'Verily I say unto you.' Comp. the previous discourse at Nazareth (Luke 4: 24, *etc.*), and Matt. 7: 28, 29.

Ver. 23. **Straightway.**—The best authorities insert Mark's favorite word at this point.—**A man with an unclean spirit.** Lit., 'in an unclean spirit,' in his power, in intimate union with him. The more usual expression is 'demoniac,' lit., 'demonized.' The Gospel accounts plainly show that in those days evil spirits ('demons') in-

24 a man with an unclean spirit; and he cried out, saying, What have we to do with thee, thou Jesus of Nazareth? art thou come to destroy us? I know thee
25 who thou art, the Holy One of God. And Jesus rebuked ¹him, saying, Hold thy peace, and come out
26 of him. And the unclean spirit, ²tearing him and
27 crying with a loud voice, came out of him. And they were all amazed, insomuch that they questioned among themselves, saying, What is this? a new teaching! with authority he commandeth even the unclean spirits,

¹ Or, *it.* ² Or, *convulsing.*

vaded the persons of men. We cannot explain how this took place; but Matt. 4: 24 and similar passages distinguish this possession from every kind of sickness. When our Lord came to earth, Satan would be most hostile.

Ver. 24. **What have we to do with thee?** Lit., 'what to us and to thee,' what have we in common; comp. Matt. 8: 29.—**To destroy us.** The language of the demon, overbearing the consciousness of the man. The plural indicates, either the presence of more than one evil spirit, or that this one speaks as the representative of the class. The destruction referred to includes banishment to torment (comp. Matt. 8: 29), and also the destruction of the empire of Satan in the world, signified and begun in such expulsions as these.—**I know thee.** Already conscious of His influence, the evil spirit with supernatural sagacity recognizes Him as the Messiah.—**The Holy One of God.** An acknowledgment of His Messiahship, but not necessarily of His Divinity. The 'unclean spirit' describes our Lord as the 'Holy One,' because this holiness torments him already, and marks Jesus as One sent by God to destroy Satan's empire.

Ver. 25. **Rebuked him.** Our Lord refuses the testimony of demons to His Person.—**Hold thy peace.** Lit., 'be thou muzzled,' silenced. A command joined with enforcing power.—**Come out of him.** Two distinct personalities are spoken of, the demon and the possessed man.

Ver. 26. **Tearing him.** A paroxysm attended the dispossession (comp. chap. 9: 26; Luke 9: 42); not a natural convulsion, but the malicious act of the demon.—**And crying with a loud voice.** The act of the demon, not a cry of pain from the demoniac. Luke (4: 35) adds that the demon 'hurt him not.' The graphic and minute description forbids the view that this was a cure of epilepsy.

Ver. 27. **They questioned among themselves.** Only a miracle could produce this effect. The people began to think and argue for themselves, not to ask the scribes.—**What is this? a new teaching!** This is the rendering of the more lively report of Mark.

28 and they obey him. And the report of him went out straightway everywhere into all the region of Galilee round about.

29 And straightway, ²when they were come out of the synagogue, they came into the house of Simon and
30 Andrew, with James and John. Now Simon's wife's mother lay sick of a fever; and straightway they tell

¹ Some ancient authorities read *when he was come out of the synagogue, he came, &c.*

They rightly inferred, that such new and unexampled power was to attest a new revelation from God.—**Even the unclean spirits.** Mark gives special prominence to Christ's power over demons. Such an exercise of 'authority' was unexampled.—Mark and Luke mention this miracle first, without saying that it was actually the *first*. That in Cana of Galilee (John 2: 1–11) was the first, since this is expressly stated. The second is recorded in John 4: 46–54. Matthew (4: 24) speaks of many miracles, but describes first the healing of a leper (chap. 8: 2–4), in accordance with the purpose of his Gospel. The Evangelists undoubtedly intended to convey the impression that Jesus wrought miracles to confirm and seal His ministry as the Saviour of men. If Christ is what He claims to be, His miracles are not only possible, but necessary. If He is not what the Gospels represent Him as being, then there is little to preserve the human race from materialistic atheism.

Ver. 28. **And the report of him went out straightway everywhere.** The correct reading presents most graphically the effect of the miracle.—**Region of Galilee round about.** Not the regions adjacent to Galilee, but the adjacent regions of Galilee.

Vers. 29, 31. THE HEALING OF PETER'S WIFE'S MOTHER.—Parallel passages: Matt. 8: 14, 15; Luke 4: 38, 39. The place was undoubtedly Capernaum. Here Matthew deviates greatly from the chronological order.

Ver. 29. **And straightway.** On the 'Sabbath day' (ver. 21) after the occurrence in the synagogue.—**The house of Simon and Andrew.** Now living in Capernaum. Bethsaida, however, is called (John 1: 45) 'the city of Andrew and Peter.' When or why they removed is unknown.—**With James and John.** Mark alone mentions these. The particularity favors the theory that Peter had told Mark of it. The Twelve were not yet chosen; though these four fishermen had been called to follow Christ (vers. 17, 20). Even as Apostles, they were more intimately associated with each other and with Jesus, than were the rest of the Twelve.

Ver. 30. **Now Simon's wife's mother.** Simon was therefore married. Jerome and modern Romanist expositors infer that the wife was dead from the fact that the mother when healed 'ministered unto them;' but were that the case, Peter must have married again (comp.

31 him of her; and he came and took her by the hand, and raised her up; and the fever left her, and she ministered unto them,

32 And at even, when the sun did set, they brought unto him all that were sick, and them that were ¹pos-
33 sessed with devils. And all the city was gathered
34 together at the door. And he healed many that were sick with divers diseases, and cast out many ²devils; and he suffered not the ²devils to speak, because they knew him.³

¹ Or, *demoniacs.*
² Gr. *demons.* ³ Many ancient authorities add *to be Christ.* See Luke 4: 41.

1 Cor. 9: 5). 'Legend says that her name was Perpetua or Concordia.' —**And straightway they tell him of her.** Matthew omits this telling; Luke says: 'they besought Him for her.'

Ver. 31. **Took her by the hand, and raised her up.** Mark is here more minute than Matthew or Luke. Our Lord could heal by a word at a distance, in the response to faith; but He generally made some outward sign of His willingness and will to cure; the sign corresponding to the cure and proving that His will healed.—The healing was instantaneous and perfect.—**The fever left her, and she ministered unto them**; thus showing her perfect restoration. The faith of her family had called for the miracle; but she shows her own faith and her gratitude by 'serving' the Lord, and that too in the natural and womanly way of household duty.

Vers. 32–34. The Healing of Multitudes at Capernaum.—Parallel passages: Matt. 8: 16, 17; Luke 4: 40, 41.

Ver. 32. **And at even, when the sun did set.** The Sabbath had ended, and they felt at liberty to bring the sick and possessed.—**Them that were possessed with devils** (or, 'demoniacs'), or, more literally, 'those demonized,' under the power of evil spirits; comp. vers. 23–27. The two afflicted classes are distinguished.

Ver. 33. **Gathered together at the door.** Peculiar to Mark, and suggesting the impression made on Peter looking out from the house.

Ver. 34. **And he healed many**, etc. This does not imply that some were not healed, either because there was not time, or because they lacked faith; both Matthew (8: 16) and Luke (4: 40) say that all were healed.—**Suffered not the devils** (more correctly, 'demons') **to speak.** This was usual. See ver. 25; comp. the more particular account of Luke (4: 41). Our Lord could be Himself the witness to His claims (comp. John 8: 14–18); practically no man ever believes in Christ without first believing Christ Himself independently of other witnesses. Besides, these were unworthy witnesses·

35 And in the morning, a great while before day, he rose up and went out, and departed into a desert place, 36 and there prayed. And Simon and they that were 37 with him followed after him; and they found him, 38 and say unto him, All are seeking thee. And he saith unto them, Let us go elsewhere into the next towns, that I may preach there also; for to this end came I

it was not the right time for the truth they stated. But Satan and Satan's emissaries can speak the truth when it will serve an evil end.

Vers. 35-39. THE CIRCUIT THROUGH GALILEE.—Parallel passage: Luke 4: 42-44; comp. Matt. 4: 23, 24. The passage in Matthew may be only a more general description of our Lord's ministry in Galilee. The paragraph has been greatly improved by the emendations of the Revised Version, restoring the vivacious style of Mark.

Ver. 35. **A great while before day**, or, 'while it was still night.' Luke: 'when it was day,' or literally, 'it becoming day.' Both refer to the same point of time, the earliest dawn. Between this and the parallel passage in Luke, there is a great difference in words, though none in matter. A proof of the independence of Mark, since Matthew does not give these details.—**Into a desert place.** Just as in Luke. 'Solitary place' really expresses the uninhabited character of the region referred to; but the word is usually rendered 'desert.' Evidently near Capernaum.—**And there prayed.** Our Lord's example enjoins secret prayer. His work and prayer are closely connected. The punctilious observance of the Sabbath in Capernaum gave the people their rest, and yet must have abridged our Lord's repose. Prayer with Him seems to have been not only intimate communion with His Father, but a necessary preparation for His ministry. How much more needful for us!

Ver. 36. **They that were with him.** 'Simon,' mentioned first as head of the house from which Jesus had withdrawn; the others were: James and John and Andrew, though perhaps more may have been with them.

Ver. 37. **And they found him.** Search and uncertainty is implied, since He had retired to an unfrequented spot.—**All are seeking thee.** The crowd soon followed Simon and his friends. See Luke 4: 42. Peter said this to induce Him to return, and the crowd besought Him to stay. The will of the multitude did not govern Him, as they supposed, hence the reply in the next verse.

Ver. 38. **Let us go elsewhere into the next towns.** Spoken to the disciples, who are invited to go with Him. The answer to the multitude is given by Luke (4: 43): 'I must preach the kingdom of God to other cities also.'—**That I may preach there also.** Not to work miracles, but to preach; though He did both (ver. 39). The crowd gathered because of the works He performed; but His great

39 forth. And he went into their synagogues throughout all Galilee, preaching and casting out ¹devils.
40 And there cometh to him a leper, beseeching him, ²and kneeling down to him, and saying unto him, If

¹ Gr. *demons.*   ² Some ancient authorities omit *and kneeling down to him.*

object was to teach. Although indifferent to the immediate wish of the multitudes, He shows His desire to really bless them, by seeking them even while all sought Him.—**For to this end came I forth,** *i. e.,* from God. Luke: 'therefore am I sent.' Probably neither the disciples nor the multitude understood this. It surely means more than that for this reason He came out of Capernaum or out of the house, because that coming forth (ver. 35) was to pray, not to preach.

Ver. 39. **In their synagogues.** Lit., 'into,' implying that He went into them, and reached the ears of the people.—**All Galilee.** Not the next towns only, but throughout the whole region; comp. Matt. 4: 23, and especially Luke 4: 44.

Vers. 40–45. THE HEALING OF THE LEPER.—Parallel passages: Matt. 8: 2–4; Luke 5: 12–14. Mark's account is fuller, showing independence, and confirming the view that Matthew has deviated from the chronological order. From Luke 5: 12–14 we conclude that the miracle occurred at some other place than Capernaum, although Mark 2: 1 suggests that it was not far from that city.

Ver. 40. **A leper.** *Leprosy* is a horrible disease of the skin, prevalent for ages in Egypt and neighboring regions. It seems to have been of a more virulent type in ancient times than at present. The form which prevailed among the Hebrews was the 'white leprosy,' as appears from the details given in Lev. 13. 'When the disease is decided in its character, it is either rapidly cured, or else spreads inward. In the former case there is a violent eruption, so that the patient is white from head to foot (Lev. 13: 12; 2 Kings 5: 27); in the latter case, the disease progresses slowly, and the symptoms are equally distressing and fatal, ending in consumption, dropsy, suffocation, and death. . . . No remedy was known for the disease itself: the leper was declared unclean, and excluded from intercourse with all other persons. He had to wear the prescribed mourning garment (Lev. 13: 45), but was permitted to associate with other lepers. Their abodes were commonly outside the city walls (Lev. 13: 46; Num. 5: 2); but they were allowed to go about freely, provided they avoided contact with other persons; nor were they even excluded from the services of the synagogue' (Lightfoot, 862). 'In this respect we note a great difference between the synagogue and the temple. On recovering from leprosy, several lustrations had to be performed (Lev. 14). The main points in the prescribed rite were, to appear before the priest, and to offer a sacrifice; the latter being preceded by religious lustrations, and introduced by a symbolical ceremony, in which the two turtles or pigeons bore a striking analogy to the scape-goat

41 thou wilt, thou canst make me clean. And being moved with compassion, he stretched forth his hand, and touched him, and saith unto him, I will; be thou 42 made clean. And straightway the leprosy departed 43 from him, and he was made clean. And he ¹strictly charged him, and straightway sent him out, and saith

¹ Or, *sternly.*

and the other goat offered in sacrifice on the day of atonement (Lev. 16:)' (Lange: *Matthew*). The disease was hereditary and infectious, but not contagious. The regulations of the Mosaic law respecting it were sanitary, it is true; but they had also a religious significance. 'The leper was the type of one dead in sin: the same emblems are used in his misery as those of mourning for the dead; the same means of cleansing as for uncleanness through connection with death, and which were never used except on these two occasions' (Alford).— **Kneeling down to him.** These words are omitted in some authorities. They state the same fact indicated by the words of Matthew's account: 'worshipped Him.'—**If thou wilt, thou canst make me clean.** In these words 'there is at once deep anguish and great faith. Other sick persons had been cured: this the leper knew, hence his faith; but he was probably the first man afflicted with his particular malady that succeeded in reaching Jesus, and entreating his aid; hence his anxiety' (Godet). One defiled by sin can now say: 'Thou wilt, thou canst make me clean.'

Ver. 41. **Moved with compassion.** Peculiar to Mark, suggesting the report of an eye-witness (Peter).—**He stretched forth his hand, and touched him.** Such touch was forbidden because of the impurity of the disease. It was not contagious, so that the courage of our Lord was not courage against disease, but against bigotry.—**I will; be thou made clean.** The same word as in ver. 40, and hence altered to correspond. All the accounts speak, not of the cure, but of the cleansing of the man, as the nature of the disease would suggest.

Ver. 42. The best authorities omit the words: 'as soon as he had spoken.'—**And straightway the leprosy departed from him.** The immediate disappearance of the disease is the point of greatest significance. Leprosy being a type of sin, a Saviour who could entirely pardon with a word (see below) must needs test that power in the case of this typical disease by instantaneous and perfect cure.

Ver. 43. **And he strictly** (or, 'sternly') **charged him.** This implies strong emotion.—**And straightway sent him out.** Not necessarily, out of the house, for there is no evidence that the miracle was performed in a house. Possibly out of the city into which the leper had come (Luke 4: 12); but away from Himself, for despite our Lord's compassion, feelings of grief seem to have been awakened by the man.

44 unto him, See thou say nothing to any man; but ¹go thy way, shew thyself to the priest, and offer for thy cleansing the things which Moses commanded, for a 45 testimony unto them. But he went out, and began to publish it much, and to spread abroad the ²matter, insomuch that ³Jesus could no more openly enter into

¹ *Go, show* (Amer. Com.).   ² Gr. *word*.   ³ Gr. *he*.

Ver. 44. **See thou say nothing to any man**, or, 'tell no man anything.' In Matthew and Luke a similar prohibition occurs. There was probably a three-fold reason for it: first, the man himself was doubtless of such a temperament that it was best for him to be silent; such characters still exist; secondly, as the rest of the verse shows, the Mosaic injunction should first be fulfilled, to prevent the miracle from awakening prejudice on the part of the ecclesiastical authorities; third, here, as elsewhere, our Lord discourages that kind of notoriety which would gather to Him masses of people with unspiritual ends in view; all the more because such concourses (see ver. 45) would awaken too early in His ministry the inevitable hostility of the rulers.—**But go thy way** (or better, 'go'), **shew thyself to the priest.** Our Lord, during His earthly life, never released men from the obligation to obey the Mosaic law. In the case of the cleansing of a leper it was usual, we are told, for the priest of the district to inspect the leper twice. After purification by this priest, a visit was made to the temple, and there an offering was presented.—**Which Moses commanded** (see Lev. 14: 30, 31), **for a testimony unto them**; that is, to the people, as a public witness that the defilement was removed.

Ver. 45. **And began to publish it much.** This he did at once ('began'). Whether he went to the priest at all, is not mentioned; but he was disobedient at all events in this matter, which is mentioned by Mark only.—**Spread abroad the matter.** Lit., 'the word,' *i. e.*, the account of what had happened, not the word of Jesus. This was wrong, a specimen and type of the injudicious zeal, all too common among those whom the Lord blesses.—**Could no more.** Moral inability. His purpose would have been defeated by entering where the people were excited by this report. The evil effect of the leper's disobedience.—**Into a city**, or, 'the city.' The latter is less probable, the sense being rather, 'into town,' not the particular city where the numbers had been healed.—**Was without in desert places.** Not to avoid the people, for it is added: **and they came to him from every quarter**, and Luke, without stating that the leper himself had spread the report, tells of this effect of the miracle. Some think our Lord, after touching the leper, was unclean according to the Jewish law, and hence remained 'in desert places.' But He would not have acted from this motive unless He

¹a city, but was without in desert places: and they came to him from every quarter.

2:1 And when he entered again into Capernaum after some days, it was noised that he was ²in the house. 2 And many were gathered together, so that there was no longer room *for them,* no, not even about the door: 3 and he spake the word unto them. And they come, bringing unto him a man sick of the palsy, borne of

¹ Or, *the city.* ² Or, *at home.*

acknowledged the uncleanness, and such an acknowledgment could not be affected by the leper's report, which is said to be the cause of His keeping away from the cities. Nor would the multitudes have come thus to an unclean person. The retirement was rather from motives of prudence, to avoid exciting the multitudes with their carnal expectations and prematurely increasing the hostility already awakened at Jerusalem (John 4: 1), and beginning to show itself in Galilee. This hostility must be regarded as much greater, if we accept the view that the events recorded in John 5, had occurred before the Galilean ministry.

Chap. II: 1-12. THE CURE OF THE PARALYTIC.—Parallel passages: Matt. 9: 2-8; Luke 5: 18-26. The account of Mark is in its proper chronological position, and it is the most minute and graphic.

Ver. 1. **Capernaum.** 'His own city.' Matt. 9: 1.—**After some days.** More than one day, but how many does not appear. Still, even this indefinite mark of time favors the view, that the order of this Evangelist is exact.—**Noised.** This suggests a private entrance into the city, and then a general report that He was there.—**In the house.** The article is wanting in the original; the phrase is equivalent to 'at home;' but with the additional idea of having come there. It is therefore probable that the house was His usual residence in Capernaum; but this is not definitely expressed.

Ver. 2. The description of Mark is here minute.—**So that there was no longer room for them, no, not even about the door.** This paraphrase brings out the sense. Another rendering is: 'So that not even the parts about (or, towards) the door (much less the house) could any longer hold them.' This suggests a constantly increasing crowd, at length filling even the porch leading from the interior court to the door.—**He spake the word unto them,** *i. e.,* 'was teaching' (Luke). He was doing this when this incident occurred. From Luke's account we infer that He had already healed others on this occasion.

Ver. 3. **Borne of four.** 'In a bed,' ver. 4 (and Luke). Mark alone mentions the **number of men.**

4 four. And when they could not ¹come nigh unto him for the crowd, they uncovered the roof where he was: and when they had broken it up, they let down the ²bed
5 whereon the sick of the palsy lay. And Jesus seeing
6 their faith saith unto the sick of the palsy, ³Son, thy sins are forgiven. But there were certain of the scribes
7 sitting there, and reasoning in their hearts, Why doth

¹ Many ancient authorities read *bring him unto him.* ² Or, *pallet* (Amer. Com.).
³ Gr. *Child.*

Ver. 4. **Could not come nigh unto him.** The doorway was full (ver. 2).—**They uncovered** (*unroofed*) **the roof where he was.** Luke says what is here implied: 'they went upon the housetop,' probably by an outside staircase. The view that they merely removed the awning from the court is forbidden by what is added: **and when they had broken it up,** or, 'dug it out.' Besides, Luke explicitly says that the man was let down 'through the tiling' (tiles). The supposition that the parapet alone was broken through is open to the same objection. It is most probable that our Lord was in the upper room, usually the largest in an Eastern house; that the crowd was in the court, as ver. 2 implies, and that these men actually removed the tiles on the roof, and broke through the plaster or clay of the roof itself. This was an evidence of their earnestness. —**The bed.** A different word from those used by Matthew and Luke. It denotes a mattress, sometimes merely a sheepskin, used for the service of the sick, or as a camp-bed. Hence the American revisers suggest the marginal rendering: or, *pallet,* in this paragraph. Of course bedsteads were and are unknown in the East.

Ver. 5. **Saw their faith.** That is, the faith of the bearers.—'Be of good cheer,' is omitted here, and in Luke's account, the latter has 'Man' instead of 'Son.'—**Thy sins are forgiven thee.** They have been and are forgiven. Some have thought from this that the man's sickness was a direct judgment for sin. There is no proof of this, although it would seem that the man's conscience had been quickened through his sickness. Our Lord, seeing that he needed both spiritual and bodily healing, shows not only His wisdom, but His true mission, by working first the spiritual cure.

Ver. 6. **Certain of the scribes sitting there.** The authorized expounders of the law. Luke defines them more particularly (5: 17). These were of the Pharisaical party. From Luke's account and from the term 'sitting,' we infer that they came early; it is probable they were in the upper room where our Lord was, nearer to Him and in the most conspicuous position.—**In their hearts.** That they did not speak, seems clear from the various accounts.

Ver. 7. **Why doth this man thus speak? He blasphemeth: Who can,** etc. This is the best established sense of the verse.

this man thus speak? he blasphemeth: who can for-
8 give sins but one, *even* God? And straightway Jesus, perceiving in his spirit that they so reasoned within themselves, saith unto them, Why reason ye these things
9 in your hearts? Whether is easier, to say to the sick of the palsy, Thy sins are forgiven; or to say, Arise,
10 and take up thy ¹bed and walk? But that ye may know that the Son of man hath ²power on earth to for-

¹ Or, *pallet* (Amer. Com.).   ² Or, *authority* (Amer. Com. read in text).

'This one,' contemptuously; 'thus,' *i. e.*, such great things; the words in the original resemble each other: 'This one in this wise.' If our Lord were what the scribes deemed Him, their judgment was correct. This occurrence is to prove the incorrectness of their estimate of Him.

Ver. 8. **In his spirit.** An immediate and supernatural knowledge is thus indicated: itself no slight evidence of His power to forgive sins.—**Why reason ye?** Comp. on Matt. 9: 4, where their thoughts are called 'evil.'

Ver. 9. **Whether is easier, to say, Thy sins,** etc. 'In our Lord's argument it must be carefully noted, that He does not ask: "Which is easiest, to forgive sins, or to raise a sick man?" For it could not be affirmed that that of forgiving was easier than this of healing; but: "Which is easiest, to *claim* this power, or to *claim* that; to *say*, Thy sins be forgiven, or to *say*, Arise and walk?" And then He proceeds: 'That is easiest, and I will now prove my right to say it, by saying with effect, and with an outward consequence setting its seal to my truth, the harder word: "Rise up and walk."' (*Trench.*) The agreement of the Evangelists in regard to this answer of our Lord is remarkably exact; the argument is a very important one.

Ver. 10. **The Son of man.** That is, the Messiah (Dan. 7: 13); but our Lord applies the term to Himself (the Apostles do not thus speak of Him) as the head and representative of the new humanity. (Comp. 'the seed of the woman:' Gen. 3: 15.) It does not deny His divinity, but is the complement of the term 'Son of God,' which also belongs to Him. 'It is the name by which the Lord ordinarily in one pregnant word designates Himself as the Messiah, the Son of God manifested in the flesh of man—the second Adam; and to it belong all those conditions of humiliation, suffering and exaltation, which it behooved the Son of man to go through' (Alford).—**Hath power**; more correctly, 'authority.' The question at issue was, whether the man among them had a right to forgive? So that the idea of authority delegated to a mere man is by no means involved.—**On earth.** Where the pardon is granted; in distinction from heaven, whence the Son of man derived this authority.

11 give sins (he saith to the sick of the palsy), I say unto thee, Arise, take up thy ¹bed, and go unto thy house.
12 And he arose, and straightway took up the bed, and went forth before them all; insomuch that they were all amazed, and glorified God, saying, We never saw it on this fashion.
13 And he went forth again by the sea side; and all the
14 multitude resorted unto him, and he taught them. And

¹ Or, *pallet* (Amer. Com.).

Ver. 11. **He saith unto the sick of the palsy.** This parenthetical remark of the Evangelist indicates a moment of solemn silence, during which our Lord turned from the doubting scribes and Pharisees to the paralytic, who certainly must have eagerly listened to this discussion, which affected both his bodily and spiritual well-being.— **Take up thy bed.** Comp. John 5: 8–12, where a similar command was given, and obeyed by the healed person, on the sabbath, thus occasioning the hostility of the Jews.

Ver. 12. **And straightway took up the bed** The instantaneousness of the cure is more fully indicated by the order of the correct reading: he had at once strength enough to take up his pallet.— **Before them all.** A hint that the account comes from an eye-witness.—**They were all amazed**, etc. Matthew, 'feared;' Luke combines all three, and tells that the man also glorified God. The impression produced was a very powerful one, and the emotions were of a mixed character: wonder, gratitude and fear.—**We never saw it on this fashion**, or, 'thus.' This was the prevalent feeling, a conviction that the kingdom of God was manifesting itself as never before. It is scarcely necessary to suppose that it is a comparison with previous *miracles*. The remarkable feature (Luke: 'strange things') was the attestation of the miracle to the power to forgive sins (Matthew: 'glorified God, who had given such authority to men').

Vers. 13–17. THE CALL OF LEVI AND THE FEAST AT HIS HOUSE.—Parallel passages: Matt. 9: 9–13; Luke 5: 27–32. These two incidents are joined together by all three Evangelists; but it is improbable that they were connected together in time (see below). According to the usual view of the chronology, the feast and discourse (vers. 15–22) occurred some time after the call of Levi, and these verses only, in the first thirteen chapters of Mark, are out of chronological order. Although the three Evangelists agree in joining together the call and feast, the relative position in the history is not the same. Mark and Luke place them immediately after the healing of the leper near Capernaum. Most harmonists are compelled to place the miracle wrought on the paralytic and the calling of Matthew together at the *earlier* period, and to insert the feast between the return from Gadara and the healing of Jaïrus' daughter. Matthew himself distinctly states that Jaïrus came to our Lord while at the feast in his house (Matt. 9: 18). That Evangelist must needs speak of the feast, and properly prefaces

as he passed by, he saw Levi the *son* of Alphæus sitting at the place of toll, and he saith unto him, Follow me. 15 And he arose and followed him. And it came to pass that he was sitting at meat in his house, and many [1] publicans and sinners sat down with Jesus and his disci-

[1] That is, *collectors or renters of Roman taxes.*

that account by telling of his call. As, however, the latter event was preceded by an instructive miraculous incident (the healing of the paralytic) in the same city, it too was inserted. Mark and Luke, having placed the call of Matthew (Levi) in its proper chronological position, mention the feast in the same connection. Levi is undoubtedly the same as Matthew the Apostle and Evangelist. The three accounts agree in matter, but with the usual variation in words.

Ver. 13 is more specific than the parallel passages.—**Went forth again.** Either with a reference to ver. 1 ('He entered again'), or possibly in allusion to the previous call of four disciples by the sea-side (chap. 1: 16, etc.).—**And all the multitude**, etc. The popularity continued.

Ver. 14. **Passed by.** Matthew: 'from thence,' thus closely joining his own call with the healing of the paralytic.—**Levi the son of Alphæus**; 'a publican named Levi' (Luke 5: 27); the accounts otherwise agree closely. The formal call seems peculiar to the Apostles, and Mark and Luke mention Matthew, not Levi, among the Twelve. The former was probably the apostolic name, the latter the ordinary one. Matthew himself mentions the former only. Although 'the son of Alpheus,' there is no evidence that he was the brother of James, the son of Alpheus.—**Sitting at the place of toll**, or, 'the toll-booth.' Like the four fishermen, at his regular employment, and probably previously acquainted with Jesus.—**Follow me.** Levi obeyed; 'forsook all, rose up and followed Him' (Luke 5: 28); certainly not simply: walked after Jesus into His place of residence.

Ver. 15. **And it came to pass.** All three accounts are indefinite as to the length of the interval. As already intimated, the arrangement of Mark and Luke is due to the natural association of the call of the publican with the feast afterwards made by him.—**In his house.** That of Levi, who made the feast for our Lord (Luke 5: 29). The passage before us does not decide this; but any other view needlessly creates a discrepancy. Our Lord did not pass directly from the custom-house to the feast. The narrative is lively in style.—**Many publicans.** These were the tax-gatherers employed by the Romans. Doubly hateful to the Jews, because they were the agents of the foreign conquerors, and themselves guilty of many exactions. The system, then prevalent, of selling to the highest bidders the privilege of collecting taxes in a given province or district, led to great abuses, and the minor officers would soon be of the most disreputable class. Hence the phrase: **publicans and sinners**, so frequently used.—

16 ples: for there were many, and they followed him. And the scribes ¹of the Pharisees, when they saw that he was eating with the sinners and publicans, said unto his disciples, ²He eateth ³and drinketh with publicans
17 and sinners. And when Jesus heard it, he saith unto them, They that are ⁴whole have no need of a physician, but they that are sick: I came not to call the righteous, but sinners.
18 And John's disciples and the Pharisees were fasting:

¹ Some ancient authorities read *and the Pharisees*.   ² Or, How is it *that he eateth* . . . *sinners*.   ³ Some ancient authorities omit *and drinketh*.   ⁴ Gr. *strong*.

For there were many, and they followed him. Mark alone gives this reason for the number of publicans and sinners gathered there, namely, that persons of these classes were numerous, and that they very generally followed Christ. The fact that the host was one of the former class (and would naturally gather his associates), is brought out by Luke.

Ver. 16. Both Mark and Luke, in different forms, say that these scribes were **of the Pharisees**, *i. e.*, of that party.—**When they saw that he was eating.** Our Lord had just returned from Gadara, and they would be on the watch for Him; or hearing that He was at a publican's feast, they pressed in. It is not probable that they came as guests, but toward the close of the feast; yet they may have actually witnessed this eating. Luke (5: 30) represents the objection as made against the disciples. Their criticism probably included both the Master and His followers. The correct form: **He eateth—sinners!** points to an exclamation of surprise, which may have preceded the hostile question.

Ver. 17. Our Lord, in figurative language, lays down a principle, applicable to the case, on their own estimate of themselves, and the 'publicans and sinners.'—**They that are whole have no need of a physician, but they that are sick.** He is the Physician; the two classes are, the objectors and those objected to. Those thinking themselves whole (although really they are not) need not (or do not admit their need of) a physician, but those thinking themselves sick (which is really their case).—**I came not**, etc. The best authorities omit, 'to repentance.' The sense remains unaltered.—**Righteous men;** those thinking themselves so; **sinners**, those convinced of their sin; not those actually righteous and sinful. The latter view is admissible; those actually righteous cannot be called to repentance, but this would not assert the existence of positively sinless men. The former view corresponds better with the previous clause, gives a more direct reply to the Pharisees, and enforces the great lesson of the whole passage; sense of need is the first step toward Christ.

Vers. 18-22. THE DISCOURSE AT THE HOUSE OF LEVI (MATTHEW).—Parallel passages:

and they come and say unto him, Why do John's disciples and the disciples of the Pharisees fast, but thy
19 disciples fast not? And Jesus said unto them, Can the sons of the bridechamber fast, while the bridegroom is with them? as long as they have the bridegroom with
20 them, they cannot fast. But the days will come, when the bridegroom shall be taken away from them, and

Matt. 9: 14–17; Luke 5: 33–38. The important lessons are: The kingdom of heaven a marriage-feast, even in the days of mourning.—New life, new forms; not new forms, new life. The old form useless when antiquated; the new form useless if it does not express the new life.—The incongruity of legalism and the gospel; the gospel bursts the restraints of the old Judaism.

Ver. 18. **And John's disciples and the Pharisees were fasting.** This explanatory remark, peculiar to Mark, may point to some particular fast, which these classes were then observing. The form of the question in Matthew and Luke indicates the habits of these classes.—**They come.** Matthew says 'the disciples of John' asked the question. Luke seems to put it in the mouth of the Pharisees, while this phrase joins both classes as inquirers. The two were gradually coming together. Mark is, in some respects, fuller than the others, showing that his account cannot be an abridgement of the others. Comp. especially the peculiar phrase: **John's disciples and the disciples of the Pharisees.** The Pharisees, it is supposed, fasted twice in the week (Luke 18: 12); the remnant of John's disciples would be led to a similar practice by his austere life.—**But thy disciples fast not?** The complaint also implies: 'if you are a teacher from God, why does your teaching result in leading your followers away from old-established forms and customs, confirmed by the example of our own teacher, John?' A demand for a compromise between the old and the new, as ver. 16 shows. External legalism here assumed to teach Christ; and John's disciples borrowed aid from the Pharisees whom John denounced.

Ver. 19. **Can the sons of the bridechamber.** The companions of the bridegroom, as the bride was brought to his father's house. The festive procession was usually in the evening, with torches, music, and dancing, and the marriage feast lasted seven days. The application is of course to the disciples of Christ; He Himself being **the bridegroom.** A common Old Testament figure. There may also be an allusion to the words of the Baptist (John 3: 29), in which he represents himself as the friend of the bridegroom, Christ. 'Mourn' and 'fast' are used interchangeably; genuine fasting springs from real sorrow.—**As long as they have the bridegroom with them, they cannot fast.** This repetition is peculiar to Mark.

Ver. 20. **The days will come,** etc. 'How sublime and peaceful

21 then will they fast in that day. No man seweth a piece of undressed cloth on an old garment: else that which should fill it up taketh from it, the new from the 22 old, and a worse rent is made. And no man putteth new wine into old [1] wine-skins: else the wine will burst the skins, and the wine perisheth, and the skins: but *they put* new wine into fresh wine-skins.

[1] That is, *skins used as bottles.*

is this early announcement by our Lord of the bitter passage before Him' (Alford).—**Then will they fast.** A simple prediction, not a command; hence 'will,' instead of 'shall.'—**In that day.** Mark, though so concise, seems fond of such solemn and specifying repetitions. Real fasting takes place where there is real occasion for it. History shows that prescribed fasts become formal; that formal fasting is closely linked with Pharisaical ritualism.

Ver. 21. Two illustrations follow, naturally associated with a wedding feast. The form is peculiar to Mark, and characteristic of his lively style. The variations show entire independence. **And no man seweth a piece of undressed** (or, 'unfulled') **cloth on an old garment; else that which should fill it up** (lit., 'the fulness') **taketh away from it, the new from the old, and a worse rent is made.** The patch of cloth that would shrink, placed on a worn garment, would tear the weaker fibre; the new rent is all round the patch that covered the old one. What is *antiquated* cannot be patched up with what is *fresh*. The worn out system of fasting for fasting's sake cannot be patched up with a piece from the new, fresh, complete gospel. It is often attempted. Many special applications may be made, but care must be taken that nothing directly appointed by God be deemed 'antiquated.'

Ver. 22. **Putteth new wine into old wine-skins,** *i. e.,* 'skins used as bottles,' as is customary in the East. Compare: **else the wine will burst the skins, and the wine perisheth, and the skins,** with Matt. 9: 17; Luke 5: 37. Old ones would burst from the fermenting of the new wine, which would distend new ones without injury. This figure, representing an internal operation, is stronger than the previous one. The living principle of the new covenant, if we attempt to enclose it in the old ceremonial man, is lost; even the form is destroyed.—**But they put new wine into fresh wine-skins.** The second adjective is not the same as the first. New emergencies require new means. In this case, God had appointed the new means. The former figure seems most applicable to the mistake of John's disciples; the latter to the subsequent dangers besetting the Apostles. Judaistic Christianity died, form and spirit were destroyed; but the freedom of the gospel for which Paul contended remained. The new life assumes an outward form, differing from the antiquated

23 And it came to pass, that he was going on the sabbath day through the cornfields; and his disciples [1] began, as they went, to pluck the ears of corn. And the

[1] Gr. *began to make* their *way plucking.*

form, and we must seek to preserve both life and form; **both are preserved together.**

Vers. 23-28. FIRST SABBATH CONTROVERSY.—Parallel passages: Matt. 12: 1-8; Luke 6: 1-5.—*Chronology:* Mark and Luke place the events of this paragraph just before the *choice of the Twelve,* which occurred during our Lord's retirement. The season of the year may have been April, at which time the barley would be ripe. It has been inferred from Luke's account (6: 1, 'second Sabbath after the first'), that the second Sabbath was in the second week after the passover; but this is not even probable (see Luke). The supposition that a passover intervened at this time, rests mainly on that phrase, which is rejected by many modern critics. It seems quite certain that the Sermon on the Mount had not yet been delivered; also that the controversy in regard to the Sabbath had already begun (John 5: 16) at Jerusalem.—The observance of the Sabbath had been the great outward mark of distinction while the Jews were in exile; the strict observance of it afterwards became an expression of national Jewish feeling. As spirituality decreased, formality increased; during our Lord's ministry the Fourth Commandment was made the basis of over-refined distinctions and petty minutiæ. Here then was the stronghold both of Jewish exclusiveness and Pharisaical formalism. To this our Lord must be antagonistic. As the Sermon on the Mount was delivered *after* these Sabbath controversies, this antagonism is one reason for the omission of any reference to the Fourth Commandment in that discourse. There is no evidence that the Fourth Commandment was abrogated, or that its requirements were curtailed. Our Lord's arguments are drawn either from Old Testament facts and principles, or from Jewish practice. He gave a spiritual character to the whole Decalogue, and His opposition was to the unspiritual observance of the Sabbath. To keep the Christian Sabbath as Christ would have us do it, also 'exceeds the righteousness of the scribes and Pharisees.'

Ver 23. **On the Sabbath day.** This phrase is rightly placed in prominent position—**Through the corn fields.** The grain was probably barley, which ripens in April in that region, and is usually harvested in May.—**His disciples.** Not the 'Twelve' exclusively, probably including most of them.—**Began.** While so doing they were interrupted by the objection of the Pharisees.—**As they went, to pluck the ears of corn;** Greek: 'began to make *their* way, plucking,' etc. That they ate the grain, appears not only from the parallel passages, but from the reference to David's eating (ver. 26). Some think the sense is: broke a way through the grain by plucking off the ears. But this would not have been necessary, since they could tread a path through. Evidently this account also in ver. 27 points to an act of necessity. Mark chooses the phrase in accordance with his graphic style.

24 Pharisees said unto him, Behold, why do they on the
25 sabbath day that which is not lawful? And he said
unto them, Did ye never read what David did, when
he had need, and was an hungred, he, and they that
26 were with him? How he entered into the house of

Ver. 24. **And the Pharisees said unto him.** Luke represents the objection as made to the disciples; both were probably addressed.—**Behold, why do they on the sabbath day that which is not lawful.** It was lawful on other days, all admitted (Deut. 23: 25); but the Pharisees claimed it was not lawful on the Sabbath. Plucking grain on the Sabbath was construed by the Rabbins into a kind of harvesting. This departure from their formal legalism was magnified by the Pharisees into a breaking of God's law.

Ver. 25. **Did ye never read what David did.** All three Evangelists record this main argument against the Pharisees. The case of David (1 Sam. 21: 1-6) was peculiarly in point. The Pharisees insisted that their mode of observing the Sabbath was needful, if a man would be a patriotic Jew and acceptable to God; but a model of Jewish piety had, according to the Scriptures, violated the law as they construed it.—**Hungry**, as His disciples had been.

Ver. 26. **The house of God.** The tabernacle at Nob.—**When Abiathar was high-priest.** The argument is the same as in Matt. 12: 3, 4. The name here introduced occasions some difficulty. According to 1 Sam. 21, 'Ahimelech' was the high-priest who gave David the hallowed bread. 'Abiathar' was the son of Ahimelech (1 Sam. 22: 20) and the friend of David. He afterwards became high-priest, being the only one of his father's family who escaped from the anger of Saul. Some have therefore supposed that the title 'high-priest' is given to him, because he afterwards held the office. But the original (according to the correct reading) is almost equivalent to: during the high-priesthood of Abiathar. The A. V. is based upon the less supported reading given in the margin of the Revised Version. The presence or absence of the article is the variation in the Greek. Probably both father and son had the two names, Ahimelech and Abiathar. In 2 Sam. 8: 17, and 1 Chron. 24: 6, 'Ahimelech the son of Abiathar' is spoken of where the same father and son are undoubtedly referred to, since the time was during the reign of David, after the father had been killed by Doeg (1 Sam. 22). In 1 Sam. 14: 3, the father is called Ahiah ('the son of Ahitub;') in 1 Chron. 18: 16, the son is called 'Ahimelech the son of Abiathar.' The father was certainly called 'Abiathar,' and, as actual high-priest, is here meant. This explanation is the simplest.—**The shew-bread.** Twelve loaves were placed in rows upon a table in the holy place, as a symbol of the communion of God with men. They were renewed every seven days, on the Sabbath, the old loaves being eaten by the priests. David probably came

God ¹when Abiathar was high priest, and did eat the shew-bread, which it is not lawful to eat save for the priests, and gave also to them that were with him? 27 And he said unto them, The sabbath was made for

¹ Some ancient authorities read *in the days of Abiathar the high-priest.*

on the day the old loaves were taken away, *i. e.*, on the Sabbath; which makes the case very appropriate. David did what was actually forbidden, yet hunger was a sufficient justification; much more might the constructive transgression of the disciples be justified by their hunger. Principle: Works of *necessity* have always been permitted on the Sabbath.

Ver. 27. **The sabbath was made for man, and not man for the sabbath.**—Peculiar to Mark, but intimately connected with the quotation from Hosea (Matt. 12: 7). The Sabbath is a means to an end; it was instituted by God (in Paradise, and, like marriage, has survived the fall), for the moral and physical benefit of man. To this gracious end, as all experience shows, *the observance of one day in seven as a day of* RELIGIOUS REST *is a necessary means.* Pharisaism makes the observance itself the *end*, and so establishes its minute rules, as shown in the days of our Lord. Irreligion *misapprehends* the end, by forgetting that man's spiritual needs are to be met, and hence despises the means, namely, a religious observance of the Christian Sabbath. But because 'the Sabbath was made for man,' because of our needs, the first day of the week which our Redeemer, as Lord of the Sabbath, has substituted for the seventh day, is to be observed by Christians, not as a day of pleasure-seeking, or even of excessive religious exertion, but as a time for *physical rest* combined with a *religious activity and enjoyment*. Like all Christian duty, Sabbath observance is to be prompted by love, by a desire for such religious enjoyment, not by any minute rules of Pharisaism. To observe the Christian Sabbath in such a way that our temporal and spiritual welfare is thereby furthered is in one aspect a far more difficult duty than to conform to Pharisaical external rules on the subject. But it becomes easy, as other duties do, under the promptings of grateful love to 'the Lord of the Sabbath.'—While Christian men may hold a different theory, the workings of that theory on the continent of Europe prove its incorrectness. While the State cannot make men religious, or secure a Christian observance of the Sabbath, it can and ought to prevent its *open* desecration, and to protect Christian citizens in their *right* to a day of rest, which is also necessary for the welfare of the state itself. 'Man' here includes children. For them, also, Sabbath observance should be a means, not an end. Too often parents, from conscientious motives, have exacted from their children only a legal, Pharisaical observance of the day, making it a burden and a dread to them. It should rather be used as a day for the training of the little ones, not in Pharisaism, but in the gospel of Jesus Christ; so that, as soon as possible, it may become to them a

28 man, and not man for the sabbath: so that the Son of man is lord even of the sabbath.

3: 1 And he entered again into the synagogue; and there was a man there which had his hand withered. 2 And they watched him, whether he would heal him on the sabbath day; that they might accuse him. And 3 he saith unto the man that had his hand withered,

day of *religious pleasure.* Neither pastor nor Sunday-school teacher can do this so well as parents.

Ver. 28. **So that the Son of man is lord even of the sabbath.** The connection here differs from that of the other accounts, and the idea is more full. Since the Sabbath was made for the benefit of man, it follows that *the Son of Man* (the Messiah, but especially in His character as the Head and Representative of humanity) is Lord (Sovereign over all that belongs to the interest of man, and hence) *also of the Sabbath;* i. e., not for its abolition, but for its true fulfilment; comp. Matt. 5: 17. As such He has the right to change the position of the day, but the language points to a perpetuity of the institution. It implies further that a new air of liberty and love will be breathed into it, so that instead of being what it then was, a badge of narrow Jewish feeling and a field for endless hair-splitting about what was lawful and unlawful, it becomes a type and foretaste of heaven, a day when we get nearest our Lord, when we rise most with Him, when our truest humanity is furthered, because we are truly made like the 'Son of man.'

CHAP. III: 1-6. SECOND SABBATH CONTROVERSY.—Parallel passages: Matt. 12: 9-14; Luke 6: 6-11.

Ver. 1. **He entered again.** On the next Sabbath (Luke 6: 6). 'Again' may refer to 1: 21. In that case the place was Capernaum.— **The synagogue.** It is doubtful whether we should render: 'the,' or, 'a synagogue.' Matthew says definitely 'their synagogue,' i. e., that of His opponents. Luke adds that 'He taught there.'—**Withered.** This word suggests disease or accident as the cause. It was the 'right hand' (Luke).

Ver. 2. **And they watched him.** Watched Him closely.— **Whether he would.** Lit., 'will;' Mark's account being in the present tense.—**That they might accuse him**, might find in His teaching and in the act of mercy they expected would follow, the basis for a formal charge before the local tribunal of which they were themselves members (see ver. 6).

Ver. 3. **Stand forth.** This command is omitted by Matthew. The account of Luke (6: 8) is fullest. Our Lord, knowing their thoughts, took the first active step by calling upon the man to 'stand forth,' and that then the questioning took place. The subsequent discourse is rendered more impressive by the position of the diseased man.

4 ¹Stand forth. And he saith unto them, Is it lawful on the sabbath day to do good, or to do harm? to save a
5 life, or to kill? But they held their peace. And when he had looked round about on them with anger, being grieved at the hardening of their heart, he saith unto the man, Stretch forth thy hand. And he stretched it

¹ Gr. *Arise into the midst.*

Ver. 4. Matt. 12: 10 shows that the question of our Lord was preceded by one from the Pharisees, just as His command had been occasioned by 'their thoughts' or, 'reasonings' (Luke 6: 8).—**Is it lawful?** *i. e.,* according to the Mosaic law.—**To do good or to do harm.** To *benefit,* or to *injure,* rather than to do right or to do wrong. This is repeated yet more forcibly: **to save a life, or to kill?** Our Lord thus establishes the propriety of works of *mercy* on the Sabbath, even according to the Mosaic law (see on Matt. 12: 11, 12, where the falling of a sheep into a pit is introduced). His opponents were silenced; and His authority as 'Lord even of the Sabbath' (chap. 2: 28) is then vindicated by the miracle.

Ver. 5. **He had looked round about on them.** So Luke, who adds 'all,' implying that He took a formal survey of those in the synagogue.—**With anger.** A holy indignation, mentioned by Mark alone, and no doubt expressed in His look.—**Being grieved at the hardening of their heart.** The original implies a compassionate sympathy for their spiritual insensibility. These two feelings, usually excluding each other, are here combined. In this, Christ manifests the character of God as Holy Love,—His anger was the result of holiness, His compassion of love. This character is revealed in the Bible alone. Of themselves men discover either God's anger, forgetting His love, or His mercy, forgetting His holiness. So, too, they are usually angry without compassion, or compassionate without being just. 'Hardening' is preferable to 'hardness,' since the original suggests a process as well as a result. This process was going on as the effect of their opposition to Him, and as a punishment for this sin against privilege. For it man is responsible, and it can put men beyond the reach of the Saviour's compassion. Not that any thing is too hard for Him, but He never saves us against our will. The manner in which the healing took place gave no legal ground for a charge on account of His actions. He did not touch the man, or even command: be healed, but simply said: **Stretch forth thine hand.** The man had no power to do this, and as in the case of spiritual healing, the act of stretching forth was both the effect and the evidence of Divine power. The man's faith was manifest in his attempt to obey, and that too in the midst of such an assembly. His act was a defiance of them, and yet it was not a forbidden act, so that they could not accuse either the Healer or the healed.

6 forth: and his hand was restored. And the Pharisees went out, and straightway with the Herodians took counsel against him, how they might destroy him.
7 And Jesus with his disciples withdrew to the sea: and a great multitude from Galilee followed: and from
8 Judæa, and from Jerusalem, and from Idumæa, and beyond Jordan, and about Tyre and Sidon, a great multitude, hearing ¹what great things he did, came

¹ Or, *all the things that he did.*

Ver. 6. **With the Herodians.** Mark alone mentions this fact. The Herodians were the court party, the adherents of the Herods. As friends of the Romans they were the political antagonists of the Pharisees.—**Took counsel.** The meaning is more exactly: 'held a consultation.' It is not implied that they 'held a council,' *i. e.*, a formal, legal assembly. Hatred of the truth produced this strange alliance. The Pharisees were 'filled with madness' (Luke), and would seek the support of those who could help them in their purpose, as they afterwards did that of Pilate. Dislike of John the Baptist may have made the Herodians hostile to Jesus also. 'Hierarchs and despots are necessary to each other,' and combine against Christ.

Vers. 7-12. THE GREAT MULTITUDES GATHERED TO JESUS.—Parallel passages: comp. Matth. 4: 24, 25; Luke 6: 17-19.

Vers. 7, 8. **Withdrew.** Not to avoid the multitudes, but rather to fulfil His ministry among them, undisturbed by the opposition of the Pharisees.—**To the sea.** To the shores of the sea of Galilee; perhaps to a boat from which He might teach (ver. 9, chap. 4: 1; comp. Luke 5: 3). This description of the crowds waiting upon His ministry is the fullest given in the Gospels. The verses are unfortunately divided in the A. V. Two classes are spoken of, *first*, **a great multitude from Galilee**, where He was teaching, who **followed him**, holding to Him in His conflict with the Pharisees, then: **from Judæa**, etc.—**a great multitude**, who in consequence of the reports of His works **came unto him**. Others prefer to distinguish the second crowd as those who came from Tyre and Sidon, but the correct reading forbids this view. The original emphasizes the greatness of the crowd in the first instance, and in the second their coming from different and distant places.—**Idumæa.** Edom, southeast of Palestine, a sort of border land between the Jews and Gentiles. The inhabitants were descendants of Esau, but had been conquered and made Jews by violence about one hundred and twenty-one years before Christ.—**Beyond Jordan**, east of Jordan.—**About Tyre and Sidon.** The leading cities of Phenicia, north of Palestine along the sea-coast. They stand here for the whole district. Probably Jews and heathen alike came from all these

9 unto him. And he spake to his disciples, that a little boat should wait on him because of the crowd, lest
10 they should throng him: for he had healed many; insomuch that as many as had ¹plagues ²pressed upon
11 him that they might touch him. And the unclean spirits, whensoever they beheld him, fell down before him,
12 and cried, saying, Thou art the Son of God. And he charged them much that they should not make him known.
13 And he goeth up into the mountain, and calleth unto him whom he himself would: and they went

¹ Gr. *scourges*.   ² Gr. *fell*.

quarters. The route of traffic between the points here specified was by Capernaum, so that reports would quickly spread and crowds easily gather.

Ver. 9. **That a small boat.** The original refers to a boat even smaller than the usual fishing-boats.—**Wait on him.** Be constantly at His service.—**Because of the crowd.** A different word from 'multitude' (vers. 7, 8), though the one usually so translated. The purpose was probably both to teach from the boat and to retire from the crowd when He wished. It was doubtless thus that He retired shortly afterwards (ver. 13). His ministry, rather than His personal comfort, was therefore furthered.

Ver. 10. **They pressed upon him.** Not merely gathered about Him to hear Him, and thus created a pressure, but actually pushed themselves upon Him, **to touch him.** The last clause shows that all were healed, as Matthew states.—**Plagues.** Lit., 'scourges;' not a particular class of diseases, as the word 'plagues' now implies. On the healing power, comp. Luke 6: 19.

Ver. 11. **And unclean spirits.** The demon identified himself with the person, since the confession was undoubtedly that of the evil spirit.—**Whenever they saw him.** This was the usual effect.—**Fell down before him and cried.** The possessed man fell down, and his voice uttered the cry; but both acts are attributed to the evil spirit; hence the intimate possession.—**The Son of God.** Comp. chap. 1: 24, 34.

Ver. 12. **And he charged them much.** Matt. 12: 16 shows that some such charge was given to all who were healed; probably to prevent a premature rupture with the Pharisees. But the prohibition to evil spirits was special, and usually given. See the addition Matthew (12: 17-21) makes to this account of our Lord's healing.

Vers. 13-19. THE CHOICE OF THE TWELVE.—Parallel passage: Luke 6: 12-16; comp. Matt. 5: 1; 10: 1-4. During the withdrawal, after the opening hostility of the Phari-

14 unto him. And he appointed twelve,¹ that they might be with him, and that he might send them forth to
15 preach, and to have authority to cast out ²devils:

¹ Some ancient authorities add *whom also he named apostles.* See Luke vi. 13.
² Gr. *demons.*

sees (ver. 7), this choice took place, followed by the Sermon on the Mount, of which Mark makes no mention. This event is to be distinguished from the *sending out* of the Twelve. Comp. chap. 6: 7; Luke 9: 1. The description of the gathering of the multitudes (vers. 7, 8) agrees closely with Luke 6: 17, and also with Matt. 5: 1, so that we can thus fix most exactly the correct position of this choice of the Twelve in the Gospel narrative.

Ver. 13. **Into the mountain.** Probably the mount of Beatitudes (comp. Matt. 5: 1); or possibly the hill country in contrast with the seashore. Our Lord spent the previous night in prayer, choosing the Apostles in the morning (Luke 6; 12, 13).—**Whom he himself would.** The freedom of choice is made prominent. He gathered a larger number of disciples about Him and chose out Twelve (Luke 6: 13). This verse probably refers to the latter act. Strictly speaking, this was rather the formal announcement of His choice, for most of them (seven at least) had been specially called before this time.— **They went,** lit., 'went away' (*i. e.*, from the others) **unto him.**

Ver. 14. **Appointed.** Literally, 'made,' nominated, set apart. The word 'ordained' may mislead. The addition 'whom also He named apostles,' found in some authorities, is probably taken from Luke.— **That they might be with him.** This hints that they were first to be trained for their work. The best preparation for doing Christ's work is being with Christ.—**Send them forth.** This took place afterwards. The word Mark uses implies that they were 'Apostles,' a title now given them (Luke 6: 13), yet rarely applied by the other Evangelists. The discipleship was the main point while Christ lived, and only through the direct choice of the Master to the most intimate discipleship, did they become Apostles.

Ver. 15. The phrase, 'to heal sicknesses,' is to be omitted. Mark gives special prominence to the power of casting out demons.

THE TWELVE APOSTLES. In the four lists given by Matthew (10: 2-4), Mark (3: 16-19), and Luke (6: 14-16; Acts 1: 13), we find the name of Peter *first,* that of Philip *fifth,* that of James the son of Alpheus *ninth;* while between, the same names occur in different order, Judas Iscariot being always put last. The Twelve seem to be thus distinguished into *three* sets of *four each.* In the first the four fishermen, who were once partners in business, are placed together. Besides these two pairs of brothers, we have two brothers (perhaps three) in the third set, while Philip and Bartholomew were friends. All but Judas were Galileans, a number had been disciples of John. Our Lord therefore had regard to natural relationship and mental affinity in the construction of the Apostolate, and the same principle holds good in all His

16, 17 ¹and Simon he surnamed Peter; and James the *son of* Zebedee, and John the brother of James; and them he surnamed Boanerges, which is, Sons of thunder; 18 and Andrew, and Philip, and Bartholomew, and Mat-

¹ Some ancient authorities insert *and he appointed twelve.*

dealings with the church. Those friendships and fraternal ties are blessed which are strengthened by common attachment to our Friend and Elder Brother.

Ver. 16. **He surnamed Peter.** It is not asserted that this name was first given on this occasion. Still the words of our Lord at His first meeting with Simon (John 1: 42) were prophetic, and Mark seems to have mentioned the name for the first time here, because it was the Apostolic name.

Ver. 17. **James ... John.** See chap. 1: 19.—**Boanerges.** A transfer into Greek of an Aramaic word, which was modified from the Hebrew. Mark, writing for other than Jews, interprets it. He alone mentions it.—**Sons of thunder.** This seems to have been occasioned by their '*vehement* and *zealous* disposition, as indicated in Luke 9: 54; comp. Mark 9: 38.' This does not imply censure; for these trials, when sanctified, would be praiseworthy. John was not, as he is often portrayed, of a soft and almost effeminate disposition. Such neutral characters are rarely heroes of faith. The Apocalypse reveals the son of thunder. The name may refer also to the corresponding character of their eloquence. Powerful, fervid preachers are still thus termed. With the ancients, thunder was the symbol for profound and solemn utterances. The name would be prophetic in this application. It was not used frequently, like Simon's surname, because it was borne by two brothers, one of whom was martyred earliest.

Ver. 18. **Andrew.** See chap. 1: 16. Matthew arranges the Twelve by pairs; Mark does not. In other respects the lists of Matthew and Mark correspond most closely.—**Philip,** not the Evangelist. The first disciple called, a native of Bethsaida. The name is Greek.—**Bartholomew,** *i. e.,* the son of Tholmai. He is probably identical with Nathanael (John 1: 43), the friend of Philip, and is also supposed to have been a resident of Cana in Galilee.—**Matthew,** the Evangelist, who, in his own account, inserts his previous employment as a token of the power of grace.—**Thomas,** *i. e.,* 'twin,' the Greek name of the same meaning being 'Didymus.' He is frequently mentioned in the Gospel according to John.—**James** (Jacob) **the son of Alphæus,** called 'James the less,' or, the younger (chap. 15: 40, where his mother Mary is mentioned). The name 'Alpheus' has been considered identical with 'Clopas' or 'Cleophas,' since 'the mother of James the less' (chap. 15: 40) is identical with 'Mary, the wife of Cleophas' (John 19: 25). His mother's sister, in John 19: 25, may refer to Salome (see above). The view that it refers to Mary, the wife of Cleophas, identifies this James with 'the Lord's brother'

thew, and Thomas, and James the *son* of Alphæus, and
19 Thaddæus, and Simon the ¹Cananæan, and Judas Iscariot, which also betrayed him.

¹ Or, *Zealot.* See Luke vi. 15; Acts i. 13.

(Gal. 1: 19); the term being taken in the wide sense of relative. Others reject the notion that the two sisters had the same name, and think that Alpheus was an older brother of Joseph, who adopted his children, and that thus they were called our Lord's 'brethren.' We hold that James the Lord's brother was the author of the Epistle, but not one of the Twelve, nor were any of 'His brethren,' who were either the younger children of Joseph and Mary, or the children of Joseph by a former wife. We only remark here: In the many varying lists of the Apostles, there is no hint that these persons were the Lord's brethren; that in Matt. 12: 46–50 these brethren are distinguished pointedly from the disciples, at a time after the Twelve were chosen; the taunt at Nazareth, which names these brethren, loses much of its force, if they were among His disciples; John (7: 5) expressly states they did not believe on him. On the whole subject, see Lange's Com., *Matthew*, pp. 255-260.—**Thaddæus**, meaning, 'courageous,' as also his other name: 'Lebbæus.' He was also called 'Judas;' was probably the brother of James, 'the son of Alpheus,' and the author of the short Epistle of Jude. Comp. Luke 6: 16; Acts 1: 13; John 14: 22. One of the Lord's 'brethren' was called Judas (Matt. 13: 55), and has been identified with this Apostle. But Matthew was also the son of Alpheus, and yet no one affirms that he was the brother of James. It is as likely that there was a *great number* of persons about our Lord called James, Judas, and Simon, as that two of the Apostles mentioned together were not brothers, although the father of each was named Alpheus.—**Simon the Cananæan.** Not 'Canaanite.' If a local term at all, it means 'an inhabitant of Cana;' but it is probably derived from the Hebrew, and is the same as 'Zelotes' (Luke 6: 15; Acts 1: 13). The *Zealots* were a sect of strict Jews, who afterwards became fierce fanatics. They were apt to take the law into their own hands, to punish offences against the Jewish law. This Apostle has also been considered one of our Lord's 'brethren;' but 'Simon' was a very common name (eight persons, at least, of this name are mentioned in the New Testament). These three are joined together in all four lists of the Apostles; but there is no other hint of relationship.

Ver. 19. **Judas Iscariot**, *i. e.* 'a man of Kerioth,' in the tribe of Judah (Josh. 15: 25). He was not, like all the rest, a Galilean.—**Which also betrayed**, or, 'delivered Him up.' The choice of this man remains a part of the great mystery concerning God's sovereignty and man's free choice. He is generally supposed to have been by nature the most gifted of the Twelve; but it is a mistake to suppose that the Twelve as a body were poor, ignorant or dull. They had fair

20 And he cometh ¹into a house. And the multitude cometh together again, so that they could not so much
21 as eat bread. And when his friends heard it, they went out to lay hold on him: for they said He is

¹ Or, *home.*

natural abilities, a teachable disposition, and the common religious education; some had been in the preparatory school of the Baptist; Peter and John were men of genius, especially the latter, as his Gospel abundantly proves; John possessed a house in Jerusalem, and was connected with the family of the high-priest. All were unsophisticated, simple-hearted, open to conviction, and fit vessels to be filled with the saving knowledge of Christ. With the last clause of ver. 19, a new paragraph begins.

Vers. 19 b-30. THE DOUBT OF FRIENDS AND THE HOSTILITY OF THE SCRIBES.—Parallel passages: Matt. 12: 25-29; Luke 11: 17-22.—*Chronology.* At this point we find the largest gap in Mark's narrative. Shortly after the choice of the Twelve, the Sermon on the Mount was delivered. See Luke 6: 12—7: 1. On and after the return to Capernaum, a number of events took place, recorded partly by Matthew and partly by Luke, and in most cases by both. The miracle immediately preceding the occurrences of the paragraph before us, was the healing of a blind and dumb demoniac (Matt. 12: 22) which called forth the charge of the scribes (ver. 22). Vers. 20, 21, are peculiar to Mark.

Ver. 19 b. **And he cometh into a house.** This indicates a return to Capernaum; as the succeeding events probably took place there. The sentence, therefore, properly begins a new paragraph. In the interval a number of important events took place; see above. If a particular house is meant, there is an undesigned coincidence. Matthew, in prefacing the parables of our Lord, tells us He went 'out of the house,' without having spoken of His entering one. Those parables were uttered just after the events next recorded by Mark, who speaks of this entering a house, without telling of His going out.

Ver. 20. **Cometh together again.** If the last clause of ver. 19 means a return to Capernaum, 'again' must refer to chap. 2: 1.— **They could not so much as eat bread.** A vivid description of the thronging. Our Lord and His disciples could not find time to have their regular meals. Notice, the excitement and popularity was at its height; but the opposition now takes definite form, and stems the tide.

Ver. 21. **His friends**, lit. 'those by him.' The exact reference is doubtful. The nearer relatives, spoken of ver. 31, may not be included, since they waited outside; but probably the whole circle was engaged in this effort with varying feelings, the immediate family persisting longer (see on Matt. 12: 46).—**Heard it**, *i. e.*, what was going on; they may have heard that the scribes had come with a hostile purpose

22 beside himself. And the scribes which came down from Jerusalem said, He hath Beelzebub, and ¹By the prince of the ²devils casteth he out the ²devils. 23 And he called them unto him, and said unto them in 24 parables, How can Satan cast out Satan? And if a

¹ Or, *In.* ² Gr. *demons.*

(ver. 22).—**They went out**, etc. Either from Nazareth, or from their house in Capernaum, since it is uncertain in which place they now lived.—**For they said.** The relatives just spoken of.—**He is beside himself.** This implies either actual insanity in a bad sense, or religious enthusiasm and ecstasy, even to derangement, in a good sense. While an accusation of madness on the part of His relatives is neither impossible nor improbable, so long as they were not true believers, it may have been a mere pretext. As His enemies had already, in all probability, said that He was possessed, His relatives, from motives of policy, may have adopted this modification of the charge to get Him away; with this, anxiety for His health may have entered as a motive. The context favors the thought that the motive was *policy* resulting from want of faith, though perhaps not from positive disbelief. This doubting, worldly policy, which could seek to shelter Him by meeting the accusations of His foes half way, is in keeping with the desire to thrust Him forward, which was afterwards shown (John 7: 3–5). Yet even among these relatives there was probably a great variety of opinions regarding Him.

Ver. 22. **The scribes which came down from Jerusalem.** Mark thus defines the parties, while Matthew (12: 23) states the occasion of the accusation. The purpose of their coming was doubtless to entrap and oppose Him, and hence the place was probably Capernaum, since they would go to His headquarters.—**He hath Beelzebub.** More correctly, 'Beelzebul.' The former ('lord of flies') was the name of a Philistine idol. 'Beelzebul' means either, (1) 'lord of dung,' the word being changed from Beelzebub to Beelzebul to admit of this contemptuous sense; or (2) 'lord of the habitation.' The latter corresponds better with the expression: 'master of the house.' Satan is referred to, but with a special reference to the indwelling of evil spirits in man; Satan being the lord.—**By,** lit., 'in,' *i. e.*, in intimate fellowship with. Mark, both here and in ver. 30, states with greatest definiteness that they charged Him, not only with exercising Satanic power, but with being Himself possessed by an evil spirit.

Ver. 23. **Said unto them in parables.** The word 'parable,' here, has its wider sense of similitude. Three illustrations are given by Mark (vers. 24, 25, 27); Matthew inserts a fourth (that of a 'divided city').—**How can Satan cast out Satan?** Peculiar to Mark. This is the statement of the absurdity of their accusation; the illustrative proof follows.

Ver. 24. **And if a kingdom be divided against itself.** The

kingdom be divided against itself, that kingdom can-
25 not stand. And if a house be divided against itself,
26 that house will not be able to stand. And if Satan
hath risen up against himself, and is divided, he can-
27 not stand, but hath an end. But no one can enter into
the house of the strong *man*, and spoil his goods, except
he first bind the strong man; and then he will spoil
28 his house. Verily I say unto you, All their sins shall
be forgiven unto the sons of men, and their blasphe-

assertion of the Pharisees assumed that there was 'an organized kingdom of evil with a personal ruler.' Our Lord uses this assumption, as a terrible fact, which, however, proves the absurdity of the charge made against Himself. This organized kingdom of darkness, because it is only evil, is racked with discords and hatred, but against the kingdom of God (ver. 28), it is a unit. The point of the argument here is: not that discords are always and at once fatal, but that an organization which acts against itself, its own distinctive aims, must destroy itself.

Ver. 25. **And if a house**, etc. The same principle is illustrated by a divided house.—**Will not be able to stand.** Mark's account here and in ver. 26 shows independence.

Ver. 26. **And if Satan hath risen**, etc. Not, 'rise up,' but 'rose,' 'hath risen,' as the accusation implied.—**He cannot stand, but hath an end**, *i. e.*, ceases to be what he is; the supposition, which His enemies advanced, would, if fully carried out, argue Satan out of existence. A man might be at war within, but even then the outward acts would not necessarily be in opposition. Satan is utterly wicked, hence good and evil do not strive within him, and his fighting against himself is not to be imagined. The argument implies: that the Pharisees had called our Lord 'Satan;' that Satan is a person; that he has a kingdom.

Ver. 27. **But no one**, etc. The third illustration introduces the antagonism between the kingdom of Satan and the kingdom of God (comp. Matt. 12: 28, 29; Luke 11: 20-22). The latter Evangelist presents this figure more fully. The course of thought is, 'If I were not the Messiah, *stronger than Satan*, how could I thus spoil him?'—**Spoil his goods.** The strong man represents Satan; his 'house' the world where he has long reigned; 'his goods,' the possessed or the evil spirit possessing them.—**Spoil his house.** The word 'spoil' in both clauses is a strong one, indicating a complete victory over Satan in this world. The parallel accounts emphasize still further the antagonism between Christ and Satan by adding: 'He that is not with me is against me,' etc.

Ver. 28. **Verily**, etc. This formula here implies Christ's Divine

29 mies wherewith soever they shall blaspheme: but whosoever shall blaspheme against the Holy Spirit hath
30 never forgiveness, but is guilty of an eternal sin: because they said, He hath an unclean spirit.

authority to speak on this subject.—**All their sins**, etc. A literal rendering would be: 'All things shall be forgiven unto the sons of men, their sins and their blasphemies wherewith,' etc.

Ver. 29. **But whosoever shall blaspheme against the Holy Spirit.** The account of Matthew makes a contrast between speaking against the Son of Man and speaking against the Holy Spirit. The latter term does not refer to the Divine nature of Christ, but to the third Person of the Trinity, as the Agent working in the hearts of men, without whom neither forgiveness nor holiness is possible.—**Hath never forgiveness**, or, 'hath no forgiveness forever.' The phrase equivalent to 'forever' corresponds with the fuller expression of Matthew: 'neither in this world, nor in that which is to come.' The Jews distinguished eternity into two worlds (æons, or, ages), one before, the other after the coming of Christ. That the sense here is 'forever' scarcely admits of a doubt.—**But is guilty of**, more than in *danger of*, or even *liable to*, indicating a present subjection to.—**An eternal sin.** Thus Mark expresses the same idea given by Matthew: 'neither in this world, nor in that to come.' The word we translate 'sin' includes the idea of guilt (Rom. 3: 25; 5: 16), but can scarcely be rendered 'punishment.' It usually refers to an *act*, rather than a state of sin, but eternal sin points to an unending state of activity in sin. Damnation, or, 'judgment,' is an explanatory alteration of the original text. The correct reading implies that the unpardonable sin, though it may begin with one act of blasphemy (ver. 30), results in a state of sinful activity which continues forever. For this reason it is unpardonable. The punishment is perpetual, because the sin is perpetual. The sin excludes pardon, because it excludes repentance. The remark of Matthew refers to the guilt, that of Mark to the sin itself, explaining the former. This is the most fearful aspect of eternal punishment, namely, being forever deprived of the needed influences of the Holy Spirit, and hence in a state of eternally growing sin and guilt. Conscious existence is evidently implied by the word chosen. Further, while the next verse suggests a particular form of the unpardonable sin, this phrase favors the view that it is an active *state* rather than a particular act.

Ver. 30. **Because they said, He hath an unclean spirit.** This does not necessarily define the sin of blasphemy against the Holy Spirit, but certainly indicates its character. Even if these accusers had not committed it, their language tended in that direction. They had attributed to an evil spirit what was the work of the Holy Spirit, that too in presence of sufficient evidence of its true character. This verse, however, is the strongest support of that view of the sin against the Holy

31 And there come his mother and his brethren; and, standing without, they sent unto him, calling him. 32 And a multitude was sitting about him; and they say unto him, Behold thy mother and thy brethren with-

Spirit which regards it as a *particular sin*, that of deliberately, persistently, and maliciously, in the presence of proper evidence, attributing the works of Christ (whether of physical healing or spiritual deliverance) to diabolical agency, instead of acknowledging the Holy Spirit as the Agent. The accusation of the Pharisees, in this instance, *may* have been such a sin. It is very different from ordinary and usual opposition to God and Christ, and also from 'grieving' or 'resisting the Holy Ghost.' It cannot be a mere denial of the Divinity of Christ. Those who fear that they have committed the unpardonable sin, give good evidence that they have *not* done so. Another view defines this sin as a *state* of determined, wilful opposition, in the presence of light, to the power of the Holy Spirit, virtually a moral suicide, a killing of the conscience, so that the human spirit is absolutely insusceptible to the influences of the Holy Spirit. Ver. 29 and Matt. 12: 32–35 favor this view. The outward manifestation of such a state will be 'the blasphemy of the Holy Spirit.' It is uncertain whether such a state is possible 'in this world,' and we should beware of imputing it to any, but the impossibility of forgiveness is quite evident. The inference from this view is, that all sin must either be repented of and forgiven, or culminate (here and hereafter) in the unpardoned and unpardonable state.

Vers. 31–36. Our Lord's Mother and Brethren seek Him.— Parallel passages: Matt. 12: 46–50; Luke 8: 19-21.

Ver. 31. Mark omits the introductory phrase: 'While He yet talked to the people' (Matt. 12 : 46), which fixes the occasion.—**And there come his mother and his brethren.** This vivacious form is peculiar to Mark; the A. V. follows an inaccurate reading.—**Standing without.** Probably, though not necessarily, outside the house referred to in ver. 19; possibly, on the outside of the crowd.—**They sent unto him, calling him.** Comp. ver. 20. Luke 8: 19 shows that they had unsuccessfully attempted to get near Him. The same Evangelist (11: 27, 28) places immediately after the discourse just narrated the exclamation of a woman, referring to His mother ('Blessed is the womb,' etc.), as if Mary's presence had occasioned it. The response there recorded is similar in character to ver. 35 of this chapter.

Ver. 32. **And a multitude was sitting about him.** Peculiar to Mark.—**And they say unto him.** Matthew is more specific: 'and one said unto him.' We need not suppose that there was any wish to interrupt the discourse, still less any purpose of calling attention to the humble relatives to prove that Jesus was not the Messiah.

33 out seek for thee. And he answereth them, and saith,
34 Who is my mother and my brethren? And looking round on them which sat round about him, he saith,
35 Behold, my mother and my brethren! For whosoever shall do the will of God, the same is my brother, and sister, and mother.

4:1 And again he began to teach by the sea side. And there is gathered unto him a very great multi-

Ver. 33. **Who is my mother and my brethren?** Implying not contempt nor carelessness, but that the family relation in His case was peculiar. He was more than man, otherwise He was not justified in thus speaking.

Ver. 34. **And looking round**, etc. Matthew; 'And He stretched forth His hand toward His disciples.' The look was probably one of affectionate recognition; contrast the look of anger and grief (ver. 5). That the look as well as the word applied to more than the Twelve is evident.—**Behold my mother and my brethren**, *i. e.*, these are as nearly allied and as dear to me (see next verse).

Ver. 35. **For whosoever shall do the will of God.** Matthew: 'my Father who is in heaven.' Mere profession of discipleship does not entitle to such a position. Our Lord does not say how we are enabled to do the will of God, but makes such a result the criterion.— **The same is my brother, and sister, and mother.** The term 'father' is excluded; His 'Father' is 'in heaven.' Christ loves His people with a love *human* as well as Divine; there can be no closer relationship to Him than that of real discipleship which manifests itself in this obedience to His Heavenly Father. Christ was 'the Son of man' as well as 'the Son of Mary,' identified with humanity in one sense, even more than with her. Those who have not seen Jesus on earth are here assured of His presence and affection in a way that should be a constant stimulant to holiness. Brethren of Christ are brethren to each other. The dearest and best of friends and relatives so often needlessly anxious about us, have no claims upon us superior to our duties to the gospel of the Kingdom. On the brethren of our Lord, see ver. 18 and chap. 6:3.

Chap. IV: 1-9. THE PARABLE OF THE SOWER.—Parallel passages: Matt. 13: 1-9; Luke 8: 4-8. A parable, in the strict sense, is thus defined by Alford: 'a serious narration within the limits of probability, of a course of action pointing to some moral or spiritual truth.' It is not necessary to suppose that our Lord's parables were always founded on fact, and generally composed of real incidents. We indeed resort to fiction in teaching moral truth, because unaware of facts adapted to convey the same lesson; while Christ's knowledge of course included such facts. It is, however, enough to say, that Christ's parables (His figures also) are based on analogies which He alone

tude, so that he entered into a boat, and sat in the sea; and all the multitude were by the sea on the land.

had wisdom to discern, and authority to proclaim. His parables give no warrant for new ones; nor do they determine the propriety of our using fiction to spread or illustrate the truth. Parables may be pressed too far; the general truth is always the central one; others are usually involved, but only *as related to* it. Resemblances which we discover at every point, although founded on analogies which God has created, are not to be placed on a level with what our Lord distinctly teaches. The uninspired lessons *from* the parables exceed in number the inspired lessons *of* the parables. The former include *possible* meanings, the latter *necessary* ones. The former may be used to enforce truth revealed elsewhere; the latter are revelations of truth. Seeking the many lessons makes us rich in spiritual knowledge, grasping the necessary one makes us confident. The purpose of our Lord in teaching by parables was two-fold (vers. 11, 12; comp. vers 21-25): to *reveal* and to *conceal* the truth. To *reveal* to those who really sought the truth; to *conceal* from those who did not desire such knowledge; thus rewarding the former, and punishing the latter. The purpose of concealing is plainly stated by our Lord Himself, and may have been in mercy, since it prevented a greater perverting of the truth to their condemnation. The hostility of the Pharisees called for the teaching by parables in its purpose of *concealing* the truth, which is most strongly expressed by Mark (ver. 12), while the choice of the Twelve (chap. 3: 14) formed the nucleus of a band of followers (comp. ver. 10), in whom the other purpose of *revealing* the truth could be fulfilled. The Old Testament parable, spoken by Nathan (2 Sam. 12: 1-6), also concealed and revealed; it called forth from David an unprejudiced judgment on his own conduct, and then produced conviction of sin. This special purpose is also evident in a few of our Lord's parables, e g., that spoken in the house of Simon (Luke 7: 41, 42). Mark, in his report of this protracted discourse in parables, gives but three, one of them not mentioned elsewhere. Each of the Evangelists independently chose some out of the many uttered. In Matthew we find the *chronological* development of the kingdom of heaven brought out; here, all three parables are drawn from familiar agricultural pursuits, presenting the one idea of the growth or development of the kingdom of God: the *first*, as respects the soil, or the difficulty of its beginnings; the *second*, illustrating the *relative independence* of this development; the last, its wonderful *extension*. Mark here introduces (vers. 21-25) what Matthew records as uttered on other occasions. Our Lord was in the habit of repeating striking figures, proverbs and aphorisms. This discourse took place the 'same day' (Matt. 13: 1) with the occurrences just mentioned (chap. 3: 20-35). It should be noted that a large section of Luke's account (chaps. 11: 27—12: 59) seems to find its most appropriate chronological position immediately before this discourse in parables. The question cannot be decided with certainty; but this view presents us with further details respecting the 'same day,' the history of which is narrated with the greatest fulness, as if to give a specimen of the busy life led by our Lord during His ministry.

Ver. 1. **And again he began.** 'Began' may refer either to this new mode of instruction, or to His beginning with the gathering of the crowd. 'Again' may point to a similar occasion (chap. 3: 7).— **A very great multitude**; lit., 'greatest.' There is every reason

2 And he taught them many things in parables, and
3 said unto them in his teaching, Hearken: Behold, the
4 sower went forth to sow: and it came to pass, as he
sowed, some *seed* fell by the way side, and the birds
5 came and devoured it. And other fell on the rocky
ground, where it had not much earth; and straightway it sprang up, because it had no deepness of earth:

to believe that this was the greatest. It was the turning point in His public teaching, since the parabolic instruction now begins.—**A boat.** Probably the one provided for this purpose (see chap. 3: 9). It is doubtful whether the definite article is here used in the Greek.—**In the sea.** The boat was small, and His position was near the surface of the water, the audience being slightly elevated above Him. This is the best way of arranging an audience; but the world seems to have discovered it quicker than the Church.

Ver. 2. **And he taught them.** The reference is to His habit of teaching.—**Many things.** Out of these Mark selects what follows. —**In his teaching,** perhaps, with a reference to this particular kind of teaching. Christ's teaching was authoritative, and in this, as in most cases, *doctrinal.* He presents new truth here, not mere exhortation (see ver. 11).

Vers. 3-9. THE PARABLE OF THE SOWER. The similarity between the accounts of Matthew and Mark is very great, as might be expected in the case of such a striking parable. Matthew was present; Mark probably heard it from Peter, who was also present. Luke's account (8: 5-8) is briefer, and he does not describe the position of the Teacher and His audience.

Ver. 3. **Hearken.** This, inserted by Mark only, seems to introduce the whole discourse, as deserving great attention.—**Behold,** calling attention to what follows, not to some object in sight, which would have distracted attention from the parable.—**The sower,** standing for the class; **went forth,** *i. e.,* as usual, pointing rather to a supposed case, than to something occurring before their eyes.

Ver. 4. **By the way-side.** The paths or roads pass close to the edge of the ploughed ground in unenclosed fields; or the reference may be to the path across the field on which the sower walked as he sowed. In any case the seed was exposed, and quickly picked up by the birds.—'Fowls' is misleading; 'of the air' is not found in the best authorities.

Ver. 5. **And other.** The various accounts present remarkable minor differences, which will appear from a comparison of expressions like this, in the Revised Version.—**Upon the rocky ground.** Not full of stones, but thin soil over rocks.—**Straightway it sprang up, because,** etc. The greater heat of the shallow soil would cause a rapid growth upwards.

6 and when the sun was risen, it was scorched; and be-
7 cause it had no root, it withered away. And other
fell among the thorns, and the thorns grew up, and
8 choked it, and it yielded no fruit. And others fell
into the good ground, and yielded fruit, growing up
and increasing; and brought forth, thirty-fold, and
9 sixty-fold, and a hundred-fold. And he said, Who
hath ears to hear, let him hear.
10 And when he was alone, they that were about him

Ver. 6. **Scorched**, or, 'burnt.' The heat of the sun, so necessary to vegetable life, did this; but the effect must be connected with the cause: **it had no root.** Plants need both sunshine and moisture; they get the first from their growth above ground, the second from their growth below ground; the root however being the principal channel of nourishment (comp. Luke; 'moisture'). Hence **it withered away.**

Ver. 7. **Among the thorns,** *i. e.*, where there were roots of thorns, etc., not necessarily among thorn-bushes.—**And the thorns grew up and choked it.** The thorns were of ranker growth.—**And it yielded no fruit.** This Mark adds, showing that his account is not an abridgment. The same result is of course implied in the other narrative.

Ver. 8. **Into the good ground.** The proportion of the harvest is large, but not unexampled. Palestine was once exceedingly fertile.—**Growing up and increasing.** The words are peculiar to Mark. This is spoken of the 'fruit,' but in the wider sense of the whole progress of the plant, since all this is necessary to the real fruit or grain, which was brought forth. This verse puts the smallest proportion first; in Matthew's account it is put last. Other verbal differences attesting the independence of the Evangelists, are indicated as far as possible in the Revised Version.

Ver 9. **Who hath ears,** etc. (In Matthew, 'he that' is correct; here, 'who'). The A. V. reverses this. The proverbial expression usually follows an important statement, intimating that he who has the discernment to understand will find the deeper meaning. It here forms an appropriate transition to what follows.

Vers. 10–20. THE PRIVATE EXPLANATION OF THE PARABLE.—Parallel passages: Matt. 13:10-23; Luke 8:9-15. The agreement with Matthew is striking; but Mark's account shows independence. In vers. 10-12 the reason is given for speaking in parables; comp. Matt. 13:10-17. The latter is fuller on this point, but Mark's statement is, in some respects, more specific and stronger.

Ver. 10. **Alone.** This refers to a temporary withdrawal, when His disciples 'came' to Him (Matthew), for He evidently spoke further to the multitude (Matt. 13:24-35).—**They that were about him**

11 with the twelve asked of him the parables. And he said unto them, Unto you is given the mystery of the kingdom of God: but unto them that are without, 12 all things are done in parables: that seeing they may see, and not perceive; and hearing they may hear, and

with the twelve. Matthew and Luke say less definitely: 'the disciples.' What follows was spoken neither to the multitude nor to the Twelve alone.—**Asked of him the parables.** The plural is the more correct form. Matthew says more definitely: 'Why speakest thou unto them in parables?' and Luke: 'What this parable might be?' The answer in all three accounts is: *first*, a reason why He thus taught, and, *secondly*, the exposition of this particular parable. Both questions must have been asked, as is implied in the indefinite statement of this verse. This was precisely the purpose: that those who would seek might know 'the mystery,' and those who would not put forth this effort, might not.

Ver. 11. **Unto you** is emphatic.—**Is** ('hath been and is') **given.** —**The mystery.** Matthew and Luke: 'the mysteries.' A mystery is not necessarily something inscrutable in its nature, but it may be that which is unknown to man in his natural condition, before it is revealed to him by God. The mysteriousness arises mainly from the sinful state of man; yet God for wise purposes often withholds the revelation without which these things remain a mystery. The great mystery is Christ Himself (1 Tim. 3: 16), making peace between God and man, between man and man (Jew and Gentile; Eph. 3: 4-11). This was not fully revealed to the Apostles until long after the death of Christ, although they already had clearer views than the mass of the people. Where this gospel mystery has been preached, sin alone hides it from men; however much may remain not fully revealed to us. To Christ's disciples 'is given the mystery of the kingdom of God.' The omission of 'to know' renders the declaration even more forcible. These parables are to reveal, not good moral advice, but *truth otherwise unknown*, the peculiar doctrines respecting 'the kingdom of God' which can be fully received only by those to whom spiritual discernment is given.—**Unto them that are without.** Matthew: 'to them.' Luke: 'to the rest.' A separation between the disciples and others had begun. (Afterwards, 'those without' meant those not Christians; 1 Cor. 5: 12.) 'Those without' did not receive this gift of God necessary for the understanding of these truths, were without its influence. But their position was according to their own choice; Christ forbade none, and the disciples in this case were not merely the Twelve chosen by Him, but all who would come.

Ver. 12. **That**, more exactly, 'in order that.' 'When God transacts a matter, it is idle to say that the result is not the purpose' (Alford). This purpose is indicated here even more strongly than in

not understand; lest haply they should turn again, and
13 it should be forgiven them. And he saith unto
them, Know ye not this parable? and how shall ye
14 know all the parables? The sower soweth the word.
15 And these are they by the way side, where the word is
sown; and when they have heard, straightway cometh
Satan, and taketh away the word which hath been

Matthew. The object of the parable is both to conceal and to reveal the truth, according to the moral state of the hearers. Mark only uses the prophecy of Isaiah (6: 9, 10), without citing it directly as Matthew does. It was already partially fulfilled when the Jews hardened their hearts against the preaching of Isaiah, the Evangelist among the prophets; it was completely fulfilled, when they rejected the gospel itself as proclaimed by the Son of God. Their moral *unwillingness* preceded their moral *inability*, and the latter was a divine judgment on the former. So Pharaoh first hardened his heart before God judicially hardened him. Here, where a separation between Christ's followers, and those without, is first plainly marked, the point of discrimination is *spiritual knowledge*. This shows the importance of Christian truth. which implies *doctrine*.

Ver. 13. **Know ye not this parable?** An answer to the second question, implied in ver. 10. It is not a reproof, but means: 'You find you cannot understand this without assistance.' The next question: **and how shall ye know all the parables?** extends the thought to all parables, but intimates further: 'The first parable of the kingdom is the basis of all the rest. If they understand not this, they could not understand any that followed. If they had the explanation of this, they had the key for the understanding of all others.' Hence our Lord gives, not rules of interpretation, but examples, one of which is here preserved, to be our guide in interpretation. To understand the parables, God must help us (ver. 11). Wrong interpretations are those which do not tend to conversion and forgiveness (ver. 12).

Ver. 14. Peculiar to Mark, though involved in the other accounts.— **The sower** is Christ (Matt. 13: 37) Himself and His ministers (1 Cor. 3: 6).—**The word.** Matthew: 'the word of the kingdom'; Luke: 'the seed is the word of God.' The *spoken* word is made most prominent, as this was almost the only means used in the Apostolic age, to which this parable primarily refers.

Ver. 15. **And these are they by the way side, where the word is sown.** In all the accounts the expressions used point, not to the ground. but to the result of the sowing in the different cases as representing the different classes of hearers. This apparent mixing of metaphors should caution us against pressing the analogies too far.—

16 sown in them. And these in like manner are they that are sown upon the rocky *places*, who, when they have heard the word, straightway receive it with joy; 17 and they have no root in themselves, but endure for a while; then, when tribulation or persecution ariseth 18 because of the word, straightway they stumble. And others are they that are sown among the thorns; these 19 are they that have heard the word, and the cares of the ¹ world, and the deceitfulness of riches, and the

¹ Or, *age*

Cometh Satan. Matthew: 'the wicked one'; Luke: 'the devil.' Being spoken of in the explanation of the parable, or in a didactic way, Satan must be a real personal being, and not merely the symbol of evil.—**And taketh away.** Almost during the act of hearing. This is done through 'birds,' passing thoughts and desires; the purpose being 'lest they should believe and be saved' (Luke 8: 12). The immediate cause is hardness of the soil.

Ver. 16. **In like manner.** 'After the same analogy carrying on a like principle of interpretation' (Alford).—**Straightway receive it with joy.**—The effect is immediate and apparently good; but beneath the surface easily stirred, is a soil harder than the trodden path. Great joy without deep spiritual conviction or conflict.

Ver. 17. This verse, as emended, presents the case more vividly.—**They have no root in themselves.** Their apparent Christian life is rooted only in the temporary excitement about them.—**Endure for a while.** The expression implies also: 'are the creatures of circumstances.'—**Then**, as might be expected, **when**, etc.—**Tribulation**, the Greek word is usually thus translated; **persecution**, a special form of tribulation; all arising **because of the word**, and intended to strengthen, as the sunshine the plant; but the plant without root is withered.—**Straightway** (as in the reception of the word) **they stumble**, or, 'are made to stumble.' They are sentimental, superficial, changeful, one-sided professors of Christianity. The parable does not decide whether such have really been subjects of grace.

Ver. 18. **And others are they that are sown among the thorns.** The form of this verse is peculiar to Mark. The *third class* hold out longer, but are unfruitful, from a divided heart, in which evil triumphs; the thorns being hardier than the wheat.

Ver. 19. **The cares of the world**, not pure worldliness, which belongs to the first class, but anxieties about worldly things distracting persons of serious mind.—**The deceitfulness of riches.** Whether in the pursuit or possession of wealth.—**The lusts of other things**, other than those presented by the word. This includes all other worldly distractions. The desires become 'lusts,' because the objects

lusts of other things entering in, choke the word, and
20 it becometh unfruitful. And those are they that were
sown upon the good ground; such as hear the word,
and accept it, and bear fruit, thirtyfold, and sixtyfold,
and a hundredfold.
21 And he said unto them, Is the lamp brought to be
put under the bushel, or under the bed, *and* not to be

interfere with spiritual growth. What is in itself innocent may become a snare. These things **choke the word, and it becometh unfruitful.** Notwithstanding the previous (and perhaps long continued) promise of fruit.

Ver. 20. The closing words of the parable (ver. 8) are repeated in the last clause of this verse, as in Matthew, and the same difference in order is preserved.—**The good ground.** This has been prepared. All is of divine grace, yet the verse plainly teaches that the persons referred to *actively* and *willingly* accept and understand the truth; the result being continued fruitfulness. The degrees vary, since characters and capacities and gifts vary. This class alone fulfils the purpose of the sower.

This parable, which begins the discourse, refers primarily to the beginnings of Christianity. The generous sowing of the Apostolic age; though the hearers differ, the sowing always the same; with good seed, a full hand, and a wise reach.—The four classes of hearers, the same in every age. The unfruitful hearers: the *first* class, careless, corrupt, utterly hardened; the *second*, enthusiastic, but fickle, full of feeling, not of faith: the *third*, earnest, but legal, self-seeking, serious-minded worldlings—the worst of the three, though often awakening most hope. The first have the faults of childhood; the second, of youth; the third, of more mature years. The good ground; broken up, deeply stirred, cleared of thorns. The proportion of fruit varies, but the whole is fruitful. Historical application: 1. The Jews (who failed to receive the word); 2. The Greeks (short-lived in their devotion); 3. The Romans (choked by temporal power); 4. As we hope, the Teutonic races (thus far the most fruitful).

Vers. 21-25. THE WARNING ABOUT HEARING.—Parallel passage: Luke 8: 16-18.—The same thoughts are found in different places in Matthew. They were doubtless repeated.

Ver. 21. Comp. Matt. 5: 15. The variations in the three forms of this verse are well reproduced in the Revised Version.—**Is the lamp.**—**The bushel.** The ordinary household measure, holding about a peck. Under this, the lamp could be hid.—**Or under the bed** (so Luke also).—**And not to be put on the stand,** *i. e.* 'lampstand;' its proper place, an elevated holder or stand, so that its light might

22 put on the stand? For there is nothing hid, save that it should be manifested; neither was *anything* 23 made secret, but that it should come to light. If any 24 man hath ears to hear, let him hear. And he said unto them, Take heed what ye hear: with what mea-

be diffused as widely as possible. The application here is to teaching in parables. Although thus spoken in secret, they were not to remain mysteries, confined to a few; the purpose, as in case of a lamp, was to give light. Hence they should take care to learn their meaning, 'not hiding them under a blunted understanding, nor when they did understand them, neglecting the teaching of them to others' (Alford).

Ver. 22. **For there is nothing hid**, etc. A proverbial statement, occurring with a different application in Luke 12: 2; in a different connection, but with the same general application in Matt. 10: 26; and in the same connection in Luke 8: 18. The course of thought is: God designs to reveal His truth ('there is nothing hid,' etc.). You are to be the agents in doing so, take heed, therefore, etc. This is a literal statement of what was figuratively expressed in ver. 21.—**Made secret** (*i. e.*, by God), **but that it should come to light.** This is the purpose of the temporary secrecy, a thought implied throughout, but more strongly expressed here. Even the *concealing* is for the purpose of revealing. Only by such a process could Christian truth be ultimately spread. The concealing, hiding purpose, mentioned in ver. 12, is not without this gracious use of revealing the truth more fully to those who see the evil effect of rejecting it.

Ver. 23. Comp. ver. 9 and Matthew. The three forms vary slightly; the saying was probably repeated.

Ver. 24. **Take heed what ye hear.** Luke: 'how ye hear.' The latter is implied in the former, for what we hear really depends on how we hear. The reference is to a proper improvement of the opportunities now graciously afforded them, as appears from what follows.—**With what measure ye mete**, etc. Comp. Matt. 7: 2. The principle is the same in both cases: but there the application is to censorious judgments, here to our Lord's mode of instruction and the way it was received. Giving and receiving are reciprocal. As you treat me as your Instructor (giving attention), you will be treated (in receiving profit).—**And more shall be given**, lit., 'added,' *i. e.*, in case you hear properly. 'That hear,' omitted in the best authorities, was probably inserted to express this obvious sense. The reference may possibly be to teaching as well as to giving attention; vers. 21, 22, allude to this, and 'mete' is more appropriately applied to giving out to others. The promise of increased knowledge is certainly given to those who faithfully teach in God's kingdom; but here the other application is the primary one, as appears from the more immediate connection.

sure ye mete, it shall be measured unto you: and
25 more shall be given unto you. For he that hath, to
him shall be given: and he that hath not, from him
shall be taken away even that which he hath.
26   And he said, So is the kingdom of God, as if a man
27 should cast seed upon the earth; and should sleep and
rise night and day, and the seed should spring up and
28 grow he knoweth not how. The earth ¹beareth fruit
of herself; first the blade, then the ear, then the full

¹ Or, *yieldeth*

Ver. 25. **For he that hath**, etc. In Matt. 13: 12, this thought precedes the explanation of the parable of the sower. It was possibly repeated, since it is equally apt in both cases. There as well as here the application is to spiritual knowledge. (In Matt. 25: 29, Luke 19: 26, the application is more general.) There is nothing arbitrary in this rule; it is a law of God's dealing in the kingdom of nature as well as of grace. Use of opportunities develops capacity; neglect produces incapacity. In spiritual things, the increased capacity is rewarded of grace, the incapacity is punished of justice. The various forms of this proverbial expression deserve attention. The Revised Version reproduces the minor differences.

Vers. 26-29. THE PARABLE OF THE SEED GROWING, WE KNOW NOT HOW.—Found here only.

Ver. 26. **And he said.** The instruction to the people is resumed, or 'to them' would probably be added:—**As if a man**, *i. e.*, any one. It is not necessary to interpret this; the main point is the *seed*, the agent being in the background throughout. Besides, it is difficult to apply it, either to Christ (except on one theory suggested below) or to His ministers; for the language of ver. 27 seems 'inappropriate in the case of our Lord, and the putting in the sickle inapplicable to His ministers.' Human agency in general may be referred to.—**Should cast seed upon the earth**, literally, shall have cast seed upon the earth. A single past act of sowing, not involving great care, as the expression plainly intimates.

Ver. 27. **And should sleep**, etc., *i. e.*, live as usual without further care of the seed sown.—**He knoweth not how.** The emphasis rests on the word 'he;' he who sows does not know how that takes place which he expects to occur, and to occur for his benefit. A true picture, since such knowledge is not permitted to the wisest of men, and what is known helps the growth very little.

Ver. 28. This verse presents the main points of the parable, *first:* **The earth beareth fruit of herself,** as if from a self-acting power. The growth in nature is according to certain laws which act indepen-

29 corn in the ear. But when the fruit ¹ is ripe, straightway he ² putteth forth the sickle, because the harvest is come.

¹ Or, *alloweth*. ² Or, *sendeth forth*.

dently of man's agency, though the agency of God who established these laws and acts through them, is not denied. The same is true in the kingdom of grace; spiritual growth is independent of human agency. That God's power is involved, appears from the whole tenor of Scripture. While, therefore, the main lesson of the parable is about spiritual things, that lesson rests on an analogy of nature, assuming that in nature God operates through the laws He has established. The growth of the kingdom of God, *in general and in individuals*, is according to a development which is natural, *i. e.*, in accordance with certain laws in the realm of grace, which are analogous to what are called natural laws, and like them acting with a certain spontaneousness; though God's constant energy is present in both. The mistakes opposed by this truth are : *first*, expecting growth without any seed ; *secondly*, taking up the seed to see how it grows, *i. e.*, perpetually exacting a certain kind of *experience*, and testing discipleship by unwise and premature measures ; *thirdly and chiefly*, trying to make the growth according to our notions, instead of according to God's law of development, and thinking our care and anxiety can accomplish this. A particular form of this error is met by the next clause : **first the blade, then the ear, then the full corn in the ear.** The maturity of the Church or of individual Christians does not come at once. The repeated 'then' marks the gradual progress better than 'after that.' The same word is used in the Greek in both clauses. The lesson is therefore one of *patience*. While we are not to press a particular meaning upon these three stages, the parable plainly implies that we must be careful not to mistake the blade from the seed of grace for ordinary grass, still less to think the immature ear will never be ripe grain. Indeed, as there is germination, we know not how (ver. 27), before the blade appear, we should not be discouraged if we notice no results, still less expect that we can tell how or when the germ begins to develop.

Ver. 29. **But when the fruit is ripe.** The Greek means either: ' when the fruit shall have yielded itself,' or, according to the more usual sense of the word used, ' when the fruit alloweth,' *i. e.*, when it is ripe. In either case the thought of independence of human agency is kept up.—**Straightway he putteth forth the sickle, because the harvest is come.** The marginal rendering, ' sendeth forth,' is more literal, and suggests that the harvest is reaped by others. The agency which sowed enters again. If it means human agency, the conclusion is simply : this development and fruitfulness is for man's benefit, though independent of his care. We reap in spiritual things, though God alone (by His laws of grace) gives the increase. If it

30 And he said, How shall we liken the kingdom of
31 God? or in what parable shall we set it forth? ¹It is like a grain of mustard seed, which, when it is sown upon the earth, though it be less than all the seeds
32 that are upon the earth, yet when it is sown, groweth up, and becometh greater than all the herbs, and putteth out great branches; so that the birds of the heaven can lodge under the shadow thereof.

¹ Gr. *As unto*.

refers to Christ, it is hinted that when the grain is ripe He harvests it, takes matured Christians to Himself. The parable possibly has a historical application: The sowing referring to Christ's instituting the Church; the intervening period to His absence, during which the growth continues according to the laws of the Spirit's influence; and the harvest to His return. Such a view suits the position of the parable between that of the *sower* (the beginnings of Christianity) and that of the *mustard-seed* (its wonderful extension). But this is not to be insisted on, since the agent is not brought into prominence. The main lesson is: Spiritual growth is independent of our agency, even though we sow the good seed and reap the harvest. Hence, *patience* with immature Christians, and *patience* with an immature Church. Both cautions are constantly needed to prevent our becoming uncharitable and schismatic.

Vers. 30–34. THE PARABLE OF THE MUSTARD-SEED.—Parallel passages, Matt. 13: 31, 32; Luke 13: 18, 19.

Ver. 30. **How shall we liken?** Opening a discussion with a question seems to have been a usual mode with Jewish teachers. Here our Lord graciously includes His disciples ('we') who were also to teach about the kingdom of God,—a hint that Christ's way of teaching is still to be followed.

Ver. 31. **A grain of mustard-seed.** The plant grows wild, but was often found in the gardens of the Jews. In the fertile soil of Palestine it reached the height of several feet. 'A grain of mustard seed' was the proverbial expression for the smallest thing conceivable (comp. Matt. 17: 20).—**In the earth.** Mark is fond of repeating the same expressions; an evidence that his Gospel is not an abridgment.— **Less than all the seeds,** *i. e.,* those sown by the Jews.

Ver. 32. **Greater than all the herbs.** The literal meaning leaves it uncertain whether the plant referred to was itself an herb. The main point is the rapid growth from a diminutive seed.—**Putteth out great branches.** Lit., 'maketh.' Peculiar to Mark.—**The birds of the heaven** represent the external adherents of the kingdom, nations nominally Christian; oftentimes 'outward Church form,' since

33 And with many such parables spake he the word
34 unto them, as they were able to hear it: and without a parable spake he not unto them: but privately to his own disciples he expounded all things.
35 And on that day, when even was come, he saith

the kingdom itself is not the Church organization.—**Can lodge under the shadow thereof.** Seeking shelter and remaining there. The permanent external adhesion is thus indicated. This parable, setting forth the wonderful extension of the kingdom of God, is an appropriate close to the selections made by our Evangelist. After the difficulties in the beginning (the sower) and the slow growth independently of human agency have been emphasized, the successful result is foretold. The lesson of *patience* is again enforced, but *hope* is more directly encouraged.

Vers. 33-34. THE CONCLUDING STATEMENT.—Comp. Matt. 13: 34.

Ver. 33. **With many such parables.** The many such expressions in the Gospels should put an end to the foolish assumption that each Evangelist intended *to tell all he knew*.—**As they were able to hear it.** Not merely as they had opportunity of listening to His instructions, but 'according to their capacity of receiving,' the ability being moral as well as mental. A wise Teacher! It is taken for granted that He intuitively knew their capacity; a point in which well-meaning instructors may fail.

Ver. 34. **And,** not 'but.' The contrast begins with the next clause.—**Without a parable spake he not.** Our Lord did instruct in other ways, but now that the separation had begun, He taught a *certain set of truths* in this way alone, since this would carry out the purpose of mercy and judgment indicated in vers. 11, 12. But this method was also necessary, in view of Jewish prejudice and misunderstanding, to prepare His disciples to extend the truth (vers. 21, 22).— **But privately to his own disciples.** The correct reading and the Greek order alike emphasize the isolation of the disciples.—**He expounded all things.** That they needed this is evident from the Gospel accounts, and we have specimens of these expositions in this chapter and Matt. 13; 15: 15. In other cases there are indications of such expositions. More are not given, because the *subsequent teaching of the Apostles* gives us the fruits of this training, revealing the truth more plainly than was possible then. A caution to those who underrate the Epistles, which embody what is not told us in the Gospels. Still the specimens recorded by the Evangelists are sufficient to guide us in interpretation.

Vers. 35-41. THE VOYAGE ACROSS THE LAKE; THE STILLING OF THE TEMPEST.—Parallel passages: Matt. 8: 18, 23-27; Luke 8: 22-25. The time of the voyage across the lake is fixed by the account before us. It was the evening of the day (ver. 35) when

36 unto them, Let us go over unto the other side. And leaving the multitude, they take him with them, even as he was, in the boat. And other boats were with 37 him. And there ariseth a great storm of wind, and the waves beat into the boat, insomuch that the boat 38 was now filling. And he himself was in the stern,

the discourse in parables had been uttered. The other accounts (Matt. 8: 18; Luke 8: 22 can readily be harmonized on this view. The conversations with some who would follow Him Matt. 8: 19-22) seem to have taken place just before He crossed the sea. It had been a busy day; our Lord had first healed a demoniac (Matt. 12: 22), then encountered the accusation of His family (Mark 3: 20, 21); afterwards the accusation of the Pharisees (chap. 3: 22-30; more fully in Matt. 12: 24-45), when His mother and brethren sought Him (chap. 3: 31-35; Matt. 12: 46-50,); then after some discourses narrated by Luke only (chap. 10: 37—12: 59), departing to the sea-side, had given the long discourse, parts of which are recorded in chap. 4 and Matt. 13, then encountered half-hearted followers (Matt. 8: 19-22), and in the evening crossed the lake. After such exhausting labors, it is not strange that He fell asleep, even amid the storm. Mark's account is vivid, and in most respects more minute than that of Matthew, giving particulars omitted by both the other Evangelists.

Ver. 35. **And on that day, when even was come.** Here Mark is most definite.—**Let us go over unto the other side.** This vivid form of the command indicates a sudden departure. Comp. Luke 8: 22. He would thus seek rest, which could be obtained more easily on a lake subject to storms than in a crowd already excited. Yet unbelief disturbed Him even on the sea.

Ver. 36. **And leaving the multitude.** They did not send the people away, but left them.—**As he was**; without preparation. He was already in the boat, and they set off at once.—**Other boats.** The best authorities do not give the diminutive form, 'little ships.' Mark alone tells of this. These other boats were probably separated from them during the subsequent gale.

Ver. 37. All three accounts of this storm and its effects differ in form, but agree in substance. From ver. 35, we infer that it was already night when the storm arose. The lake was and is still subject to sudden storms; but very few boats are seen there now.—**The boat was now filling.** The boat, probably without a deck, was shipping seas every moment, and 'they were in jeopardy' (Luke 8: 23).

Ver. 38. **In the stern, asleep on the cushion.** The ordinary cushion, at the stern of the boat, used for a seat, sometimes for the rowers. The position is mentioned by Mark only; but Matthew and Luke speak of the disciples' coming to Him, which indicates the same thing. His weary body needed the rest, and this the disciples must have known; hence there is a tone of unkindness as well as unbelief in the language here recorded: **Carest thou not that we perish?**

asleep on the cushion: and they awake him, and say unto him, ¹Master, carest thou not that we perish? 39 And he awoke, and rebuked the wind, and said unto the sea, Peace, be still. And the wind ceased, and 40 there was a great calm. And he said unto them, Why 41 are ye fearful? have ye not yet faith? And they feared exceedingly, and said one to another, Who then is this, that even the wind and the sea obey him?

¹ Or, *Teacher.*

The various accounts indicate a variety of expressions, as of fear, though this includes a complaint. The same want of faith is still manifest in Christians in times of trial, even though not thus expressed.

Ver. 39. **Peace, be still.** Mark alone preserves these words. Matthew places the rebuke of the disciples first; Mark and Luke that of the elements.—**A great calm.** Not only a cessation of the wind, but a sudden and remarkable quietude of the water.

Ver. 40. **Why are ye fearful?** 'Afraid' would be too weak, and 'cowardly' too strong.—**Have ye not yet faith?** 'Yet,' in view of the late instruction, and His numerous miracles. Mark, in many instances, brings out the weakness of the disciples most prominently, a significant fact, if we remember that Peter was his authority. Matthew says: 'O ye of little faith.' Fear while the Saviour was with them, evidence of 'little faith;' the cry to Him evidence they were not faithless. He rewards the faith they had, but rebukes them, because of their 'little faith.'

Ver. 41. **Feared exceedingly,** lit., 'feared a great fear.'—**And said one to another.** This seems to have been the language of all in the boat.—**Who then is this?** Mark and Luke have a different expression from that given by Matthew: 'What manner of man.' 'Who then,' *i. e.*, in view of all this new exhibition of power we have seen.—**Even the wind and the sea obey him.** Such a miracle, wrought before those to whom the terrors of the lake were the highest natural danger, was best adapted to convince them of His power to save the soul. By it He also taught a lesson of faith and warned against unbelief, as well as attested to the mere lookers-on His Divine power. All His miracles are displays not only of power, but of love to lost men. Alford: 'The symbolic application of this occurrence is too striking to have escaped general notice. The Saviour, with the company of His disciples in the ship tossed on the waves, seemed a typical reproduction of the Ark bearing mankind on the flood, and a foreshadowing of the Church tossed by the tempests of this world, but having Him with her always. And the personal application is one of **comfort and strengthening of faith in danger and doubt.'**

5 : 1 And they came to the other side of the sea, into the
2 country of the Gerasenes. And when he was come
out of the boat, straightway there met him out of the
3 tombs a man with an unclean spirit, who had his
dwelling in the tombs: and no man could any more
4 bind him, no, not with a chain; because that he had
been often bound with fetters and chains, and the
chains had been rent asunder by him, and the fetters
broken in pieces: and no man had strength to tame

Chap. V. 1-20. THE DEMONIAC AT GERASA.—Parallel passages: Matt. 8: 28-34; Luke 8: 26-39. Luke's account more nearly resembles that of Mark, and both are fuller than that of Matthew.

Ver. 1. **The Gerasenes.** The preferable form here. 'Gergesenes' is found in some of the best authorities. The latter is probably the preferable reading in Luke, although there is good authority for 'Gerasenes' there also. The A. V. is incorrect in all three places. We know who changed the word 'Gadarenes' into 'Gergesenes' in the Gospel of Matthew (Origen), and his reasons for doing it.

The variety in names has occasioned much discussion as to the exact locality. The common view is that the city referred to in vers. 14, 15, was *Gadara*, the capital of Perea, situated south-east of the southern end of the lake. It was about seven miles from Tiberias, on a mountain near the river Hieromax; was probably inhabited by Gentiles, and is now called *Omkeis*. This place was not too far away to be 'the city' referred to, since the events occured before 'the city' was reached. The name 'Gergesenes' is then to be regarded as derived from the old 'Girgashites,' who lived there before the conquest of the Israelites. (Josephus says the name survived.) 'Gerasenes' was probably a corruption, or derived from the city *Gerasa*, which was situated in the same district, though at a great distance. Another theory, coming more and more into favor, is, that a place, called *Gerasa* or *Gergesa*, existed near the lake shore. So Dr. Thomson (*The Land and the Book*) and others.

Ver. 2. **Straightway.** Mark's favorite word.—**A man.** Matthew tells of 'two,' being more particular in this respect. Luke speaks of but one.—**With,** lit., 'in,' **an unclean spirit.** Mark usually prefers this form of describing demoniacal possession.

Ver. 3. Mark's description of the man is most full and striking. Both he and Luke tell in different words that his dwelling was **in the tombs,** a fact only hinted at by Matthew. Peculiar to this narrative is the mention of the fact that **no man could any more bind him.**

Ver. 4. Gives the proof of the last statement from the unsuccessful attempts which had been made. The case was probably one of long

5 him. And always, night and day, in the tombs and in the mountains, he was crying out, and cutting himself
6 with stones. And when he saw Jesus from afar, he
7 ran and worshipped him; and crying out with a loud voice, he saith, What have I to do with thee, Jesus, thou Son of the Most High God? I adjure thee by
8 God, torment me not. For he said unto him, Come

standing, and repeated efforts had been made to confine him (Luke 8: 29).—**Fetters** were for the feet, **chains**, for any other part of the body.—**To tame him**, by any means. The necessity for attempting to tame him was the danger to those passing that way (Matt. 8: 28).

Ver. 5. This untamable demoniac spent his time in self-laceration crying, **night and day**, deprived of sleep in all probability, and wandering not only **in the tombs** in which he dwelt, but **in the mountains**, so common in that district. That he was usually naked is implied here, but stated in Luke only. A fearful picture, agreeing in most points with certain forms of insanity. It cannot be argued from these symptoms that it was merely a case of insanity. The writers who so accurately describe the symptoms, define the malady; their statements must be accepted or rejected as a whole. (See below.) Mark's Gospel, more fully than any of the others, shows Christ's power over evil spirits. The power is measured by the difficulty of the case.

Ver. 6. **And when he saw Jesus from afar.** The prominent thought is that he ran from a distance. This running would look like a violent attack, but instead of this, he **worshipped him**; Luke: 'fell down before Him,' which may be all that the word 'worshipped' means. But the next verse intimates that it was an acknowledgment of Christ's power, even if still hostile in its tone. If the man were merely insane, how could he have known of Jesus?

Ver. 7. **And crying out**, etc. Instead of attacking.—**What have I to do with thee**, lit., 'What (is) to me and thee,' what have we in common? The language of the demons, who recognized Him as the **Son of the Most High God**. Peculiar to Mark is the strong expression: **I adjure thee by God**. The language of the demon, not of the man; not a mere blasphemy, but a plausible argument: 'We implore thee to deal with us as God Himself does, that is, not to precipitate our final doom, but to prolong the respite which we now enjoy' (J. A. Alexander). The highest acknowledgment comes from the most virulent demon.—**Torment me not**. Matthew: 'Art thou come hither to torment us before the time?' The language is that of opposition, blended with consciousness of weakness. It is demoniacal to defy and oppose, even when aware that it is useless! According to Luke, our Lord had already begun to exercise His power, and they knew they must obey.

Ver. 8. **For he said**, or, 'was saying.' This and the next verse

9 forth, thou unclean spirit out of the man. And he asked him, What is thy name? And he saith unto
10 him, My name is Legion; for we are many. And he besought him much that he would not send them away
11 out of the country. Now there was there on the
12 mountain side a great herd of swine feeding. And they besought him, saying, Send us into the swine,
13 that we may enter into them. And he gave them

show that the language just used was that of the demon speaking through the man. The adjuration of the demon and the command of our Lord were uttered about the same moment, the conversation (vers. 9–12) taking place immediately afterwards.

Ver. 9. **What is thy name?** Probably addressed to the man, since there would be no special object in finding out the name of the demon, who however answered: **My name is Legion.** Matthew omits this, and Luke abbreviates it. The Latin word 'legion' (used also in Greek and rabbinical Hebrew), was applied to a division of the Roman army, numbering from three to six thousand men. But it also denotes, indefinitely, a large number (compare our popular use of the word regiment); so that the answer means: 'I am a host,' as the next clause shows: **for we are many.** Luke narrates the fact without putting it in the mouth of the demon. Our Lord had already commanded the demon to come out (ver. 8): the question 'what is thy name' assumed that the command would be obeyed, leaving the man free to answer: but the demons still lingered, and one of them, as leader, answered thus, in pride and partial resistance. 'Legion' implies, not a collection, but an organized host (comp. Eph. 6: 12; Col. 2: 15).

Ver. 10. **He besought—send them away.** The singular and plural here used confirm the explanation just given.—**Out of the country,** *i. e.*, the Gerasene district. Luke says: 'into the deep;' comp. Matt. 8: 29. This request seems to have been a preparation for the subsequent one (ver. 12). It was less definite than the first adjuration, but still uttered in the spirit of resistance. Their desire to remain in that district was probably connected with its lawless character, though it may have been merely the wish to stay where they were, in the man.

Ver. 11. **On the mountain side.** A slight change of reading gives a peculiar expression which is thus paraphrased in the Revised Version. Matthew: 'afar off from them.'—**A great herd of swine feeding.** With herdsmen (ver. 14). The animals were unclean, according to the Mosaic law, and probably not owned by Jews.

Ver. 12. **And they besought him.** So the best authorities. The full, direct form of the request is peculiar to Mark.

Ver. 13. **Entered into the swine.** In all the accounts the fact

leave. And the unclean spirits came out, and entered into the swine; and the herd rushed down the steep into the sea, *in number* about two thousand; and they 14 were choked in the sea. And they that fed them fled, and told it in the city, and in the country. And they 15 came to see what it was that had come to pass. And they come to Jesus, and behold ¹him that was possessed with devils sitting, clothed and in his right mind, *even* him that had the legion; and they were 16 afraid. And they that saw it declared unto them how it befell ¹him that was possessed with devils, and con-

¹ Or, *the demoniac.*

of possession is plainly stated: the animal soul has appetites that can be influenced by demons.—**The herd.** Few animals are so individually stubborn as swine, yet the rush was simultaneous: **down the steep into the sea.—In number about two thousand,** or, '*being* about two thousand.' The correct reading makes the parenthesis of the A. V. unnecessary. The two thousand animals were speedily destroyed by demons that made two men violent without destroying them. There may be some connection between merely sensuous life and demoniacal influence. No difficulty ought to be raised in regard to the propriety of our Lord's permission. All such objections only show how perfect is the character of our Lord.

Ver. 14. **And they that fed them,** the herdsmen.—**Fled.** Affrighted.—**And told it.** Matthew emphasizes the report about the destruction of the swine.—**In the city.** Possibly Gadara, but far more probably some other city nearer the lake.—**In the country,** lit., 'in the fields,' *i. e.*, the villages and houses by which they passed. So Luke; Matthew is less minute.—**They,** *i. e.*, the people who heard the report. Matthew: 'the whole city.'—**What it was that had come to pass.** A more exact rendering than that of the A. V.

Ver. 15. The order of the Greek, which is reproduced in the Revised Version, is vivid.—**Sitting,** not wandering as before; **clothed,** not naked now: **and in his right mind,** sane, not a maniac, as he had been under the demoniacal influence.—**Even him that had the legion.** The reality of the possession is emphasized by the fact that they identified this man as the former terror to the district.— **They were afraid,** terrified, awe-struck.

Ver. 16. **And they that saw it.** Probably the swineherds, who had returned; possibly those who had accompanied our Lord in the boat.—**How it happened.** Not merely the fact, which those coming already perceived, but the way in which the cure had occurred.

17 cerning the swine. And they began to beseech him
18 to depart from their borders. And as he was entering into the boat, he that had been possessed with ¹devils
19 besought him that he might be with him. And he suffered him not, but saith unto him, Go to thy house unto thy friends, and tell them how great things the Lord hath done for thee, and *how* he had mercy on
20 thee. And he went his way, and began to publish in Decapolis how great things Jesus had done for him; and all men did marvel.

¹ Gr. *demons.*

Ver. 17. **Began to beseech him.** The imperfect tense, here used, has this force. They were heathen, and were alarmed at the supernatural power of Jesus. Such an effect was but natural.—**To depart from their borders.** He departed, and probably never returned. The possessed received Him more readily than the Gadarenes. Christ healed madmen where calculating selfishness drove Him away.

Ver. 18. **As he was entering into the boat.** The correct reading shows that He had not yet entered.—**Besought him.** The same word used in the last verse. The reason of this request was probably personal gratitude to our Lord. He would thus separate himself from those who rejected his Deliverer. Possibly he feared a relapse.

Ver. 19. **Go to thy house unto thy friends,** etc. He may have been in danger of despising his friends in the district that rejected Christ. His previous life may have harmed them; our Lord would make his future life a blessing to them.—**Tell them.** The command to those healed was often to keep silence; here it is the reverse, and for a good reason. There was no danger of tumult attending the proclamation in that region as there was in Galilee. Then our Lord, even when rejected, would leave a preacher behind Him.—**How great things the Lord hath done for thee.** Luke: 'God hath done for thee.' So that 'the Lord' means *Jehovah,* but it is also a fair inference that it means Christ Himself (see ver. 20).—**How he had mercy on thee.** This hints at a spiritual blessing.

Ver. 20. **In Decapolis.** Comp. Matt. 4: 25. The region (of ten cities east of the Jordan) of which this immediate district formed a part. The healed man became a preacher, not only where Christ had been rejected, but where He had not gone. His message was his own experience: **how great things Jesus had done for him,** which he understood to be the same as 'how great things the Lord hath done for thee.' Our Lord was not altogether unknown in this region, but His personal ministry did not extend further than this visit and ano-

21 And when Jesus had crossed over again in the boat unto the other side, a great multitude was gathered
22 unto him: and he was by the sea. And there cometh one of the rulers of the synagogue, Jaïrus by name;
23 and seeing him, he falleth at his feet, and beseecheth him much, saying, My little daughter is at the point

ther through the northern part of Decapolis (chap. 7: 31). In Pella, a city of Decapolis, the Christians found refuge at the destruction of Jerusalem.

This miracle, the only one which tells of a transfer of demoniacal possession and of its effect upon other creatures than man, shows (1) that demoniacal possession was not identical with any bodily disease. (2) It also opposes the view that while the influence was indeed demoniacal, there was no actual bodily possession; the persons possessed identifying themselves in their own minds with the demons. The plain language of the narrative is against such a theory, which moreover explains nothing. The main trouble is the admission, not of bodily possession, but of demoniacal influence of any kind. (3) The most natural and tenable position is, that in the time of Christ persons were, actually and bodily, *possessed* by personal evil spirits. The New Testament accounts show, even by their grammatical peculiarities, the existence of a 'double will and double consciousness' (Alford) in the demoniac. Sometimes the evil spirit speaks, sometimes the poor demoniac himself. That sensual sin prepared the way for possession has often been supposed, and is not improbable.

Vers. 21-24. THE RETURN AND THE REQUEST OF JAÏRUS.—Parallel passages: Matt. 9: 1, 18, 19; Luke 8: 40-42.— *Chronology.* The miracles narrated in the remainder of chap. 5: were performed very shortly after the return from the country of the Gadarenes. From Matthew, however (9: 18), we learn that Jaïrus came while our Lord was discoursing after the feast at his (Matthew's) house. In order of time, the paragraph (chap. 2: 15-22), should immediately precede ver. 22 of this chapter.

Ver. 21. **A great multitude was gathered unto him** Luke (8: 40) tells us, 'the multitude welcomed Him; for they were all waiting for Him.' The night after the discourse was probably passed on the lake, so that this was the day after; possibly the second day.— **By the sea side.** He resumed His teaching there. As indicated above, there was an interval before the coming of Jaïrus.

Ver. 22. **There cometh,** to the house of Matthew (Levi). Mark is fond of using the present tense.—**Jaïrus.** So Luke. The Rev. Version indicates that the word has three syllables. Matthew omits the name. The original is vivid: **seeing him, he falleth at his feet.**

Ver. 23. **My little daughter.** 'Little daughter,' one word in the original, a diminutive of affection; comp. the German *Töchterlein*.

of death: *I pray thee,* that thou come and lay thy hands on her, that she may be ¹made whole, and 24 live. And he went with him; and a great multitude followed him, and they thronged him.

25 And a woman, which had an issue of blood twelve 26 years, and had suffered many things of many physicians, and had spent all that she had, and was nothing

¹ Or, *saved*

Mark probably gives the exact words of the ruler; Luke narrates in his own language the state of the case; Matthew, in his briefer account, combines in one sentence the substance of what the ruler said and the actual state of the girl as reported on the way thither (ver. 35), omitting any special reference to the latter fact.—**Is at the point of death.** A correct paraphrase of a Greek expression which cannot be literally translated.—**That thou come,** etc. The language of the original is peculiar and broken, indicating great emotion. Hence 'I pray thee' has been supplied, but the strong word 'that' (in order that) should not be omitted. The best explanation is: He states the condition of his daughter 'in order that coming thou mayest lay thy hands on her, in order that she may be made whole and live.' He thus expresses his faith.—**Made whole,** lit., 'saved,' from her disease, **and live,** since it threatened death.

Ver. 24. **A great multitude.** The thronging of the people is prominent in the accounts of Mark and Luke. That so important a person as Jaïrus had asked our Lord's help may have occasioned unusual excitement, though multitudes usually followed Jesus.

Vers. 25-34. THE HEALING OF THE WOMAN WITH THE ISSUE OF BLOOD.—Parallel passages: Matt. 9: 20-22; Luke 8: 43-48. Mark's account of this miracle is the most full, and is very vivid.

Ver. 25. **A woman which had an issue of blood.** The disease involved uncleanness, according to the ceremonial law, and on the part of the sufferer a sense of shame as well as fear. 'However commonplace the case may seem to many, there are some in whose experience when clearly seen and seriously attended to, it touches a mysterious cord of painful sympathy.' (J. A. Alexander.)—**Twelve years.** The length of time is significant, both as accounting for the remainder of the description, and as contrasted with the instantaneous cure.

Ver. 26. **Suffered many things of many physicians.** Luke, himself a physician, also states that she 'had spent all her living on physicians,' without any good result. Mark emphasizes the fact that she 'suffered' at their hands, and grew worse instead of better. In those days such diseases especially would be poorly treated, and treated without tenderness, first because the patient was Levitically *unclean,*

27 bettered, but rather grew worse, having heard the things concerning Jesus, came in the crowd behind, 28 and touched his garment. For she said, If I touch 29 but his garments, I shall be ¹made whole. And straightway the fountain of her blood was dried up; and she felt in her body that she was healed of her 30 ²plague. And straightway Jesus, perceiving in himself that the power *proceeding* from him had gone forth, turned him about in the crowd, and said, Who 31 touched my garments? And his disciples said unto

¹ Or, *saved*   ² Gr. *scourge*.

second because she was a *woman*. Our Lord's conduct was a protest against both these. Just in proportion as His influence permeates society, is woman not only elevated, but tenderly dealt with, especially in the matter of delicate diseases. All, physicians included, may learn a lesson here in the treatment of invalids of the female sex.

Ver. 27. **Having heard.** It is not indicated how long it was since she heard, but she came because she had heard.—**The things concerning Jesus.** This paraphrase brings out the correct sense. She had heard of His doings, as well as His name.—**In the crowd** (the word usually translated 'multitude'). Mark alone mentions this.—**His garment.** Matthew and Luke are more particular: 'the hem of His garment.'

Ver. 28. **For she said,** literally, 'was saying.' Matthew: 'within herself,' but it is possible that she may have murmured it again and again, as she tried to get through the crowd.—**If I touch but his garments.** The original is very emphatic. 'May' (A. V.) is incorrect. She was timid, not doubtful. It is implied that she wished only to touch some part of His clothes, no matter which. She may have looked for some magical influence, but twelve years in the hands of physicians in those days may well excuse such a thought in a weak woman.

Ver. 29. **Felt in her body.** Lit., 'knew (*i. e.*, by feeling) in the body.' The first clause tells of the cessation of the ordinary symptom of her disease, this points to a new sense of health.

Ver. 30. **That the power proceeding from him had gone forth.** The power, which was His and which proceeded from Him, He felt had on this occasion also gone forth to heal. The rendering of the Rev. Ver. is awkward, but exactly expresses the sense of the Greek. —**Who touched my garments?** The question of our Lord constrained her to make public confession, sealed and strengthened her faith, presenting her to the world as healed and clean.

Ver. 31. **His disciples.** Luke: 'Peter and they that were with Him.' The denial of all is mentioned by the same Evangelist. This natural answer of the disciples, according to Luke, called forth an

him, Thou seest the multitude thronging thee, and
32 sayest thou, Who touched me? And he looked round
33 about to see her that had done this thing. But the
woman fearing and trembling, knowing what had been
done to her, came and fell down before him, and told
34 him all the truth. And he said unto her, Daughter,
thy faith hath ¹ made thee whole; go in peace, and be
whole of thy ² plague.
35 While he yet spake, they come from the ruler of the

¹ Or, *saved thee*   ² Gr. *scourge*.

express declaration from our Lord, that He perceived power had gone out from Him.

Ver. 32. **And he looked round about.** Peculiar in this form to Mark.—**To see her.** This indicates, what is implied in any fair view of the whole transaction, that He knew who had done it.

Ver. 33. **Fearing and trembling.** Luke inserts: 'saw that she was not hid.' The two accounts agree remarkably and yet differ. Her experience in the past well accounts for her conduct; rough physicians, painful treatment, loss of means, constant diminution of health, the nature of her disease, all led to the secret mode she adopted, and this was in keeping with that.—**Told him all the truth**, and that too 'before all the people' (Luke 8: 47). Her faith is brought out and triumphs thus over her timidity. To this day, physicians complain of want of candor in female patients, or at least of a failure to accurately state their symptoms, etc. So that the naturalness of the picture is remarkable.

Ver. 34. **Be whole**, or, 'healed.' Not the same word as that in the previous clause, which also means 'saved,' see marginal renderings. —**Of thy plague**, scourge, affliction. Peculiar to Mark. These words were a gracious and solemn ratification of the healing, which had been stolen, as it were.—**Go in peace.** Lit., 'into peace.' The state in which she could now live, in contrast with her previous suffering and her unquiet up to this moment. The healing of the woman suggests: All believers do not show their faith in the same way (comp. the paralytic); retiring faith should be encouraged and brought to public confession; the timid, shrinking ones may be very near Christ; the many afflicted women, whose sufferings must be kept concealed, have special need of Christ; faith is only a hand to lay hold of Christ, if it but touch His garment He will strengthen it.

Vers. 35-43. THE HEALING OF THE DAUGHTER OF JAÏRUS.—Parallel passages: Matt. 9: 23-26; Luke 8: 49-56. Here Mark is much more full than Matthew; but Luke gives a few details not found in this account.

Ver. 35. **While he yet spake.** So Luke. Matthew is less spe-

synagogue's *house*, saying, Thy daughter is dead: why
36 troublest thou the ¹Master any further? But Jesus,
²not heeding the word spoken, saith unto the ruler of
37 the synagogue, Fear not, only believe. And he suffered no man to follow with him, save Peter, and
38 James, and John the brother of James. And they come to the house of the ruler of the synagogue; and he beholdeth a tumult, and *many* weeping and wailing

¹ Or, *Teacher*. ² Or, *overhearing*.

cific.—**They come.** Luke: 'there cometh one.'—**From the ruler of the synagogue's house.** This awkward expression is retained in the Rev. Ver. The Greek has no word answering to 'house,' but uses a form equivalent to our colloquial phrase: 'from A's.'—**Why troublest thou the Master** (Greek: 'teacher') **any further?** The underlying thought is: the case is now beyond the help of Jesus, who might have cured, but cannot raise her. The language is kind, and indicates faith.

Ver. 36. **But Jesus not heeding, or, overhearing, the word spoken.** The correct reading introduces a word, which usually means, to pass by as unheard, not to heed: more rarely, to overhear. In either case, it is a mark of accuracy in this account. The message was addressed to the ruler, not to our Lord. Either He did not heed it, though He heard it; or He heard it, when it was not addressed to Him, the former seems preferable.—**Fear not, only believe.** Luke adds: 'and she shall be made whole.' Otherwise the language is exactly the same; the A. V. makes two needless variations in the accounts. The delay seemed fatal, was in itself a trial to the faith of Jaïrus, especially now that the crisis had come. Yet what had just happened, for the message came 'while He yet spake' (ver. 35), would encourage Jaïrus, especially as faith had been exalted in the miracle which the ruler himself witnessed.

Ver. 37. **And he suffered no man to follow with him,** &c. The three disciples here named, who had a certain pre-eminence among the Twelve (comp. chap. 9: 2), were permitted to enter into the house with the father and mother of the maiden (comp. ver. 40 with Luke 8: 51). But this verse indicates that they were singled out of the crowd before reaching the house.

Ver. 38. **Beholdeth a tumult.** There was always a horrible clamor at Eastern funerals; and the preparations had begun, for early burial was usual among the Jews. The lamentation often began as the last breath left the body. Mark gives prominence to the noise common in such circumstances; Matthew, to the 'minstrels;' Luke, to the weeping. Evidently the same scene is described and the accounts derived from eye-witnesses.

39 greatly. And when he was entered in, he saith unto them, Why make ye a tumult, and weep? the child is
40 not dead, but sleepeth. And they laughed him to scorn. But he, having put them all forth, taketh the father of the child and her mother and them that were
41 with him, and goeth in where the child was. And taking the child by the hand, he saith unto her, Talitha cumi; which is, being interpreted, Damsel, I say
42 unto thee, Arise. And straightway the damsel rose up, and walked; for she was twelve years old. And

Ver. 39. **When he was entered in.** The crowd was kept outside, the three disciples accompanying Him. He then speaks to the crowd *inside*, and after their scornful reply (ver. 40), they are put out of the house, at least kept from entering into the chamber of death.— **The child** (so Mark only) **is not dead** (lit., 'did not die'), **but sleepeth.** A direct reference to the miracle which He was about to perform. She did not die, as others die; but she is as one who sleepeth, for I am about to raise her, as one is wakened from a sleep. This view is sustained by the fact that the same words were used of Lazarus, in whose case the raising from actual death is distinctly asserted (John 11:11, 14, 44). There is also a deeper and more general meaning; for Christ, by His own resurrection and His promise to raise believers, has declared death to be but a sleep.

Ver. 40. **And they laughed him to scorn**, lit., laughed Him down; not sharing the father's faith.—**Having put them all forth.** From the fact that the crowd outside was dismissed, and the crowd inside put forth, we may infer, not so much, not to crowd the Saviour, as not to crowd into family grief, and rudely enter the sacred circle of deepest sorrow.—**Goeth in where the child was.** The whole account, just here, seems to have been derived directly from Peter, who was present.

Ver. 41. **Talitha cumi.** These were the words used, in the dialect of the country. Mark cites such Aramaic expressions a number of times (3:17; 7:11, 34; 14:36). The addition of an interpretation shows that he wrote for other Jewish readers, but the insertion of the very words is a mark of accuracy, and of the strong impression made upon the eye-witness.—**Damsel, I say unto thee, Arise.** 'Damsel' is a word of endearment, as if it were: 'Rise, my child,' and 'Talitha' has precisely that sense. 'I say unto thee,' is inserted so that the meaning shall be as plain as possible. Some suggest that it was to show that the words used were not a magical formula, but an actual address or command; this, however, is not probable.

Ver. 42. **Straightway the damsel rose up.** Luke, the physician, speaks of her spirit returning.—**And walked.** Peculiar to

they were amazed straightway with a great amazement. 43 And he charged them much that no man should know this; and he commanded that *something* should be given her to eat.

6: 1 And he went out from thence; and he cometh

Mark, and an incident which would be impressed upon an eye-witness.—**For she was twelve years old.** Before her death she was old enough to walk, and was now restored just as before. Up to this point there was nothing to indicate that she was other than an infant. Luke mentions her age much earlier in his narrative, while Matthew omits it altogether. It is impossible to believe that these three Evangelists copied from each other, or from a common source, in regard to this occurrence. The attempt to differ and agree in this way would either be altogether unsuccessful or cost more than it was worth.—**Amazed.** A stronger word than that usually translated 'astonished.'—**Straightway.** Here again Mark uses his favorite word, which the early transcribers omitted as unnecessary.

Ver. 43. **Charged them much.** A tumult might be excited, the carnal expectations about the Messiah might be roused. Comp. 1: 43; Matt. 9: 30, etc.—**Something should be given her to eat.** The miraculous power now ceased: she needed food; her strength would be recovered by natural means. At the same time it was an evidence that she was actually restored.—Matthew, who was probably *outside* with the other disciples, tells of the spreading of the report of this miracle, while Mark, probably informed about it by Peter, who was inside the house, gives the particulars of what occurred there.

Chap. VI: 1-6. THE VISIT TO NAZARETH.—Parallel passages: Matt. 13: 54-58; comp. Luke 4: 16-30.—*Chronology.* This visit to Nazareth is the same as that mentioned by Matthew (13: 54-58), but different from that recorded by Luke (4: 14-30), this one occurring at the beginning of the Galilæan ministry, the latter later, just before the murder of John the Baptist. On this view we have a reason for our Lord's removal from Nazareth to Capernaum (Matt. 4: 13; Luke 4: 31), which became 'His own city' (Matt. 9: 1). Two such occurrences are not unlikely. If He went there twice, He would be rejected twice, and in much the same way. The narratives of Matthew and Mark point to a later period, and Mark is usually more exact in the matter of chronology. Besides, there is no mention of violence in the accounts of Matthew and Mark, which would scarcely omit this, if referring to the event recorded by Luke. Mark expressly speaks of disciples being with Him, and of a few cases of healing. This seems irreconcilable with the account before us, on the theory that all speak of the same visit. If there was but one rejection, it occurred at the earlier period (that assigned by Luke).—Some other miracles intervened between the raising of Jairus' daughter and this rejection (Matt. 9: 27-34).

Ver. 1. **Went out from thence.** From Capernaum.—**His own country,** *i. e.,* Nazareth, 'where He had been brought up' (Luke

into his own country; and his disciples follow him. 2 And when the sabbath was come, he began to teach in the synagogue; and ¹many hearing him were astonished, saying, Whence hath this man these things? and, What is the wisdom that is given unto this man, and *what mean* such ²mighty works wrought by his 3 hands? Is not this the carpenter, the son of Mary,

¹ Some ancient authorities insert *the.* ² Gr. *powers.*

4: 16), and where some of the family still resided (ver. 3).—**His disciples follow him.** Mentioned by Matthew also; this opposes the identity with the visit mentioned by Luke.

Ver. 2. **The sabbath.** Mark, here as so often, is more specific than Matthew.—**Many,** according to many ancient authorities, 'the many,' the multitude of this city.—**Whence hath this man.** As if to say: This is our townsman, what better schooling did he have than we; what his family is, we all know, etc.—**What is the wisdom that is given unto this man?** This acknowledgment of His wisdom conveys a sneer. More graphic than Matthew's statement.—**And such mighty works** (or, 'powers') **wrought by his hands.** We may supply either 'whence are,' or, 'what mean.' The latter seems to give the sense of the correct reading. It is plain, from ver. 5, that they referred to miracles in other places.

Ver. 3. **The carpenter.** Matthew: 'the carpenter's son.' The word rendered 'carpenter' is sometimes applied to artisans in general, but it means strictly a worker in wood. Our Lord had probably wrought at the trade of Joseph; though the Nazarenes would in any case naturally identify Him with the occupation of His reputed father. All Jewish young men learned a trade. The legends and fancies about the infancy of Christ are very foolish ; but the Son of man would doubtless share in the primal curse (Gen. 3: 19). The question, though not contemptuous, implies: He is one of us, no better than we are, etc.—**The son of Mary,** etc.—They knew His family, and mention the name of His mother and brothers, speaking also of His sisters, who possibly still resided in Nazareth.—**And they were offended in him,** or, 'caused to stumble.' They were led into error and sin with regard to Him.

The brothers of our Lord. Mention is made fourteen or fifteen times in the New Testament of the brothers of our Lord, named in ver. 3. In an ordinary history, this would naturally imply that they were the younger children of Joseph and Mary, or possibly the children of Joseph by a former marriage. The well-known terms, 'cousin' and 'kinsman,' would have been used, had the relationship been more remote. Notwithstand'n ; this, *three* views have been held : (1) That they were the children of Joseph and Mary; the theory of Tertullian, Helvidius, and many of the best modern Protestant commentators.

and brother of James, and Joses, and Judas, and Simon? and are not his sisters here with us? And they

(2) That they were the children of Joseph by a former marriage; the theory of Epiphanius, and the ancient Greek Church. (3) That they were the children of Mary, the wife of Alphæus (Clopas), the sister of our Lord's mother, and hence his cousins. This was the theory of Jerome, adopted by the Roman Catholic Church, and by the older (and some modern) Protestant commentators. Lange modifies this view, by supposing that Alphæus was the brother of Joseph, and that in consequence of his early death the children were adopted by Joseph.

1. The first view is not only the most natural one, but involves fewest difficulties. Objections: (*a.*) It denies the perpetual virginity of Mary. But this is nowhere asserted, while Matt. 1: 26 and Luke 2: 7, suggest that Mary had other children. (*b.*) Gal. 1: 19, seems to intimate that James, our Lord's brother, was an Apostle, while this view involves the non-identity of this James with James the son of Alphæus, who undoubtedly was an Apostle. But the passage in Galatians does not necessarily imply the Apostleship of our Lord's brother. The identity of names in the list of Apostles and in that of our Lord's brothers is, of itself, no proof of identity of persons; the name of James being especially common among the Jews. Further, at a point in the history *after* the choice of the Twelve (John 7: 5), our Lord's brethren did not believe on Him; they are distinguished from the 'Apostles' in Acts 1: 14; 1 Cor. 9: 5, and by implication in Matt. 12: 46–50. (*c.*) Our Lord on the cross commended His mother to the care of John, which is regarded as indicating that she had no other sons. But the spiritual nearness of John, and the probable kinship (see below, and notes on John 19: 25) will account for this preference of that disciple.

2. The view that they were the sons of Joseph by a former marriage, though not open to any great objection, is supported by no positive evidence. It, too, fails to identify 'James the son of Alphæus' and 'James the Lord's brother.'

3. The cousin-theory is beset with difficulties. (*a.*) It assumes that two sisters had the same name (Mary). (*b.*) It does not account for 'Simon' and 'Judas,' who were our Lord's brothers. Indeed, the better supported reading in Matt. 13: 55 ('Joseph,') destroys the identity of name with Mark 15: 40 ('Joses'). (*c.*) It is probable that 'Salome,' and not 'Mary' (John 19: 25), was the sister of our Lord's mother. The view of Lange is free from some of these difficulties, but assumes what is extremely improbable, namely, that Joseph, a poor carpenter, adopted at least half a dozen children into his family. Besides, it is a pure hypothesis.

The view that Mary had other children furnishes an argument in favor of the historical character of the Gospels. Had the story of the miraculous conception been a fiction, the Evangelists, to give consistency to the tale, would have denied that our Lord had any brothers,

4 were ¹offended in him. And Jesus said unto them, A prophet is not without honour, save in his own country, and among his own kin, and in his own 5 house. And he could there do no ²mighty work, save that he laid his hands upon a few sick folk, and healed 6 them. And he marvelled because of their unbelief.

And he went round about the villages teaching
7 And he called unto him the twelve, and began to

¹ Gr. *caused to stumble*.   ² Gr. *power*.

instead of speaking of them without reserve. For a full presentation of all the views, see Lange's Comm., *Matthew*, pp. 255-260.

Ver. 4. **A prophet is not without honour**, etc. The rejection is accounted for by a proverbial expression, verified by human experience. 'Familiarity breeds contempt,' 'Distance lends enchantment to the view,' are still more general expressions of the same principle. —**Among his own kin.** This is peculiar to Mark.

Ver. 5. **And he could there do no mighty work.** His power was not changed. His miracles were not feats of magic, but required two conditions to call them forth: an opportunity and a sufficient moral purpose. 'Unbelief' prevented both. The unbelieving would not come for healing; to heal such would be contrary to His purpose in the miracles, the demonstration of His spiritual power. Hence, He 'could not.' When men do not believe, they do not give Him the opportunity to save them, and to save the unbelieving is contrary to His purpose, and impossible. The few miracles of healing in Nazareth were of the most usual character; but these too were doubtless according to the faith of the subjects.

Ver. 6. **He marvelled because of their unbelief.** To be taken literally. On another occasion our Lord 'marvelled' (Matt. 8: 10; Luke 7: 8) at the great faith of a heathen centurion. Both indicate the great importance of faith.—**Went round about.** The unbelief of Nazareth did not stop our Lord's activity. This circuit was closely connected with the sending forth of the Twelve (ver. 7); hence it seems to be identical with that mentioned in Matt. 9: 35, if we refer the latter to a distinct journey. It would be the *third circuit* through Galilee, which began with this rejection at Nazareth, and continued until the return of the Apostles, when they all withdrew (ver. 30).

Vers. 7-13. THE SENDING OUT OF THE TWELVE.—Parallel passages: Matt. 10: 1, 9-14; Luke 9: 1, 3-5. Comp. also Luke 10: 4-11. Matthew prefaces his fuller account by telling of our Lord's compassion for the multitudes (Matt. 9: 36-38). Luke gives a very brief statement (Luke 9: 1-6). The *choice* of the Twelve took place some time before (chap. 3: 13-19), within the same year. The locality from which the Twelve were sent out, and the length of their tour are unknown. But Galilee, where our Lord

send them forth two by two; and he gave them
8 authority over the unclean spirits; and he charged
them that they should take nothing for *their* journey,
save a staff only; no bread, no wallet, no ¹money in
9 their ²purse; but *to go* shod with sandals: and, *said*
10 *he*, put not on two coats. And he said unto them,

¹ Gr. *brass*.   ² Gr. *girdle*.

had Himself labored so long, was doubtless the scene of this first mission, which probably covered some time. The instruction given, though directly applicable to the Twelve on that occasion, 'may be taken as the type of all the commissions given by Christ to His servants.' (Lange.) Mark gives only a portion of the *first part* of the discourse recorded in Matthew. CONTENTS: their *outfit* or *want of outfit* (vers. 8, 9); the *manner of proceeding* (vers. 10, 11); vers. 12, 13 describe their activity.

Ver. 7. **The twelve**; already chosen, and named in chap. 3: 16–19.—**By two and two.** These pairs seem to be indicated in the list given by Matthew, although he does not mention that they were thus sent out. A proof both of truthfulness and of independence.—**Authority over the unclean spirits.** Peculiar to Mark, and characteristic of his narrative.

Ver. 8. **And he charged them that they should take nothing for their journey.** Peculiar in form to Mark, though Matthew and Luke present verbal resemblances.—**Save a staff only**, *i. e.*, if, as was usual, each had a staff for walking, let him take it, but not provide one especially. This explanation, which is strictly grammatical, removes the apparent difference between the command as recorded here and by Matthew and Luke. Our Lord did not prescribe minutely what each should wear and carry, as monkish rules do. The point is: make no special preparation, take no special care: 'for the workman is worthy of his food' (Matthew), a thought involved in the words: **no bread**, which Matthew omits.—**No wallet.** A leathern pouch. 'Scrip' (A. V.) is now unintelligible. The correct order is as here indicated.—**No money in their purse**, lit., 'not brass into the girdle.' Here Matthew is fuller.

Ver. 9. **With sandals**, *i. e.*, such as they had on at the time, without waiting for shoes especially adapted for the journey (Matthew: 'nor shoes').—The construction changes into a direct command in the last clause, as if the memory of one present had supplied it. Hence the Rev. Ver. inserts the clause in Italics: **saith he.** Neither here nor in Luke is there any reference to the prohibition against visiting Gentile regions or entering into a city of the Samaritans (Matt. 10: 5); a prohibition removed after the Resurrection (Acts 1: 8), and pertinent to the purpose of Matthew's Gospel only.

Ver. 10. **Wheresoever.** The emendations in the Rev. Ver. at the beginning of vers. 10, 11 are in accordance with corrections of the

Wheresoever ye enter into a house, there abide till ye
11 depart thence. And whatsoever place shall not receive
you, and they hear you not, as ye go forth thence,
shake off the dust that is under your feet for a testi-
12 mony unto them. And they went out, and preached
13 that *men* should repent. And they cast out many
¹ devils, and anointed with oil many that were sick,
and healed them.

¹ Gr. *demons.*

Greek text sustained by the best authorities.—**Ye enter into a house.** This was to be done after proper inquiry (Matt. 10: 11).—**There abide till ye depart thence,** *i. e.*, out of that city or, 'place' (ver. 11); the clause, therefore, is not tautological. In this fixed abode they were not to give unnecessary trouble (Luke 10: 7). They were not social visitors but messengers of the gospel. The time of the ministry may be wasted by social exactions.

Ver. 11. **Whatsoever place,** etc. The A. V. here conforms to Matthew, following the less correct text.—**And they hear you not.** This implies that they made an effort to obtain hearing.—**As ye go forth thence.** Not the same expression as 'depart' (ver. 10), but pointing to the actual movement out of the place.—**Shake off the dust that is under your feet.** The form is peculiar to Mark, who adds: **for a testimony unto them** (comp. Matt. 10: 13). Luke says, 'against them.' This solemn act, which meant a cessation of intercourse, was a testimony to them, and against them also, a token that the truth was still the truth, and their rejection would be a ground of judgment.—The remainder of the verse is properly omitted in the Rev. Ver. It is not found in four out of five of the oldest manuscripts, nor in the best versions, and was inserted from the parallel passage in Matthew (10: 15), where it is fully sustained.

Ver. 12. **That men should repent.** Not simply, preached repentance, but preached in order that men might be led to repentance; the latter including the former.

Ver. 13. **Anointed with oil many sick.** Peculiar to Mark. To suppose that the oil was used medicinally is contrary to the whole tenor of the narratives. It was 'the vehicle of healing power committed to them' (Alford), an external sign such as our Lord sometimes used to connect Himself and the person cured. It was probably also a symbol of anointing by the Holy Spirit. A practice of this kind continued in the Apostolic Church (see Jas. 5: 14); but neither the fact nor the symbolical meaning justify the Roman sacrament of extreme unction (observed also in the Greek Church, with the difference that it may be repeated, while the Roman Church administers it only once, at the approach of death).

14 And king Herod heard *thereof*; for his name had become known: and ¹he said, John ²the Baptist is risen from the dead, and therefore do these powers
15 work in him. But others said, It is Elijah. And others said, *It is* a prophet, *even* as one of the prophets.
16 But Herod, when he heard *thereof*, said, John, whom

¹ Some ancient authorities read *they*.   ² Gr. *the Baptizer.*

Vers. 14-29. THE MURDER OF JOHN THE BAPTIST.—Parallel passages, Matt. 14: 1-13; comp. Luke 9: 7-9. Mark's account is detailed, going back to the imprisonment of John, which occurred before our Lord began His Galilæan ministry. The narrative presents a fearful picture of the Herodian family, in their lust, ambition, and cruelty. No scene in history presents in a single group more of the vices characteristic of corrupt courts: arbitrary imprisonment, dread of the multitude, adultery and incest, illegal divorce, continued oppression of one whose words demand respect, feminine intrigue working against a conscience that is not yet dead, feasting and intoxication, voluptuous and immodest dancing, lavish promises and foolish oaths to the dancer, weak fear of court flatterers, and the murder of a faithful reprover; the picture completed by the superstition of the murderer, who sees in the power of the Messiah only a token that his victim has reappeared.

Ver. 14. **King Herod.** Herod Antipas, the 'Tetrarch' (Matt., Luke), was a son of Herod the Great, and now ruler in Galilee; a light-minded, prodigal, and luxurious prince, superstitious and cunning (Mark 8: 15; Luke 13: 32). He was at Jerusalem when our Lord suffered, and showed utter heartlessness on that occasion. He died in Spain, a defeated and banished man (see on ver. 17).—**Heard.** The activity of the Apostles, preaching and performing miracles as the messengers of Jesus, now specially attracted his attention.—**For his name had become known.** The necessary result of the labor of the Apostles.—**John the Baptist**; the form is peculiar; 'he that baptized,' or, 'the Baptizer'; and so throughout this account.—**Is risen from the dead.** Such an opinion was not singular (see ver. 16).—**Therefore,** etc. John had wrought no miracle (John 10: 41), but Herod supposed that the rising from the dead had resulted in higher powers.—**Powers,** or, 'mighty works,' as in ver. 5. Herod's desire to see our Lord (Luke 9: 9) was at best a patronizing condescension to the gospel.

Ver. 15. **Others said,** were in the habit of saying. The current popular opinions are here given (comp. chap. 8: 28; Matt. 16: 14; Luke 9: 19), and not what was said to Herod.—**A prophet, even as one of the prophets.** The meaning is: A prophet like the old prophet, not Elijah nor the Prophet.

Ver. 16. **Heard.** Probably of these opinions as well as of the acts which occasioned them.—**John, whom I beheaded, he is risen.** The emphasis rests on '**I**,' and the correct reading is more graphic

17 I beheaded, he is risen. For Herod himself had sent forth and laid hold upon John, and bound him in prison for the sake of Herodias, his brother Philip's 18 wife: for he had married her. For John said unto Herod, It is not lawful for thee to have thy brother's 19 wife. And Herodias set herself against him, and

than the common one. His guilty conscience suggested the thought, which was uttered to his servants (Matt. 14: 2). Others held the same view (Luke 9: 7).

Ver. 17. **For** introduces the explanation of both the fact and the feeling indicated in ver. 16.—**For Herod himself,** &c. This imprisonment took place not long after our Lord began His ministry (comp. chap. 1: 14; Matt. 4: 12; John 3: 24). The place, according to Josephus, was the strong fortress of Machærus, on the borders of Perea.—**For the sake of Herodias, his brother Philip's wife.** Herodias, the daughter of Aristobulus (the half-brother of Herod Antipas), the wife of Herod Philip (not to be confounded with Philip the Tetrarch, Luke 3: 1), who was disinherited by his father, Herod the Great, and lived as a private citizen.—**For he had married her.** This is only implied in other accounts. Herod Antipas was first married to a daughter of Aretas, king of Arabia (mentioned 2 Cor. 11: 32). Becoming enamored of Herodias, his niece and sister-in-law, he married her secretly, while her husband was still living, repudiating his own legal wife. Aretas made war against him in consequence, and having defeated him was prevented by the Romans from dethroning him (A. D. 37). At the instigation of Herodias he went to Rome to compete for the kingly power bestowed on Agrippa, but was banished by the Emperor Caligula to Cyprus.

Ver. 18. **For John said**: not once, but habitually, as the original hints. John was a bold preacher of righteousness and repentance, not 'a reed shaken by the wind' (Matt. 11: 7). His fidelity led to his imprisonment.—**It is not lawful for thee to have thy brother's wife.** Here Mark is more full and explicit. The act of Herod was primarily a crime against his brother, but also against his wife, and in itself incestuous, since Herodias was his niece (comp. Lev. 18: 16; 20: 21).

Ver. 19. **And Herodias set herself against him.** 'Had a quarrel' (A. V.) is inexact. The original indicates her continued conduct. She doubtless frequently urged Herod to kill John, and Matthew (14: 5) intimates that he was half-persuaded to do so.—**And she could not.** For the reasons, see ver. 20.

Ver. 20. **For Herod feared John.** Herod's feelings toward John are detailed by Mark only. The impression made upon Herod grew stronger after the imprisonment, so that Herodias 'could not' kill John. Matthew says that Herod 'feared the multitude.' Both

20 desired to kill him; and she could not; for Herod feared John, knowing that he was a righteous man and a holy, and kept him safe. And when he heard him, he ¹was much perplexed; and he heard him gladly. 21 And when a convenient day was come, that Herod on his birthday made a supper to his lords, and the 22 ²high captains, and the chief men of Galilee; and when

---

¹ Many ancient authorities read *did many things*. ²Or, *military tribunes*. Gr. *chiliarchs*.

motives necessarily entered. Without the political motive the moral one would not have sustained Herod against the will of the woman he had adulterously married.—**Holy.** A recognition of John's dignity as a prophet, one consecrated to God's service.—**Kept him safe,** or, 'preserved him,' *i. e.*, from Herodias.—**Was much perplexed.** The reading here followed is that of the two oldest manuscripts, and of some minor authorities. This is one of the cases where the discovery of the Sinaitic manuscript has determined a question previously very doubtful. Even now the Rev. Ver. gives the other reading in the margin. The clause, thus corrected, shows most strikingly the peculiar and divided state of Herod's mind.—**Heard him gladly.** Some real influence for good was beginning to operate. The description is not unnatural.

Ver. 21. **A convenient day,** *i. e.*, for the purpose which Herodias cherished, not for Herod's feast, which took place at the fixed time.—**That Herod on his birthday.** Probably the anniversary of his ascension to power. Herodias planned the scheme beforehand. —**Lords,** etc. Political servants and military officials, then leading men of the land. 'His' belongs to the first class only. Strictly speaking, Herod had no **high captains** (chiliarchs) of his own.—**And the chief men of Galilee.** The A. V. ('chief *estates* of Galilee') is misleading.

Ver. 22. **The daughter of Herodias herself.** She sent, for the accomplishment of her purpose, not a common dancing girl, but her own daughter, 'Salome,' whose father was Herod Philip. She married her uncle Philip the Tetrarch, and after his death her cousin Aristobulus. Some of the best authorities, however, read: 'his daughter Herodias.' She was now, in law, his daughter, and thus a member of his own family is made to arouse feelings, which, while sinful in themselves, led him into a crime he did not wish to commit. The dance was a pantomime, probably of a voluptuous character, and was performed 'in the midst' (Matt. 14: 6), with the intoxicated party forming a circle about her. Such conduct was deemed immodest by Jews, Greeks, and Romans; in this case there was added a criminal purpose, and a sin against her own forsaken father. Public dancing (and often private dancing) calls forth evil passions, even if not de-

¹the daughter of Herodias herself came in and danced, ²she pleased Herod and them that sat at meat with him; and the king said unto the damsel, Ask of me 23 whatsoever thou wilt, and I will give it thee. And he sware unto her, Whatsoever thou shalt ask of me, I will give it thee, unto the half of my kingdom. 24 And she went out, and said unto her mother, What shall I ask? And she said, The head of John ³the 25 Baptist. And she came in straightway with haste unto the king, and asked, saying, I will that thou forthwith give me in a charger the head of John ³the 26 Baptist. And the king was exceeding sorry; but for the sake of his oaths, and of them that sat at meat, he

¹ Some ancient authorities read *his daughter Herodias*.   ² Or, *it*.
¹ Gr. *the Baptizer*.

signed to do so. It should be noted that the opening clause of this verse is joined closely to the first clause of ver. 21, the day having come,—the damsel having come in; what intervenes describes the convenient day. The main thought is: **she pleased Herod.**—The fact that the whole company was pleased is mentioned by Mark only, who also gives the words of Herod.

Ver. 23. **Unto the half of my kingdom.** The full form of the oath is here preserved. Ahasuerus (Esther 7: 2) made a similar oath to his queen; this was to a girl whose graceful immodesty had pleased the king.

Ver. 24. **She went out.** The studied vindictiveness of Herodias is here brought out. She asks not simply for the death, but for **the head of John the Baptist.**

Ver. 25. **With haste.** She shows no reluctance, but is a genuine daughter of the Herodian family. Her request is put most strongly: **I will,** *i. e.*, this is my choice.—**Forthwith,** after as short an interval as possible. (Not the word which Mark so often employs.)—**In a charger,** *i. e.*, a platter, a large dish. The Revised Version leaves this word to puzzle many readers. This phrase seems to have been added by Salome herself, 'as a hideous jest, implying an intention to devour it' (J. A. Alexander).

Ver. 26. **Exceeding sorry.** Mark's language is stronger than that of Matthew. The emotion was in keeping with Herod's character and feelings toward John, but was of no avail; compliance with the murderous request was the more criminal because he was 'exceeding sorry.' Herod is called 'the king' by both Evangelists, although he did not really possess the title.—**But for the sake of his oaths.** The oath was foolish, and was sinfully kept. Better

27 would not reject her. And straightway the king sent forth a soldier of his guard, and commanded to bring his head: and he went and beheaded him in the
28 prison, and brought his head in a charger, and gave it to the damsel; and the damsel gave it to her mother.
29 And when his disciples heard *thereof,* they came and took up his corpse, and laid it in a tomb.
30 And the apostles gather themselves together unto

break our word than God's Word. Herod was scrupulous on this point, and yet an adulterer and murderer.—**And of them that sat at meat.** His courtiers were probably hostile to John. In any case the fear of men, so powerful for evil, influenced him.

Ver. 27. **A soldier of his guard.** The word is a peculiar one, derived from the Latin. The members of the body-guard would be entrusted with the execution of capital sentences; but that was not their special office.—**In the prison.** If the feast took place in Machærus, the head was brought in before the feast closed. Some, however, infer from this account that the messengers went some distance, and hence that the feast was given in a royal palace at Livias (not far from Machærus), while others think the nobility of Galilee would more probably be invited to Tiberias, the usual residence of Herod. But 'forthwith' (ver. 25) indicates that the prison was near.

Ver. 28. **Gave it to her mother.** 'A Jezebel was not wanting in the history of the second Elijah.' The vindictive adulteress was served by the immodest dancer; the sixth and seventh commandment stand next each other.

Ver. 29. **His disciples,** *i. e.,* those of John. They 'went and told Jesus' (Matt. 14: 12), after burying their teacher.

Vers. 30-44. THE FEEDING OF THE FIVE THOUSAND.—Parallel passages: Matt. 14: 13-21; Luke 9: 10-17; John 6: 1-13. The entire independence of Mark's Gospel is fully apparent in this paragraph, which tells of one of the few events recorded by all four Evangelists. (The emendations reproduce, to some extent, the vivacity of the original.) This miracle, therefore, furnishes a definite chronological point for a comparison of the Gospels. It is in many respects the most incomprehensible of all the miracles. Various suggestions have been made as to the mode of increase, as involving a higher order of nature; an acceleration of the natural process; a removal of the ban of barrenness resting on our earthly bread, showing the positive fulness which it contains when Christ's blessing descends upon it. It is safest to accept a supernatural increase without seeking to know the method, and then to seek and accept the spiritual lessons it teaches. The attempts to explain it as a natural event have been utter failures. The four Evangelists could not write as they have done, of a 'myth,' a 'parable,' or a 'symbol.' Either this was a miracle, or the Evangelists have wilfully falsified. The great lesson is: Christ the Bread of the world; its type is the manna in the wilderness. Christ's people partake of Him to the nourishment of their souls. As in the miracle,

Jesus; and they told him all things, whatsoever they
31 had done, and whatsoever they had taught. And he
saith unto them, Come ye yourselves apart into a desert
place, and rest a while. For there were many coming
and going, and they had no leisure so much as to eat.
32 And they went away in the boat to a desert place apart.
33 And *the people* saw them going, and many knew *them*,
and they ran there together ¹on foot from all the
34 cities, and outwent them. And he came forth and saw
a great multitude, and he had compassion on them,

¹ Or, *by land.*

the means may be visible, but the mode unknown; of the fact we may be assured, and may assure others.—Notice the contrast between the feast at Herod's court, and this feast in the wilderness. Our Lord gave freely in the wilderness: healed, taught, and fed all.—'The Bible, so little in bulk, like the five barley loaves and the two fishes, what thousands upon thousands has it fed, and will it feed, in every age, in every land of Christendom, to the world's end!'

Ver. 30. **And they told him all things.** This report was probably given at a time previously appointed for their reassembling.

Ver. 31. **Come ye yourselves** (*i. e.*, you alone) **and rest a while.** The motive was that *they* should rest. Another reason for this departure was Herod's state of mind (comp. Matt. 14: 13), which would lead him to regard with suspicion any gathering of the multitudes.

Ver. 32. **A desert place.** Not a 'desert' in the modern sense, but a thinly-inhabited district; in Gaulonitis (Luke 9: 10) Julias, on the *eastern* shore of the lake of Tiberias (John 6: 1), in the dominions of Philip the Tetrarch. Our Lord would avoid Herod, as well as seek rest for His disciples.—**Apart.** The same word as in ver. 31. 'Privately' (A. V.) points to concealment, which was scarcely designed. The departure was not in secret (ver. 33).

Ver. 33. A striking picture of the continued popularity of our Lord. The Greek text of the verse must be corrected in several places. The Rev. Ver. gives an accurate rendering of the better supported, approved reading.

Ver. 34. **And he came forth.** Either disembarked from the boat, or, more probably, came out from His retirement. Upon landing they went up some hill or cliff, and from that point saw the great crowd (John 6: 3, 5). It is not certain that the needed rest was obtained.—**Had compassion,** etc. Comp. Matt. 9: 36, which tells of the same feelings on an earlier, but similar occasion.—**He began to teach them many things.** This shows what He deemed their greatest need to be, although at the same time 'He healed their sick'

because they were as sheep not having a shepherd:
35 and he began to teach them many things. And when the day was now far spent, his disciples came unto him, and said, The place is desert, and the day is now far
36 spent: send them away, that they may go into the country and villages round about, and buy themselves
37 somewhat to eat. But he answered and said unto them, Give ye them to eat. And they say unto him, Shall we go and buy two hundred ¹pennyworth of
38 bread, and give them to eat? And he saith unto them, How many loaves have ye? go *and* see. And when
39 they knew, they say, Five, and two fishes. And he

¹ The word in the Greek denotes a coin worth about eight pence half penny.

(Matthew); comp. Luke 9: 11. 'Began' may mean, either that He began at once, or that He only began, the day being already far spent. The former is more probable.

Ver. 35. **And when the day was now far spent.** In the afternoon, since ver. 47 refers to the second evening of the same day.—**The place is desert,** etc. The disciples probably interrupted His discourse with this suggestion. Our Lord had continued His work of teaching and healing, until He had an opportunity to show how He could supply other wants. Those who wait on Him shall be fed! John tells us He 'knew what he would do,' inserting a question our Lord put to Philip (who was probably the spokesman) to try him. (See John 6: 5–7.)

Ver. 37. **Give ye them to eat.** 'Ye' is emphatic. Obedience seemed impossible, but they did obey through Christ's power providing the means for them. Duty is measured by Christ's command, not by our resources.—**Two hundred pennyworth.** This sum is mentioned mainly because it was an estimate of how much it would cost to give to each one a little (John 6: 7). Some have supposed that this was the amount of money they had in their common treasury, but it seems rather to be mentioned as a sum *beyond* their ability to pay. It was = $30, or £6, 5, a large amount of money then, since a denarius, or, 'penny,' was the hire of a day's labor.

Ver. 38. **Go and see,** lit., 'go, see.' Peculiar to Mark.—**When they knew.** By finding a lad with these provisions; see John 6: 8, 9. The answer was given by Andrew.

Ver. 39. **Upon the green grass.** 'Green' is inserted by Mark alone, in his usual graphic way, though John speaks of 'much grass.' The time of year was in April, since the Passover 'was at hand' (John 6: 4).

commanded them that all should ¹sit down by com-
40 panies upon the green grass. And they sat down in
41 ranks, by hundreds, and by fifties. And he took the
five loaves and the two fishes, and looking up to heaven,
he blessed, and brake the loaves; and he gave to the
disciples to set before them; and the two fishes divided
42 he among them all. And they did all eat, and were
43 filled. And they took up broken pieces, twelve bas-

¹ Gr. *recline.*

Ver. 40. **In ranks, by hundreds, and by fifties.** This is the fullest account of the way they were placed, though all four Evangelists intimate that the crowd was arranged in an orderly manner. Some have thought there were 50 ranks in breadth and 100 in length, thus making 5,000 (ver. 44). Gerlach: 'Two longer rows of 100, a shorter one of 50 persons. The fourth side remained, after the manner of the ancient's tables, empty and open.' Such an arrangement precluded deception. There was no disorderly running after 'the loaves and fishes'; Christ's blessings were received through those He commanded to impart them.

Ver. 41. Mark here agrees most closely with Matthew and Luke, while John is less full—**Looking up to heaven, he blessed, and brake the loaves.** The description recalls the Last Supper, of which this miracle is a premonition. The word 'bless' in the Bible means God's favoring us, our asking favors of Him and our thanksgiving for such favors; the three senses are always more or less connected. The form of the Greek disconnects the 'loaves' from the word 'bless.' The blessing was therefore mainly a thanksgiving (comp. John: 'when he had given thanks'), not simply a blessing of the loaves. Thus the eucharistic reference becomes prominent.—**And he gave to the disciples to set before them.** The word 'gave' is more exactly 'was giving,' continued giving, the miracle seems to have taken place in His hands, not in theirs.—**And the two fishes divided he among them all.** In the case of the fish there is no mention made of a distribution through the disciples. The greater detail in regard to the bread was probably due to its higher symbolical meaning. Moreover all did not partake of the fishes; comp. John 6: 11. Mark's mention of the division of the fishes is another evidence of the exactness so characteristic of this Gospel.

Ver. 42. **And were filled.** Philip had said that 200 pennyworth of bread would only give each a little, but now all had received enough.

Ver. 43. Among the many peculiarities of the various accounts of this miracle and the similar one (Matt. 15: 32-39; Mark 8: 1-9), none are more remarkable than the variety of expressions used to tell of what was gathered by the disciples. Among the six accounts no

44 ketfuls, and also of the fishes. And they that ate the loaves were five thousand men.

45 And straightway he constrained his disciples to enter into the boat, and to go before *him* unto the other side to Bethsaida, while he himself sendeth the

two are precisely alike. The Revised Version reproduces in part the variety of form.—**And they took up broken pieces.** The pieces they distributed, not the refuse.—**Twelve basketfuls**, lit., 'the fulnesses of twelve baskets.' The word for 'baskets' is the same in all four accounts (comp. chap. 8: 8-19, 20). These 'baskets' were such as travellers carried with them. They may have belonged to the disciples, who collected the broken pieces. What was gathered exceeded what was first given out. Christ was no waster; He enjoined (John 6: 12) carefulness and economy at the close of His most abundant bestowment. These fragments were probably for the use of the Twelve, since such miraculous increase was not the rule, but the exception. This circumstance was designed to impress the miracle upon the disciples (comp. chap. 8: 19, 20).—**And also of the fishes.** This, as well as the conclusion of the previous statement (ver. 41), is peculiar to Mark. What remained of the fishes was probably included in the contents of the twelve baskets, although John seems to limit these to the fragments of the loaves.

Ver. 44. **And they that ate the loaves**, not, 'of the loaves.' Here also Mark's expression differs from that of the other Evangelists. —**Five thousand men.** The 'women and children' (Matthew) are not mentioned, though Mark is usually so exact. All four accounts give the number of men; an important point in view of the question respecting the miracle narrated in chap. 8: 1-9.

Vers. 45-52. JESUS WALKS UPON THE SEA.—Parallel passages: Matt. 14: 22-33; John 6: 15-21.—*Connection.* Immediately after the miraculous feeding, the people wished to proclaim Jesus a king and were ready to take violent steps for that purpose (John 6: 14, 15). The disciples were probably ready to join the people in an enterprise, which would fulfil their remaining carnal expectations regarding the Messiahship of their Master. Hence our Lord dismissed them, sending them where they would feel their need of His presence. Matthew and John narrate this occurrence, but the attempt of Peter is mentioned only by the former (Matt. 14: 29-31).

Ver. 45. **Constrained his disciples.** See above.—**To go before him unto the other side to Bethsaida.** The prepositions used are different, and it is not necessarily implied that Bethsaida 'was on the other side.' In the only other case where Mark uses this name (chap. 8: 22), it undoubtedly refers to Bethsaida Julias on the *eastern* shore of the lake. It is most likely that the same place is meant here. Bethsaida, the city of Andrew and Peter, is supposed to have been on **the western shore, and ver. 45 seems to point to a place across the**

46 multitude away. And after he had taken leave of
47 them, he departed into the mountain to pray. And
when even was come, the boat was in the midst of the
48 sea, and he alone on the land. And seeing them distressed in rowing, for the wind was contrary unto them, about the fourth watch of the night he cometh unto them, walking on the sea; and he would have passed
49 by them: but they, when they saw him walking on

lake. But the disciples were driven westward, across the lake, against their will, and this can be best explained by supposing that while the ultimate destination was 'the other side,' they were to go first to Bethsaida on the same side and there take up our Lord, after He had sent away the people. It is not certain that there was a western Bethsaida (see Schaff's Bible Dictionary, and comp. Matt. 12: 21). The view suggested accords best with all the details as given by the three Evangelists.—**While he himself sendeth the multitude away.** They were in an excited condition (see above and John 6: 15); hence great prudence, perhaps an exercise of some constraining power, was necessary.

Ver. 46. **After he had taken leave of them,** *i. e.*, the multitude. This detail is peculiar to Mark. The A. V. renders the two Greek phrases (ver. 45 and here) in the same way.

Ver. 47. **And when even was come.** The second evening (comp. Matt. 14: 15 with ver. 35).—**The boat was in the midst of the sea.** When Jesus came to them, they were 'about twenty-five or thirty furlongs' from shore (John 6: 9), *i. e.*, about the middle of the lake, driven out by an easterly wind, while they attempted to reach Bethsaida which was in a northerly direction.

Ver. 48. **Distressed in rowing.** Lit., 'tormented.'—**The wind was contrary,** etc. It had arisen after they started, John 6: 18. They must have been thus engaged for some time, since it was not until **about the fourth watch of the night** (three to six in the morning) that our Lord appeared. Their danger had lasted nearly all night. Deliverance is often long delayed, but while the Master prayed, the disciples could not be lost.—**Would have passed by them.** Mentioned by Mark only. This was to try them. It seems best to suppose, not that both were going in the same direction, but that their courses crossed, and that, seeing Him go on His path over the sea, they were affected as ver. 49 describes. This too will best account for Peter's loss of courage in the boisterous (contrary) wind. See Matt. 14: 30. Lange thinks that this passing on was, as it were, to show them the way, to show that they need no longer toil to meet Him at eastern Bethsaida, but might pass directly over.

Ver. 49. **Supposed that it was an apparition.** An unreal

the sea, supposed that it was an apparition, and cried
50 out: for they all saw him, and were troubled. But he
straightway spake with them, and saith unto them, Be
51 of good cheer: it is I; be not afraid. And he went
up unto them into the boat; and the wind ceased: and
52 they were sore amazed in themselves; for they understood not concerning the loaves, but their heart was hardened.

53 And when they had ¹crossed over, they came to the

¹ Or, *crossed over to the land, they came unto Gennesaret*

appearance of a real person. The word is not that usually rendered 'spirit.'—**And cried out.** All three Evangelists recognize this superstitious fear. As Matthew and Mark here discriminate between 'an apparition' and a real bodily appearance of our Lord, they cannot mean the former when they write of the resurrection of Christ.

Ver. 50. **For they all saw him and were troubled.** A proof that this story was not due to the over-heated imagination of a few of them.—**Be of good cheer: it is I.** An assurance, through a living voice, of His bodily presence.—**Be not afraid.** The presence of Christ always brings with it this cheering injunction. At this point occurred the attempt of Peter to walk upon the sea.

Ver. 51. **And he went up unto them into the boat.** John (6: 21) speaks of the boat being immediately 'at the land whither they went.' This was on the western side of the lake, and we may either suppose that the wind during the night had driven them near that shore, or accept another miracle.—**Were sore amazed in themselves.** That their amazement was not altogether praiseworthy appears from ver. 52. The longer reading followed in the A. V. seems to have arisen from an attempt to explain the connection of the two verses. Matthew's account (14: 33) emphasizes another side of the effect: 'And they that were in the boat worshipped Him, saying, Of a truth thou art the Son of God.'

Ver. 52. **For they understood not concerning the loaves**, lit., '*on* the loaves.' 'There was no intelligent comprehension *founded* on the miracle of the loaves. They did not from the miracle they had seen, infer the power of the Lord over nature' (Alford).—**But their heart was hardened.** 'Had been hardened' is equally near the meaning. Not in the sense in which we now use these terms, but rather suggesting slowness of intellect. Yet there is a tone of censure in the verse. This state of mind was in keeping with their character as portrayed throughout the Gospels, and true to human nature.

Vers. 53–56. JESUS HEALS IN THE LAND OF GENNESARET.—Parallel passages: Matt. 14: 34–36; comp. John 6: 24–25. Mark's account gives fuller details of the healing

54 land unto Gennesaret, and moored to the shore. And when they were come out of the boat, straightway *the*
55 *people* knew him, and ran round about that whole region, and began to carry about on their beds those that were
56 sick, where they heard he was. And wheresoever he entered, into villages, or into cities, or into the country, they laid the sick in the marketplaces, and besought him that they might touch if it were but the border of his garment: and as many as touched ¹him were made whole.

¹ Or, *it.*

work in Gennesaret. John introduces other incidents and an important discourse uttered to those who sought our Lord.

Ver. 53. **And when they had crossed over.** The correct reading, which is more exactly rendered in the margin, strengthens the view that there was no miraculous sailing, since it distinguishes the passing over to the land, and the coming to Gennesaret. The natural course of things is further apparent from the last phrase: **moored to the shore,** or, simply 'moored there,' *i. e.*, came to anchor, or, made fast, possibly ran the boat on shore, although there is nothing in the original answering to the phrase: 'to the shore.' 'Gennesaret' was a fertile district, with a mild climate, on the western shore of the lake (also called the Lake of Gennesaret). It was about four miles long and half as broad. Capernaum was at its northern end, near Khan Minyeh, but according to others further north at Tell Hûm (see Schaff's *Bible Dict., Capernaum*).

Ver. 54. **Ran round about that whole region.** Several minor corrections in the Greek text are indicated in this rendering. It is evident that the people of the unknown place where they landed are referred to. Matthew says: 'they sent unto all that region round about.'—**To carry about in their beds.** Some carried to one place, others to another, as they heard where our Lord was; some may have been carried from place to place after Him, but it is not meant that this was generally necessary.

Ver. 56. **Wheresoever he entered.** This implies that a journey of some kind followed.—**Into the country,** lit., 'fields.'—**Market-places**; here with a wide sense.—This description may refer to a period of some length, and indicates the great number of miracles performed by our Lord. The passover was at hand (John 6: 4).—**If it were but the border of his garment.** In that very region a woman had been thus healed in the presence of a crowd (chap. 5: 25-34), so that these people were not superstitious, but had strong faith. As our Lord was only passing through, a greater number could be healed in this way. Christ's miracles were always performed so as to

7:1 And there are gathered together unto him the Pharisees, and certain of the scribes, which had come 2 from Jerusalem, and had seen that some of his disciples ate their bread with ¹defiled, that is, unwashen

¹ Or, *common.*

show a connection between Himself and the person cured, even though it were so slight a one as this touch. It is this fact which gives the permanent spiritual significance to the simple statement: **and as many as touched him were made whole,** a significance not diminished by referring to the touch (as is done in the margin) to the 'border of his garment.'

Chap. VII: 1-23. DISCOURSE IN REGARD TO EATING WITH UNWASHEN HANDS.—Parallel passage: Matt. 15: 1-20. The history of the last year of our Lord's ministry begins here. The discourse at Capernaum (John 6: 22-71), respecting the manna from heaven, followed the feeding of the five thousand. The passover, which was nigh at hand (John 6: 4), was not attended by our Lord (John 7: 1). The larger half of each Gospel is devoted to this 'year of conflict,' the story of which here begins with an account of a covert attack on our Lord. Certain scribes from Jerusalem (chap. 3: 22) some time before had openly opposed Him. Then they expressed a blasphemously hostile opinion respecting the miracles of our Lord; now these remonstrate against the conduct of His disciples. The opposition now, though apparently less bitter, was really more dangerous. The interview with the Pharisees (vers. 1-13) shows that it is characteristic of sticklers for the external customs and ceremonies of religion (Pharisees in all ages) to be intolerant about little and belittling questions, to be inconsistent, unrighteous (even according to their own standard), and hypocritical. This ever-recurring mistake of making religion consist in 'meat and drink,' is further rebuked in the saying to the multitude (vers. 14, 15), while the exposition of the 'parable' shows the nature of real defilement. Moral purity or impurity is from the heart, not from the food, still less from the observance or neglect of the ceremonial 'washing' of the hands before eating bread. On this point the Lord's words (ver. 18) are still applicable: 'Are ye so without understanding also?' Mark introduces several independent details: the fact that the opposers came from Jerusalem (ver. 1), the explanation of the Jewish washings (vers. 3, 4); but he omits the remarks to the disciples about the Pharisees taking offence (Matt. 15: 12-14).

Ver. 1. **And there are gathered together unto him.** Against Him, as we see.—**The Pharisees,** etc. A party of the Pharisees, including **certain scribes.**—**Which had come from Jerusalem.** They had recently come, apparently with a hostile purpose. It is possible, but not probable, that this was a formal deputation from the Sanhedrin. 'Had come' refers to the entire party.

Ver. 2. **And had seen.** On some recent occasion. They gathered unto Him, because they 'had seen' this (lit., 'having seen;' but the pluperfect is required in English). The close connection with ver. 1 was overlooked by the transcribers, and 'they found fault' inserted to complete the sentence.—**That some of his disciples ate their**

3 hands. For the Pharisees, and all the Jews, except
they wash their hands [1] diligently, eat not, holding the
4 tradition of the elders: and *when they come* from the
marketplace, except they [2] wash themselves, they eat
not: and many other things there be, which they have
received to hold, [3] washings of cups, and pots, and

[1] Or, *up to the elbow*, Gr. *with the fist.*
ancient authorities read *sprinkle themselves.*
[2] *bathe* (Amer. Com.), Gr. *baptize.* Some
[3] Gr. *baptizings.*

bread. 'This incident naturally brings to view the constant and intrusive *surveillance* to which our Lord and His disciples were subjected' (J. A. Alexander).—**Defiled,** or, 'common.' Comp. Acts 10: 14, 15.—**That is, unwashen hands.** This explanation shows that the Gospel was written for Gentile readers.

Ver. 3. **All the Jews.** Pharisaism had the upper hand.—**Diligently,** lit., 'with the fist.' The two interpretations now most generally adopted are: (1) Actually 'with the fist,' as a peculiar ceremony on such occasions. ' Probably it was part of the rite, that the washing hand was shut; because it might have been thought that the open hand engaged in washing would make the other unclean, or be made unclean by it, after having itself been washed' (Lange). (2) 'Diligently,' thoroughly, in accordance with a Hebrew expression, which uses the fist as meaning *strength.* But Mark is giving an explanation to Gentile readers, and he would hardly use a Hebrew expression. 'Up to the elbow' is an interpretation, not a translation. The literal sense is the correct one; but it conveys no meaning to the ordinary reader without a long explanation. The main point is, that the ceremony was formal.

Ver. 4. **And from the market.** It is doubtful whether this means: when they come from the market, or, what comes from the market. We prefer the former (see below).—**Except they bathe** (so the Amer. Com., to indicate that this is not the same word as that used in ver. 3), lit., 'baptize;' according to another reading, 'sprinkle themselves.' The original means, either baptize themselves, or, for themselves. The former is the more obvious sense. In either case, it was a *religious* ceremony.—**Washings,** or, 'baptisms,' *i. e.*, ceremonial, religious washings. The passage clearly proves the wider usage of the terms 'baptism' and 'baptize' in Hellenistic Greek, whether by immersion, or pouring, or sprinkling. Christianity does not prescribe any particular mode as essential. Disputes about the form of baptism savor much of what our Lord is rebuking in the discourse which follows.—**Cups.** Drinking vessels.—**Pots.** The word here used is derived from the Latin, meaning a vessel holding the sixth part of a larger one. It was probably wooden, holding about a pint and a half.—**Brasen vessels.** Earthen ones were broken when defiled (Lev. 15: 12).—'Couches,' not 'tables,' is the meaning of the word which

5 brasen vessels¹. And the Pharisees and the scribes ask him, Why walk not thy disciples according to the tradition of the elders, but eat their bread with ²de-
6 filed hands? And he said unto them, Well did Isaiah prophesy of you hypocrites, as it is written,
This people honoureth me with their lips,
But their heart is far from me.

¹ Many ancient authorities add *and couches*. ² Or, *common*.

is found here in many authorities (see foot note), the couches on which persons then reclined at meals. All these things were ceremonially washed, or baptized, in case of defilement. Ordinary washing for cleanliness is not referred to. It is probable that the Pharisees multiplied the *occasions* of defilement, as they had done the *articles* which could be defiled, but it is scarcely possible that these baptisms took place before or after every meal. These usages were based on Lev. 12-15, but the main authority for them was not derived from this source, as is evident from the language of the Pharisees (ver. 5) and of our Lord (vers. 8, 9).

Ver. 5. **Why walk not thy disciples.** In reality a cautious and artful attack upon our Lord Himself.—**The tradition of the elders.** Certain rules handed down by word of mouth from Moses and the fathers of the nation (comp. Gal. 1: 14). 'Elders' refers to the authors, not the upholders, of these traditional customs. 'The Jews attached greater value to tradition than even to the written law, appealing in support of it to Deut. 4: 14; 17: 10. More especially did they pay respect to the traditionary injunction of washing the hands before meals, to which it was thought Lev. 15: 11 referred' (Meyer).—**But eat their bread with defiled hands.** See vers. 3, 4. 'Rabbi Akiba, being imprisoned, and having water scarcely sufficient to sustain life given him, preferred dying of thirst to eating without washing his hands' (Alford). Our Lord opposes, not the custom, but the authority of this tradition, which was assumed by the Pharisees. Notice the belittling influence of legalism.

Ver. 6. This citation is placed in a different position by Matthew, but the sense is precisely the same.—**Well did Isaiah prophesy of you hypocrites** (Is. 29: 13). 'Well,' *i. e.*, aptly. Our Lord assumes that the prophecy properly referred to the Jewish people then, while He does not imply that this was its exclusive or even original application. The word 'hypocrites' had not quite so strong a sense then as now. It included those self-deceived.—**Their heart is far from me.** In the Hebrew: 'Their heart they have removed far from me.' Applicable first to the contemporaries of Isaiah, but descriptive of the unbelieving Jews in all ages, and, as our Lord declares, peculiarly 'apt' at that time.

7 But in vain do they worship me,
   Teaching *as their* doctrines the precepts of men.
8 Ye leave the commandment of God, and hold fast the
9 tradition of men. And he said unto them, Full well
   do ye reject the commandment of God, that ye may
10 keep your tradition. For Moses said, Honour thy
   father and thy mother; and, he that speaketh evil of
11 father or mother, let him ¹die the death: but ye say,

¹ Or, *surely die.*

Ver. 7. **In vain.** This phrase (only implied in the original passage in Isaiah) refers to the *emptiness* of such worship. It is both *groundless* (without true principle) and *fruitless* (without proper results). The Hebrew means literally: 'their fearing of me has become a precept of men, a thing taught.' The Greek here might be rendered more exactly: 'teaching *as* teachings precepts of men.' A rebuke of such religion as rests only on human authority. In this case, as applied to the Pharisees, it shows that such religion becomes contrary to God's commandments, and hence *positively false.*

Ver. 8. **Ye leave the commandment of God,** etc. 'Let go' would form a more exact contrast to 'hold fast.' This verse is peculiar to Mark, 'setting forth their *depreciating* of God's command in comparison with human tradition, before their absolute *violation* of that command in vers. 10, 11' (Alford).—**Tradition of men.** 'Men' as in contrast to 'God,' implying that the 'elders' (ver. 5) had no other than human authority.—The rest of the verse is to be omitted, according to the best authorities.

Ver. 9. **Full well.** Ironical; the same word as in ver. 6.—**Your tradition.** The tradition of the elders was that of 'men,' and they had made it theirs, living by it, contrary to the laws of God. 'At the bottom of all rigorous enforcement of traditional observances there is an unconscious, or half-conscious, repugnance to submit perfectly to the law of God' (Lange).

Ver. 10. **For Moses said.** Matthew: 'For God said,' assuming that God spoke through Moses in the law (Exod. 20: 12). The precepts cited are apt, since the Pharisees upheld tradition as delivered by the 'fathers.'—**He that speaketh evil,** etc. Exod. 21: 17. Our Lord quotes, not the promise in the Decalogue, but the penalty given elsewhere. Comp. chap. 9: 39, which shows that 'curseth' is too strong a term —**Die the death.** In the original Hebrew: 'dying he shall die;' in the original Greek of this passage: 'let him end with death,' both equivalent to: 'he shall surely die;' this penalty is to be inflicted upon him.

Ver. 11. **But ye say.** God (through Moses) said one thing, 'ye say' another, and though you quote tradition, it has only your own

If a man shall say to his father or his mother, That wherewith thou mightest have been profited by me is
12 Corban, that is to say, Given *to God*; ye no longer suffer him to do aught for his father or his mother;
13 making void the word of God by your tradition, which ye have delivered: and many such like things ye do.
14 And he called to him the multitude again, and said
15 unto them, Hear me all of you, and understand: there is nothing from without the man, that going into him

authority.—**That wherewith thou mightest**, etc. The Rabbins taught, that, by saying **Corban** of his possessions, a man was absolved from the duty of caring for his parents, yet the brief expression was not considered sufficient to bind the party to devote his property to religious uses. The Hebrew word used, is translated by the Evangelist into Greek for his Greek readers. Both mean a gift to God. The term 'Corban' seems to have included all kinds of offerings, though some think it was applied, in the time of Christ only to offerings without a sacrifice. The Rev. Ver. makes this difficult passage more intelligible. The correct text makes it unnecessary to supply 'he shall be free.' The construction in Matthew is still more difficult.

Ver. 12. **Ye no longer suffer him**, etc. . Not necessarily that they actively forbade it, but their teachings virtually permitted him to neglect his father and mother altogether. This is the comment of our Lord, not the language of the Pharisees. Comp. Matt. 15: 6.

Ver. 13. **Making void**, not merely transgressing, but rejecting, **the word of God.** Modern Pharisaism does the same. Church tradition leads to dogmas which deny God's direct commands. Its upholders persecute, not only for infractions of their interpretations of God's laws, but for disregard of precepts of their own making. Or at least, they constantly break Christ's law of love, through zeal for external things about which Christ gave no express command.—**By your tradition, which ye have delivered.** Peculiar to Mark. They made void God's word themselves, and by handing down these traditions would make others do the same. The last clause of ver. 8, was probably taken from this verse.

Ver. 14. **And he called to him the multitude again.** 'Again' (which the best authorities read, instead of 'all') implies that during this questioning the crowd was not so closely about Him as usual, but it does not follow that He had been judicially examined in the synagogue.—**Hear me all of you.** 'All' is peculiar to Mark.
—**And understand.** He turns to the people, as if to say, these hypocrites, though the zealous expounders of the law, cannot understand its real sense.

Ver. 15. **There is nothing**, etc. In the remainder of the paragraph (and in the parallel passage) a number of verbs of motion are

16 can defile him: but the things which proceed out of
17 the man are those that defile the man.¹ And when he
was entered into the house from the multitude, his
18 disciples asked of him the parable. And he saith
unto them, Are ye so without understanding also?
Perceive ye not, that whatsoever from without goeth
19 into the man, *it* cannot defile him; because it goeth not
into his heart, but into his belly, and goeth out into
the draught? *This he said,* making all meats clean.

¹ Many ancient authorities insert ver. 16 *If any man hath ears to hear, let him hear.*

used, the exact force of which is reproduced in the Revised Version.— **Can defile the man**, *i. e.*, make him common, impure or profane. The Mosaic law, by a variety of ceremonial regulations, made external distinctions to teach the importance of *moral* purity. This purpose had been lost sight of, and the external regulation not only made the main matter, but so extended it that ceremonial impurity was considered worse than moral impurity. Our Lord opposes only this perversion of the Mosaic law. Pharisees in all ages have exalted the sign and symbol at the expense of the reality.

Ver. 16 is not found in some of the best early manuscripts. The words were a common close to instruction difficult to understand, and would easily creep into the text.

Ver. 17. **Into the house.** The remarks about the Pharisees (Matt. 15: 12-14) were uttered first, then **his disciples** ('Peter,' Matthew) **asked of him the parable.** If Peter was Mark's informant, there is modesty in this variation. The declaration in ver. 15, was a 'hard saying' to those who were born Jews, and hence Peter might have called it a 'parable,' especially as our Lord had so often taught the deeper truths in that form. Or the disciples, with their Jewish education, might have thought: this saying to which the Pharisees so much object (Matt. 15: 12) is not to be taken literally, it must be a parable. The censure of the next verse favors this explanation.

Ver. 18. **Are ye so,** in this way, as indicated by the question, **without understanding also,** as well as the multitude (ver. 14). —**Perceive ye not?** The truth affirmed was one easy to be perceived by the spiritually minded.

Ver. 19. **Because it entereth not into his heart.** The thought of the verse is that food affects the body not the heart, that the moral and spiritual state of man is not dependent on the food or drink he uses, much less on certain ceremonial observances in regard to these things.—**Into the draught,** 'drain' or 'privy.'—**Making all meats clean.** Mark inserts this new detail. The clause may be joined with 'draught;' it then refers to the purifying process, which takes place in the impure matter coming from the body. God having thus pro-

20 And he said, That which proceedeth out of the man,
21 that defileth the man. For from within, out of the
22 heart of men, [1] evil thoughts proceed, fornications, thefts, murders, adulteries, covetings, wickednesses, deceit, lasciviousness, an evil eye, railing, pride, fool-
23 ishness: all these evil things proceed from within, and defile the man.

[1] Gr. *thoughts that are evil.*

vided for a purifying (physical) process, how absurd to make the spiritual condition depend on food, especially upon certain ceremonies connected with it. A grammatical difficulty, however, attends this view. Many therefore consider this an explanation of the Evangelist = *This he said;* making all meats clean. This view is very old, but open to grave objections. The variation in readings is against it, there is no similar instance of interpretation in Mark's Gospel, and it gives an unusual sense to the word 'purify,' or, 'make clean.' But it has been accepted in the Revised Version.

Ver. 20. Expresses in another form the same thought, indicating plainly that the heart is unaffected by what goes into the mouth, while what comes out of the mouth indicates what is in the heart.

Ver. 21. **For from within, out of the heart of men.** This represents, even more emphatically than the form preserved by Matthew, that the heart of man is 'the laboratory and fountain-head of all that is good and bad in the inner life of man,' hence his responsibility, etc. That the body is the seat of sin is here denied. Both materialism and asceticism are opposed. Mark's catalogue of sins is fuller than that of Matthew. Here, as there, the plural seems to indicate that the sins are common and notorious.

Ver. 22. **Covetings**, lit., 'covetousness,' grasping, greedy desires, with the attending peculiarities.—**Wickednesses.** 'Malignities;' evil dispositions.—**Deceit.** Fraud, as distinguished from actual theft.—**Lasciviousness.** Sensual excess.—**An evil eye.** A figure for *envy.*—**Blasphemy.** Proud and spiteful anger, manifesting itself in abusive language against God.—**Pride.** Self exaltation, leading to arrogance towards God and man.—**Foolishness.** Senselessness, unreasoning folly, in thought, as well as in the words and acts which result. A fearful catalogue, true to nature still. How well our Lord, the purest of the pure, knew the depths of iniquity from which He would save sinful men!

Ver. 23. **All these evil things proceed,** &c. An emphatic re-statement, after the dreary catalogue of sins. Ceremonial impurity is insignificant compared with moral impurity. Yet Christians now are as slow to learn this as the disciples were.

24 And from thence he arose, and went away into the borders of Tyre ¹and Sidon. And he entered into a house, and would have no man know it: and he could
25 not be hid. But straightway a woman, whose little daughter had an unclean spirit, having heard of him,
26 came and fell down at his feet. Now the woman was a ²Greek, a Syrophœnician by race. And she besought him that he would cast forth the ³devil out of her

¹ Some ancient authorities omit *and Sidon.*   ² Or, *Gentile.*   ³ Gr. *demon.*

VERS 24–30. THE VISIT TO THE BORDERS OF TYRE AND SIDON; THE MEETING WITH THE SYROPHENICIAN WOMAN.—Parallel passage: Matt. 15: 21-28. This visit of our Lord to Gentile regions immediately followed the attack from the Pharisees. (Comp. the course of Paul; Acts 13: 46.) The interview with the heathen woman is striking and prophetic. The Jews reject the blessing; the Gentiles seek it with longing desire. The heathen world had been prepared for Him who was 'a light to lighten the Gentiles.' The incident was timely. It prepared the Apostles for their universal mission, and also for the prophecy (chap. 8: 31) of His death at Jerusalem. They must see the faith of the Gentiles, before they could learn the faithlessness of the Jews.

Ver. 24. **And from thence.** Probably Capernaum, though the locality is nowhere specified.—**Went away.** Matthew: 'withdrew,' to avoid the Pharisees.—**The borders of Tyre and Sidon.** Some ancient authorities omit 'and Sidon,' probably to avoid a difficulty in ver. 31. He may not have passed much beyond the frontier. Phenicia, here named from its chief cities, was north of upper Galilee, and inhabited by Gentiles. The Jewish world was closing against our Lord; the Gentile world was not yet open.—**Entered into a house.** To avoid notice.—**And he could not be hid.** From the desire of the mother who came. She entered the house, and afterwards followed Him in the way. Some, however, suppose that the first entreaty (Matt. 15: 22) took place outside the house and the final entreaty within it, so that 'He could not be hid,' because she pressed in. The heathen mother found Him: she was a type of the longing, suffering Gentile world.

Ver. 25. **Whose little daughter,** as in chap. 5: 23, the only places where the Greek word occurs.—**Had an unclean spirit.** Such possession was, therefore, not confined to Jews.—**Having heard of him, came.** Probably into the house.—**Fell at his feet.** In her final entreaty also she 'worshipped Him' (Matt. 15: 25).

Ver. 26. **A Greek,** *i. e.*, a Gentile in religion.—**Syrophœnician by race,** such a nation no longer existed. There were Phenicians at Carthage in Libya (Africa), as well as in Syria. The Phenicians were Canaanites by extraction (comp. Matt. 15: 22).—**She besought him.** Here occurred all the details given in Matt. 15: 23-25: the

27 daughter. And he said unto her, Let the children first be filled: for it is not meet to take the children's
28 ¹bread and cast it to the dogs. But she answered and saith unto him, Yea, Lord: even the dogs under the
29 table eat of the children's crumbs. And he said unto her, For this saying go thy way; the ²devil is gone
30 out of thy daughter. And she went away unto her house, and found the child laid upon the bed, and the ²devil gone out.

¹ Or, *loaf*. ² Gr. *demon*.

silence of the Lord; the request of the disciples, to get rid of her; the answer to them, and her second and more urgent request.

Ver. 27. **Let the children first be filled.** 'This important addition in Mark sets forth the whole ground on which the present refusal rested. The Jews were *first* to have the gospel offered to them for their acceptance or rejection; it was *not yet time* for the Gentiles' (Alford).—**It is not meet.** The reply is not harsh, nor is it a refusal. It calls forth the woman's faith, and convinces the disciples that it is 'proper' to bless this heathen woman.—**To take the children's bread.** All present understood this as referring to the blessing provided for the Jews.—**To the dogs,** lit., 'little dogs.' A reference to the large savage dogs so common in the East, would be very contemptuous; household dogs are meant; a sense the woman skilfully used.

Ver. 28. **Yea, Lord.** She accepts the Lord's word and makes an argument of it.—**Even,** not, 'yet,' **the dogs.** Not as one of the children; but as a humble dependent, she asks only what falls to such: **the crumbs.** Possibly a reference to the pieces of bread on which, according to the ancient usage, the hands were wiped; but the usual sense is more natural. The woman had been *earnest* in gaining a hearing at all. Her answer shows a quickness of mind, approaching wit, humility also, joined with true wisdom; in her persevering faith she saw the mind of Christ even in the seemingly repulsive figure.

Ver. 29. **For this saying.** As an evidence of her *faith.* Matthew: 'great is thy faith.'—**The devil (demon) is gone out.** As He spoke, the miracle was performed (Matt. 15: 28).

Ver. 30. **And she went away unto her house.** This sketch of her return is peculiar to Mark. She had obeyed the command: 'Go thy way.'—**Laid,** or, 'thrown,' **upon the bed.** Just as the demon left her, but in a quiet condition, which was the evidence that the demon had gone. The correct order favors this view. The exhaustion was natural, and a sign of complete dispossession.—As in the case of the Gentile centurion, this cure was performed at a distance. The intermediate link in both cases was strong faith combined with affec-

31 And again he went out from the borders of Tyre, and came through Sidon unto the sea of Galilee,
32 through the midst of the borders of Decapolis. And they bring unto him one that was deaf, and had an impediment in his speech; and they beseech him to
33 lay his hand upon him. And he took him aside from the multitude privately, and put his fingers into his

tion for the person healed. A hint is thus given in regard to intercessory prayer.

Vers. 31-37. THE MIRACLES OF HEALING IN DECAPOLIS.—Parallel passage: Matt. 15: 29-30. The miracle here narrated in detail is peculiar to Mark and of special interest.

Ver. 31. **And came through Sidon.** Not the city, but the district thus termed. The course was first northward, then eastward, then southward or southwestward, **through the midst of the borders of Decapolis.** This refers to the northern part of the Decapolis at the foot of the Lebanon range. Passing through this He reached the mountainous (and solitary) district on the *eastern* shore of the sea of Galilee. In making this circuit, our Lord was seeking needed retirement. Matthew (15: 29-30) tells of His going up into the mountain and adds: 'And there came unto him great multitudes, having with them the lame, blind, dumb, maimed, and many others, and they cast them down at his feet; and he healed them.' Even here 'He could not be hid.'

Ver. 32. **Had an impediment in his speech.** Lit., 'hardly speaking.' It is more probable that he was 'deaf and dumb' than a 'stammerer,' etc. Deafness usually causes dumbness. An actual and separate defect in the vocal organs is, however, suggested by both the form here used and the mode of healing. This man was not possessed, as many thus afflicted were. Possession and such diseases and deformities are to be distinguished; the more so, since Mark is specially apt to tell of our Lord's power over unclean spirits.—**To lay his hand upon him.** They thought this was necessary.

Ver. 33. **Took him aside from the multitude privately** (or, 'by himself'). This may have been in consequence of some peculiarity in the *man* himself, or in the spectators. The people of that district were probably rude and more or less under heathen influence. The peculiar manner of the miracle was not occasioned by the difficulty of the case. The design seems to have been, still to connect the miraculous effect with His own person, yet to show that He was not bound to one mode. It is not necessary to find a symbolical meaning in each act.—**And he spat and touched his tongue.** Probably moistening His finger with saliva, He touched his tongue. The two parts affected by disease were touched, to show that our Lord could choose His own mode. We may, however, regard the miracle as a literal ful-

34 ears, and he spat, and touched his tongue; and looking up to heaven, he sighed, and saith unto him, Ephpha-
35 tha, that is, Be opened. And his ears were opened, and the bond of his tongue was loosed, and he spake
36 plain. And he charged them that they should tell no man: but the more he charged them, so much the more
37 a great deal they published it. And they were beyond measure astonished, saying, He hath done all things well: he maketh even the deaf to hear, and the dumb to speak.

filment of Is. 35: 5: 'Then shall the ears of the deaf be unstopped,' etc.

Ver. 34. **And looking up to heaven.** In *prayer*, perhaps to show His connection with God the Father in heaven, over against the magical influences which may have been assumed by the people of that district; perhaps to affect the deaf and dumb man, who could perceive this.—**He sighed.** In sympathy, always felt, but here expressed; perhaps also in distress at the ignorance and superstition He would overcome.—**Ephphatha.** The precise word used, translated into Greek by Mark, meaning **be opened** (thoroughly) It is closely related to the Hebrew word used in Is. 35: 5. The command was addressed to the man, as shut up from the world by the defect of these two senses.

Ver. 35. **The bond of his tongue**, the impediment, whatever it was, **was loosed**, was removed. **And he spake** (more exactly: 'was speaking') **plain** (or, 'rightly'). It is not necessarily implied that he was able to speak in some way before the cure 'Mark shows, in his account of the miracles, a preference for those healings, in which the gradual process of the cure, as connected with the instrument and the development of it, is vividly presented' (Lange).

Ver. 36. **Charged them.** etc. The prohibition was mainly to prevent excessive zeal among these mountaineers. As usual, the command to be silent was not obeyed. It often seems harder to make men keep silence than to make the dumb to speak.

Ver. 37. **Beyond measure.** Their excessive zeal was equalled by their excessive astonishment.—**He hath done all things well.** Perhaps an allusion to Gen. 1: 31; the same Power and Beneficence were manifested in His healing as in God's work of creation.—**The dumb to speak.** This favors the view that the cured man was entirely speechless. The whole verse intimates that this was but one of many miracles. Matthew adds: 'and they glorified the God of Israel.' They were, however, not heathen, but Jews. Yet living on the borders, they seem to have been affected by heathen nations, and half recognized other gods.

8 : 1 In those days, when there was again a great multitude, and they had nothing to eat, he called unto
2 him his disciples, and saith unto them, I have compassion on the multitude, because they continue with
3 me now three days, and have nothing to eat: and if I send them away fasting to their home, they will faint in the way; and some of them are come from far.
4 And his disciples answered him, Whence shall one be able to fill these men with ¹bread here in a desert
5 place? And he asked them, How many loaves have

¹ Gr. *loaves.*

Chap. VIII: 1-10. THE FEEDING OF THE FOUR THOUSAND.—Parallel passage: Matt. 15: 32-39. The two Evangelists (Matthew and Mark) here show unusual agreement, thus indicating the greater improbability that this is another account of the miracle narrated in chap. 6: 30-44. The circumstances of the two miracles differ in many ways: as to the number fed, the amount of provision present, the fragments gathered, even the kind of baskets used, a different word being found here, and also in the question of our Lord about the two miracles (Matt. 16: 9, 10; chap. 8: 19, 20).

Ver. 1. **In those days.** Indefinite; but the interval between this and the last miracle must have been very brief.—**He called unto him his disciples.** Our Lord Himself takes the first step (comp. chap. 6: 35). This case was more urgent; the crowd was not composed of those on the way to the passover, and had been three days with Him.

Ver. 2. **Three days.** The third day was passing; so they were hungry and destitute of provisions, but not yet in actual distress.

Ver. 3. **Faint in the way,** *i. e.,* because exhausted from the want of food on their way home in that mountainous region.—**And some of them are come from far.** Peculiar to Mark. The Lord's compassion was called out by their physical want, which, however, resulted from their desire to be near Him.

Ver. 4. **Whence shall one be able to fill?** The long fast would call for plentiful provision. The question may seem strange after the miraculous feeding of the five thousand. But it was not so strange as their subsequent reasoning about the leaven of the Pharisees (vers. 15-21). Our own forgetfulness and unbelief should make us wonder less at the 'little faith' of the disciples. In the previous case the disciples emphasized the amount of bread ('two hundred pennyworth'); in this, the fact that they are in a **desert place.** The place was certainly mountainous, and probably sterile (comp. ver. 6).

Ver. 5. **How many loaves have ye?** In the other case a lad had the provisions; here the disciples themselves. The loaves were **seven** in this case, *five* in the other.

7

6 ye? And they said, Seven. And he commandeth the multitude to sit down on the ground: and he took the seven loaves, and having given thanks, he brake, and gave to his disciples, to set before them; and they set
7 them before the multitude. And they had a few small fishes: and having blessed them, he commanded
8 to set these also before them. And they did eat, and were filled: and they took up, of broken pieces that
9 remained over, seven baskets. And they were about
10 four thousand; and he sent them away. And straightway he entered into the boat with his disciples, and came into the parts of Dalmanutha.

Ver. 6. **And he commandeth**, etc. In the other case the disciples arranged the multitude (Luke 9: 14; John 6: 10).—**On the ground**, not, 'upon the green grass' (chap. 6: 39); the region was probably barren.

Ver. 7. **A few small fishes**. The number is unknown. Mark speaks of them separately. The language intimates that they were separately blessed and distributed.—**Having blessed**. A different word from that used in ver. 6. The distinction is slight, however: this one implying *praise*, and the other *thanksgiving*. The Revised Version brings out with exactness the minor variations of the various accounts of the two miracles. The mode of distribution (and the miracle itself) was precisely the same.

Ver. 8. **And were filled**. The same word as in the doubting question of the disciples (ver. 4); a correspondence obscured in the A. V.—**Of broken pieces that remained over, seven baskets**. Comp. with chap. 6: 43; in that case the baskets were 'twelve' in number. The word rendered 'baskets' is a different one (probably larger ones are meant), and the same difference is observed in vers. 19, 20, and in Matt. 16: 9, 10.

Ver. 9. **Four thousand**, instead of 'five thousand.' In this case the material miracle seems not to have been so great, as respects the number fed and the fragments remaining. All these variations, which show no gradation between the miracles, and betray no special design, prove that the Evangelists give true accounts of two distinct miracles.

Ver. 10. **Into the boat**. Probably one awaiting Him.—**With his disciples**. Implied, but not stated, in the account of Matthew. —**Into the parts of Dalmanutha**. Matthew: Magadan (according to the correct reading; Magdala, A. V.). The site of Magdala (Magadan), now called *Madschel* ('Migdol,' Josh. 19: 38), is north of Tiberias and directly east of Cana, on the *western* shore of the lake, since the next voyage (chap. 8: 13; Matt. 16: 5) was across the lake to the

11 And the Pharisees came forth, and began to question with him, seeking from him a sign from heaven,
12 tempting him. And he sighed deeply in his spirit, and saith, Why doth this generation seek a sign? verily I say unto you, There shall no sign be given

eastern side. The theory which places the site on the south-eastern shore of the lake is altogether unsupported, and makes of these journeys of our Lord an aimless wandering. Our Lord, pursued by the hostility of the Jews and seeking retirement, seems to have landed at an obscure locality between the two neighboring places named by the two Evangelists.

Vers. 11-13. THE PHARISEES DEMAND A SIGN.—Parallel passage: Matt. 16: 1-4. In consequence of the opposition of Pharisees and scribes from Jerusalem (chap. 7: 1-23), our Lord had withdrawn to heathen and unfrequented regions. On His return, He lands at a retired locality in Galilee; the Pharisees seek Him, tempting Him again. He then withdraws to the eastern side of the sea (ver. 13), not far from Bethsaida (ver. 22). The connection of events shows the reason for these repeated voyages, which seem purposeless to many readers. Galilee being almost completely closed to Him, it was time for the decided confessions and revelations (ver. 27—9: 1) which follows. In the account of this meeting with the Pharisees, Matthew is much fuller.

Ver. 11. **And the Pharisees.** Matthew adds: 'with the Sadducees'; but the former were the leaders on this occasion when, as so often, extremes of error combined from hatred of the truth.—**Came forth.** This implies spying hostility. He had landed at some retired locality (see on ver. 10), but their opposition speedily found him, since they began, at once, **to question with him.** These details are peculiar to Mark.—**A sign from heaven.** This had been done before (comp. Matt. 12: 38). It was the common belief that visible signs from heaven would attend the Advent of the Messiah. Their request implied that the many mighty works He had already wrought were not of heavenly origin. 'The Jews require a sign' (1 Cor. 1: 22); formalism and self-righteousness tend to superstition.—**Tempting** (or, 'trying') **him,** putting Him to the proof. But He never responded to doubt and disbelief; only to faith. To accede to their wish, would foster their carnal hopes.

Ver. 12. **And he sighed deeply in his spirit.** This sigh, or groan, came from His heart, showing how deeply He felt the opposition He encountered. They showed more decided enmity, but the plain prediction of His death which so soon followed (ver. 31), shows that He knew the crisis was approaching. ('The sign of the prophet Jonah,' Matt. 16: 4, points in the same way.) It may have been a sign of His entering, though with human pang, upon the appointed path of tribulation. But the sigh was mainly for these who would reject the atoning sorrows they were the instruments in producing.—**This**

13 unto this generation. And he left them, and again entering into *the boat* departed to the other side.
14 And they forgot to take bread; and they had not in
15 the boat with them more than one loaf. And he charged them, saying, Take heed, beware of the leaven
16 of the Pharisees and the leaven of Herod. And they reasoned one with another, ¹saying, ²We have no bread.

¹ Some ancient authorities read *because they had no bread.*
² Or, It is *because we have no bread.*

generation. A term of rebuke; comp. Matt. 16: 4: 'An evil and adulterous generation seeketh after a sign.'

Ver. 13. This presents more distinctly than the parallel in Matthew the immediate departure in the waiting boat.—**To the other side.** He returned to Galilee but once again, and then as quietly as possible (chap. 9: 30, etc.).

Vers. 14–21. THE DISCOURSE ABOUT LEAVEN.—Parallel passage: Matt. 16: 5–12. The unbelief and ignorance of the Twelve are frankly set forth in both accounts.

Ver. 14. **Forgot to take bread.** Both accounts suggest that the neglect occurred after they landed.—**In the boat with them more than one loaf.** The conversation, therefore, did not take place in the boat. When they landed (Matthew), they forgot to supply themselves with provisions for their land journey, although they had brought but one loaf with them in the boat. No stock of provisions was needed for the short voyage.

Ver. 15. **The leaven of the Pharisees.** 'Leaven;' figure for a permeating spiritual influence, generally an evil one (comp. however Matt. 13: 33). Their want of bread made the illustration apt. They were now withdrawing, both bodily and spiritually, from the Jews; hence there is probably a reference to Exod. 12: 15–17; comp. 1 Cor. 5: 7.—**The leaven of Herod.** Matthew: 'of the Sadducees.' Herod was not a professed Sadducee, but our Lord was warning against what all these had in common. On the alliance of the Pharisees and the Herodians, see on chap. 3: 6. The one common characteristic of the Pharisees, Sadducees, and Herodians was 'hypocrisy' (see Matt. 16: 12), the last named party coquetting with the other two as politicians do, and of course acting hypocritically.

Ver. 16. The sense of this verse is clear, but the form varies in the early authorities; see the margin of the Revised Version.—**And they reasoned with one another.** Matthew: 'among themselves.' In their own hearts and then with each other; not in dispute, but in earnest conversation.—**We have no bread.** An unspiritual but not altogether unreasonable thought. As Jews they would naturally think about not eating bread with these sects; but this would imply separation from the whole nation, and separate provision for their

17 And Jesus perceiving it saith unto them, Why reason ye, because ye have no bread? do ye not yet perceive, neither understand? have ye your heart hardened?
18 Having eyes, see ye not? and having ears, hear ye not?
19 and do ye not remember? When I brake the five loaves among the five thousand, how many ¹baskets full of broken pieces took ye up? They say unto him,
20 Twelve. And when the seven among the four thousand, how many ¹basketfuls of broken pieces took
21 ye up? And they say unto him, Seven. And he said unto them, Do ye not yet understand?
22 And they come unto Bethsaida. And they bring to him a blind man, and beseech him to touch him.

¹ *Basket* in ver. 19 and 20 represents different Greek words.

wants, which they had forgotten. General anxiety about worldly things would follow.

Ver. 17. **And Jesus perceiving it saith.** This rendering avoids the incorrect notion, that He took some time to discover it. The reproofs here given are somewhat fuller than in the parallel passage. After such miracles their cares were unbelieving. Besides want of faith, they had shown great want of perception.

Ver. 18. Many authorities join the last clause of ver. 18 with ver. 19.

Ver. 19. **When I brake**, etc. Comp. chap. 6: 30–44.—**Twelve.** Mark alone presents the answer of the disciples.

Ver. 20. **Baskets.** A different word in the original from that used in ver. 18, but the same one we find in the account of the miracle (chap. 8: 1–10). This difference incidentally confirms the truthfulness of the account.

Ver. 21. **Do ye not yet understand.** *i. e.*, after these miracles. The recent instruction (chap. 7: 15–19) that eating did not defile a man, should have prevented the surmise about not eating bread with the Pharisees and Sadducees; the miracles should have shown them that lack of earthly bread was not referred to. Mark stops with this brief question, because in writing for Gentile readers his main design was to show the condition of the Twelve. But the whole conversation warns against false ' teaching '"(Matt. 16 : 12). Principles, tendencies, ' teachings,' are most permeating, and if evil, most dangerous. To those who after all the lessons of history, and of experience, fail to see this, we may apply the words of our Lord: 'Do ye not yet understand?'

Vers. 22–26. THE HEALING OF THE BLIND MAN AT BETHSAIDA.—Peculiar to Mark. This miracle is of peculiar interest, as exhibiting a *gradual* cure. In this case, as in

23 And he took hold of the blind man by the hand, and brought him out of the village; and when he had spit on his eyes, and laid his hands upon him, he asked
24 him, Seest thou aught? And he looked up, and said, I see men; for I behold *them* as trees, walking.
25 Then again he laid his hands upon his eyes; and he looked steadfastly, and was restored, and saw all things

the last miracle (chap. 7: 32-36), there was a suggestion from the people as to the mode of healing, a separation from the crowd, a different mode from that suggested, including the application of saliva. The place was undoubtedly Bethsaida Julias on the eastern side of the lake. It is probable that there was no other Bethsaida (see on chap. 6: 47). Moreover, the next occurrence took place in the neighborhood of Cæsarea Philippi (ver. 27), in journeying toward which they would not pass near the supposed site of western Bethsaida.

Ver. 22. **And they come** (so the best authorities read) **to Bethsaida.** They had not landed there, but probably stopped there to procure provisions. Our Lord did not intend to remain there; He was seeking retirement, to prepare His disciples for the future.—**To him.** The correct order is restored in the Rev. Ver.—**A blind man.** Probably not born blind. See on ver. 24.—**To touch him**, as though the touch was necessary to heal him.

Ver. 23. **Brought him out of the village.** A more decided separation even, than in the last case (chap. 7: 33). The reason may have been the unbelief of the place, since the man was particularly commanded not to go back there (ver. 26). The application of saliva came first, then the laying on of hands (which had been requested), which was repeated (ver. 25). Three successive acts instead of the usual word or touch.—**Seest thou aught?** The correct reading gives this vivacious form.

Ver. 24. **I see men** (lit., 'the men'); **for I behold them as trees, walking.** The first exclamation is one of joyous surprise: 'I see the men,' *i. e.*, the men who were near, the disciples, and perhaps the man's friends. But the cure was not complete, and, as he had been asked to tell what and how he saw, he adds: 'because as trees,' *i. e.*, indistinctly, 'I behold them' (the men, not trees, as some infer from the A. V.) 'walking.' Perhaps his friends, or even the disciples, were restlessly moving about, awaiting the result. The mention of men and trees suggests that the man had once had his eyesight.

Ver. 25. The Greek text in this verse has been altered by transcribers. There is general agreement among modern editors as to the correct readings.—**He looked steadfastly.** A single act is here indicated; he made a special effort in consequence of the second laying of hands upon him. But the sense may be: 'he saw clearly' (as in Matt. 7: 5); the word, however, differing from that in the last

26 clearly. And he sent him away to his home, saying, Do not even enter into the village.

27 And Jesus went forth, and his disciples, into the villages of Cæsarea Philippi: and in the way he asked his disciples, saying unto them, Who do men say that

clause.—**And was restored, and saw all things clearly.** The last clause represents a continued action. If the previous clause means: 'he saw clearly,' this one must refer to the subsequent condition of the man. 'All things' is preferable to 'every man.' Of course our Lord *could* have healed the man with a word; but He was not confined to one method. The gradual cure would remove the notion of magical influence. There may have been something in the man's spiritual condition which called for this method to develop his faith. Nor was the mode without an important lesson for the disciples, at this juncture. We need not and ought not to expect Christ's work of grace to be manifested in all cases through the same experience; a mistake which has caused much distress among real Christians, and encouraged hypocrisy. The work of grace, though always wrought by Christ, is often a gradual process, in which other agencies are apparently involved; a protest against the notions, which look for magical power in sacramental forms, or insist upon sudden illumination and joy as a necessary accompaniment of conversion. Comp. the parable (chap. 4. 36–39) peculiar to this Gospel. The man is not represented as active in curing himself; yet he follows Christ, who leads him by the hand, looks up when Christ bids, and tells our Lord both of the cure and its imperfection.

Ver. 26. **To his home.** This was not in the village, but elsewhere. Our Lord forbids his return to the village. He was now seeking retirement, and avoiding publicity, and there may have been some special reason why it should not be published there.—The last clause (A. V.) is omitted, though found in many ancient authorities.

Vers. 27–9: 1. THE DISCOURSE NEAR CÆSAREA PHILIPPI.—Parallel passages: Matt. 16: 13–28; Luke 9: 18–27.—*Contents.* The confession (ver. 29), and the revelation (ver. 31), constitute an epoch in the training of the Apostles. Despite their little faith and want of understanding, they cling to Jesus as the Christ of God. He calls for a confession of this. Peter, the usual spokesman, makes it. Then He reveals His passion and the sufferings of His people with Him and for His sake. This revelation was at first rejected, never received by the disciples in its full force until it became a fact. The important statement regarding the foundation of His Church (recorded in Matt. 16: 18) is not, as many suppose, the central thought. Neither Mark nor Luke make any reference to it. The former, though probably deriving his information from Peter, omits in this account the *blessing* bestowed on Peter, and the subsequent *promise*, but inserts the *rebuke*. A significant fact, showing the humility of Peter. The reference to the institution of the Church as a separate communion, is also wanting. Hence the **Passion of Christ** is the central truth, involving the *active* and *passive* confession of His

28 I am? And they told him, saying, John the Baptist: and others, Elijah; but others, One of the prophets. 29 And he asked them, But who say ye that I am? Peter answereth and saith unto him, Thou art the Christ.

people, and not the institution of the Church, much less the primacy of Peter. It is remarkable that this fundamental confession of faith was called forth by our Lord, not in Galilee or Judea, but near Cæsarea Philippi (Danias), a Roman settlement on the extreme northern boundary of Palestine. The hostility of the Jews had banished Him thither, but its ultimate effect would be to banish them from the Land of Promise.

Ver. 27. **Into the villages of Cæsarea Philippi.** Retired localities in the neighborhood, better adapted for private intercourse. The city was situated at the foot of Mount Hermon, and formerly bore the name *Paneas*. Philip the Tetrarch beautified it, and called it Cæsarea; his name (Philippi) being commonly added to distinguish it from Cæsarea on the sea-coast (where Paul was afterwards imprisoned). The name was changed to *Neronias* by Agrippa II., but the village which now marks the site is called *Banias*.—**In the way.** Luke (9·18), without naming the locality, tells that He had been 'alone praying;' an important preparation for the important revelation which was to follow. This was not necessarily 'in the way' from Bethsaida to Cæsarea Philippi, but may have been during some journey while in those regions.—**Who do men say that I am?** The form of Matthew is fuller: 'that the Son of Man is?' thus bringing the implied thought: 'I am the Son of Man, the Messiah.'

Ver. 28. **They told him.** The people had never been fully convinced that He was the Messiah, In the presence of opposition they only held that He was a remarkable personage.—**John the Baptist.** Herod's opinion, see chap. 6: 14-16.—**Elijah.** The forerunner of the Messiah.—**One of the prophets**, comp. chap. 6: 15. Some really believed that the old prophets would reappear in another form

Ver. 29. **But who say ye**, etc. The question does not imply that they doubted His Messiahship, but is a demand for a decided expression of their belief. In the fuller account of Matthew the main point in Peter's reply is respecting what He was *as the Messiah*.—**Peter answereth**; speaking for the others as well as for himself.—**Thou art the Christ**, *i.e.*, the Messiah. Matthew adds: 'the Son of the living God;' Luke: 'the Christ of God.' The confession of Peter is the germ of the true and full statement respecting the Divine Human Person of Christ. The germ itself was a revelation (Matt. 16: 17), and its development was through subsequent revelation to the Apostles. The doctrine of Christ's Person is not the result of human speculation, but a truth revealed by the Father of our Lord respecting His only Begotten Son. As at the beginning of His ministry our Lord received an attestation from man (John the Baptist) preceding the attestation of His Sonship from heaven (chap. 1: 11), so at this turning-point a

30 And he charged them that they should tell no man of
31 him. And he began to teach them, that the Son of man must suffer many things, and be rejected by the elders, and the chief priests, and the scribes, and be killed,
32 and after three days rise again. And he spake the saying openly. And Peter took him, and began to
33 rebuke him. But he turning about, and seeing his disciples, rebuked Peter, and saith, Get thee behind me, Satan: for thou mindest not the things of God, but

confession from man precedes the renewed attestation from heaven on the mount of Transfiguration (chap. 9: 7).

Ver. 30. **That they should tell no man.** Until our Lord Himself announced His Messiahship before the Sanhedrin (chap. 14: 62), the Christian acknowledgment was to be kept separate from the carnal expectations of the Jews.

Ver. 31. **And he began.** The confession prepared them for the revelation. We may infer that He spoke often and familiarly on this topic, to prepare them for their own trials, and to impress upon them the truth they deemed so strange. (Comp. chaps. 9: 12; 10: 31, and the parallel passages in Matthew and Luke.)—**He must suffer.** The *necessity* of His sufferings was revealed: not in all its bearings, since after His resurrection He must still ask: 'Behoved it not the Christ to suffer,' etc. (Luke 24: 26).—**Many things.** His sufferings included more than the outward persecutions.—**Be rejected by the elders,** etc. These classes represented the whole Jewish nation. Christ did not reject the covenant people; they rejected him.—**And be killed.** A startling announcement to the disciples, and yet Daniel (9: 26) and Isaiah (53: 4-10) had foretold it. 'The cross' is the *necessary* climax of His sufferings.—**After three days.** Matthew and Luke: 'the third day.' The latter is the more definite expression for the same period.

Ver. 32. **And he spake the saying openly.** Not necessarily *in public*, but rather without *concealment*, explicitly, not indirectly. Peculiar to Mark.—**And Peter took him.** Probably laid hold on Him to interrupt Him. Matthew gives the language. The explanation, 'took by the hand,' for friendly entreaty, is unwarranted.—**And began to rebuke him.** He did not proceed far in this chiding.

Ver. 33. **And seeing his disciples.** This look, mentioned by Mark only, shows that Peter had not taken Him aside, but publicly interrupted Him. Luke omits altogether the rebuke of Peter.—**Get thee behind me,** 'avaunt,' 'begone.' Comp. Matt. 4: 10, where the same words are addressed to Satan himself.—**Satan.** The meaning 'adversary' is too weak. There was a Satanic influence at work in Peter, though he was not conscious of it. 'Has Satan come again?'

34 the things of men. And he called unto him the multitude with his disciples, and said unto them, If any man would come after me, let him deny himself, and 35 take up his cross, and follow me. For whosoever would save his ¹life shall lose it; and whosoever shall lose his ¹life for my sake and the gospel's shall save

¹ Or, *soul.* Am. Com. omit this margin.

The Apostle himself was no doubt startled.—**Thou mindest not the things of God**, *i. e.*, as represented by Christ, not regarding God's purpose in the foretold death.—**The things of men**, *i. e.*, he had carnal views, expected the temporal exaltation of the Messiah. Human nature is here represented as opposed to God, and under the influence of Satan.—A rebuke for all who have a sentimental admiration for Jesus of Nazareth, but stumble at the cross, which belongs to 'the things of God.'

Ver. 34. **Called unto him the multitude.** The crowd was never far off. What he would now say was of universal application. He would prepare the multitude to hear what He had just revealed to the Twelve, and test their willingness to follow Him to death. He thus showed His wisdom as a Teacher, in adapting the truth to the audience. —**If any one would come after me.** A general statement, involving on this occasion the question, will you follow me even to the death, which, I have assured you, must come. Unlike worldly leaders, Christ declares the darker side of His service; He asks for willing followers. A religion of *force* cannot be Christ's religion.—**Deny himself.** Let him renounce self as the object of supreme regard; this involves the relinquishment of all that interferes with the higher object. —**Take up his cross.** The person to be crucified bore his own cross; the death was a painful and shameful one. The reference is to readiness to *endure* for Christ, even death in its worst form. It includes of course all minor forms of endurance. Comp. Luke 9: 23, where 'daily' is added.—**Follow me.** Here in the path of suffering, but also in the path of holiness and in the path to glory, as the following verses suggest. Continuous action is indicated by this verb.

Ver. 35. **For whosoever would save his life,** etc. 'Life' is here used in two senses; otherwise the paradoxical statement would have no meaning at all. In both clauses it means, in the first instance, the outward, earthly life, with all its pleasures and comforts; and in the second ('it') the inward, spiritual life, beginning here in faith, and to be perfected in heaven. Life, worldly, selfish, fleshly, is opposed to life eternal, Christian and spiritual. 'The fear of death subjects to the bondage of death (Heb. 2: 15); while readiness to suffer a holy death for Christ's sake opens up before us true life.' It is not said, that we must lose the one life in order to gain the other; nor that each one is called to make the sacrifice literally.—**For my sake and**

36 it. For what doth it profit a man, to gain the whole
37 world, and forfeit his ¹life? For what should a man
38 give in exchange for his ¹life? For whosoever shall
be ashamed of me and of my words in this adulterous
and sinful generation, the Son of man also shall be
ashamed of him, when he cometh in the glory of his

¹ Or, *soul.* Am. Com. omit this margin.

the gospel's. The last phrase is peculiar to Mark (comp. chap. 10: 29). But 'for my sake' remains the leading thought: for the sake of the gospel, because it tells of the personal Redeemer. The meaning is: Christ must be loved more than life itself, or more fully: 'he that gains or saves his earthly life, saving it by unfaithfulness, shall lose his true life; but he that loses it by faithfulness to Christ, shall find eternal life.' The standard is not too high. Salvation must consist in an overcoming of selfishness by bringing the heart back to God. This has been done only by Christ, and by His becoming supreme in the heart. He gave His life *for us,* and therefore asks us to give our lives *for Him;* He gives His life *to us,* so that we can give our lives both *to* and *for Him.*

Ver. 36. The peculiar form of this and the next verse is restored in the Revised Version.—**For what doth it profit,** etc. In view of this saving and losing.—**Forfeit his life.** Same word as in ver. 35. The variation in the A. V. is unfortunate. The word has the double meaning 'life' and 'soul.' But here 'life' in the higher sense is meant, not 'soul' in distinction from 'body;' hence the Am. Com. object to the marginal rendering. It is plainly implied that gaining the world in a selfish manner involves the loss of true life; that such a gain is really only an apparent gain of the world, while the loss is real, irreparable, irretrievable. The usual inferences, based on the sense 'soul,' are true enough, but not suggested here.

Ver. 37. **Life,** same word as in ver. 35; comp. Matt. 16: 25, 26. —**In exchange,** lit., 'as a ransom price.' The price which the earthly-minded gives for the world is his 'life,' in the highest sense. But after having laid that down as the price, what has he as a counter price (that is the exact sense of the Greek word), to buy the life back again?

Ver. 38. **For.** The reason this transaction is so unprofitable is now given.—**Shall be ashamed of me and of my words.** Disown me and reject my words. The two terms correspond with those in ver. 35; 'for my sake and the gospel's.' There is a hint of the same thought in Matthew's account (16: 27), and something analogous is found in Matt. 10: 33.—**In this adulterous and sinful generation.** Comp. Matt. 12: 39. These words, peculiar to Mark in this connection, suggest that being ashamed of Christ is the result of paying attention to the verdict of such a generation.—**The Son of man** (now lowly, despised and

9: 1 Father with the holy angels. And he said unto them, Verily I say unto you, There be some here of them that stand *by*, which shall in no wise taste of death, till they see the kingdom of God come with power.

rejected) **also shall be ashamed** (disown and reject).—**Cometh.** At the Second Advent.—**In the glory of his Father.** See Matt. 16:27. Luke is fuller: 'In His own glory, and the Father's, and of the holy angels.' Through suffering to glory. He spoke first of His own sorrows, then of His people's; now He predicts glory and triumph; theirs also, because His. In this second coming, afterwards more fully spoken of (chap. 13), He shall appear as Judge of all, in the glory of God the Father, and the attendants shall be **holy angels.** Matthew: 'His angels.' Both a threatening and a promise, in view of the judgment which it involves.

IX: 1. **And he said unto them.** The Revised Version does away with the unfortunate effect of beginning a new chapter here.— **Verily I say unto you.** Solemn preface.—**There be some here of them that stand by.** The Twelve and the people about (chap. 8:34).—**Shall in no wise taste of death.** Death is represented under the figure of a bitter cup. Some of those present should be still alive when the event referred to in the next clause should take place, though they should afterwards die.—**The kingdom of God come with** (lit., 'in') **power.** The last clause is peculiar to Mark and characteristic, since he presents our Lord mainly in His power. This coming is probably distinct from that spoken of in the preceding verse. (1) That was 'in the glory of His Father;' this, a coming of the kingdom of God 'with power' (comp. Luke 9:27). (2) So definite a prediction of the final coming is inconsistent with chap. 13:32: 'But of that day and hour knoweth no one, ... neither the Son,' etc. Nor is it the transfiguration, which was a temporary revelation, but the establishment of the new dispensation, which was the coming of the kingdom of God with power. The more precise reference can scarcely be to the coming of our Lord after the resurrection; for all of them except Judas lived to see that, and it is implied that some would die; nor to the day of Pentecost, since this is open to the same objection. It probably refers to the *destruction of Jerusalem*, which ended the old dispensation. This was a coming 'in power,' *i. e.*, its principal manifestation was an exhibition of power. That event was, moreover, of awful significance. In view of the circumstances, the hostility of the Jews now manifest, the prediction that Jerusalem would be the place of His sufferings, the announcement of His Church as distinguished from the old economy to be abrogated fully in the ruin of that city, it seems likely that if one event be referred to, it is this, which was in so many respects 'a *type* and *earnest* of the

2 And after six days Jesus taketh with him Peter, and James, and John, and bringeth them up into a high mountain apart by themselves: and he was trans-

final coming of Christ' (Alford). Some, however, adopt a wider view, referring it 'to a gradual or progressive change, the institution of Christ's kingdom in the hearts of men and in society at large' (J. A. Alexander), extending from the day of Pentecost to the destruction of Jerusalem.

Chap. IX: 2–8. THE TRANSFIGURATION.—Parallel passages: Matt. 17: 1–8; Luke 9: 28–36. *Contents:* After our Lord's prediction of His sufferings and hint of His glory (chap. 8: 31—9: 1), three chosen disciples receive a supernatural testimony and pledge of that glory. But the primary purpose probably was to give to our Lord, at this crisis, consolation from His Father, who by an attesting voice ushered in the sufferings as He had done the successes. The scene of the Transfiguration, according to tradition, was Mount Tabor, in Galilee; but it was more probably *Hermon*, which was near Cæsarea Philippi, an uninhabited and lofty mountain, and better fitted to be the scene of a secret revelation. Mount Panium and a mountain near the lake have also been suggested, but with less reason.—The *Transfiguration*, a Sabbath revelation ('after six days'); an earnest of the resurrection, a prophecy of Sabbath rest and privilege.— Three witnesses, three accounts; the same human company in Gethsemane, but a different heavenly visitant.—Our Lord's inherent glory burst forth, an anticipation and prophecy of His future glory.—Moses and Elijah: the one had represented Christ's sufferings in type, the other in prophecy: the Old and New Testament agree, and centre in the cross; Christ is revealed as Lord of the invisible world, as well as of the future kingdom of glory.—Peter's proposal; an expression of fear and perplexity, and yet of gratitude for privilege; like privilege often produces like desires to rest before the time.—The dark cloud on Mount Sinai; the bright cloud on the Mount of Transfiguration.—The attesting voice, now a command to hear Him, as He went to death.— Jesus only; the new covenant established on its own evidence, the Master's authority proclaimed as sufficient.

Ver. 2. **Six days.** So Matthew. Luke more generally, or perhaps including the day of Peter's confession: 'about an eight days' (*i. e.*, a week).—**Peter, and James, and John.** His companions in Gethsemane (chap. 14: 37; Matt. 26: 35), Peter the leader, James the first to suffer martyrdom, and John the beloved disciple, who lingered longest on earth.—**A high mountain apart.** The Transfiguration probably took place in the *night*. 1. Jesus had gone up into the mountain to pray (Luke 9: 28), which He usually did at night (Luke 6: 12; 21: 37; 22: 39; Matt. 14: 23, 24). 2. The Apostles were heavy with sleep. 3. They did not descend till the next day (Luke 9: 37). 4. The transfiguration itself could be seen to better advantage at night than in daylight. On Mount Hermon snow would be visible, adding a natural splendor to the scene.—**By themselves.** Not simply *in private* ('apart'), but actually 'alone.' The immediate purpose was 'to pray' (Luke), the ultimate purpose this revelation.—**And he**

3 figured before them: and his garments became glistering, exceeding white; so as no fuller on earth can
4 whiten them. And there appeared unto them Elijah
5 with Moses: and they were talking with Jesus. And Peter answereth and saith to Jesus, Rabbi, it is good

was transfigured before them, as witnesses. Peter afterwards mentions the fact (1 Pet. 1: 16–18), and John alludes to it (John 1: 14). The change in His appearance took place while He was praying (Luke 9: 29).

Ver. 3. **And his garments.** All three Evangelists speak of this; but Mark gives the most vivid description of it, omitting the other details.—**Became.** This graphic touch brings out 'the glistening of each separate portion of His clothing' (Alford) — So as (or, 'such *garments* as') **no fuller on earth can whiten them.** This indicates that the splendor was preternatural. The fuller's business was to wash soiled white garments, and to make them clean and glistening. Persons of high rank were often distinguished by the brightness of their white garments. Beyond all these efforts of human splendor was the glory of our Lord's raiment, Matthew: 'and His face did shine as the sun, and His garments became white as the light.' Luke: 'The fashion of His countenance was altered, and His raiment became white and dazzling.' No explanation is possible that denies the supernatural element. Our Lord's inherent glory burst forth; added to this there was an external heavenly illumination affecting His garments and surrounding Moses and Elijah, reaching its highest manifestation in the cloud spoken of in ver. 7, which Matthew tells us was luminous. An anticipation of His future glory as the Son of man.

Ver. 4. **There appeared unto them.** These persons were really present. It was not a vision, as is plain from the account of Luke.— **Elijah with Moses.** Elijah is more prominent in this account, and probably was in the scene as witnessed by Peter. The two chief representatives of the Old Testament (the law and the prophets). Both were forerunners of the Messiah, and had also fasted forty days. They came from the invisible world, appearing 'in glory' (Luke 9: 31), in a glorified form. They were recognized by the disciples, probably by intuition.—**And they were talking with Jesus** 'Of His decease which He was about to accomplish at Jerusalem' (Luke). Even on the mount of transfiguration the cross is in the foreground, and these Old Testament saints were probably then instructed in regard to it. The appearance of these two persons has been connected by some with the manner of their departure from earth. But this point cannot be pressed.

Ver. 5. **Rabbi.** Peculiar to Mark.—**It is good for us to be here,** etc. Luke, 'not knowing what he said.' He wished to remain there,

for us to be here; and let us make three ¹tabernacles; one for thee, and one for Moses, and one for Elijah. 6 For he wist not what to answer; for they became sore 7 afraid. And there came a cloud overshadowing them; and there came a voice out of the cloud, This is my 8 beloved Son: hear ye him. And suddenly looking

¹ Or, *booths.*

and perhaps to detain Moses and Elijah, since they were about to depart (Luke 9: 33). The glory was so dazzling, the privilege seemed so great, the companionship so choice, that he would cling to the enjoyment, and let the toils and duties of the future go.—**Let us make.** Matthew (correct reading): 'I will make.'—**Three tabernacles,** or, 'booths.' Peter speaks of a tabernacle (2 Pet. 1: 13, 14) just before referring to this event.—**One for thee,** etc. Lange: 'That form of antichristian error which appeals to the authority of Peter has given rise to the erection of three tabernacles (Moses: the Greek Church; Elijah: 'the Roman Church; Christ: the Evangelical Church).' This analogy is not to be pressed. Peter, in his inconsiderateness, may have thought of inaugurating a new communion, with Christ for its centre, Moses its law-giver, and Elijah its zealot, thus amalgamating *externally* the Old and New Testaments.

Ver. 6. **For they became sore afraid.** All three Evangelists speak of this fear, or religious awe: Mark here, Luke: 'as they entered into the cloud.' Matthew: when 'they heard' the voice. This indicates a continued and growing awe. It is placed earliest by Mark, who thus accounts for Peter's words.

Ver. 7. The account of Mark is the more vivacious, according to the correct readings.—**And there came a cloud** (Matthew: 'a bright cloud'). 'A sign from heaven' granted to the Apostles, though refused to the Jewish leaders. A luminous cloud, not dark like that on Sinai. It was analogous to the pillar of cloud by day and fire by night in the wilderness and to the Shekinah of the Old Testament; a *symbol* of the glory resting on the New Testament Church, separating between the holy and the unholy, and a *type* of the splendor of the New Jerusalem. —**Overshadowing them,** *i. e.,* our Lord, Moses, and Elijah, since the voice came from 'out of the cloud.' (But see Luke 9: 34.) A bright cloud could render them invisible as readily as a dark one.—**And there came a voice,** etc. The culmination. The 'visible presence' of God was followed by an 'audible presence,' giving a solemn attestation to the Messiah and Son of God, at a time when His rejection by the chosen people had begun and His death been foretold to His disciples.—**Hear ye him.** Obey Him, as well as listen to Him. Hear *Him,* more than law or prophecy (Moses and Elijah). Their remaining carnal Messianic hopes were thus opposed.

Ver. 8. **And suddenly,** etc. Mark omits some details here. The

round about, they saw no one any more, save Jesus only with themselves.

9 And as they were coming down from the mountain, he charged them that they should tell no man what things they had seen, save when the Son of man should 10 have risen again from the dead. And they kept the saying, questioning among themselves what the rising

withdrawal itself was not necessarily sudden, but their perception of it was.—**Save Jesus only.** Without Moses and Elijah. The hour of glory was over, and the Lord now in His usual lowliness, resumed His intercourse with them, and returned to the labors of His ministry, which were awaiting Him at the foot of the mount. The sufficiency of His authority is implied, in view of the command of ver. 7.—**With themselves.** Peculiar to Mark; it hints at the self-consciousness of an eye-witness, and suggests that our Lord was near them as they looked. Matthew tells that they looked up after He touched them.

Vers. 9-13. The Questioning of the Three Disciples.—Parallel passage: Matt. 17: 9-13. When Christ should come forth from the grave, the truth about Him could come out from secresy (ver. 9). Elijah had appeared; the true fulfilment of prophecy was in the coming of John the Baptist; what was done to him, a prelude of what the rulers of the Jews would do to Christ. Those who reject the preacher of repentance will soon crucify the preacher of salvation.

Ver. 9. **As they were coming down.** This would require some time.—**Charged them.** A special prohibition.—**Save when the Son of man should have risen again from the dead.** It was too soon to tell of it; even the three understood very little (ver. 10). This injunction would also serve to impress the occurrence on their minds; discussion of it during the intervening period of persecution would occasion doubts or carnal expectations. Besides, it involved new light concerning the state of the dead, which could not be received until the Resurrection of Christ. The necessity for concealment then ceased.

Ver. 10. **And they kept the saying.** Probably this particular saying about the Resurrection, as the limit of their silence about what they had seen on the mount. Obedience to the command of ver. 9, is assumed in the account of Matthew, and asserted in that of Luke, and is of course implied here.—**Questioning among themselves,** etc. The perplexity was about this Resurrection. 'What is the shall have risen again from the dead,' would be a literal rendering. However much they believed in a general resurrection, it was difficult for them to conceive of a resurrection *after which* they could tell of these things. The unexampled fact, now the basis of our faith in a Living Saviour, could not be understood in advance. They doubtless continued wondering when and how the time would come when they could speak.

11 again from the dead should mean. And they asked him, saying, ¹The scribes say that Elijah must first
12 come. And he said unto them, Elijah indeed cometh first, and restoreth all things: and how is it written of the Son of man, that he should suffer many things and
13 be set at nought? But I say unto you, that Elijah is come, and they have also done unto him whatsoever they listed, even as it is written of him.
14 And when they came to the disciples, they saw a

¹ Or, How is it *that the scribes say ... come?*

Mark derived his exact information from Peter, who also alludes to this event in his second Epistle.

Ver. 11. **Elijah indeed cometh.** Our Lord confirms the view that Elijah should come (Mal. 4: 5).—**And restoreth** (or, 'establisheth anew') **all things.** Comp. Mal. 4: 6. The actual work of restoration was, however, the work of the Messiah, for which Elijah should prepare the way (comp. Luke 3: 4; Acts 3: 21). Three renderings are possible: 'saying, The scribes say,' etc., 'How is it that the scribes,' etc., 'Why,' etc. The last, which is not indicated in the Rev. Ver., is probably the sense here. See on ver. 28.

Ver. 12. The connection with what precedes is, according to Alford: 'If this was not the coming of Elijah, *was he yet to come?* If it was, how was it so *secret* and so *short?*' The punctuation is in dispute. The A. V. does not give 'how' its proper meaning. Most later scholars take the first half only as a question: **And how is it written of the Son of man?** then the answer: **That he should suffer,** etc. Others take the whole as one question (so the Rev. Ver.). The next verse shows that the main point is not so much to prove that the Son of man must soon suffer, as that the predicted Elijah had come, and, like the Old Testament Elijah, had suffered as the Messiah also would, hence that this Elijah was *John the Baptist* (Matt. 17: 13).

Ver. 13. **Even as it is written of him.** There is no direct prophecy of the sufferings of the predicted Elijah. But as the prophet Elijah suffered, it might be inferred from the Old Testament that the forerunner of the Messiah (called Elijah) would suffer, especially in view of the predicted sorrows of the Messiah Himself. So the disciples understood it; see Matt. 17: 13. The passages bearing on the subject indicate strongly another appearance of Elijah (whether the same person or not is of course unknown to us) before the second coming of Christ, to do a similar preparatory work. In every great spiritual movement there must be one who precedes 'in the spirit and power of Elijah.'

Vers. 14–29. THE HEALING OF THE DEMONIAC BOY.—Parallel passages: Matt. 17: 14–18; Luke 9: 37–42.—*Contents.* All three Evangelists place this miracle immediately

great multitude about them, and scribes questioning
15 with them. And straightway all the multitude, when
they saw him, were greatly amazed, and running to
16 him saluted him. And he asked them, What question
17 ye with them? And one of the multitude answered
him, ¹Master, I brought unto thee my son, which hath

¹ Or, *Teacher.*

after the Transfiguration (Luke: 'the next day'). This 'may be regarded as one of the evidences of the genuineness and authenticity of the narrative, and against the mythical hypothesis.' Meyer. Lesson: On earth we may not rest on the mount of spiritual delight, but must go down into the valley of duty (Raphael has grouped the two events in his masterpiece). The subject of this miracle had all the symptoms of epilepsy and was also possessed. The inability of the disciples to cure him, the questionings of the scribes (mentioned by Mark), and the faith of the father, all give additional interest to the occurrence. Thus the training of the Twelve, now the all-important matter, was carried on. The nine disciples in the valley had ventured without sufficient faith into a conflict with Satan and the scribes. The Master came to their aid, to enforce the needed lesson. The people, on whom the failure of the disciples had produced an effect, now wondered again (Luke 9: 43); but the current of hostility was not checked. Mark's account is most detailed and vivid. He alone mentions the contention with the scribes, the amazement of the people, their running to Jesus. The wretched state of the possessed youth is most vividly represented, and the effect of the presence of Jesus upon him. The description of the interview with the father (vers. 21-25) is as valuable as it is touching. The report of the subsequent conversation with the disciples is brief, and no mention is made of the effect upon the people.

Ver. 14. **And when they came.** 'The next day' (Luke).—**The scribes questioning with them.** The disciples were not yet prepared to defend themselves, and their failure to cure the lunatic boy was probably used, not only against them, but against their master.

Ver. 15. **Were greatly amazed.** Our Lord's countenance may have retained some traces of the glory on the mount, as in the case of Moses. The word here used (struck with awe) indicates more than surprise at His sudden coming.—**Running to him.** Luke: 'Much people met Him.'—**Saluted him.** Welcomed Him, whatever had been the influence of the debate with the scribes. Christ's presence put an end to this debate. The evidence of Christ's presence and the exhibition of His power always produce a similar effect.

Ver. 16. **Asked them.** Probably the scribes. The opposition was thus transferred from the disciples to our Lord.—**What question ye with them?** About what, what is the subject of discussion?

Ver. 17. **One of the multitude.** The scribes were silent, but the person most deeply interested answers. The subject of dispute was connected with the cure of the lunatic boy. The scribes feared to

18 a dumb spirit; and wheresoever it taketh him, it ¹ dasheth him down: and he foameth, and grindeth his teeth, and pineth away: and I spake to thy disciples that
19 they should cast it out; and they were not able. And he answereth them and saith, O faithless generation, how long shall I be with you? how long shall I bear
20 with you? bring him unto me. And they brought him unto him: and when he saw him, straightway the spirit ² tare him grievously; and he fell on the ground,
21 and wallowed foaming. And he asked his father, How

¹ Or, *rendeth him*.   ² Or, *convulsed*.

repeat their objections, lest our Lord should convict them in the presence of the multitude by working a miraculous cure. The hostility to our Lord was always cowardly!—**I brought.** He actually brought his son, expecting to find Christ, **unto thee**, not knowing of His absence. It was his only son (Luke 9: 38) —**A dumb spirit.** A spirit causing the boy to be speechless; not that the demon was a silent one.

Ver. 18. **Wheresoever it taketh him.** The symptoms, as described here and by the other Evangelists, are those of *epilepsy*. The fits were sudden, but the dumbness seems to have been continuous. Many of those possessed had symptoms altogether different. The peculiar difficulty in this case was the combination of this possession and epilepsy.

Ver. 19. **Answereth them.** Not to the man alone (as the incorrect reading implies), though he was included, but to the multitude, whom our Lord addresses as representing that **faithless,** or, 'unbelieving,' **generation.** The failure to cure, the catechizing of the scribes, and the effect produced on the people, proved that all present were unbelieving and liable to be led astray. But the term 'generation' requires a still wider reference to the race and generation, whom this company represented.—**How long,** etc.? This indicates 'holy impatience of their hardness of heart and unbelief. In this the father, disciples, scribes, and multitude are equally interested' (Alford). Less probably, it means that the disciples soon could not have Him to come thus personally to supply their lack of faith and power.—**Unto me,** emphasizing His power, despite the failure of the disciples.

Ver. 20. **And when he saw him.** When the lad saw Jesus, the spirit convulsed him. But the original gives a stronger hint of the intimate connection between the demon and the possessed person. 'The kingdom of Satan, in small and great, is ever stirred into a fiercer activity by the coming near of the kingdom of Christ. Satan has great wrath, when his time is short' (Trench).

Ver. 21. **And he asked his father.** To bring out his faith.

long time is it since this hath come unto him? And
22 he said, From a child. And oft-times it hath cast him both into the fire and into the waters, to destroy him: but if thou canst do anything, have compassion
23 on us, and help us. And Jesus said unto him, If thou canst! All things are possible to him that be-
24 lieveth. Straightway the father of the child cried out,

Ver. 22. **To destroy him.** The father describes the case still further, representing the demon as a malignant enemy seeking to kill his only son.—**If thou canst do anything.** The father's sense of need is stirred by the recital; but his faith is very weak. Not strong at first, it had probably been weakened by the failure of the disciples.—**Have compassion on us, and help us.** The father's feelings are intense, as he naturally and properly identifies himself with the misery of his son (comp. Matt. 15: 25). But intense feeling is not *faith!*

Ver. 23. **If thou canst!** The sense of the passage is: 'The question is, not what is possible on my part, but on yours.' The best authorities omit the word 'believe.' The man's words were repeated by our Lord, either as a *question:* 'Did you say, If thou canst?' or as an *exclamation:* 'As to thy words, *If thou canst,* all depends upon faith,' etc.—**All things are possible,** etc. The fundamental law of the kingdom of God. The measure of faith is the measure of our ability, because according to our faith Christ's power is ours. Christ is the object of faith; faith can only be omnipotent as Christ is omnipotent.

Ver. 24. **And straightway the father of the child cried out.** A touching description, true to nature and drawn from life. The full form: 'the father of the child,' not only implies that the son was a child in years, but suggests the spiritual connection between 'father' and 'child' in this matter, and the effect of the faith of the former upon the cure of the latter. When the father's faith had been sufficiently tested, the helpless child was healed.—**I believe, help thou mine unbelief,** *i. e.,* want of faith. The man's faith is further awakened by the challenge of our Lord; but this increase of faith only shows him how great his doubt is; and he at once adds to his confession of belief a new prayer for help—help for himself, that thus help might come to his only son. This will seem natural to all who have any faith, and paradoxical only to outright unbelievers. Weak faith is yet faith, and when it leads to prayer, it becomes stronger. Alford: 'Nothing can be more touching and *living* than this whole most masterly and wonderful narrative. The poor father is drawn out into a sense of the unworthiness of his distrust, and "the little spark of faith which is kindled in his soul reveals to him the abysmal deeps of unbelief which are there" (Trench).'

25 and said,¹ I believe; help thou mine unbelief. And when Jesus saw that a multitude came running together, he rebuked the unclean spirit, saying unto him, Thou dumb and deaf spirit, I command thee, come 26 out of him, and enter no more into him. And having cried out, and ²torn him much, he came out: and *the child* became as one dead; insomuch that 27 the more part said, He is dead. But Jesus took him 28 by the hand, and raised him up; and he arose. And when he was come into the house, his disciples asked 29 him privately, ³*saying,* We could not cast it out. And

¹ Many ancient authorities add *with tears*. ² Or, *convulsed*.
³ Or, How is it *that we could not cast it out?*

Ver. 25. **A multitude came running together.** Our Lord would avoid too great publicity (comp. ver. 30); the father's faith had been sufficiently tested, hence the command to the evil spirit was now uttered. The words are preserved by Mark only: **I** (emphatic, *I*, although my disciples could not cast thee out) **command** (authoritatively) **thee.—Enter no more into him.** These unusual words show the unusual malignity of this kind of a spirit (ver. 29).

Ver. 26. **Crying out,** uttering an inarticulate cry. Spoken of the demon, but with the same hint of intimate connection alluded to in ver. 20.—**And the child became as one dead.** The Rev. Ver. properly supplies 'the child' in italics. Exhaustion followed the excitement; but this very quietude was a token that the demon was gone.—**The more part,** lit., 'the many,' according to the correct reading. This was the general verdict.

Ver. 27. **Took him by the hand.** The usual external act which connected His person with the subject of a miracle.—**And he arose,** or, 'stood up.' The cure was now complete, the child's own activity appearing. Mark alone tells of the successive steps. This mode of healing would serve to strengthen the father's faith, and, by showing the difficulty of the case, make the more powerful impression on the multitude, before whom the failure of the disciples and the debate with the scribes had occurred. The effect of the miracle is described by Luke (9 : 43). The vivid and detailed narrative must have been obtained from the recollections of an eye-witness.

Ver. 28. **Into the house.** Peculiar to Mark. The question may mean: 'We could not,' etc., since the word with which it begins is often a mere mark of quotation. But it sometimes means 'why.' In that case the A. V. is correct. Others paraphrase: 'How is it that we,' etc. The same difficulty occurs in ver. 11, but the word 'saying' there, renders the first view less abrupt than here.

Ver. 29. Matthew's account is fuller, but the answer here given is

he said unto them, This kind can come out by nothing, save by prayer.¹
30 And they went forth from thence, and passed through Galilee; and he would not that any man
31 should know it. For he taught his disciples, and said unto them, The Son of man is delivered up into the hands of men, and they shall kill him; and when he
32 is killed, after three days he shall rise again. But

¹ Many ancient authorities add *and fasting*.

to be omitted there.—**This kind.** Probably evil spirits in general. The disciples had cast out evil spirits before; their failure in this case of remarkable malignity was for their admonition.—**By prayer.** On the part of those who would exorcise the demon. The words 'and fasting' are to be omitted. Even if retained, they cannot refer, as the Sermon on the Mount shows, to stated or ceremonial observances, but to proper spiritual discipline, in which fasting (private and personal) holds an important place. Nothing is implied about the power to cast out evil spirits in later times. The 'prayer and fasting' would not work the miracle, but were necessary to sustain the faith which would successfully call upon Christ's power in such a case.

Vers. 30-32. THE SECOND PREDICTION OF THE PASSION.—Parallel passages: Matt. 17: 22-23; Luke 9: 43-45. *Contents:* The definite details as to time and place show that our Lord repeated His prediction of His sufferings (chap. 8: 31). Our Lord now left the foot of the mount and passed through Galilee; the prediction was made while the people were still wondering (Luke 9: 43). We infer that they passed directly from Mount Hermon into Galilee. Mark alone tells us that the journey from the mount of Transfiguration to Capernaum was private (ver. 30). The education of the disciples called for this, and the hostility of the Pharisees had in fact closed Galilee against His labors. The incident about the temple-tribute (Matt. 17: 24-27) is omitted, probably on account of Peter's desire not to make himself too prominent in the narrative. This was the last visit to Galilee; that, the last miracle there. It is unlikely that a visit to Jerusalem (at the Feast of Tabernacles, John 7: 2-14) intervened.

Ver. 30. **Passed through Galilee**; probably over by-ways, since **he would not that any man should know it.** The purpose was that opportunity might be given for instructing the disciples about His approaching sufferings.

Ver. 31. **For he taught,** or, 'was teaching,' habitually, during this private journey.—**His disciples.** The Twelve, as is indicated by the parallel passages. Others may, however, have been included.—**Is delivered up.** Matthew: 'shall be delivered up;' hence the present tense here is prophetic. The delivery was **into the hands of men,** *i. e.,* by God. This was a new point in the prediction.

Ver. 32. **But they understood not the saying.** Matthew:

they understood not the saying, and were afraid to ask him.

33 And they came to Capernaum: and when he was in the house he asked them, What were ye reasoning in
34 the way? But they held their peace: for they had disputed one with another in the way, who *was* the
35 ¹greatest. And he sat down, and called the twelve;

¹ Gr. *greater*.

'they were exceeding sorry.' They understood enough to disturb their false hopes, and to awaken proper regret at the prospect of His death.—**And** (yet) **were afraid to ask him.** We may infer from the strife which followed, that this fear did not spring from proper motives. Men are still slow to learn the meaning of the death and resurrection of our Lord.

Vers. 33–37. Discourse about who should be Greatest.—Parallel passages: Matt. 18: 1-5; Luke 9: 46–48. This is a brief report of a discourse, which occupies an entire chapter in Matthew's narrative. Evidently the disciples felt that the kingdom of heaven was approaching, since this dispute had reference to position in that kingdom (Matt. 18: 1). But they needed to learn what was necessary to enter that kingdom, before they could understand who would be the greatest in it. The disciples, therefore, had not understood our Lord's previous saying (Matt. 16: 18) as conferring any primacy upon Peter.

Ver. 33. **To Capernaum.** Our Lord's usual residence; hence the question about the temple-tax was asked Him here (Matt. 17: 24-27).—**When he was.** Literally, 'being;' but in the singular number. It was immediately after their entrance.—**In the house.** Probably a particular house, where He usually resided.—**In the way.** Probably during the journey to Capernaum.

Ver. 34. **But they held their peace.** In shame and confusion. The thought of their heart had been perceived (Luke 9: 47).—**Disputed.** The discussion had been animated, probably heated.—**Who was the greatest**; lit., greater. The question was not one of primacy, but of priority. The dispute was occasioned by the preference given to Peter, James, and John, rather than by the promise to Peter (Matt. 16: 18, 19). They probably thought that their rank *now* would determine their rank in the future kingdom. The question of Matt. 18: 1, may have been put after the saying of the next verse and before the child was brought (ver. 36). In any case it was more humble than the dispute had been.

Ver. 35. **If any man would.** Comp. chap. 10: 43; Matt. 20: 26; 18: 4; 23: 12, etc. The form is that of an Oriental paradox. If the desire is selfish, the plan will fail, **he shall be last of all**; if he would be truly first then he will take this lower position voluntarily, **and be minister of all.** The word 'minister' is used in all the similar passages. It has reference, not to servitude, but to help-

and he saith unto them, If any man would be first,
36 he shall be last of all, and minister of all. And he
took a little child, and set him in the midst of them:
37 and taking him in his arms, he said unto them, Whosoever shall receive one of such little children in my name, receiveth me: and whosoever receiveth me, receiveth not me, but him that sent me.
38 John said unto him, [1]Master, we saw one casting out [2]devils in thy name: and we forbade him, because

[1] Or, *Teacher.* [2] Gr. *demons.*

ful service. The functions of officers in Christ's Church are ministerial, not magisterial.

Ver. 36. **And taking him in his arms.** Peculiar to Mark. The child seems not to have been brought in, but to have been a member of the household. Tradition says it was the martyr Ignatius, of Antioch, who therefore was called *Christophores* (borne by Christ). The little one may have been the child of one of the Apostles, perhaps of Peter, at whose house this may have occurred.—**Set him in the midst of them.** The whole transaction would of itself show the child's 'submission and trustfulness.'

Ver. 37. **And whosoever shall receive,** etc. The primary reference is to children in years, but the context (in Matthew) extends it to children in spirit. The general application is to those apparently small, those needing and receiving instruction, forbidding pride and a hierarchical spirit on the part of Christ's disciples. 'Shall receive,' *i. e.,* into spiritual fellowship. This implies that little children can be Christians and members of Christ's Church.—**In my name,** *i. e.,* on the ground of my name; referring either to those who receive, or to those who were received, probably to both.—**Receiveth me,** since the 'little one' represents Christ.—**Him that sent me.** Also said to them, when they were first sent out (Matt. 10: 40).

Vers. 38-50. DISCOURSE ABOUT CAUSING TO OFFEND.—Parallel passages: Luke 9: 49-50 (to vers. 38-40); Matt. 18: 4-9. Strictly speaking the account as a whole has no exact parallel. The paragraph is one of the most difficult as well as one of the most peculiar in this Gospel.

Ver. 38. **John said unto him.** Luke: 'answered,' so the A. V. here also. It was an answer in the wide sense; for the command to receive a child in His name would suggest the question of John.—**We saw.** Probably on their missionary tour.—**One casting out devils (demons) in thy name.** This unknown man wrought such miracles as the Apostles did and by the same power, though it had not been directly committed to him as to them. He was not a follower of Jesus, yet he believed in the power of our Lord sufficiently to attempt

39 he followed not us. But Jesus said, Forbid him not:
for there is no man which shall do a ¹mighty work in
40 my name, and be able quickly to speak evil of me. For
41 he that is not against us is for us. For whosoever
shall give you a cup of water to drink, ²because ye are
Christ's, verily I say unto you, he shall in no wise lose

¹ Gr. *power.*   ² Gr. *in name that ye are.*

this exorcism. The needed power was given him; undoubtedly to teach the lesson here recorded.—**We forbade him.** This forbidding may have so disturbed his faith, that he could no longer exorcise.—**Because he followed not us.** They probably demanded that the man should either stop his activity or join them. How natural, especially in their circumstances!

Ver. 39. **Forbid him not,** *i. e.*, such a man.—**For there is no man,** etc. The success of the miracle would strengthen the faith, the germs of which were manifested in the attempt to work it in the name of Christ.—**Be able quickly to speak evil of me** (the word is usually rendered 'revile'). The use of so strong a word points to a sharp distinction between the two classes: 'for' and 'against us.' This is a warning against limiting 'the work of the Spirit of God to any sect, or succession, or outward form of church' (Alford). The Apostles lost no authority from this exceptional case. The two mistakes have been: either denying that such exceptions exist; or, regarding these cases as the rule not the exceptions, for while the Apostles were taught the lessons in toleration, the man receives only negative praise. There are always earnest Christian laborers who decline to be orderly in their methods. Their irregularity calls for toleration, not approval.

Ver. 40. **Against us is for us.** Matt. 12: 30; 'He that is not with me, is against me.' As regards Christ and His people, there is no neutrality. In certain cases, the absence of hostility is a proof of friendship; in others, the failure to co-operate is the proof of enmity; and both might occur in the experience of the same person. But in all cases there is *either friendship or enmity.* The apparently contradictory proverbs suggest the need of discrimination in applying them. The saying in Matthew refers more to *inward unity* with Christ; this one to *outward conformity* with His people. The former may exist independently of the latter, and its existence unites real Christians, whatever their name and outward differences.

Ver. 41. **For whosoever shall give you,** etc. Comp. Matt. 10: 42. Here the lesson is intended directly for the Apostles.—**A cup of water to drink.** A figure for the smallest act of kindness. —**Because ye are Christ's,** *i. e.*, because ye belong to Christ (see the margin). It may include a reference to the recognition of Christ's name on the part of the giver.—**Verily I say unto you.** A solemn de-

42 his reward.   And whosoever shall cause one of these little ones that believe ¹on me to stumble, it were better for him if ²a great millstone were hanged about
43 his neck, and he were cast into the sea. And if thy hand cause thee to stumble, cut it off: it is good for

¹ Many ancient authorities omit *on me*.   ² Gr. *a millstone turned by an ass*.

claration that for such an act, **he shall in no wise lose his reward.** Not as before, the reward a disciple receives, but a reward due to himself, measured, not by our estimate of the act, but by God's. In His sight it may be more worthy than the great benefactions which the world applauds. He always recognizes what is done to His people, but His people are so slow to recognize what is done for Him, if not done by them and in their way!

Ver. 42. The connection is probably with ver. 37, as represented in Matt. 18: 6; but the question of John and the answer to it prepared for this advance of thought. The Apostles, by their conduct in that case, had been in danger of causing a little one to stumble.—**Cause . . . to stumble.** The Greek word from which 'scandalize' is derived, is properly rendered 'cause to stumble' in the Rev. Vers. 'Offend' is misleading, since that is referred to effect upon the feelings, rather than upon the conduct or religious conviction. Here the reference is to causing others, by our pride, to fall into unbelief (the opposite of 'receiving'); not a mere wounding of over-sensitive feelings, or offending a morbid and incorrect sense of right. Such an application would destroy all right as well as all hope. A warning in regard to our treatment of humble Christians, especially of Christian children. —**One of these little ones that believe on me.** The child (ver. 36) was probably still in His arms. The weak, unpretending, outwardly insignificant, the children, the poor, the ignorant, and the weak-minded, are all included. Only he who feeds the lambs can feed the sheep (John 21: 15).—**It were better for him if a great millstone.** The large stone used in a mill driven by asses.—**He were cast into the sea.** Capital punishment by drowning was common among the Greeks and Romans, probably not among the Jews. —The profit of dominating over the conscience is a burden about the neck of the offender, which involves his destruction. A warning both to individual and ecclesiastical bodies. The principle proved true in the case of the Jewish hierarchy.

Ver. 43. **And if thy hand**, etc. Comp. Matt. 5: 29, 30 (where the order is different) and 19: 8, 9. Here the reference is more general than in the Sermon on the Mount, namely, to whatever in us, however dear or necessary, which would lead us astray, sever our fellowship with Christ.—**Cut it off.** We should resist 'the first springs and occasions of evil desire, even by the sacrifice of what is most useful to us.'—**It is good**, etc. The surgeon does not hesitate to ampu-

thee to enter into life maimed, rather than having thy two hands to go into ¹hell, into the unquenchable fire.²
45 And if thy foot cause thee to stumble, cut it off: it is good for thee to enter into life halt, rather than having
47 thy two feet, to be cast into ¹hell. And if thine eye cause thee to stumble, cast it out: it is good for thee to enter into the kingdom of God with one eye, rather
48 than having two eyes to be cast into ¹hell; where their worm dieth not, and the fire is not quenched.
49, 50 For every one shall be salted with fire.³ Salt is

¹ Gr. *Gehenna*.
² Vers. 44 and 46 (which are identical with ver. 48) are omitted by the best ancient authorities.
³ Many ancient authorities add *and every sacrifice shall be salted with salt*. See Lev. 2: 13.

tate a limb, if he hopes thereby to save a life; no earthly sacrifice is too great where eternal life is concerned.—**Hell**, Gehenna, not Hades; the place of punishment, not the place of the dead; hence spiritual, not physical, death is referred to.—**Unquenchable fire**. Certain and awful future punishment is threatened in cases where some darling sin (or, cause of sin) is preferred to Christ. The omission of vers. 44, 46, and other variations indicated in the Rev. Vers., alter the form, but not the sense of the passage. In reading it we must avoid a slavish literalism, and remember the main thought, which is to spare nothing which hinders our salvation. A literal execution would turn the Church into a house of invalids, since every Christian is more or less tempted to sin by his eye or hand; nor would the cutting off of all the members, of itself, destroy lust in the heart. Here, too, the rule applies: 'The letter killeth, the spirit maketh alive.'

Vers. 45, 47. As regards the repetition of the thought, we may suggest this special application (not to be pressed): the hand denotes aptitude for *government*, the foot for *exertion*, the eye for *knowledge*, all in *ecclesiastical* matters. The context suggests that all these members (representing talents, etc.) should be used, not for purposes of pride, but to the edification of the little ones.

Ver. 48. **Where their worm dieth not, and the fire is not quenched.** There is a reference to Isa. 66: 24. These awful words, though figurative (worm and fire), plainly point to a future state of never-ending punishment.

Vers. 49, 50. These verses, which have no parallel, form the most difficult passage in this Gospel. The difficulty is perhaps lessened by following the most ancient authorities and omitting the second clause. It is agreed that the interpolated clause, 'every sacrifice,' etc., refers to Lev. 2: 13. As the salt is there expressly called 'the salt of the covenant of thy God,' a good sense was designed to be given by the

good: but if the salt have lost its saltness, wherewith will ye season it? Have salt in yourselves, and be at peace one with another.

interpolation, and ver. 50 equally requires such a good sense. As to the 'fire,' the immediate connection would point to eternal fire; but as there is a refiner's fire also, this sense is not absolutely necessary; nor, on the other hand, must the 'fire' and 'salt' be regarded as two different figures for exactly the same thing. Nor will any interpretation be satisfactory which does not fully bring out the meaning of the word 'for.' Explanations: (1) **For** (giving a reason why *it is better to cut off*, etc.) **every one** (all, without exception, those who thus deny themselves and those cast into hell) **shall be salted with fire** (as the symbol of Divine purity, which either *purifies* or *consumes*, so that *both* refining fire and eternal fire are included under the same figure). The interpolated clause will then be explained: 'And every sacrifice' (those accepted of God are here referred to, not those rejected) 'shall be salted with salt' (with 'the salt of the covenant of thy God'). All must enter the fire of God's purity in some way; those who offer themselves 'a living sacrifice' are seasoned with salt, are preserved in the fire; while others are salted only with fire, the same fire of Divine purity becoming eternal fire of judgment to them. This is a strong reason why the self-denials just enjoined should be made, while the connection with the next verse becomes plain.—**Salt is good** (see Matt. 5: 13, and in this case it is the preservative salt, whether the doubtful clause be omitted or not, the salt of the covenant, so that the 'fire' only purifies): **but if the salt have lost its saltness** (if you profess to be in the covenant, and are not; if the failure to cut off the offending member shows this to be the case), **wherewith will ye season it? Have salt in yourselves** ('this grace of God, this spirit of adoption, this pledge of the covenant'), **and** (as a fruit, with a reference now to the strife with which the conversation began, ver. 34) **be at peace one with another**. This view is unaffected by the omission of the doubtful clause. (2) Another interpretation agrees with this, except in making the salt and fire identical: this difference appears only in the clause, 'and every sacrifice shall be salted with salt,' which is thus interpreted: this very fire with which every one shall be salted, becomes preserving salt. The objection to this is that it takes 'and' as $=$ *just as*, and makes two figurative expressions identical. (3) Another view takes the two clauses of ver. 49 as opposed: 'Every one' (*i. e.*, of those condemned) 'shall be salted with fire, and' (on the contrary) 'every sacrifice' (God's people) 'shall be salted with salt.' This unnecessarily limits the words 'every one,' and does not account for the use of the word 'salted' in the same clause. Such a direct opposition would be expressed by 'burned with fire' and 'salted with salt.' Further, the idea of purification is obscured, and the reason presented for the preceding exhortations is less forcible. (4) The

10:1 And he arose from thence, and cometh into the borders of Judæa and beyond Jordan: and multitudes come together unto him again; and, as he was wont,

most objectionable view is that which applies the whole of ver. 49 to the lost. 'For,' in that case, introduces merely a reason for the eternal punishment. This view, too, takes 'and' as = just as: 'Every one' (condemned) 'is salted with fire' (preserved from annihilation, so that the punishment can be eternal), 'just as every sacrifice,' etc. The connection with ver. 50 is very forced on this view: 'Salt is good' (*i. e.*, although thus used as a figure for preservation to punishment, it is also a figure for what is good), etc. Besides, 'the salt of the covenant,' which is the most obvious reference, is thrown out of view, and meanings given to the figures which are contrary to the analogy of Scripture. The first view is to be preferred as most grammatica , most true to the correct reading, and most in keeping with the context.

Chap. X: 1-12. DISCOURSE ABOUT DIVORCE.—Parallel passage: Matt. 9: 1-9. *Chronology.* Shortly after the discourse recorded in chap. 9 our Lord finally left Galilee, passing toward Jerusalem. This chapter takes up the history after an interval of some length, omitting a number of events which are recorded by Luke and John. Intervening occurrences (Robinson): the sending out of the Seventy (Luke 10: 1-16); the final departure from Galilee, passing through Samaria Luke 9: 51-56; John 7: 2-10); the healing of the ten lepers (Luke 17: 11-19); the public teaching of Jesus at the feast of Tabernacles John 7: 11-53); the account of the woman taken in adultery (John 8: 1,; the reproof of the unbelieving Jews, and the escape from their hands (John 8: 12-59); the instruction of the lawyer, and the parable of the good Samaritan (Luke 10: 23-37); the incidents in the house of Martha and Mary (Luke 10: 38-42); the return of the Seventy (Luke 10: 17-24), which should probably be placed earlier; then in regular order the events narrated in John, chaps. 9-11; 'Ephraim' (John 11: 54) being in Perea, and this chapter taking up the history at that point. The early part of this chapter gives us lessons concerning the marriage relation in the Church (vers. 2-12), children in the Church (vers. 13-16), and property in the Church (vers. 17-31.)

Ver. 1. **From thence.** From Capernaum, this being the final departure from Galilee.—**The borders of Judæa.** John's narrative shows that he visited Jerusalem at least twice in the interval, and hence this account is literally correct.—**And beyond Jordan** (Perea). The common reading is 'through the farther side of (beyond) the Jordan.' He had already been in Perea, or at least on the borders (John 10: 40). after the feast of dedication and before the raising of Lazarus. Perea proper is probably meant. This was part of the territory of Herod Antipas, and extended from the Arnon on the south to Pella on the north; or, from the head of the Dead Sea to a point nearly opposite the boundary between Samaria and Galilee. The name was also given to the territory between the Arnon and the sources of Jordan, and sometimes included the whole eastern part of the Jordan valley down to the Elamitic Gulf. The breadth of the district in all

2 he taught them again. And there came unto him Pharisees, and asked him, Is it lawful for a man to
3 put away *his* wife? tempting him. And he answered and said unto them, What did Moses command you?
4 And they said, Moses suffered to write a bill of di-
5 vorcement, and to put her away. But Jesus said unto

three senses was not very great. The Christians of Jerusalem sought refuge in Perea (in Pella) just before the destruction of that city.—**And multitudes.** Matthew: 'great multitudes.'—**Come together unto him again.** As they had done on the previous visit (John 10: 41, 42), or, more probably, as occurred in Galilee.—**He taught them again.** Matthew: 'and He healed them there.' The harmonists insert here the record of Luke, chaps. 13: 22—18; 14; consisting mainly of parables appropriate to the advanced stage of our Lord's ministry. This assumes that He was already on the way toward Jerusalem, when the Pharisees came. The accounts of Mark and Matthew agree closely, but the former puts the law of Moses first, and then that of Paradise.

Ver. 2. **Came unto him Pharisees.** Even in remote Perea, almost the only remaining field of labor, Christ's opposers sought Him.—**Is it lawful**, etc. A matter of dispute between the schools of Hillel and Shammai. Herod Antipas, in whose dominions Christ now was, had imprisoned John the Baptist for too free an utterance on this point. Mark omits 'for every cause' (Matthew), but the whole subject is brought into discussion.—**Tempting him**, or, 'trying Him.' Matthew's account shows that they wished, not only to entangle Him in their party disputes, but also to place Him in opposition to the law of Moses. As an affirmative answer would probably have called forth the charge of lax morality, there was a double snare laid for Him.

Ver. 3. **What did Moses command you?** Peculiar to Mark. This question at once takes the matter out of the sphere of tradition and Rabbinical hair-splitting, into that of Divine law.

Ver. 4. **Moses suffered.** This answer implies the purely permissive character of the Mosaic provision (Deut. 24: 1–4), since the **bill of divorcement** was not designed to encourage divorce, but to render it more difficult; being in effect a protection of the repudiated wife. Comp. Matt. 5: 31.

Ver. 5. **For your hardness of heart.** Their general sinfulness, with special reference to harshness toward their wives, which this regulation was designed to counteract. It was not to encourage divorce.—**He wrote.** This implies that some of the precepts of the Mosaic law were of temporary validity, designed only to educate the chosen people. The law of Paradise is, in one sense, more permanent, just as Paul exalts the Abrahamic covenant above the law (Gal. 3).

them, For your hardness of heart he wrote you this
6 commandment. But from the beginning of the crea-
7 tion, Male and female made he them. For this cause
shall a man leave his father and mother, and ¹ shall
8 cleave to his wife; and the twain shall become one
9 flesh: so that they are no more twain, but one flesh. What
therefore God hath joined together, let not man put
10 asunder. And in the house the disciples asked him

¹ Some ancient authorities omit *and shall cleave to his wife.*

Ver. 6. **But from the beginning of the creation.** In the original state in Paradise. Polygamy appears first (Gen. 4 : 19) in conjunction with murder, and in the line of Cain. The historical truth of the narrative in the first two chapters of Genesis, is assumed as the basis of an important argument. The *creation* of man is affirmed. —**Male and female** (Gen. 1 : 27). The question of the Pharisees is answered by citing what God *did.* In the original creation of man He instituted the sexual relation, and marriage as an indissoluble union between one man and one woman.

Ver. 7. Our Lord sanctions the words of Gen. 1 : 24, by making them His own. Whether at first spoken by Adam, or a comment by Moses, they are the words of God (Matthew).—**For this cause.** Comp. Eph. 5 : 31, where the passage is applied also to Christ and the Church. God says, Christ says, that the relationship between a man and his wife is closer, higher, and stronger, than even that between children and parents. Notice: it is the man who leaves his parents.

Ver. 8. **The twain shall become one flesh.** 'Unity of soul and spirit,' is not mentioned. The absence of it, however great a source of unhappiness, is not a ground of divorce. The essential bond is the fact that the twain, by marriage, 'become one flesh,' one man within the limits of their united life in the flesh, for this world. This is the first precept or prophecy of Holy writ; again and again referred to.

Ver. 9. **What therefore God hath joined together,** etc. More literally 'did join together,' at the time of creation. Our Lord's conclusion. The sentence forms a proper part of every Christian marriage ceremony. It is Christ's protection of this holy relation. It also implies a warning against hasty marriages, against ignorance and forgetfulness of the fact that it is *God* who forms the indissoluble tie. As a *remnant of Paradise* the marriage relation suffers many attacks from 'the seed of the serpent.'

Ver. 10. **And in the house.** An accurate detail peculiar to Mark. The fuller private teaching was needed, for these disciples were to teach the world new lessons on the subject of marriage and divorce, and thus elevate woman. Sadly enough, women who have been elevated by these teachings are seeking to overthrow their au-

11 again of this matter. And he saith unto them, Whosoever shall put away his wife, and marry another,
12 committeth adultery against her: and if she herself shall put away her husband, and marry another, she committeth adultery.
13 And they ¹brought unto him little children, that he should touch them: and the disciples rebuked them.
14 But when Jesus saw it, he was moved with indignation, and said unto them, Suffer the little children to come unto me; forbid them not: for of ²such is the kingdom

¹ *were bringing* (Am. Com.)   ² *To such belongeth* (Am. Ver.).

thority, thus unwittingly laboring for the renewed degradation of their sex.

Ver. 11. See on Matt. 19: 9, where the case of one marrying a divorced woman is added.—**Against her.** It is not clear whether this means the first or second woman. But the marriage with the second is a crime against the first, as well as adultery with the second. The one justifiable ground of divorce is omitted here, being understood as a matter of course.

Ver. 12. **And if she herself shall put away,** etc. Mark's account is peculiar in representing the woman as seeking the divorce. This was unusual among the Jews (exceptional cases: Michal, 1 Sam. 25: 44; Herodias, Matt. 14: 4), though it occurred among the Greeks and Romans. Probably in this confidential interview, the delicate subject was discussed in all its bearings (Matthew preserves particulars omitted here), and Mark preserves a specification more applicable to Gentile readers.

Vers. 13-16. THE BLESSING OF LITTLE CHILDREN.—Parallel passages: Matt. 19: 13-15; Luke 18: 15-17. The latter at this point resumes the parallelism with Matthew and Mark. The account before us is the fullest and most striking of the three.

Ver. 13. **They brought unto him**; probably their parents (Luke: 'their babes'). An encouragement to parents to bring even 'babes' to Christ. Thus the doubts of the disciples about the marriage state were answered.—**That he should touch them.** So Luke; Matthew: 'lay His hands on them and pray.' A recognition of Christ's power to bless, since He healed by laying on His hands.—**And the disciples rebuked them.** They were engaged in an interesting discussion about marriage, etc. Abstract theories about household relations should not stand between the Lord and little children.

Ver. 14. **Much displeased,** *i. e.*, at the rebuke of the disciples. Peculiar to Mark. Some sign of displeasure was probably on His countenance. How careful we should be not to call forth His displeasure, by keeping children from Him.—**Suffer the little children,**

15 of God. Verily I say unto you, Whosoever shall not receive the kingdom of God as a little child, he shall 16 in no wise enter therein. And he took them in his arms, and blessed them, laying his hands upon them.

etc. The natural impulse would be to bring children to Him, do not check it.—**Forbid them not,** as the disciples did, and many since then.—**To such belongeth the kingdom of heaven.** This rendering, preferred by the Am. Com., seems more clear than that of the A. V. Children may be Christians; heaven is full of such. Probably a majority of the redeemed is made up of children, lost in Adam but saved in Christ, who were sinners by nature though not in act. But ver. 15, Luke 18 : 17, and similar passages show that children in spirit are referred to in the wider application. All who are in the 'kingdom' are of a childlike spirit; many in it are actual children. It follows: that the earlier children are brought to Christ, the better; that they too need salvation from the Saviour of sinners; that, as we are privileged to bring them, we may mistakenly forbid them both by neglect and injudicious teaching: (*a*) by not failing to teach them of Christ, through word and example; (*b*) by teaching them legalism, *i. e.*, 'Be good, or God will not love you,' instead of this: 'Christ loves you, therefore go to Him in order to be good.' It seems fair to infer that through the faith of parents *a seed of faith* may exist in the heart of a child, so that the infant members of a Christian family *ought to be* Christian children, and their education conducted in the confident expectation that they will show the fruits of faith. None are too small for Him to notice; none too small for Him to save.

Ver. 15. Comp. Matt. 18 : 3. The connection here is remarkable. Not only may infants be brought to Christ, but adults, in order to enter the kingdom, to come to Him, must become *like them.* Only **as a little child** can any one enter the kingdom. It is fairly implied that children in years can be Christians, recognized as such by their parents' act and the Master's act through His ministers, trained as such by parents and pastors, and a promise that His grace will not fail, where our faith does not fail.

Ver. 16. **And taking them in his arms.** Mark loves to tell of our Lord's gestures. Christ did more for the children than those who brought them asked, as He always does. The servants of such a Master should welcome children to His fold.—**Laying his hands on them.** 'In the Christian Church men are ordained to the ministry by laying-on of hands; and about the question of proper ordination much has been said and written: on this question churches have been divided. But it is remarkable that we are not definitely told of Christ's ordaining His Apostles by laying His hands on them. Yet on children, infants, He did lay hands, thus ordaining them for the kingdom of God. The fact is also of importance in determining whether the Church should openly receive infants.'

17 And as he was going forth ¹ into the way, there ran one to him, and kneeled to him, and asked him, Good ² Master, what shall I do that I may inherit eternal
18 life? And Jesus said unto him, Why callest thou me
19 good? none is good save one, *even* God. Thou know-

¹ Or, *on his way.*   ² Or, *Teacher.*

Vers. 17-22. THE YOUNG MAN WHOM JESUS LOVED.—Parallel passages: Matt. 19: 16-22; Luke 18: 18-23. The position of this paragraph is the same in all three Gospels. Ver. 17 shows that our Lord had already started on His journey to death. This gives the greater emphasis to His demand for self-denial from the rich young man. The connection with ver. 15 is also significant; the love of riches is the very opposite of receiving 'the kingdom of God, as a little child.' Our Lord first presented the high ideal of marriage, the closest human tie, with a hint that even this must be subordinate to the claims of His kingdom; then the position of children, next in order of intimacy; now comes the relation to earthly possessions, which men value next (though through the influence of sin sometimes most of all). Our Lord meets the young ruler, whom He loved, on his own ground, leads him to a recognition of the idol that prevents him from entering the kingdom.—Going away sorrowful is not entering into life.

Ver. 17. **Into the way.** On His journey to Jerusalem, as He finally left Perea.—**There ran one,** etc. Peculiar to Mark. This eagerness and respect were the more remarkable, since the man was a 'ruler' (Luke), and 'very rich.' Still the enthusiasm was also that of youth (Matthew: 'the young man'). This person must not be confounded either with the lawyer to whom the parable of the Good Samaritan was addressed (Luke 10: 25), or with the lawyer who tempted our Lord in the temple (chap. 12: 28-33; Matt. 22: 35-40). Some slight correspondences in the conversations lead the careless reader into such confusion. The circumstances, character of the questioner, &c., differ greatly in all three cases. The first question here is, however, similar to that in Luke 10: 25.—**Good Master, what shall I do?** Matthew: 'Master, what good thing?' Both ideas were no doubt included in the original question, but in Matthew's narrative the one point ('good thing') is taken up, in Mark and Luke the other ('good master'). Both *what* was good, and *who* was good, had been misapprehended by the questioner.

Ver. 18. **Why callest thou me good?** Matthew (the correct reading): 'Why askest thou me of that which is good?' In applying the term 'good' to our Lord, the young ruler was honest, but mistaken. He used it without fully apprehending its meaning. On the connection of this answer with the one 'good thing,' see Matt. 19: 17. *Either* 'there is none good, but God: Christ is good; therefore Christ is GOD' —*or*, 'there is none good, but God: Christ is not God: therefore Christ is NOT GOOD' (Stier). Since but one is good, God, then giving up all for Him is the last test, and following Christ (ver. 21) is doing that.

Ver. 19. **Thou shalt not kill,** etc. Those commandments involv-

est the commandments, Do not kill, Do not commit adultery, Do not steal, Do not bear false witness, Do 20 not defraud, Honour thy father and mother. And he said unto him, ¹Master, all these things have I 21 observed from my youth. And Jesus looking upon him loved him, and said unto him, One thing thou

¹ Or, *Teacher*

ing duties toward our fellow men are cited, so as to meet the young man on his own ground.—**Do not defraud.** This probably answers to the tenth commandment.—**Honour thy father and thy mother.** This commandment connects the two classes of duties enjoined in the Decalogue, but is here presented as involving duty to man. Hence the position it occupies in all three accounts. Matthew gives the sum of the second table of the law. Our Lord would show the young man how much he falls short of keeping of even these commandments. What follows shows that his obedience, however strict, failed to recognize God as the supreme good.

Ver. 20. **All these things have I observed from my youth.** Externally moral, perhaps self-righteous, he yet felt that he lacked something. Peace of conscience had not been attained by his keeping of 'all these things.' But he had not yet learned how much he lacked of even comprehending the spirituality of the law.

Ver. 21. **And Jesus looking upon him loved him.** A touching particular, peculiar to Mark. The young man made no immediate response to this love. How then could Jesus have loved him in his self-righteousness and worldliness? The phrase 'looking upon him' indicates that the love was called forth by the loveliness of the young ruler. Despite all his mistakes, there was in him something lovely. To this loveliness there was a response in the heart of Him who shared our humanity so entirely. It may have been a part of the sorrows of His early life, that such affection met no proper spiritual response. This view neither diminishes the *power* of our Saviour's affection, nor assumes, what is nowhere hinted, that the young man was at heart right.—**One thing thou lackest.** The ruler had asked what he lacked (Matthew). Judged from his own point of view, one duty was as yet undone. Our Lord does not imply that he had done all but this one duty: He rather proposes this as a test, to show that the entire obedience was imperfect.—**Sell whatsoever thou hast.** In his case wealth was the hindrance; in another case it might be something else. All we have belongs to Christ, and we hold it aright only when it is subordinate to Him. Hence the command is not literally applicable to all. The gospel is here put in legal form to reach the legalistic young man's conscience.—**Give to the poor.** Not, however, to buy eternal life (1 Cor. 13: 3).—The **treasure in heaven** is not bought by voluntary poverty (comp. Matt. 5: 12; 6: 20).—**Come, follow me.**

lackest: go, sell whatsoever thou hast, and give to the poor, and thou shalt have treasure in heaven: and 22 come, follow me. But his countenance fell at the saying, and he went away sorrowful: for he was one that had great possessions.

23 And Jesus looked round about, and saith unto his

(This briefer form is sustained by the best authorities; the clause: 'take up thy cross,' was easily transferred from similar passages, such as chap. 8: 34.) This is the final test. Whenever property interferes with following Christ, it must be given up; and he who would be a Christian, must be *ready* to relinquish it for Christ's sake, not to win salvation nor to buy a superior place in heaven.

Ver. 22. **But his countenance fell.** A strong expression, peculiar to Mark, who loves such minute details of look and gesture.—**He went away sorrowful.** Whether he ever obeyed, we are not told. Our Lord's love may have followed him, but of the three similar cases this is the least hopeful.—**For he was one that had great possessions.** It was, however, not the greatness of his wealth, but its great hold on him, which led him away. This was his idol. Up to the point of decision, Christ or Mammon, the Master had wisely led him; but now he chose for himself, and chose foolishly, perhaps fatally, as many another amiable young man has done. Our Lord's comments on 'riches' show that this young man's pride was intrenched in his wealth; a part of it he might have been willing to pay for 'eternal life;' but, being his idol, it must be entirely relinquished before he could enter the kingdom of heaven. The hindrance is often removed by God's Providence. Some practical inferences: Respect for Christ is not reception of Christ. Earnest religious inquiry is not of itself the way to eternal life. No words are so keen as Christ's, in cutting away false hopes. His presence reveals our idols. If 'character' saves, why was this young man not saved?

Vers. 23-31. DISCOURSE ON RICHES.—Parallel passages: Matt 19: 23-30; Luke 18: 24-30. This discourse was our Lord's comment upon the conduct of the young ruler. It suggests many lessons: Riches are a hindrance so great, that just here comes in the declaration of God's saving omnipotence.—Our Lord speaks the truth to rich and poor alike. There is no word here that points to a 'community of goods,' though this was the occasion, were that doctrine correct. The giving up of wealth when it is an idol, the crucifixion to the world, here enjoined, have a moral quality. There is none in a forced equality of possessions, nor in voluntary poverty with the hope of winning heaven. Agrarianism, no less than avarice, makes wealth the chief good; trusting in poverty, no less than trusting in riches, fosters pride.—The highest lesson is, Trust in Almighty God, not in uncertain riches.

Ver. 23. **Looked round about.** A second look of Jesus, in earnest sadness, we may well suppose.

disciples, How hardly shall they that have riches enter
24 into the kingdom of God! And the disciples were
amazed at his words. But Jesus answereth again,
and saith unto them, Children, how hard is it [1] for
them that trust in riches to enter into the kingdom of
25 God! It is easier for a camel to go through a needle's
eye, than for a rich man to enter into the kingdom of
26 God. And they were astonished exceedingly, saying
27 [2] unto him, Then who can be saved? Jesus looking

[1] Some ancient authorities omit *for them that trust in riches*.   [2] Many ancient authorities read *among themselves*.

Ver. 24. **Were amazed.** The word is a strong one. Mark introduces this astonishment of the disciples earlier than Matthew, and adds the Lord's explanation : **Children** (a term of affection to tranquillize them), **how hard is it for them that trust in riches,** etc. That this trust is almost inseparable from the possession of riches, is implied by the connection with ver. 25. Some ancient authorities omit: 'for them that trust in riches,' thus making the statement more general.

Ver. 25. **Easier for a camel,** etc. A strong declaration of impossibility (comp. ver. 26). This has been weakened in two ways: (1.) by the change of a single letter (in some manuscripts) of the original, altering 'camel' into 'rope;' (2.) by explaining **a needle's eye** to mean the small gate for foot-passengers at the entrance to cities. The first is incorrect, the second uncertain and unnecessary. The literal sense is not too strong, as both the context and abundant facts show. Our Lord elsewhere speaks of a 'camel' as a figure for something very large (Matt. 23: 24); and in the Talmud the same saying occurs about an elephant. 'The camel was more familiar to the hearers of the Saviour than the elephant, and on account of the hump on its back, it was especially adapted to symbolize earthly wealth as a heavy load and serious impediment to entrance through the narrow gate of the kingdom of heaven.'

Ver. 26. **Astonished exceedingly.** Driven out of their wonted state of mind, dismayed. Evidently they felt that having riches almost inevitably led to 'trusting in riches.' In fact many who have *not* riches are seeking wealth as the chief good, because they already *trust* in it. Because the impossibility was thus extended, the question, **Then who can be saved?** was so natural.

Ver. 27. **Looking upon them.** The third look is mentioned by Matthew also. The first (ver. 21) was a look of affection, the second (ver. 23) a look of sorrow, the third of kindness bringing hope, for the grace of God is declared to be equal to this task.—**With men it is impossible.** Not only in their judgment, but with their power.

upon them saith, With men it is impossible, but not with God: for all things are possible with God. 28 Peter began to say unto him, Lo, we have left all, 29 and have followed thee. Jesus said, Verily I say unto you, There is no man that hath left house, or brethren, or sisters, or mother, or father, or children, 30 or lands, for my sake, and for the gospel's sake, but he shall receive a hundredfold now in this time, houses, and brethren, and sisters, and mothers, and children, and lands, with persecutions; and in the ¹world to

¹ Or, *age*.

—**All things are possible with God.** God's grace not only can, but does, save some who are rich in spite of all the hindrances their wealth occasions.—This passage opposes the love of money in every form and among all conditions of men. The desire for wealth, even more than the actual possession of it, interferes with entering into a kingdom where humility is a cardinal virtue and self-denial an essential prerequisite. He has learned the lesson right, who applies this mainly to *himself*, seeking the almighty grace which can save him from his trust in earthly things.

Ver. 28. **Peter began to say.** Probably under the influence of the astonishment just mentioned. On the special promise to the Apostles, see Matt. 19: 28. Mark's account presents a few peculiar features.

Ver. 29. **For the gospel's sake.** A similar addition occurs in chap. 8: 38. Mark perhaps inserts this in both places, in consequence of his own shrinking from suffering on account of the gospel (Acts 13: 13; 15: 38); so, also, 'with persecutions' (ver. 30). He would guard others against his own mistake.

Ver. 30. **Now in this time.** So Luke. It is implied, though not very plainly, in Matthew's account.—**Houses**, etc. This repetition is peculiar to Mark, and characteristic.—**Mothers.** 'Nature gives us only one; but love, many' (see Rom. 16: 13). We do not find 'fathers' here, or 'wives' ('wife' being of doubtful authority in ver. 29), the new relations being spiritual. The former is omitted, probably for the reason suggested in Matt. 23: 9 ('One is your father,' etc.), and the omission then contains a lesson. Christian love and hospitality literally fulfil this promise. But the hope of such a reward is not the proper motive. The promise is made only to those who do this 'for my sake and the gospel's sake.'—**With persecutions.** According to the gospel, the persecutions are a part of our best possessions (Matt. 5: 12; Rom. 5: 3, etc.), and really prevent the others from becoming a curse. This phrase not only serves to spiritualize the whole promise, but to guard against its misuse.

31 come eternal life. But many *that are* first shall be last; and the last first.

32 And they were in the way, going up to Jerusalem; and Jesus was going before them: and they were

Ver. 31. **But many**, etc. The form differs slightly from that in Matthew, but in each case the proverb is a caution against trusting to appearances or to the permanence of present circumstances and conditions. The Twelve were liable to mistake priority in time of calling for priority in position—a frequent mistake in every human society, but doubly a mistake where God's free grace is concerned. The proverb is illustrated in Matthew's account by the parable of the laborers in the vineyard (Matt. 20: 1-16). Lange: 'Believers are to find a new and eternal home and country, new and eternal relationships, and new and eternal possessions, of which the blessings enjoyed by them on earth are to be the earnest and foretaste. All these promises are summed up in that of being made heirs of eternal life (Rom. 8).'

Vers. 32-34. THE THIRD PREDICTION OF THE PASSION.—Parallel passages: Matt. 20: 17-19; Luke 18: 31-34. This prediction was made during the direct journey to Jerusalem, from Perea through Jericho, just before the last Passover. The raising of Lazarus is, however, placed by some between the departure from Perea and this final journey. The approach of His death calls for a more specific prediction to the Twelve. The *crucifixion* is mentioned only in Matthew's account.

Ver. 32. **They were in the way**. Actually on the public road. —**Going up to Jerusalem**; continuing the journey already begun. —**Jesus was going before them**, leading the way. Probably implying some remarkable energy in His gait, some determination or eagerness in His manner.—**And they were amazed**. At His eagerness. By this time they knew that great danger awaited Him at Jerusalem.—**And they that followed** (him) **were afraid**. Of this known danger to Himself, which they may have thought threatened themselves also. This graphic description is peculiar to Mark. The better supported reading is followed here, which distinguishes between those who were 'amazed,' and those who were 'afraid.' Explanations: (1) The whole body were amazed, so much so that only some continued to follow, and these were afraid. But multitudes attended Him all the way. Besides, according to Luke 18: 34, even the revelation of the Twelve was not understood by them; how then should His manner of walking frighten away most of the crowd? (2) The better view is: The Twelve nearest to Him were amazed, and the larger company of followers were afraid, though further away from Him.—**And he took again the twelve** (aside), as He frequently did.—**Began to tell**. Opened up this subject again, for the third time, exclusive of the intimation to the three chosen disciples (chap. 9: 9). This was a fuller and more detailed revelation of the *time* and the *mode* of His sufferings

amazed; ¹and they that followed were afraid. And he took again the twelve, and began to tell them the
33 things that were to happen unto him, *saying*, Behold, we go up to Jerusalem; and the Son of man shall be delivered unto the chief priests and the scribes; and they shall condemn him to death, and shall deliver
34 him unto the Gentiles: and they shall mock him, and shall spit upon him, and shall scourge him, and shall kill him; and after three days he shall rise again.
35 And there come near unto him James and John, the sons of Zebedee, saying unto him, ²Master, we would that thou shouldest do for us whatsoever we shall ask

¹ Or, *but some as they followed were afraid.* ² Or, *Teacher.*

and of the *agents* who should be engaged therein.—**That were to happen**, not, 'that should.' Certainty and nearness are implied.

Ver. 33. **We go up to Jerusalem.** On the journey to death which He had previously predicted (Matt. 16 : 21).—**Delivered unto the chief priests.** More detailed than chap 9 : 31 : 'into the hands of men.' A double betrayal is implied: first by His professed friends to His declared enemies; then by His own people to the Gentiles.—**They shall condemn him to death.** A reference to the judicial condemnation on the part of the Sanhedrin (chap. 14 : 64).—**And shall deliver him unto the Gentiles.** Comp. chap. 15 : 1.

Ver. 34. **Spit upon him.** See chap. 15 : 19. Omitted by Matthew.—**Kill him.** Matthew: 'crucify Him,' which is implied here, as the 'Gentiles,' to whom the whole verse refers, were to put Him to death. The Twelve failed to understand this detailed prediction (Luke 18 : 34). That danger threatened they felt, but they may have given this prediction *figurative* interpretations.—**After three days.** This form is given by Mark in all three predictions (chaps. 8 : 31 ; 9 : 31, and here).

Vers. 35-45. THE REQUEST OF THE SONS OF ZEBEDEE.—Parallel passage: Matt. 20: 20-28. On the way from Perea (see vers. 32-34) to Jericho, this ambitious request was made by the two sons of Zebedee and their mother Salome (Matthew). This was probably occasioned by the prediction, and leads to further instruction.

Ver. 35. **And James and John.** The request doubtless originated with them. (The priority of the name of James suggests that he was the older brother.) In the account of Matthew (20 : 20-22), the answer is addressed to them, and Salome appears as an intercessor for them. Either both mother and sons preferred the request, or the mother *for* the sons.—**We would that thou shouldest do,**

36 of thee. And he said unto them, What would ye that
37 I should do for you? And they said unto him, Grant unto us that we may sit, one on thy right hand, and
38 one on *thy* left hand, in thy glory. But Jesus said unto them, Ye know not what ye ask. Are ye able to drink the cup that I drink? or to be baptized with
39 the baptism that I am baptized with? And they said unto him, We are able. And Jesus said unto them, The cup that I drink ye shall drink; and with the baptism that I am baptized withal shall ye be baptized:
40 but to sit on my right hand or on *my* left hand is not

etc. The form of the request is more fully stated here, but in both accounts there appears the same consciousness that what was desired was of doubtful propriety.

Ver. 36. **What would ye,** etc. This question also is fuller in Mark's account.

Ver. 37. **One on thy right hand, and one on thy left hand, in thy glory.** (Matthew: 'in thy kingdom'.) The highest places of honor, implying special authority also, as is indicated by the answer (ver. 42). The request was based upon ignorance (comp. ver. 38), was prompted by ambition (comp. vers. 42-44), however natural it may have been.

Ver. 38. **Ye know not what ye ask.** Addressed to James and John (according to both accounts), who had prompted their mother. The request could scarcely have been occasioned by jealousy of Peter. Had he been appointed 'primate,' this would have been an opportunity for upholding him in that position. When John saw the crucified thieves on the right and left hand of his dying Lord, he knew what he had asked.—**To drink the cup?** A frequent Scriptural figure for the Providential portion assigned to any one; especially for a suffering lot. It refers to inward anguish here.—**Or to be baptized,** etc. The two clauses about our Lord's baptism (vers. 38-39) are peculiar to this Gospel; the best authorities omit them in Matthew. We find a vividness too in use of the present tense: **that I drink—that I am baptized with** (so in ver. 39). 'The Lord had already the cup of His suffering at His lips; was already, so to speak, sprinkled with the first drops of the spray of His baptism of blood' (Alford).

Ver. 39. **We are able.** They were not the least courageous of the Twelve (comp. John 18: 15), but they also forsook Him and fled (chap. 14: 50) in the hour of trial.—**The cup that I drink ye shall drink.** James was the first martyr among the Twelve; John died a natural death at an advanced age, but in a spiritual sense his was the longest martyrdom.

Ver. 40. **Is not mine,** etc. Either, it is not a favor to be gained

mine to give: but *it is for them* for whom it hath been
41 prepared. And when the ten heard it, they began to be moved with indignation concerning James and John.
42 And Jesus called them to him, and saith unto them, Ye know that they which are accounted to rule over the Gentiles lord it over them; and their great ones
43 exercise authority over them. But it is not so among you: but whosoever would become great among you,
44 shall be your ¹minister: and whosoever would be first

¹ Or, *servant*.

by asking; or, it is not in my power, but it will be assigned to those **for whom it hath been prepared**, according 'to the eternal predestination of eternal positions in the kingdom of God.' (Matthew adds: 'of my Father'.) Yet these two might occupy the position. Christ asserts that His will as Ruler in His kingdom accords with the eternal purpose of God; this purpose, because its individual objects were as yet concealed, forbade their ambitious solicitation.

Ver. 41. **The ten**, so Matthew also, including himself. A proof of humility and truthfulness.—**They began.** Peculiar to Mark, suggesting that their feeling was soon interrupted.—**Moved with indignation** (so the verb is usually rendered in the Rev. Ver.). —**Concerning James and John.** This displeasure was no more praiseworthy than the ambition of the two, and was speedily discountenanced.

Ver. 42. **Accounted to rule over the Gentiles**, have the *title* of rulers (God being the real Ruler), or, are recognized as rulers, the essence of all heathen government being despotism. The latter is perhaps the more suggestive sense. The Jewish form of government, as ordained by God, was designed to exclude tyranny.—**Lord it over them**, *i. e.*, exercise tyrannical and arbitrary power.—**Their great ones.** Either conquerors and usurpers, or, the officers of state.

Ver. 43. **But it is not so among you.** The present tense, used by Mark, according to the best authorities, agrees with his vivacious style. To maintain superiority of rank by force is not Christian, even if encouraged by ecclesiastical organizations. In such organizations it is most hurtful, for freedom in the Christian communion is necessary to true civil freedom.—**But whosoever would become great among you**, *i. e.*, great in the next life, **let him be your minister**, *i. e.*, in this life.

Ver. 44. **Would be first**, &c. This is a repetition of the same thought, but with increased emphasis, since 'be first' is stronger than 'become great,' and **servant** here (Gr. 'bond-servant') is stronger than the related word 'minister' in the previous clause. Deep humility expressing itself in a service of love is the measure of

45 among you, shall be ¹servant of all. For verily the Son of man came not to be ministered unto, but to minister, and to give his life a ransom for many.
46 And they come to Jericho: and as he went out from Jericho, with his disciples and a great multitude, the son of Timæus, Bartimæus, a blind beggar, was sitting

¹ Gr. *bondservant.*

Christian greatness, actually constituting it here, but acknowledged hereafter. Official orders in the Church are not forbidden, but real greatness is independent of such orders. However necessary, they are intended to advance the liberty of the Church. Service rendered to Christians ranks higher than office in the Church.

Ver. 45. **For verily the Son of man.** What He asked of them was on the ground of what He did Himself.—**Came.** His appearing in the world was **not to be ministered unto**, not to be personally served by others, nor to exercise an external authority for His own external interest, **but to minister**, to serve others, as His whole ministry showed. Christ's *example* enforces the lesson of humility, but a deeper truth is now for the first time declared.—**And to give his life.** The crowning act of His ministering to others.—**A ransom for many.** 'Ransom' may mean only the payment for a life destroyed (Exod. 21: 20), the price paid for the redemption of a slave (Lev. 25: 5). As however it also means 'propitiation' (Prov. 13: 8), and the word translated 'for' means 'in the place of,' this passage affirms that our Lord's death was vicarious; by His death as a ransom-price the 'many' are to be redeemed from the guilt and power of sin. As soon as the disciples could bear it, they were taught this central truth of the gospel, to which they gave such prominence, after the Holy Ghost came upon them. This tender rebuke of their ambition bases the cardinal grace of humility upon the cardinal doctrine of the Atonement.

Vers. 46-52. THE HEALING OF BLIND BARTIMÆUS.—Parallel passages: Matt. 20: 29-34; Luke 18: 35-43. Reaching Jericho about a week before the Passover, our Lord performed the miracle here detailed. Matthew mentions two blind men, Mark and Luke but one, the former giving his name. Matthew and Mark say that the miracle occurred as they went out of Jericho; Luke 'as He drew nigh unto Jericho.' The latter also narrates the interview with Zaccheus and the parable of the ten pounds, as following this miracle and immediately preceding the journey to Jerusalem. Accepting Luke's order, we suppose that our Lord remained for a day at Jericho, and that the healing occurred during some excursion into the neighborhood. Our Lord left Jericho for Bethany during the afternoon of Friday (8th of Nisan), a week before the crucifixion. On Saturday He was in Bethany (John 12: 1).

Ver. 46. **And they come to Jericho.** Our Lord entered the city *before* the blind man was healed, so that Luke's account (chap. 18: 35) refers to a *second* entrance.—**As he went out from**

47 by the way side. And when he heard that it was Jesus of Nazareth, he began to cry out, and say, Jesus,
48 thou son of David, have mercy on me. And many rebuked him, that he should hold his peace: but he cried out the more a great deal, Thou son of David,
49 have mercy on me. And Jesus stood still, and said, Call ye him. And they call the blind man, saying

Jericho. Jericho was in the tribe of Benjamin on the borders of Ephraim, about two hours journey from the Jordan, and the road thence to Jerusalem was difficult and dangerous (Luke 10: 30–34). The district was a blooming oasis in the midst of an extended sandy plain, watered and fruitful, rich in palms, roses, and balsam: hence probably the name ('the fragrant city'). Built by the Canaanites, and destroyed by Joshua (Josh. 6: 26), it was rebuilt and fortified at a later day, and became the seat of a school of the prophets. Herod the Great beautified it, and it was one of the most pleasant places in the land. In the twelfth century scarcely a vestige of the place remained, there is now on the site a wretched village, Richa or Ericha, with about 200 inhabitants. Robinson, however, locates the old Jericho in the neighborhood of the fountain of Elisha (two miles northwest of Richa).—**The son of Timæus, Bartimæus.** Some think the father was well known, but the order in the original suggests that the son was the well-known personage. 'Bar' = son, as Mark seems to explain.—**A blind beggar.** He was probably begging as he sat, as the A. V. states, but the original does not necessarily mean this. Why Matthew (20: 30–34) mentions *two* blind men, and Mark and Luke but *one*, has been variously explained; but it is altogether unnecessary to find a contradiction in the accounts. The prominence of this *one* is evident from the narrative before us, which is in many respects the most exact and vivid of the three.

Ver. 47. **Jesus of Nazareth**, lit., 'the Nazarene.' Mark alone (with one exception) uses this form. It was sometimes a term of contempt. In any case we can contrast the title given by the crowd with that in the cry of the blind beggar: **Son of David** (Messiah).

Ver. 48. **That he should hold his peace.** The multitude did not object to the title, 'son of David,' but thought the cry would annoy our Lord.—**But he cried out the more a great deal.** In persistent faith. The continued crying is set forth even more strongly here than in the account of Matthew.

Ver. 49. **And Jesus stood still.** He now allows Himself to be publicly called: 'Son of David.' Peculiar in this form to Mark, and omitted altogether by Matthew. This was a 'reproof to the reprovers.' It seems to have had an effect, for the words now addressed to the blind man are full of sympathy: **Be of good cheer: rise, he calleth thee.** The order is that of *kindness, faith* would put: 'He

unto him, Be of good cheer: rise, he calleth thee.
50 And he, casting away his garment, sprang up, and
51 came to Jesus. And Jesus answered him, and said, What wilt thou that I should do unto thee? And the blind man said unto him, [1] Rabboni, that I may re-
52 ceive my sight. And Jesus said unto him, Go thy way; thy faith hath [2] made thee whole. And straightway he received his sight, and followed him in the way.

11 : 1 And when they draw nigh unto Jerusalem, unto

[1] See John xx. 16. [2] Or, *saved thee*

calleth thee' first. The forbidding and the cheering address represent the priestly spirit which would keep men from applying directly to Christ, and the true spirit of the gospel messengers.

Ver. 50. **Casting away his garment.** A detail indicating that the narrative comes from an eye-witness. Bartimæus did not stop to care for the cloak that might be lost, if it impeded his progress. Nay, if he received his sight, it could easily be found again.—**Sprang up.** This mark of eagerness is also peculiar to this account.

Ver. 51. **What wilt thou,** etc. The question was to call forth an expression of his faith in Jesus.—**Rabboni,** or, '*my* Master,' (as in John 20 : 16), the most respectful of the three titles, Rab, Rabbi, Rabboni.—**That I may receive my sight,** or, 'see again.' Not *how* or *why,* but the *desire,* which he believes the Lord can grant in the best way.

Ver. 52. **Go thy way.** Not necessarily a command to depart, but a token that his prayer was granted. The commendation is omitted by Matthew, who speaks of our Lord touching the blind man, but this seems more accurate.—**Followed him in the way.** Not simply for the time being, we suppose, but joined the multitude who went up to Jerusalem with our Lord. The effect on the people is described by Luke. Our Lord thus proved that He came to minister (ver. 45). This is the last miracle recorded in detail in the Gospels, and one of the most encouraging. 'Thousands have read this simple and touching story as a truthful history of their own spiritual blindness, and its removal through the abounding grace of Jesus Christ' (J. J. Owen).

Chap. XI: 1-11. THE PUBLIC ENTRY INTO JERUSALEM.—Parallel passages: Matt. 21 : 1-11; Luke 19 : 29-44; John 12 : 12-19.—*Chronology.* The date of the public entry into Jerusalem (narrated by all four Evangelists) was *Sunday, the 10th of the month Nisan.* The narrative of Mark is the most exact. We hold that our Lord ate the Passover at the usual time (comp. chap. 14 : 17), and was crucified on Friday. Reckoning back from this date, we infer that He left Jericho on Friday, the 8th of Nisan, reached

Bethphage and Bethany, at the mount of Olives, he
2 sendeth two of his disciples, and saith unto them, Go
your way into the village that is over against you: and
straightway as ye enter into it, ye shall find a colt tied,

Bethany the next day ('six days before the passover;' John 12: 2). On the evening of that day, after the Sabbath had ended, the anointing by Mary in the house of Simon the leper took place (see John 12: 2). On the reasons for preferring this date, see on chap. 14: 3-9. John explicitly says (12: 12) that the entry took place 'the next day.' The date is significant, for on the 10th of Nisan the Paschal lamb was selected (Exod. 12: 3), being kept until the 14th. This public entry was intentional, not accidental, nor caused by the zeal of His followers, as is evident from all the details, from the prophecy cited, and from the reply to the Pharisees (Luke 19: 40: 'If these should hold their peace the stones would immediately cry out'). It prepared the way for His sufferings by a public avowal of His mission, was a temporary assumption of His rightful royal prerogative, to hasten a decision in Jerusalem. A merciful measure to believing hearts, one of judgment to His enemies. A glimpse of glory given to men, but only increasing the hatred of the rulers, and hastening His death. A remarkable contrast to the procession to Golgotha (Luke 18: 26 ff), both strictly in keeping with the purpose of His mission, 'to give His life a ransom for many.'

Ver. 1. **Unto Jerusalem.** The words 'to' and 'unto' (A. V.) are the same in the original.—**Bethphage** ('house of figs'), **and Bethany** ('house of dates'). So Luke. The two places were probably near each other, but of the former no trace remains. Bethphage was probably nearer to Jerusalem. Some suppose that Bethany lay off the road from Jericho to Jerusalem, and our Lord having turned aside to visit it, now returned to Bethphage on the direct route.—**The mount of Olives.** This lay between Bethphage and Jerusalem, about 'a sabbath day's journey' from the city (Acts 1: 12). There were three roads to the city: a winding northern one, a steep footpath directly over the summit, and a southern road, usually taken by horsemen and caravans. The usual opinion has selected the middle road as that taken by our Lord on this occasion, but the view that He passed over the southern or main road, accords best with the various accounts of the procession and its incidents. See Luke 19: 41. The hill is about seven hundred feet high, overlooking every part of Jerusalem, which lies west of it, separated from it by the valley of the Kidron ('brook Kidron,' John 18: 1). The garden of Gethsemane is on the west side of the mount. The temple was in the foreground, as one looked down on the city from this elevation.—**He sendeth two of his disciples.** Their names are not given. This sending was a royal act in all its details.

Ver. 2. **Into the village.** Bethphage; not Bethany, from which He had just come.—**A colt.** Matthew mentions the mother, but Mark and Luke the colt only.—**Whereon no man ever yet sat.** This agrees with the account that the mother was with it. Animals

whereon no man ever yet sat; loose him, and bring him. And if any one say unto you, Why do ye this? say ye, The Lord hath need of him; and straightway he [1]will send him [2]back hither. And they went away, and found a colt tied at the door without in the open street; and they loose him. And certain of them that stood there said unto them, What do ye, loosing the colt? And they said unto them even as Jesus had said: and they let them go. And they bring the colt

[1] Gr. *sendeth*.   [2] Or, *again*.

never yet worked were used for sacred purposes (Num. 19: 2; Deut. 21: 3; 1 Sam. 6: 7). The unbroken animal would be quieter, if the mother was with him.—**Loose him, and bring him.** This act was to be significant of Christ's royal prerogative. Yet in His exercise of power the willingness of men concurs.

Ver. 3. **If any one say unto you.** Probably a prediction, as well as a measure of prudence.—**The Lord hath need of him.** The tone is still royal, whether 'the Lord' here means 'Jehovah,' or simply 'the Master.' In the former case, the animals would be claimed for religious purposes, by Divine authority; in the latter, for the well-known prophet. The two meanings coincided in our Lord's intention, whatever the owner would understand.—**He will send** (Greek, 'sendeth') **him back hither.** This rendering of the Rev. Vers. makes Mark's account agree with that of Matthew, where the clause corresponding to this is a declaration of what the owner or those objecting would do. But 'again' (found in the best authorities), which is the more literal rendering, makes the clause a part of the message, a promise to return the colt soon.

Ver. 4. **Found a colt.** Mark is more detailed here: perhaps Peter was one of those sent; comp. Luke 22: 8, where Peter and John are the two sent into the city.—**At the door without.** Probably the door of the owner's house.—**In the open street,** or, 'lane.' The A. V., following the Latin Vulgate, paraphrases: 'in a place where two ways meet.' The phrase refers first to a way round, *i. e.*, round a block of houses; then to the street of a town (usually winding in the East).

Ver. 5. **And certain of them that stood there.** It was done openly. These persons were 'the owners' (Luke 19: 33), probably members of the family of the owner.

Ver. 6. **And they** (the questioners) **let them** (the two disciples) **go,** or, let them alone to do what they wished. Peculiar to Mark, and corresponding with the message of ver. 3. The reference to the prophecy of Zechariah (Matthew, John) is omitted by Mark and Luke.

Ver. 7. **On him, their garments.** Upper garments, to serve as a

unto Jesus, and cast on him their garments; and he
8 sat upon him. And many spread their garments upon
the way; and others ¹branches, which they had cut
9 from the fields. And they that went before, and they
that followed, cried, Hosanna; Blessed *is* he that
10 cometh in the name of the Lord: Blessed *is* the king-

¹ Gr. *layers of leaves.*

saddle.—**Sat upon him.** On the colt. Luke and John specify this.

Ver. 8. **And many.** Some (probably the greater number, as it would seem from Matt. 21: 11) had come from Galilee and accompanied the Lord from Jericho, others had come out from Jerusalem (John 12: 12), now crowded on account of the passover.—**Spread their garments.** 'Oriental mark of honor at the reception of kings, on their entrance into cities: 2 Kings 9: 13.' (Lange.)—**Others, branches,** not the same word as in Matthew, but more exactly: 'layers of leaves,' one word in Greek. It might be paraphrased: 'leaves and boughs.' The common reading seems to have been an alteration for the sake of uniformity.—**Which they had cut from the fields.** This, which is the more correct expression, shows that those who did not spread their clothes in the way, went off from the highway, in their zeal, to obtain a substitute. This minute stroke is peculiar to Mark, but corresponds with John 12: 13, where the providing of palm branches is implied.

Ver. 9. **And they that went before,** etc. In responsive chorus. Such 'antiphonies' were common in Jewish worship, especially in the recitation of the Psalms. Those going before had probably come from Jerusalem to meet Him.—**Hosanna.** The Greek form of a Hebrew word found in Ps. 118: 25, meaning: 'Save now,' or, 'grant thy salvation.' Used as a congratulatory expression, here applied in the highest sense to the Messiah, (Matthew: 'the son of David.')—**Blessed is he that cometh.** etc. The greeting to the pilgrims at their entrance to Jerusalem on festival occasions (Ps. 118: 26), and a part of the passover hymn (Ps. 115–118).

Ver. 10. **Blessed is the kingdom that cometh, the kingdom of our father David.** This form of the Hosannas is preserved by Mark alone. It brings out most clearly the recognition of our Lord as the royal Messiah, who was to restore the throne of David. It is asserted that the Messiah Himself was called 'David' by the Rabbis. —**Hosanna in the highest,** *i. e.*, May our Hosanna be ratified in heaven. Other exclamations are mentioned by Matthew and Luke, since in such a multitude they would differ. The former tells of the impression on the city; the latter of the weeping of the Lord over Jerusalem, as the sacred city came in sight. The crowd thus hail Him with enthusiasm as the Messiah, probably cherishing political hopes.—

dom that cometh, *the kingdom* of our father David: Hosanna in the highest.

11   And he entered into Jerusalem, into the temple; and when he had looked round about upon all things, it being now eventide, he went out unto Bethany with the twelve.

What strange mingling of truth and error in the thoughts and hopes of the multitude that day! And the error was the more fatal, because combined with the truth.

Ver. 11. THE FORMAL ENTRANCE INTO THE TEMPLE. Peculiar to Mark.—**Into Jerusalem, into the temple.** He passed at once into the temple, and visited no other point. The afternoon of Sunday seems to have been occupied with this solemn inspection of the temple, as if to take formal possession of it. Our Lord's presence there was a fulfilment of the prophecy of Haggai (2: 9): 'The glory of the latter house shall be greater than of the former.' The night as well as the succeeding one was spent in Bethany, **with the twelve.**

The Temple was built on Mount Moriah, the top of which had been enlarged by building walls from the valley (of Jehosaphat) and filling in. The first edifice was erected by Solomon, in seven years (B. C. 1005), destroyed by Nebuchadnezzar (B. C. 584). The *second* by Zerubbabel, on the same site, seventy years afterwards. It was inferior to the first, not in size but in magnificence; the ark had been burnt with the first temple, and the Shekinah (or, visible Glory) did not return. (Its real return was the visit of Christ.) This building had been frequently desolated and profaned, last of all by the Romans under Herod the Great, who, to gain favor with the Jews, afterwards restored it and rendered it in some respects more magnificent than before. The word 'temple' was applied to the whole inclosure, which was square in form. Inside its high wall were the 'porches,' or, covered walks. Of these there were two rows; on the south side three. Solomon's porch was on the east side towards the Mount of Olives, and so was the 'Beautiful Gate,' a magnificent entrance to the inclosure, directly facing the entrance to the temple proper. A second wall within the first divided the more sacred part of the inclosure from that into which Gentiles might enter: hence the outer court was called the *court of the Gentiles*. This was largest on the south side. The more sacred inclosure was an oblong square; the part nearest the Beautiful Gate was called the *court of the women*, and here the Jews commonly worshipped. On the western side of this court was a high wall; beyond this the *court of the Israelites*, entered after an ascent of fifteen steps by the *Gate Nicanor*. All around this court were rooms for the use of the Levites, and within it, separated from it by a low wall. was the *court of the priests*. At the eastern end of this court stood the altar of burnt offering and the laver, and here the daily service of the temple was performed. Within this court was

12 And on the morrow, when they were come out from
13 Bethany, he hungered. And seeing a fig tree afar off
having leaves, he came, if haply he might find any-

the temple proper. In front of it was an elevated porch, and by the entrance, on the east side, stood the pillars Jachin and Boaz. The *Holy Place*, a room sixty feet long and thirty broad, contained the golden candlestick, the table of shew-bread and the altar of incense. Beyond this was the *Holy of Holies*, a square apartment, separated from the Holy Place by a costly veil. Into this the High Priest entered once a year. White marble was the material chiefly used in the whole structure, and gold and silver plating was frequent in the more sacred parts of the edifice. Elevated as it was, and dazzling to the eye, as one came over 'the mountains of Jerusalem,' it could not fail to produce a powerful impression. Designed to convey a spiritual lesson, it too often only awakened pride. It has been regarded as the symbol of the dwelling-place of Jehovah; a figure of the human form; a symbol of heaven; a figure of the Jewish theocracy. But its highest significance was as a type of the body of Christ (John 2: 21). In this view it was none the less the dwelling-place of Jehovah.

The *court of the Gentiles*, out of which the traders were driven (vers. 15-17), did not exist in the first or second temple. Owing to the advancement of proselytism and the fact that devout Gentiles ('proselytes of the gate') brought gifts to the temple, it grew in importance.

Vers. 12-14. THE CURSING OF THE BARREN FIG TREE.—Parallel passage: Matt. 21: 18, 19.—*Order of Events:* On *Monday morning* the fig tree was cursed (vers. 12-14), on the same day the temple cleansed (vers. 15-19), the chief priests murmuring at the children's Hosannas there (Matt. 21: 14, 15); on *Tuesday morning* the fig tree was found to be withered (ver. 20), and the subsequent discourse (vers. 21-26) delivered on the way to Jerusalem (ver. 27), where the whole day was spent. Here Mark is more exact than the other Evangelists.

Ver. 12. **And on the morrow** (Monday). This definite statement must explain the indefinite accounts.—**From Bethany**. This too is a mark of accuracy. To give point to the incident, Matthew unites the two morning walks from Bethany (on Monday and Tuesday).
—**He hungered.** An actual physical want; it may have been occasioned by His leaving Bethany very early in His zeal to purify the temple, where He had seen the abuses as He looked about on the previous evening. Human want and Divine power are simultaneously exhibited. On Sunday He entered Jerusalem amid hosannas, on Monday in hunger. This hunger may symbolize His longings for some better fruit from His chosen people.

Ver. 13. **A fig tree.** Matthew indicates that it was a solitary one, 'by the way-side.'—**Afar off**, or, 'from afar.' Mark presents the appearance of the tree in the distance: **having leaves.**—**If haply.** Because it had leaves. This scarcely implies doubt in *His* mind, since

thing thereon: and when he came to it, he found nothing but leaves; for it was not the season of figs.
14 And he answered and said unto it, No man eat fruit from thee henceforward forever. And his disciples heard it.
15 And they come to Jerusalem: and he entered into the temple, and began to cast out them that sold and them that bought in the temple, and overthrew the tables of the money-changers, and the seats of them that

the design was to teach the Apostles a very important lesson.—**For it was not the season of figs.** According to the usual view, the full season had not come; yet the leaves gave promise of fruit. The failure was then in the *barrenness* of the tree, a fit symbol of the pretentious hypocrisy of the Jewish hierarchy. A recent traveller in Palestine (T. W. Chambers) gives the following explanation: 'The tree bears two crops,—an early ripe fig, which is crude and without flavor and valueless, and a later fig, which is full of sweetness and flavor, and highly esteemed. All trees bear the first; only good ones have the second. Now, the tree our Lord saw had not the second, for the time of that had not yet come; but it had not even the first, for it had nothing but leaves, and the lack of the first was sure evidence that the second would also be wanting.'

Ver. 14. **No man eat fruit from thee henceforward forever.** This is more exact than Matthew, and the Rev. Vers. brings out its force better than the A. V.—**His disciples heard it.** Another mark of accuracy, suggesting the report of an eye-witness. The reference to Peter in ver. 21 favors the thought that it was he whose recollection supplied the details of this most graphic account.

Vers. 15-18. THE CLEANSING OF THE TEMPLE.—Parallel passages: Matt. 21: 12-16; Luke 19: 45-47; comp. John 2. 14-17. At the beginning of His ministry (at the first Passover) our Lord had performed a similar cleansing, narrated by John (2: 13-17). Such a cleansing was appropriate both at the beginning and the close of Christ's ministry. In the former instance it was more the act of a reformer; here it assumes a Messianic character. In both we find power, as well as zeal for the honor of the Lord of the temple; hence an outbreak of passion is inconceivable.

Ver. 15. **And they come to Jerusalem.** Still another mark of accuracy.—**Began to cast out,** from the court of the Gentiles.—**Them that sold and them that bought.** A market was held there, for the sale of animals and those things necessary for the temple service. Not the less a desecration because so great a convenience.—**Money changers.** The temple tribute must be paid in Jewish coin (Exod. 30: 13), while Roman money was at that time the currency of Palestine. The agents for collecting this tribute proba-

16 sold the doves; and he would not suffer that any man 17 should carry a vessel through the temple. And he taught, and said unto them, Is it not written, My house shall be called a house of prayer for all the 18 nations? but ye have made it a den of robbers. And the chief priests and the scribes heard it, and sought how they might destroy him: for they feared him, for all the multitude was astonished at his teaching.
19 And [1] every evening [2] he went forth out of the city.

[1] Gr. *whenever evening came.*   [2] Some ancient authorities read *they.*

bly found it more convenient to exchange money at Jerusalem, and may have themselves been the 'money changers.'—**The seats**, or, ' stands.'—**The doves.** Needed for offerings by the poor and at the purification of women.—No resistance seems to have been offered. The traffickers were doubtless awed by the superhuman authority and dignity of our Lord.

Ver. 16. **And he would not suffer that any man**, etc. Peculiar to Mark. How He stopped this profanation, we do not know. —**Should carry a vessel**, including utensils, tools, etc.—**Through the temple,** *i. e.*, the court of the Gentiles, which seems to have been used as a thoroughfare. This practice involved the same sin as the others (ver. 15), and expressed the same contempt for the Gentiles.

Ver. 17. **It is written.** The first clause is from Is. 56: 7; the second from Jer. 7: 11.—**For all the nations.** Part of the original prophecy (Isaiah 56: 7) and of the quotation also; but the stress cannot be laid upon it, since Matthew and Luke omit it. It shows the independence and accuracy of this Evangelist.—**Ye have made it a den of robbers.** What they did here was a sign of the general venality and corruption, a desecration of a place of worship for purposes of gain, ill-gotten often enough. This driving of bargains in the place where the Gentiles could come and pray, was a robbery, a contemptuous disregard of the rights and privileges of the Gentiles.

Ver. 18. **And the chief priests,** etc. Matthew (21: 14–16) tells of other occurrences, at which the rulers took offence.—**Might destroy him.** The determination to kill Him had been formed before (see John 11: 53). ' How,' was now the question. The answer was the treachery of Judas, who probably meditated this step already (from the time of the supper at Bethany on Saturday evening), but first treated with them on the next (Tuesday) evening.—**For all the multitude,** etc. All the accounts, in various ways, tell of the wonder and attention of the multitude.

Ver. 19. The change of reading justifies the Rev. Vers. in making this verse a paragraph by itself.—**Every evening.** The correction of the Greek text, from ' when ' to ' whenever,' sustained by the best

20 And as they passed by in the morning, they saw the
21 fig tree withered away from the roots. And Peter
  calling to remembrance saith unto him, Rabbi, behold,
22 the fig tree which thou cursedst is withered away. And
  Jesus answering saith unto them, Have faith in God.

authorities, gives this more general sense. The reference is therefore, not to that particular evening, but to what happened several times during that week; comp. Luke 21: 37.—**Out of the city.** To, or near, Bethany, as the accounts suggest.—The marginal reading: 'they' (Rev. Vers.), is fairly supported, but seems to have arisen from a desire to make a more exact agreement with what follows.

Vers. 20-25. THE WITHERING OF THE FIG TREE.—Parallel passage: Matt. 21: 19-22. The cleansing of the temple and the cursing of the barren fig tree were closely connected. Matthew, in accordance with his habit and purpose, points out more emphatically the unbelief of the chief priests and scribes (whom the fig tree represented), by joining together the curse and the discovery of the effect. This is a miracle of punishment, both a parable and prophecy in action: a 'parable,' teaching that false professors will be judged; a 'prophecy' in its particular application to the Jews. (In the Old Testament the fig tree appears as a symbol of evil.) There is no evidence that this miracle affected private property.

Ver. 20. **Withered away from the roots.** The day before, the 'leaves' were visible 'afar off;' to-day (Tuesday), the blasting was complete. Our verse does not say when this took place, but when they 'saw' it. Matthew says that it took place 'immediately.'

Ver. 21. **Peter.** Mark is more definite here than Matthew.—**Calling to remembrance.** Peter himself probably informed Mark of the circumstance. This minute detail, implying an interval, confirms the view that Mark gives the more exact account.—**Which thou cursedst.** The language of Peter; yet our Lord's act was a curse, *i. e.*, a judicial word and act of condemnation (comp. Matt. 21: 19). That it was judicial and just, not passionate and wanton, is evident not only from the character of our Lord, but from the lessons He connects with it. Mark, who inserts Peter's language, which might be misunderstood, alone tells us about forgiving (ver. 25). The application to the Jewish people is unmistakable. Both the actual desolation of the land and the judgment on the people are prefigured. The curse was for falsehood as well as barrenness. The true fruit of any people before the Incarnation would have been to own that they had no fruit, that without Christ they could do nothing. The Gentiles owned this; but the Jews boasted of their law, temple, worship, ceremonies, prerogatives, and good works, thus resembling the fig tree with pretensions, deceitful leaves without fruit. Their condemnation was, not that they were sick, but that, being sick, they counted themselves whole (condensed from Trench and Witsius).

Ver. 22. **Have faith in God**; the true object of faith. This miracle

23 Verily I say unto you, Whosoever shall say unto this mountain, Be thou taken up and cast into the sea; and shall not doubt in his heart, but shall believe that what he saith cometh to pass; he shall have it. 24 Therefore I say unto you, All things whatsoever ye pray and ask for, believe that ye ¹have received them, 25 and ye shall have them. And whensoever ye stand

---

¹ Am. Com. *receive.* Gr. *received.*

was a sign of the condemnation on Israel, and so understood by the Apostles. Still their views on the whole subject were indistinct. Our Lord thus answers a sense of weakness which the Apostles had in view of the glory and strength of the visible temple and its supporters. They are therefore directed to Almighty God as the object of their faith. The words have in themselves the widest application, but the next two verses show that the Apostles were directed to God as the source of power for themselves, miraculous power in their case, in view of their special mission. Such faith, in its full extent, could perhaps exist only in Christ Himself, but as it was approximated by the disciples their power would correspond.

Ver. 23. **Whosoever shall say unto this mountain.** Either the Mount of Olives, the size and exceeding difficulty being thus emphasized, or more probably referring to Mount Moriah, where stood the temple, the centre of the Jewish worship and the bulwark of the hypocritical hierarchy. The latter reference suggests that they in their faith should bring about the destruction of that theocracy. Punitive power is spoken of; hence the faith required forbids arbitrariness and also an unforgiving spirit. This promise has a spiritual application to all believers, but gives no encouragement to fanatical attempts at working miracles.—**What he saith cometh to pass.** The present tense of *certainty.*

Ver. 24. **Therefore**, connects the promise with the *faith of miracles*, and hence the *primary* application is to the Twelve.—**All things.** 'All' is emphatic.—**Pray and ask for.** The correct reading is more striking.—**Believe that ye have received.** See note of Am. Com. The original implies, that when you asked *you received*, God at once granted your request, so that the answer comes before the fulfilment, which is spoken of as future: **ye shall have them**, lit., 'it shall be to you.' The Rev. Ver. seeks to reproduce the striking form of the original; but it is needlessly harsh. When applied to Christians in general, the promise implies agreement with the will of God, thus excluding its abuse. Christ defines believing and effective prayer to be prayer in His name (John 14: 13; 15: 16; 16: 24.)

Ver. 25. **When ye stand praying.** A common and proper posture in prayer (comp. Luke 18: 13).—**Forgive if ye have aught**

praying, forgive, if ye have aught against any one; that your Father also which is in heaven may forgive you your trespasses.¹

27 And they come again to Jerusalem: and as he was walking in the temple, there come to him the chief 28 priests, and the scribes, and the elders; and they said unto him, By what authority doest thou these things? or who gave thee this authority to do these things?

¹ Many ancient authorities add ver. 26 *But if ye do not forgive, neither will your Father which is in heaven forgive your trespasses.*

against any one. Comp. Matt. 5: 23, where the converse is presented: 'thy brother hath aught against thee,' and Matt. 6: 14, etc. That such sayings should be repeated almost word for word, is not at all strange. A forgiving temper is necessary for them in working miracles, as well as faith and believing prayer; their faith and the power it wields should never be used in the service of hate. A caution against passing judicial condemnation on the evil and unfruitful, as He had just done, even though their faith should be strong enough, to effect like results (Matt. 21: 21; 'ye shall not only do this which is done to the fig tree,' etc.). The best authorities omit ver. 26, which was probably inserted here from Matt. 6: 15.

Vers. 27–33. The First Assault of the Rulers; the Counter Question about John the Baptist.—Parallel passages: Matt. 21: 23–27; Luke 20: 1–8.—Time. Tuesday, in the temple, after the discourse about the fig tree. The events recorded in chap. 12 took place on the same day; the discourse in chap. 13 was delivered in the evening as our Lord returned from Jerusalem to Bethany (on the Mount of Olives).— Matthew is much fuller, devoting nearly five chapters (21: 20—25: 46) to his account of this busy day. In telling of this assault, the accounts agree closely; Matthew alone inserts the parable of the Two Sons.

Ver. 27. **Again into Jerusalem.** Mark is more particular here. —**Walking in the temple.** 'As if at home, or in His Father's house' (J. A. Alexander); possibly to see if the profanation had been renewed, but according to Matthew: 'as He was teaching' (so Luke); so that He seems to have taught as He walked, which was not at all singular.—**The chief priests,** etc. Mark and Luke mention all three classes of the Sanhedrin; perhaps a formal delegation had been sent to oppose Him.

Ver. 28. **By what authority doest thou these things?** Referring both to His teaching there, and to His cleansing of the temple on the previous day. They were the proper persons to challenge His authority.—**And who gave thee,** etc. 'Even if you assume to be a prophet, who sent you?' A hint at the old charge of Satanic power. Mark, with his fondness for solemn repetitions, adds to the second question: **to do these things.** This implies that the only author-

29 And Jesus said unto them, I will ask of you one
¹question, and answer me, and I will tell you by what
30 authority I do these things. The baptism of John,
31 was it from heaven, or from men? answer me. And
they reasoned with themselves, saying, If we shall say,
From heaven; he will say, Why then did ye not be-
32 lieve him? ²But should we say, From men—they
feared the people: ³for all verily held John to be a
33 prophet. And they answered Jesus and say, We
know not. And Jesus saith unto them, Neither tell
I you by what authority I do these things.

¹ Gr. *word.*
² Or, *But shall we say, From men?*   ³ Or, *for all held John to be a prophet indeed.*

ity which could justify such acts was one given for this *purpose*. Their challenge thus becomes even more definite.

Ver. 29. **I will ask,** etc. Our Lord places His authority and that of John together. If they were incompetent to decide in the one case, they were in the other. The opportunity to decide aright was given them; but they refused it.

Ver. 30. **The baptism of John.** As representing his whole ministry.—**Answer me.** Peculiar to Mark, bringing out yet more decidedly His challenge of their *moral competency*, to decide as to His authority. The tone is peremptory, implying confidence of victory in this encounter.

Ver. 31. **And they reasoned,** consulted, so as to agree upon the answer.

Ver. 32. **But should we say, From men**—Matthew carries out the reasoning of the rulers; but Mark puts the second part of their pondering in the form of a question, as indicated in the margin of the Rev. Vers. ('shall we say, From men'?)—then abruptly answers in his own words (not theirs): **they feared the people: for all verily held John to be a prophet.** This rendering is due to the order in the correct Greek text; but the marginal rendering has much to recommend it. Luke tells that the fear of being stoned entered into the thoughts of the rulers. Demagogues usually fear the people.

Ver. 33. **We know not.** A falsehood; as vers. 31, 32, show.—**Neither tell I you,** etc. Christ answers their thought: we *will* not tell. This refusal is similar to that made when a sign from heaven was demanded (chap. 12: 38 sq.). The answer assumes their proven and confessed incompetency to decide on the authority of a prophet, and consequently His superiority to their questioning. Their opposition was naturally increased by this defeat.

12: 1 And he began to speak unto them in parables. A man planted a vineyard, and set a hedge about it, and digged a pit for the winepress, and built a tower, and let it out to husbandmen, and went into another

Chap. XII: 1-12. THE PARABLE OF THE WICKED HUSBANDMEN.—Parallel passages: Matt. 21: 33-46; Luke 20: 9-19.

Ver. 1. **And he began to speak unto them in parables.** A series of parables was spoken. Matthew records three; Mark and Luke preserve the principal one only. Comp. the emphatic language of Luke (20: 9): 'this parable;' and the words: 'Hear another parable' (Matt. 21: 33). All three accounts show that the parable was spoken in the presence of the people, but directly to the parties who had assailed Him ('to them'), and 'against them' (ver. 12), much embittered as they were, by the result of their attack. This parable points out the crime to which their enmity was leading them, though still spoken in love.—**A man planted a vineyard**; the most valuable plantation, but requiring the most constant labor and care; an apt figure of the theocracy (Is. 5: 1-7, 3: 14; Cant. 2: 15), here representing the Jewish people, as the Old Testament kingdom of God. A secondary application to the external Church in later times is required by ver. 9, where the vineyard is represented as passing over from the husbandmen to others.—**Set a hedge about it.** Probably a hedge of thorns, possibly a wall. God had separated His people from other nations, and guarded them from heathen influences, by the law (comp. Eph. 2: 14) and by external marks of distinction. God's special proprietorship and care are plainly seen.—**A pit for the wine-press.** A verbal variation from Matthew's account: 'digged a wine-press in it.' The 'pit' was a receptacle into which the juice flowed, and where it was kept cool; the 'wine-press,' the place where the grapes were trodden out. This seems to be added merely to complete the description. Some suppose it represents the altar of the Old Testament economy, others the prophetic institution.—**Built a tower.** For the watchman who guarded the vineyard against depredations. In the time of the vintage, used for recreation, no doubt, as in European countries. Such towers are still common in the East, and are of considerable height. A shed or scaffold sometimes served the same purpose. This represents the provision made by God for the protection and prosperity of His people, especially the Old Testament Church.—**Let it out to husbandmen**; probably for a part of the fruit, as is indicated by comparing Matt. 21: 34 ('his fruits') with ver. 2 ('of the fruits, of the vineyard'). It has pleased God that in His kingdom of *grace* laborers should receive a reward. 'of grace' (comp. 1 Cor. 3: 8; 2 Tim. 2: 6). The 'husbandmen' represent the rulers of the Jews (Matt. 21: 45), but the people as individuals may be included. The vineyard is the people as a chosen nation.—**And went into another country**, not, 'far country,' there being no reference to distance.

2 country. And at the season he sent to the husbandmen a ¹ servant, that he might receive from the hus-
3 bandmen of the fruits of the vineyard. And they
took him, and beat him, and sent him¹ away empty.
4 And again he sent unto them another servant; and
him they wounded in the head, and handled shame-
5 fully. And he sent another; and him they killed:
and many others; beating some, and killing some.
6 He had yet one, a beloved son: he sent him last unto

¹ Gr. *bond-servant.*

The peculiar presence of God, necessary at the institution of the Theocracy (Mount Sinai, etc.), ceased, though His spiritual care did not. A period of human development followed. The same is true, in a secondary application, of the Church since the Apostolic times. Luke adds: 'for a long time,' and these developments require time.

Ver. 2. **And at the season.** Probably no definite time is here represented. God expects fruit after such careful preparation; His people, especially those in official stations, are responsible for the trust committed to them.—**He sent a servant.** The servants represent the prophets of the Old Testament, calling for the fruits of righteousness from the Jewish people.

Ver. 3. The description of the maltreatment of the servants differs in all three accounts, showing that no special interpretation is to be given to the different sendings. In general, however, this treatment points to the persecution of the prophets (Elijah, Jeremiah, Isaiah): comp. Neh. 9: 26; Matt. 23: 29-31, 34, 37; 1 Thess. 2: 15; Heb. 11: 36-38, Rev. 16: 6; 18, 24. God's messengers in later times have often suffered at the hands of the official personages in the external Church.

Ver. 4. **Again,** etc. The second sending probably does not refer to any definite time, but sets forth God's long-suffering.—**Him they wounded in the head.** The servants are represented as not being allowed even to enter the vineyard; the first one was stoned at a distance, with the purpose of killing. The gradation is: beating, trying to kill, actually killing.

Ver. 5. **Him they killed.** Here the climax is the killing of a servant, in Matthew the stoning. The former respects the actual suffering of the servants, the latter the hostility of the husbandmen. The close of the verse is peculiar to Mark, and is in his characteristic manner.

Ver. 6. **He had yet one, a beloved son.** Mark's account is graphic and touching here.—**He sent him last unto them.** 'Last' is peculiar to Mark, while Luke represents the man as asking, 'What shall I do?' etc. The sending of 'His son,' whose superiority to the

7 them, saying, They will reverence my son. But those husbandmen said among themselves, This is the heir; come, let us kill him, and the inheritance shall be 8 ours. And they took him, and killed him, and cast 9 him forth out of the vineyard. What therefore will the lord of the vineyard do? he will come and destroy the husbandmen, and will give the vineyard unto

prophets is so distinctly marked, is the last and crowning act of God's mercy; to reject Him was therefore to fill up the measure of human sin and guilt. 'The Son appears here, not in His character of Redeemer, but in that of a preacher—a messenger demanding the fruits of the vineyard' (Alford). Hence this is the real answer to their challenge of His authority (chap. 11 : 28).—**They will reverence my son.** This implies that God is not willing that any should perish (2 Pet. 3 : 9).

Ver. 7. **This is the heir.** 'Heir' in virtue of His human nature, Heb. 1 : 1, 2.—**The inheritance shall be ours.** An expression of folly (in addition to the wicked resolve), since it implied that the death of the heir would permit them to hold the possession, while the householder lived. This assumes an unwilling conviction of the Messiahship of Jesus, on the part of the rulers. Up to this point, the parable was History; here it becomes Prophecy. In the attempt to maintain their own authority, which He had challenged, by putting Him to death, they foolishly defied God. Some of them might have thought, if we try to kill Him, He will save Himself, if He is the Messiah; but this prophetic word should have banished that thought.

Ver. 8. **Killed him, and cast him forth out of the vineyard.** Matthew and Luke invert the order. This variation is perhaps a caution against interpreting the details of the parable too closely. Our Lord here recognizes the fixed purpose of the rulers to kill Him. Yet there is still love in the warning. The casting forth refers either to the excommunication which preceded death, or to the crucifixion outside the gates of Jerusalem; perhaps to both, the latter being a result of the former.

Ver. 9. **What therefore will the Lord,** etc. The question is asked that they may be warned and condemned out of their own mouth. —**He will come and destroy.** The full answer of the hearers is given by Matthew. Here the substance of the answer is given, not as coming from them, but as spoken by our Lord Himself.—**And will give the vineyard to others.** The transfer of the kingdom of God to the Gentiles is undoubtedly predicted; comp. the language of the rulers (Matt. 21 : 41). The destruction of the husbandmen points to the destruction of Jerusalem, which is therefore the coming of the Lord of the vineyard. In that case the heir who was killed becomes Himself 'the lord of the vineyard;' comp. what follows with Peter's

10 others. Have ye not read even this scripture;
   The stone which the builders rejected,
   The same was made the head of the corner:
11 This was from the Lord,
   And it is marvellous in our eyes?
12 And they sought to lay hold on him; and they feared the multitude; for they perceived that he spake the parable against them: and they left him, and went away.

citation of the same passage shortly after the day of Pentecost (Acts 3 : 10).

Ver. 10. **Have ye not read even this scripture?** The form of Mark is vivacious.—**The stone,** etc. From Ps. 118 : 22. The 'Hosannas' at our Lord's entry to Jerusalem were taken from the same Psalm. The original reference to the passage is doubtful, whether to David or to Zerubbabel (Zech. 3 : 8, 9 : 4 : 7); but it is properly applied to the Messiah. Comp. Is. 28 : 16, which Peter cites in connection with it (1 Pet. 2: 6, 7; comp. Rom. 9 : 33).—**The builders rejected.** The rulers of the Jews ('the husbandmen'), whose duty it was to build up the spiritual temple, now addressed in rebuke and warning.— **The head of the corner.** The most important foundation stone, joining two walls. A reference to the union of Jews and Gentiles in Christ (as in Eph. 2 : 19-22) may be included; but the main thought is, that the Messiah, even if rejected by the 'builders,' should become the corner-stone of the real temple of God. This involves the important idea that the 'builders' would be themselves rejected; the parable left the Son dead outside of the vineyard; this citation, representing Him as victor and avenger, points to the Resurrection of Christ.

Ver. 11. **This** (head of the corner) **was from the Lord,** etc. 'This' must grammatically refer either to 'head' or 'corner.' Others understand it as 'this thing,' this exaltation of the despised one. Both Matthew and Luke add comments of our Lord.

Ver. 12. **And they sought to lay hands on him.** The three accounts supplement each other here. The purpose to seize Him is plainly stated in all. Mark shows that it was a continued effort (literally 'they were seeking'); while Luke tells that they would have done so on the spot, had they not been afraid of the people.—**For they perceived,** etc. Matthew gives the more general reason for this fear: 'because they held him as a prophet.' Their desire to seize Him was increased by this parable, but their fear of the people was also increased, since they (*i. e.*, the rulers) perceived **that he spake the parable against them,** and in the presence of the people (Luke 20 : 9), so that they felt themselves convicted before the people. Conscience made them cowards.

13 And they send unto him certain of the Pharisees and of the Herodians, that they might catch him in
14 talk. And when they were come, they say unto him, ¹Master, we know that thou art true, and carest not for any one: for thou regardest not the person of men, but of a truth teachest the way of God: Is it lawful to give tribute unto Cæsar, or not? Shall we give, or

¹ Or, *Teacher.*

Ver. 13–17. THE INSIDIOUS QUESTION ABOUT TRIBUTE TO CÆSAR.—Parallel passages: Matt. 22: 15–22; Luke 20: 19–26. Matthew inserts before this assault another parable ('the marriage of the king's son'), which was also a warning to the Pharisees and rulers. Three attacks are then made. First, the defeated and embittered Pharisees send the Herodians to ensnare our Lord with a political question concerning tribute to Cæsar. The reply astonishes them. The narrative of Mark is graphic, but presents no peculiar details.

Ver. 13. **They send unto him.** Implying deliberate stratagem. —**Herodians.** A political party supporting the Roman rule. These two classes were antagonistic, yet they united in opposition to Christ. Luke (20: 20) is more detailed in his account, calling the deputation 'spies' of the rulers. This part was probably assigned to 'their disciples' (Matthew) as young and unknown persons, who were accompanied by the Herodians.—**To catch him in talk**, lit., 'by word;' to lay hold of Him by means of their word as a snare. Some word of His, in answer to their questions, would be laid hold of, but the figure requires a reference to *their* discourse. The dispute about tribute, however natural between these two classes, was made for the occasion.

Ver. 14. **Master, we know,** etc. This was true, but not truthfully spoken. 'The devil never lies so foully as when he speaks the truth.'—**And carest not for any one.** His independence and security had just been demonstrated, but their acknowledgment of these peculiarities was to tempt Him: as if one party would say, You do not care for the Roman authorities; the other, You do not care for the authority of the Pharisees and Jewish rulers.—**Thou regardest not the person of men.** Comp. Lev. 19: 15; Jude 16; Deut. 16: 19; 2 Sam. 14: 14; Acts 10: 34; James 2: 1–3, 9; 1 Pet. 1: 17.— **Of a truth.** The Rev. Ver. restores the variation between Matthew and the other two Evangelists, who agree here.—**Teachest the way of God,** *i. e.*, the true doctrine. This was certainly hypocritical, for both the Pharisees and Herod condemned this Teacher of the truth.— **Is it lawful.** According to Jewish law.—**Tribute,** the poll-tax which had been levied since Judea became directly subject to Rome. —**Cæsar,** the Roman Emperor, at that time, Tiberius. To say Yes, would alienate the people, who hated the Roman yoke; to say No, would give good ground for accusing Him to the Roman authori-

15 shall we not give? But he, knowing their hypocrisy, said unto them, Why tempt ye me? bring me a ¹penny, 16 that I may see it. And they brought it. And he saith unto them, Whose is this image and superscrip- 17 tion? And they said unto him, Cæsar's. And Jesus said unto them, Render unto Cæsar the things that are

¹ The word in the Greek denotes a coin worth about eight pence halfpenny; *denarius*, Am. Com.

ties. Themselves 'regarding the person of men,' the Pharisees did not avow their own belief, that it was not lawful. Their motive now was not their usual hostility to Rome, but hatred of Christ. They afterwards actually accused Him of forbidding to pay tribute (Luke 23: 2), and the chief priests, despite their Pharisaism, from the same hatred of Him, cried out: 'We have no king but Cæsar' (John 19: 15).—**Shall we give**, etc. This repetition occurs in Mark only.

Ver. 15. **Their hypocrisy.** Matthew: 'wickedness'; Luke: 'craftiness.' This hypocrisy was shown both in their flattering address and in their cunning question (ver. 14). Men may rightly carry their religious convictions into politics, and religious questions may become political ones; but when this is the case hypocrisy usually flourishes.— **Bring me a penny (denarius)**: the Roman coin (Matthew: 'tribute money'). The whole point of the occurrence turns on the fact that it was a *Roman* coin.—**That I may see it.** Peculiar to Mark.

Ver. 16. **Whose is this image.** The likeness of the ruler at the date of the coin.—**Superscription.** The name, etc., on the coin.— **Cæsar's.** Imperial money was current among them. 'Wherever any king's money is current, there that king is lord;' is reported as a Rabbinical saying. The standard currency is an indication or symbol of the civil authority; the right to coin has usually implied the right to exact tribute.

Ver. 17. **Render unto Cæsar**, etc. Render to 'the powers that be,' the service due them. Comp. Rom. 13: 1-7. Obedience to this precept would have spared Jerusalem, but the subtlest snare they devised for our Lord became their own destruction.—**Unto God the things that are God's.** Religious duties are to be rendered to God. Possibly a hint that in denying Him, they denied the honor due to God, and also a reference to man as bearing the image of God, so that political and religious duties are distinguished, but not divided. The Jews themselves were under tribute to Cæsar, because they had not rendered God His dues.—**They marvelled greatly at him.** The original is stronger than in the parallel passages. It also intimates that they continued to do so. The other accounts are fuller as to the effect of His answer. These young Pharisees (Matthew) and Herodians with feigned scruples of conscience, the flower of the youth of Jerusalem, scarcely expected such a blow from a Galilean—and their

Cæsar's, and unto God the things that are God's. And they marvelled greatly at him.

18 And there come unto him Sadducees, which say that there is no resurrection; and they asked him, saying,

19 ¹ Master, Moses wrote unto us, If a man's brother die, and leave a wife behind him, and leave no child, that his brother should take his wife, and raise up seed

¹ Or, *Teacher.*

astonishment was more than momentary. No wonder: the answer of Christ is the wisest ever given to an entangling question, and contains in principle the solution of the great problem of Church and State, or the relation of the spiritual and secular power. Real religion makes men better citizens, since it enjoins a religious fulfilment of political obligations. The few exceptional cases that arise are to be decided by the principle of Acts 5: 29. Under a free government, this religious fulfilment of political duties is essential to preserve the State against anarchy. Both Church and State are of Divine origin and authority: the one for the temporal, the other for the eternal welfare of men. They ought to be kept distinct and independent in their respective spheres, without mixture and confusion, and yet without antagonism, but rather in friendly relation in view of their common Divine origin, and their common end and completion in 'the kingdom of glory' where God shall be all in all.

Vers. 18-27. SECOND ASSAULT: THE QUESTION CONCERNING THE RESURRECTION.—Parallel passages: Matt. 22: 23-33; Luke 22: 27-40. Luke is fuller, especially in vers. 34-36. The description of the successive marriages is graphic, though not more so than Luke's. The Sadducees are mentioned only here, in this Gospel. They were so named from Zadok, the supposed founder of the sect, and represented the tendency to scepticism and rationalism, over against the strict Pharisees. They either rejected parts of the Scriptures, or explained them away. They were worldly, flippant, and scoffing, as indicated in this sneering attack.

Ver. 18. **There is no resurrection.** Comp. Acts 23: 8, where their views are shown to include a denial of the immortality of the soul as well as of the resurrection of the body. They correspond to the Skeptics and Epicureans among the Greek philosophers.

Ver. 19. **And they asked him.** A scoffing question, in ridicule of the doctrine and of Christ Himself. This sneering spirit is prominent in Sadducees of every age. Afterwards they became earnest enough. It is possible they hoped for an answer that might show sympathy with them. Errorists often think that opposition to their opponents is agreement with them. But truth must always oppose two contrary errors. In this case, first the Pharisees, then their antagonists the Sadducees.—**Moses wrote.** Deut. 25: 5, freely quoted;

20 unto his brother. There were seven brethren: and
21 the first took a wife, and dying left no seed; and the second took her, and died, leaving no seed behind him;
22 and the third likewise: and the seven left no seed.
23 Last of all the woman also died. In the resurrection whose wife shall she be of them? for the seven had
24 her to wife. Jesus said unto them, Is it not for this cause that ye err, that ye know not the scriptures, nor
25 the power of God? For when they shall rise from

comp. the regulations added in that chapter. Such a marriage was called a Levirate marriage. The object was to preserve families, a matter of great importance in the Jewish economy.—**Seed to his brother.** The first-born son would be registered as the son of the dead brother.

Ver. 20. **There were.** Probably a purely fictitious case, though in Matthew 'with us' is added.

Ver. 23. **In the resurrection,** *i. e.*, in the state after the resurrection.—**Whose wife shall she be of them?** The point of the entangling question is now evident. They had quoted the law of Moses and then given an example of obedience to it, to prove the absurdity of the doctrine of the resurrection. Our Lord at once rebukes and denies their false assumption in regard to human relations in the future state.

Ver. 24. The form here given is peculiar to Mark:—**Is it not for this cause that ye err**, etc., which is answered by the positive statement: 'ye greatly err' (ver. 27).—**That ye know not the scriptures.** 'In that ye do not understand the Scriptures,' *i. e.*, the Old Testament, which they professed to hold free from tradition. The Scriptures plainly imply the resurrection.—**Nor the power of God.** His power to raise the dead. Modern Sadduceism usually knows the meaning of the Scriptures, but denies 'the power of God,' in this as in many other things.

Ver. 25. **For when they shall rise from the dead;** *i. e.*, at the resurrection.—**Neither marry,** spoken of the man; **nor are given in marriage,** of the woman, since the father gave away the bride in marriage. This relation is not to be reëstablished in the state after the resurrection, because those raised up **are as angels in heaven.** Comp. especially the fuller answer in Luke 20: 35, 36, where the fact of immortality is brought out; as there is no death in that state there will also be no birth. Personal intercourse doubtless remains, but the Jews looked at marriage more in its physical relations. Equality with angels in mode of existence is affirmed, but the redeemed are distinguished from them. This answer opposes another error of the Sadducees, a denial of the existence of angels.

the dead, they neither marry, nor are given in marriage; but are as angels in heaven. But as touching the dead, that they are raised; have ye not read in the book of Moses, in *the place concerning* the Bush, how God spake unto him, saying, I *am* the God of Abraham, and the God of Isaac, and the God of Jacob? 27 He is not the God of the dead, but of the living: ye do greatly err.

Ver. 26. **But as touching the dead.** Proof that the doctrine was implied in the writings of Moses. Luke 20: 37 is against the view that our Lord only makes an authoritative statement without really basing His proof on the passage quoted.—**In the book of Moses, in the place concerning the Bush**; lit., 'in the bush.' It can scarcely mean, when Moses was at the bush, or, when God spake at the bush. Christ assumes the truth of the book of Exodus. The Sadducees are said to have doubted the authority of the prophetical books. The proof is drawn from the Pentateuch, which they acknowledged.— **I am the God of Abraham**, etc. Exod. 3: 6. Spoken to Moses from the burning bush. The name given by Jehovah to Himself, setting forth His self-existence and eternity (Exod. 3: 14, 15), supports the doctrine of our immortality, body and soul. God continues ('I am,' not, 'I was') in covenant relation to Abraham, Isaac, and Jacob ('the God of Abraham,' etc.). As these patriarchs had in their bodies the sign of this covenant, the body is included in whatever promise is involved.

Ver. 27. **God is not the God of the dead, but of the living.** This saying, added by our Lord, may be thus expanded: This personal, living God is the God of living persons. He calls Himself the continuing covenant God of Abraham, Isaac, and Jacob, therefore the statement of Moses involves the truth, that after their death Abraham, Isaac, and Jacob are still living. The argument derived from this designation of God in favor of the immortality of the soul, against the Sadducees who denied it, reveals the marvelous insight of our Lord into the deepest meaning of the Scriptures. The personal ever-living God calls Himself the God—not of the dead which would be dishonoring—but of those who live in perpetual communion with Him, to whom He has communicated His own immortality. The Bible treats man as a unit, and while it implies the separation of body and soul after death until the resurrection, plainly intimates that the blessedness of the future state will be incomplete until body and soul are reunited (comp. especially Rom. 8: 11, 23). Only then will we be like Christ, who has a glorified body (Phil. 3: 21, etc.). The effect of our Lord's words, which is added at this point by Matthew and Luke, is narrated by Mark in ver. 34.

28 And one of the scribes came, and heard them questioning together, and knowing that he had answered them well, asked him, What commandment is the first 29 of all? Jesus answered, The first is, Hear, O Israel; 30 ¹The Lord our God, the Lord is one: and thou shalt love the Lord thy God ²with all thy heart, and ²with all thy soul, and ²with all thy mind, and ²with all thy

¹ Or, *The Lord is our God; the Lord is one*.   ² Gr. *from*.

Vers. 28-34. THIRD ASSAULT; QUESTION RESPECTING THE GREAT COMMANDMENT.—Parallel passage: Matt. 22: 34-40. Comp. Luke 20: 39. Matthew states that this question was put, 'tempting' (or, 'trying,' *i. e.*, putting to proof) our Lord. The scribe may have been chosen by the Pharisees as their unconscious tool, because of his candor. The question was probably designed to draw forth in response the first commandment: 'Thou shalt have no other gods before me,' so that this might be used against His claim to be the Son of God. This design of the hostile Pharisees was defeated by His citing the second table of the law (ver. 31) as well as the first. They expected by His answer, either to disprove His Messiahship, or to find in His own words a basis for the charge of blasphemy in making Himself the Son of God. This charge they did bring forward in the council (chap. 14: 61-64), and before Pilate (John 19: 7), and it was probably in their thoughts when they put this question a few days before.

Ver. 28. **Knowing that he had answered them well.** This scribe no doubt rejoiced in the defeat of the Sadducees, but was also really pleased with our Lord's answers. They accorded with his intellectual convictions, perhaps with his moral tendencies, and he probably desired further instruction.—**What commandment is the first of all?** The fearful belittling tendencies of Pharisaical legalism may be inferred from the following statement: 'The Jews enumerated six hundred and thirteen ordinances; three hundred and sixty-five prohibitions, according to the days of the year; two hundred and twenty-eight commandments, according to the parts of the body. The Pharisees distinguished between lesser and greater commandments' (Braune). The phrase may mean: 'first of all things,' however.

Ver. 29. **Hear, O Israel; the Lord our God, the Lord is one.** This is the form of the LXX. (Deut. 6: 4), here quoted more fully than in Matthew. Notice the briefer reading of the first part of the verse, as indicated in the Rev. Vers.

Ver. 30. **Thou shalt love the Lord thy God**, etc. Quoted from the LXX. (Deut. 6: 6).—**With all thy heart**, literally, 'from' (Matthew: 'in'). The whole is a demand for supreme affection. The distinctions of Hebrew psychology differ from those of modern times; but if we distinguish between the phrases, the first refers to 'the whole energy of the reason and the intellect;' **soul**, 'the whole energy of sentiment and passion;' **mind**, 'the whole energy of thought and will in its manifestation;' **strength** (peculiar to Mark) probably

31 strength. The second is this, Thou shalt love thy neighbour as thyself. There is none other command-
32 ment greater than these. And the scribe said unto him, Of a truth, ¹Master, thou hast well said that he
33 is one; and there is none other but he: and to love

¹ Or, *Teacher.*

refers to moral energy. (The LXX. employs a different word of similar import.) This 'unqualified surrender of our whole being to God' is to be the aim of our strivings after holiness. God's essential perfections and His manifested grace alike demand this.

Ver. 31. **The second is this.** The common text here has been conformed to Matthew: 'And a second like unto it is this.'—**Thou shalt love thy neighbour as thyself.** From Lev. 19: 18. 'Man ought to love his neighbor, 1, not as he *does* love himself, but as he *ought* to love himself; 2, not in the same degree, but after the same manner, *i. e.*, freely and readily, sincerely and unfeignedly, tenderly and compassionately, constantly and perseveringly' (W. Burkitt). Cases arise where man ought to love his neighbor more than his life, physical life, and has done so, sacrificing it for his fellows, his country, and the church, in imitation of the example of Christ and the martyrs.—**There is none other commandment greater than these.** The unity of the moral law prevents any discrimination between its precepts: it is *one* law of love, the hinge (Matt. 22: 40) of the whole Old Testament revelation. There can be none greater. No one can love God without loving his fellow-men, and no one can truly love man without loving God. The former is the source of the latter. Hence the first table (the first five commandments) enjoins love to God; the second table (the last five commandments), love to our neighbor. Pharisaism puts the second in a lower place, thinking that seeming service of God can atone for want of charity to men. But supreme love to God is to manifest itself in love to men. Alike binding, the two are correspondent, not contradictory. The mistake of humanitarianism is making the 'second' 'the first' commandment.

Ver. 32. **Of a truth, Master, thou hast well said.** Without doubt the scribe spoke candidly; our Lord's words may have awakened in him a spiritual apprehension of the law. He represents a large class, outside the kingdom, in a more hopeful condition than Pharisees in the visible church; but he had not yet taken the decisive step.—**That he is one; and there is none other but he.** The form is impressive.

Ver. 33. **With all the understanding.** The scribe substitutes 'understanding' for 'mind,' which seems to express the same thought less abstractly. Mark preserves the answer in full.—**Is much more than.** Better, 'more acceptable to God, and more useful to the worshipper.'—**All whole burnt offerings and sacrifices.** 'Burnt

him with all the heart, and with all the understanding, and with all the strength, and to love his neighbour as himself, is much more than all whole burnt offerings
34 and sacrifices. And when Jesus saw that he answered discreetly, he said unto him, Thou art not far from the kingdom of God. And no man after that durst ask him any question.
35 And Jesus answered and said, as he taught in the temple, How say the scribes that the Christ is the son

offerings,' *i. e.*, those commanded in the law. Such things took up the whole attention of legalists. It was a bold saying in those times and in that place. Christ's atoning sacrifice is the centre of the gospel, but he who has a correct theory on this subject, without being led to the love here spoken of, is but a Pharisee at heart, below the standard of this man.

Ver. 34. **Discreetly.** Understandingly, intelligently, wisely; more than 'discreetly,' in the more modern sense.—**Thou art not far from the kingdom of God.** Intellectually on the right road, nearer to the kingdom than a mere formalist could be, recognizing the spirituality of the law, perhaps conscious of the folly of self-righteousness; but, though standing as it were at the door, still outside.—'While the worst of His opponents were unable to convict Him of an error, or betray Him into a mistake, the best of them, when brought into direct communication with Him on the most important subjects, found themselves almost in the position of His own disciples' (J. A. Alexander). This man, who asked a theological question, seems to have been in a more hopeful condition than the lawyer and the young ruler who asked what they should do to inherit eternal life (comp. chap. 10: 17-22 and Luke 10: 25-37). The three must not be confounded.—**And no man after that durst ask him any question.** A natural effect of the previous experiments. No further question is put *to* Him, but He asks one which they cannot answer. Matthew however, gives more prominence to the fact that no one 'was able to answer Him a word,' and so puts this statement after the victorious question of our Lord. Such independent testimony is the most valuable, especially here where our Lord asks a question respecting *His own Person*, in some respects the central question of Christianity.

Vers. 35-37. THE VICTORIOUS QUESTION OF OUR LORD RESPECTING HIS OWN PERSON. —Parallel passages: Matt. 22: 41-46; Luke 20: 41-44. The victory was won on the great theological battle ground—the doctrine of the Person of Christ, the central fact of Christianity.

Ver. 35. **Answered.** The whole controversy (vers. 13-37) is regarded as one; and this is our Lord's reply to their attempts to

36 of David? David himself said in the Holy Spirit,
  The Lord said unto my Lord,
  Sit thou on my right hand,
  Till I make thine enemies ¹the footstool of thy feet.
37 David himself calleth him Lord; and whence is he his son? And ²the common people heard him gladly.

¹ Some ancient authorities read *underneath thy feet*.   ² Or, *the great multitude*.

'catch him in talk.'—**As he taught** (lit., 'was teaching') **in the temple.** Of course on the same day. Matthew brings out the triumph over the Pharisees. Mark the impression on the people, in whose presence (ver. 37) the Pharisees were confounded. The account of the former is fuller and more accurate, as regards the opening of the discussion on this point.—**How say the scribes?** Matthew shows that the question was addressed to the Pharisees ('what think ye of the Christ?')—**That the Christ** (the Messiah) **is the son of David?** The 'scribes' were the acknowledged interpreters of the Old Testament. Our Lord would prove the insufficiency of their interpretation on a point which they rightly deemed of most importance. The title 'son of David' was frequently applied to the Messiah, but our Lord proved that it was an incomplete designation. On this one-sided view of the Messiah, as a descendant of David, the king and warrior, their political false hopes had been based. What they thought of Himself, He does not ask them. Since He has been abundantly proven to be 'the Christ,' the question comes to *us* in this form, as an all-important one. One answer only can be correct.

Ver. 36. **David himself said in the Holy Spirit.** Luke: 'in the book of Psalms.' The influence of the Holy Spirit upon David in penning the Psalms is assumed.—**The Lord** (Jehovah) **said unto my Lord.** From Ps. 110:1, entitled 'a Psalm of David,' probably written after the prophetic address of Nathan, 2 Sam. 7:12. ('My' is represented in the Hebrew by the little letter called 'jot' in Matt. 5:18.) It is quoted frequently in the New Testament, as referring to Christ. The Jews referred it to the Messiah, since no objection was raised at this point. 'My lord' implies superiority, not only to David himself, but to his own royal race and the people of Israel, or the inquiry would not cause perplexity.—**Sit thou on my right hand** (the place of honor and trust and power), **till I make thine enemies the footstool of thy feet** (until He is complete victor). This refers to an exaltation, exceeding any attainable by a mere man; and to a triumph beyond any political one. The latter thought opposes the false hopes of the Jews, while the whole passage shows the superhuman exaltation of the Messiah. (The marginal reading corresponds with the correct reading in Matt. 22:44.)

Ver. 37. **And whence.** From what source shall we seek an explanation of the fact that He is his Son? Or perhaps simply: 'how

38 And in his teaching he said, Beware of the scribes, which desire to walk in long robes, and *to have* saluta-

can He be his Son?' The solution is not given here, but plainly preached by the Apostles from the day of Pentecost: the Messiah was Son of David according to the flesh, yet the pre-existent eternal Son of God—the God-man (comp. Rom. 1: 3, 4). If the Pharisees were ignorant of this solution, it was their own fault, since the Old Testament plainly pointed to it. Probably they were not ignorant. (The words of Caiaphas, chap. 14: 61, indicate knowledge on this point.) Our Lord's claims involved this: He had been called the 'Son of David' (John 10: 24-38), and they afterwards accused Him of so doing. They at least knew what His solution was, and that He claimed to be both 'Son of David' and 'Lord.' They left Him. Pharisaical Judaism and Christ parted company forever at this point. Henceforth they sought to kill him by treachery.—**And the great multitude.** This multitude was made up of 'the common people,' since the upper classes were withdrawing; but that is not the prominent idea. A great multitude still listened to Him.—**Heard him gladly.** Lit., 'sweetly,' with relish, with pleasure. This was after He had virtually claimed to be the Messiah—David's Lord, as well as David's Son. See on Matt. 22: 45. Had He desired to establish a temporal kingdom, the multitude would now have followed Him. But hearing Christ with relish, is not necessarily accepting Him as a Saviour. Knowing all men (John 2: 24, 25), and faithful to His mission of Atoning Love, our Lord remains in the temple to deliver His fearful denunciation of the Pharisees (Matt. 23), briefly alluded to by Mark (vers. 38-40), pauses to praise a poor widow (vers. 41-44), and then withdraws from His foes and from the listening multitude. In the short interval before His foes seize Him, He devotes Himself to the instruction of those who should tell the story and meaning of His death to the world, and explain the mystery of David's Lord and Son, in announcing the crucified and risen Jesus as the incarnate God, able and willing to save all who believe in Him.

Vers. 38-40. DENUNCIATION OF THE SCRIBES. Parallel passages: Matt. 23: 1-39; Luke 20: 45-47. The accounts of Mark and Luke agree here very closely. Matthew, writing for Jewish Christians, gives a full report of this denunciatory discourse; but early Gentile readers only heeded a brief outline. This paragraph and the next one form a striking contrast. Comp. 'devour widows' houses' (ver. 41) and the 'poor widow' (ver. 42). Both expressions are peculiar to Mark and Luke (Matt. 23: 14 is omitted by the best authorities). Those who find our Lord's language here too severe forget that God has revealed Himself in Christ as Holy Love. This awful severity proves Christ's divine mission and character no less than His tender invitations to the sinner to come to Him. Indeed it is a part of His mercy, since it warns His sheep against the coming of the wolf, guards us against the Pharisaism of our own hearts, which is so quick to rise against Him who redeemed us.

Ver. 38. The phrase 'unto them' is properly omitted. The dis-

39 tions in the marketplaces, and chief seats in the synagogues, and chief places at feasts: they which devour widows' houses, ¹and for a pretence make long prayers; these shall receive greater condemnation.

41 And he sat down over against the treasury, and be-

¹ Or, *even while for a pretence they make.*

course was both to the multitude (ver. 39) and to His disciples (comp. Matt. and Luke).—**In his teaching**; implying that much more was said.—**Beware**, be on your guard against.—**The scribes.** Matthew: 'the scribes and the Pharisees.' Comp. Matt. 23: 2.—**Desire.** A description of the scribes as a body, not of a certain class among them. There were few to whom this description could not apply.—**To walk in long robes**, displaying their flowing robes as a sign of their official position. Desiring to display a sign of ecclesiastical dignity is here condemned. Monks have generally adopted 'long robes,' and too often the length of a clerical coat is the measure of the Pharisaical tendency among Protestants.—**Salutations in the market places.** The places of public resort, where their importance would be recognized. Salutations of courtesy and kindness in public places are certainly not forbidden.—**Chief seats in the synagogues.** The places nearest the reading desk, where the elders sat. Being in such places (at feasts, in synagogues or elsewhere) is not rebuked, but *loving* to be there. Pharisaism may now show itself in taking the lowest place, if this is done in a slavish obedience to the letter of the gospel.—**And chief places at feasts.** The places on the middle couch at the upper table (which joined the other two) were considered most honorable.

Ver. 40. This verse is substantially the same as Matt. 23: 14 (which is poorly supported in that Gospel) and identical with Luke 20: 44.—**Devour widows' houses**, *i. e.*, seize upon the property of the unprotected, here represented by a particular class.—**And for a pretence**, etc. The marginal rendering, 'even while,' expresses the sense better: 'they devour widows' houses, and that too while they are praying at great length.' The guilt was thus aggravated and **the greater condemnation** is threatened. There are many ways of swindling the defenceless, but to do it with pretended piety, is worst of all. Ecclesiastical officials may repeat this crime, by attaching to themselves the defenceless classes here represented by 'widows' with the design of obtaining control of their property. Pharisaism, in all ages and organizations, has encouraged this.

Vers. 41-44. THE WIDOW'S MITES.—Parallel passage: Luke 21: 1-4. Our Lord tarried in the temple to find an opportunity for praising one act of real religion amidst all the hypocrisy He had just denounced. (Reformers may find a lesson here.) In perfect quietude of spirit, not in haste nor anger, He finally forsook 'His own' who received Him not.

held how the multitude cast ¹money into the treasury:
42 and many that were rich cast in much. And there
came ²a poor widow, and she cast in two mites, which
43 make a farthing. And he called unto him his disciples, and said unto them, Verily I say unto you, This
poor widow cast in more than all they which are cast-
44 ing into the treasury: for they all did cast in of their
superfluity; but she of her want did cast in all that
she had, *even* all her living.

¹ Gr. *brass*. ² Gr. *one*.

Ver. 41. **And he sat down over against the treasury.** He did not leave at once, after predicting the desolation of the temple (Matt. 23: 38) but remained quietly sitting in the court of the women, opposite 'the Treasury.' This was the name given to thirteen brazen chests, called by the Rabbins 'trumpets,' probably from the shape of the mouths into which the money was cast. They were for various kinds of gifts. The reference here is probably to the place, or room (comp. John 8: 20), where these chests stood.—**And beheld**, or, 'was beholding.'—**Money.** Lit., 'brass,' copper-money, which probably formed the usual offering.—**Cast in much**, lit., 'were casting many things,' perhaps many pieces of copper, since in that form the gift would seem larger and make more noise. That Pharisaism could do this is certain; thus they would cause these 'trumpets' to sound before them.

Ver. 42. **And a poor widow.** 'One' (so the Greek) in contrast with the 'many' just spoken of, not without a suggestion of her loneliness. Possibly this widow was 'poor,' because her house had been 'devoured' (ver. 40).—**Two mites.** The 'mite' (lepton) was the smallest Jewish copper coin. The Greek name means 'fish-scale,' suggesting its diminutive size. Its value was about one tenth of an English penny, one fifth of a cent. She had two and gave both.—**A farthing.** Mark (not Luke) adds for his Roman readers an explanation, using a Greek word (taken from the Latin) meaning the fourth part, as our word 'farthing' does.

Ver. 43. **And he called unto him.** Peculiar to Mark. Our Lord directed their special attention to this act of the widow.—**More than all they which are casting into the treasury.** Not more than a specific number, but than the many who had given and were still giving. The reason follows.

Ver. 44. **For.** The worth of a gift is to be determined not by its intrinsic value, but *by what it costs* the giver. The measure of that cost is what is *left*, not what is given.—**Even all her living** (or, 'life'). All at her disposal for her present subsistence. She could not have owned much else, since she is said to be a 'poor widow.' She could

13 : 1 And as he went forth out of the temple, one of his disciples saith unto him, ¹Master, behold, what man-
2 ner of stones and what manner of buildings! And Jesus said unto him, Seest thou these great buildings? there shall not be left here one stone upon another, which shall not be thrown down.

¹ Or, *Teacher*.

not have hoped for 'glory of men' (Matt. 6: 2), but she received praise from *One* who spake as never man spake. We are here taught, not simply to give, but how to measure the cost of gifts. Since Christ alone can bless contributions for the extension of His kingdom, this incident shows that the success He has accorded has been on account of the gifts which involved self-denial, these being the only valuable ones in His sight.

Chap. XIII: 1, 2. THE PROPHECY OF THE DESTRUCTION OF THE TEMPLE.—Parallel passages: Matt. 24: 1, 2; Luke 21: 5, 6. As our Lord was finally leaving the temple, one of His disciples pointed out the magnificence of the various structures composing it. This brought out a prediction of its entire destruction.

Ver. 1. **Out of the temple,** *i. e.*, the exclusively Jewish part, inclosed from the court of the Gentiles. This was the final departure; He never returned, and henceforth the temple was virtually desolate. The Apostles returned, holding out mercy still; the last rejection recorded is that of Paul (Acts 21 : 27 sqq.), who was even accused of polluting it.—**One of his disciples.** Matthew: 'His disciples;' Luke is quite indefinite.—**What manner of stones and what manner of buildings!** Luke (21 : 5): 'How it was adorned with goodly stones and gifts.' His attention was called to all the structures in the inclosure (see note on chap. 11 : 11), especially the stones. The immense stones (some of them forty-five cubits long, five high, and six broad) could be best seen from the court of the Gentiles; so also the great number of outer structures, some of them still in process of erection. The latter fact gives additional point to the prediction. The disciples seemed almost to intercede for the temple He was leaving.

Ver. 2. **These great buildings.** Our Lord takes up the thought of His disciples, and prophesies the complete destruction of this great edifice.—**Verily I say unto you,** etc. This prophecy was uttered in a time of profound peace, when the possibility of the destruction of such a magnificent work of art and sanctuary of religion seemed very unlikely; but was literally fulfilled forty years afterwards; and that, too, in express violation of the orders of Titus, who wished to save it.

3 And as he sat on the mount of Olives over against the temple, Peter and James and John and Andrew
4 asked him privately, Tell us, when shall these things be? and what *shall be* the sign when these things are

Vers. 3–8. THE DISCOURSE ON THE MOUNT OF OLIVES: OPENING WARNING.—Parallel passages: Matt. 24: 3–8; Luke 21: 7–11. This discourse is recorded by three Evangelists (Matthew, Mark, and Luke). All the accounts correspond remarkably; that of Matthew is the fullest. Mark introduces a few thoughts not included there. It refers both *to the destruction of Jerusalem* and *to the second coming of Christ*, one prophecy respecting *two* analogous events, though all is not necessarily applicable to both. Reasons: 1. An exclusive reference to either the destruction of Jerusalem, or the second coming of Christ involves insuperable difficulties. 2. The disciples asked about both, joining them in time (comp. Matt. 24: 3 with ver. 4). The answer therefore refers to both, joining them in character, not necessarily in time. The disciples needed instruction on both points, for immediate and more remote guidance. 3. The preceding discourse in Matthew plainly points to the destruction of Jerusalem, but Matt. 25: and vers. 32–37 of this chapter, seem to apply exclusively to the Christian dispensation. Great care is necessary in deciding what refers to each of the two sets of events (or, how far the analogy holds good). The two interpretations probably run parallel as far as ver. 23, the judgment upon the Jewish Church being the predominant thought; after that (vers. 24–31) the Lord's second coming is prominent, until in the close of the chapter (vers. 32–37) it is exclusively treated of. Concerning the end of the world nothing definite as to time is made known (see ver. 36), and the part that Jerusalem will sustain is and must be unknown, since prophecy is rarely designed to enable us to foretell future events. On the minor divisions, see notes on the several paragraphs. The *occasion* and *circumstances* of delivery (vers. 1–4) are described most fully by Mark.

Ver. 3. **The Mount of Olives.** Opposite the temple. The siege of Jerusalem began from this place, and at the same season of the year. It was from the side of this mount, that our Lord two days before had prophesied the destruction of Jerusalem (Luke 19: 43, 44). —**Over against the temple.** A graphic stroke, peculiar to Mark. The summit of Olivet is directly opposite the temple, the city lying spread out like a map before one sitting there.—**Peter and James and John and Andrew**, the four fishermen first called and first named in all the lists of the Apostles, the confidential disciples, but only the three first were on the Mount of Transfiguration; 'Andrew' (the brother of Peter) is added to the more private company on this occasion.

Ver. 4. **When these things are all about to be accomplished.** In all three accounts 'the sign' is asked for. The full form of the question here given (especially the position of 'all') shows that they classed together the destruction of Jerusalem, the return of our Lord and the end of the world, as one great series of events, about which He had often spoken to them. 'These things' refer primarily to the destruction of the temple, but being Jews, they would not think

5 all about to be accomplished? And Jesus began to say unto them, Take heed that no man lead you astray.
6 Many shall come in my name, saying, I am *he*; and
7 shall lead many astray. And when ye shall hear of wars and rumours of wars, be not troubled: *these things* must needs come to pass; but the end is not yet.
8 For nation shall rise against nation, and kingdom

of the destruction of the holy city without a personal presence of the Messiah in its stead. As the two events were blended in their minds, they are not sharply distinguished in the answer.

Ver. 5. **Began to say.** Began His first explanation, which probably took a wider range than they had expected.—**Take heed.** The opening sentence is the same as in Matthew, but Mark repeats this word several times (vers. 9, 23, 33).—**That no man lead you astray.** The word usually rendered 'deceive' is a different one; that meaning 'lead astray' occurs in all three accounts, referring to practical error, the following of wrong leaders into wrong-doing. The admonition is prophetic, intimating the perplexity of the whole subject. A caution to Christians regarding specific teaching about these unfulfilled predictions.

Ver. 6. **Come in my name**; as the Messiah. The Messianic hopes of the Jews were at fever-heat, as the destruction of their holy city drew near; many enthusiasts appeared as seducers of the people, and awakened false expectations. It is not known that they claimed the authority of the Christian Messiah. The prophecy goes beyond this and intimates that Christians would be in danger of supposing some other person to be the Lord Himself. In latter times fanaticism among Christians has taken this direction, *e. g.*, the Anabaptists in the sixteenth century.—**Lead many astray.** The same word as in ver. 5. An overweening desire to understand this prophecy in its final application, combined with too material conceptions of the Second Advent, fosters such deception.

Ver. 7. **Of wars and rumors of wars.** The primary reference is to the threats of war against the Jews before the campaign which ended in the destruction of Jerusalem. During this period there were unusual commotions among the Jews in all countries, and in Rome too. It is also a prediction of unexampled convulsions before the second coming of Christ. As wars have been well-nigh continuous, something greater than ordinary war is probably meant.—**Be not troubled.** Be watchful (ver. 5), but be not disturbed. There will be nothing even in the last days to terrify the Lord's people.—**The end is not yet,** *i. e.*, this state of commotion is to continue.

Ver. 8. **Nation shall rise against nation,** etc. Primarily, national uprisings of the Jews; then, wars of races, political revolutions, migrations, etc. Even the times preceding the dissolution of

against kingdom: there shall be earthquakes in divers places; there shall be famines: these things are the beginning of travail.

9 But take ye heed to yourselves: for they shall deliver you up to councils; and in synagogues shall ye be beaten; and before governors and kings shall ye 10 stand for my sake, for a testimony unto them. And the gospel must first be preached unto all the nations.

the Roman Empire have not exhausted this prediction.—**Earthquakes in divers places.** Five great earthquakes occurred in thirteen years.—**Famines.** A famine is prophesied in Acts 11: 28; others are mentioned by Latin historians. The best authorities omit: ' and troubles.'—Luke speaks of 'terrors, and great signs from heaven.' **The beginning of travail,** *i. e.*, birth *pangs*. The physical woes are the basis of the greater succeeding moral woes. 'The death-throes of the Jewish state precede the " regeneration " of the universal Christian Church, as the death-throes of this world the new heavens and new earth' (Alford).

Vers. 9-13. Persecutions Predicted.—Parallel passages: Matt. 24: 9-14; Luke 21: 12-19. All the reports here differ slightly. Luke adds a few particulars, which point more directly to the destruction of Jerusalem.

Ver. 9. **But take ye heed to yourselves.** Peculiar to Mark. —**Deliver you up to councils.** Here Mark is more detailed.— **In the synagogues.** The punctuation is doubtful. The literal meaning is: 'into synagogues.' This may be explained: 'ye shall be taken into synagogues and beaten;' the synagogue being the place where such punishments were inflicted for greater publicity. (So the punctuation of the Rev. Vers.) Others join this with what precedes; ' to councils and to synagogues; ye shall be beaten,' etc. This is less likely.—**Governors.** Compare Paul before Felix and Festus (Acts 24, 25).—**Kings.** Compare the conduct of Herod (Acts 12: 1-3), Paul before Agrippa (Acts 25, 26), before Cæsar (2 Tim. 4: 16).— **For my sake.** It is not persecution, but persecution for Christ's sake, that is predicted; a distinction with a difference which fanatics fail to perceive. Compare the similar prediction made to the Apostles just before they were sent out (Matt. 10: 17, 18).—**For a testimony unto them.** This persecution shall enable you to bear witness of your faithfulness; giving you an opportunity to testify for the Lord, and unto your persecutors. This may become a testimony against them; but that is not the necessary sense.

Ver. 10. **And the gospel must first.** Their martyrdom would spread the gospel, and this spread should precede the end of the woes, in distinction from the beginning (ver. 8). A two-fold fulfilment of

11 And when they lead you *to judgment,* and deliver you up, be not anxious beforehand what ye shall speak: but whatsoever shall be given you in that hour, that speak ye: for it is not ye that speak, but the Holy
12 Ghost. And brother shall deliver up brother to death, and the father his child; and children shall rise up against parents, and ¹cause them to be put to death.

¹ Or, *put them to death.*

this verse is most probable.—**Be preached**, *i. e.*, proclaimed, which is the proper conception of preaching.—**Unto all the nations.** The preaching of the gospel throughout the Roman world preceded the end of the Jewish state; the promulgation of the gospel throughout the whole world will be the sign of the end of this world. The result of the preaching is not indicated. But Matthew says: 'for a testimony unto all the nations.' *To* them, if they accept it; *against* them, if they reject it. In any case, the duty of sending the gospel everywhere remains. The universal extension of missions, no less than the great apostasy, is a sign of the approach of our Redeemer. This prediction stimulated the Apostles, and should stimulate us.

Ver. 11. **Lead you to judgment.** The words supplied in Italics (Rev. Vers.) are necessary to complete the sense.—**Be not anxious beforehand.** Peculiar to Mark, though Luke 21: 14, 15, resembles it. The same thought occurs in Matt. 10: 19, 20. The two discourses have other points of resemblance. 'Neither do ye premeditate,' is to be omitted, according to the best authorities.—**What ye shall speak.** In Matt. 10: 10, both form and substance are referred to.—**But whatsoever shall be given you.** A promise of special inspiration for particular emergencies, **in that hour**; hence not an encouragement to laziness regarding pulpit preparation.—**For it is not ye**, etc. Inspiration for their defence is an indirect proof of the inspiration of the apostolic writings, since the purpose of both is 'testimony' (ver. 9), and writing was a permanent, and hence the most important, testimony.—**But the Holy Ghost.** Comp. Matt. 10: 20: 'For it is not ye that speak, but the Spirit of your Father that speaketh in you,' and Luke 21: 15: 'For I will give you a mouth and wisdom, which all your adversaries shall not be able to withstand or to gainsay.'

Ver. 12. **And brother**, etc. The omission of the article, in conformity with the original, adds to the force of the verse.—**Deliver up.** Become informers. Prophecy of actual martyrdom. The idea of persecution in general is of course included.—**Shall rise up.** A strong word, implying first, rebellion against parental authority, and then, in this connection, a parricidal course of conduct.—**And cause them to be put to death.** The marginal rendering is more literal; and such murders have occurred.

13 And ye shall be hated of all men for my name's sake: but he that endureth to the end, the same shall be saved.

14 But when ye see the abomination of desolation

Ver. 13. **And ye shall be hated of all men**; other than believers, referred to in 'ye.' The Roman historian Tacitus speaks of the early Christians as a hated race. It is difficult for us in these days to understand how literally this was fulfilled. The most shameful practices were attributed to Christians; and partly in consequence of these falsehoods, partly from hatred of good, they were treated as the offscouring of the earth. Perhaps something like this may occur again. But this need not discourage. While thus hated, Christians won their greatest victories. If like treatment must precede 'the end,' it may well be hoped that like success will attend the gospel in the last days.—**For my name's sake.** Even the heathen early caught up the name of Christ, and deemed it odious; probably the name 'Christian' was given in jest (Acts 11: 26). Bad men, however, have been universally abhorred; but it was the Christianity of the early disciples, not their errors or personal faults, which called forth this hatred. Now as then, the world often hates most what it is forced to respect and even to admire. Only God's Spirit can break down this hostility.—**He that endureth**, or, 'shall have endured,' *i. e.*, in his confession of Christ.—**To the end.** The reference is primarily, in this case, to the destruction of Jerusalem. But for the individual, 'the end' is the day of his death; for the Church, it is the Advent of Christ, the end of all things. The last sense is the more important one, giving character to the others.—**Shall be saved.** Literally fulfilled in the escape of the Christians from that doomed city, but with a wider application, and higher fulfilment, in the everlasting salvation. Perseverance to the end, however bitter, is the evidence of genuine faith.

Vers. 14–23. THE SIGNS OF THE COMING DESTRUCTION.—Parallel passages: Matt. 24: 15-25; Luke 21: 20-24. The prominent reference is to the destruction of Jerusalem, answering the question of the disciples more directly than what precedes. Luke, in this connection, distinctly refers to the siege of Jerusalem and its desolation. Another fulfiment is probable, in accordance with the parallel lines of prophecy traced in the preceding paragraph. But precisely because the details are so minute, we must be cautious in applying it to the final catastrophe.

Ver. 14. **But when ye see**, etc. This direct address points to a speedy fulfilment, whatever may be the ulterior reference.—**The abomination of desolation.** 'Spoken of by Daniel the prophet,' is to be omitted; probably inserted from Matthew. The phrase refers to 'abominations, which shall be the desolator,' the coming of which to the sanctuary (where the sacrifice is offered) is prophesied. Most of the Jews applied the original prophecy to the desecration of the temple

standing where he ought not (let him that readeth understand), then let them that are in Judæa flee unto
15 the mountains: and let him that is on the housetop not go down, nor enter in, to take any thing out of his
16 house: and let him that is in the field not return back
17 to take his cloke. But woe unto them that are with

by Antiochus Epiphanes (comp. 1 Macc. 1: 54), who set up there an idol statue of Jupiter. Our Lord points to a fulfilment, then future. The favorite interpretation refers it to the Roman eagles, so hateful to the Jews, and worshipped as idols by the soldiers, the standards of those who desolated the temple. This is favored by the addition in Luke's account (21: 20): 'but when ye see Jerusalem compassed with armies.' Others refer it to some desecration of the temple by the Jewish zealots under the pretence of defending it, which occurred at the same time with the approach of the first Roman army (under Cestius, A. D. 66) against Jerusalem. This makes Luke's account refer to an external sign, and those of Matthew and Mark to the *internal* sign, an abomination committed by the Jews themselves, which should fill up the cup of their iniquity. But it is not certain that such a desecration by the Zealots took place just at that time, and the sign for their flight (ver. 16) was to be a definite and marked one.—**Where he ought not** is less definite than 'in the holy place' (Matthew). The near approach of the Roman army is probably meant. The Roman eagles, rising on the heights over against the temple, were the sign of the fall of the city. In fact they stood on the Mount of Olives, 'the holy place,' in a higher Christian sense, where our Lord was now teaching and whence He ascended. The other view of internal desecration refers the phrase to the temple.—**Let him that readeth understand.** A remark of the Evangelist, and as there is here no direct reference to Daniel, the reader of this Gospel, not of the prophecy, is meant. Such an understanding was very important for the early Christians. Any ulterior reference, as, for example, to 'the man of sin' (2 Thess. 2: 4), will be understood by Christians, when necessary for their safety.—**Flee unto the mountains.** The Christians in Judea accordingly fled to Pella, over the mountains in Perea, and were safe in all those days of horror.

Ver. 15. **On the housetop.** The flat roofs of the eastern dwellings were a favorite place of resort.—**Not go down.** Some suppose this is a command to flee along the house-tops or to go down by the outer stairs as a quicker way. What is distinctly forbidden is to go down **to take any thing out of his house.** Extreme haste is enjoined; and being hindered by motives of selfishness or convenience is prohibited. There is probably an allusion to the flight of Lot from Sodom (comp. Luke 17: 32).

Ver. 17. **Woe unto them,** etc. Natural affection is not forbidden,

18 child and to those that give suck in those days! And
19 pray ye that it be not in the winter. For those days
shall be tribulation, such as there hath not been the
like from the beginning of the creation which God
20 created until now, and never shall be. And except
the Lord had shortened the days, no flesh would have

and this verse expresses compassion for mothers who were thus delayed.

Ver. 18. **Pray ye.** The trying events were distinctly predicted, yet prayer is distinctly enjoined.—**That it be.** 'Your flight' is properly omitted; it was taken from Matt. 24: 20.—**Not in the winter,** which would not only make it more disagreeable, but might prevent their fleeing far enough. Matthew adds: 'neither on a Sabbath.'

Ver. 19. **For those days.** Notice the striking form of Mark's account.—**Shall be tribulation,** etc, Josephus, a Jew by birth and education, but a Roman in religion and sympathies, in describing the siege of Jerusalem, almost repeats the words of our Lord. From this 'great tribulation' the Jewish Christians escaped by fleeing to Pella. The siege began at the time of the passover feast, when the city was crowded. Internal dissensions combined with scarcity of food to multiply the horrors. One woman of rank, named Mary, too, killed and roasted her own babe (comp. Deut. 28: 53, 56, 57), and was discovered only by those who sought to rob her of food; yet even they shrank back at the sight. The resistance to the Romans was fanatical, despite the bloody discord within the city. When at last it was successfully stormed by Titus, the rage of the Roman soldiers, raised to the utmost by the stubborn resistance, was permitted to wreak itself unchecked upon the inhabitants. The sword made the whole city run with blood; while crucifixions by way of jest were very frequent. *Eleven hundred thousand* persons perished; the remainder were sold into slavery, or distributed throughout the Roman provinces to be destroyed by wild beasts. Thus the prophecy of Luke 21: 24 was literally fulfilled. Yet the Roman leader who conducted these operations was one of the most excellent among the heathen.—**The like.** Peculiar to Mark, as also the phrase: **the creation which God created.—And never shall be.** This seems to indicate that nothing analogous will occur again. But ver. 20 is so closely connected with this verse, that a double reference is probably even in vers. 14-19, which were most strikingly fulfilled in the first century. The final application would be to a *sudden catastrophe* before the coming of our Lord, which His people will be enabled to avoid by recognizing the appearance of the signs He has given. Still these verses, of themselves, shed little light as yet on the subject of the last days. The final catastrophe is more plainly indicated in the subsequent part of the chapter.

Ver. 20. **Except the Lord had shortened the days,** etc. (A

been saved: but for the elect's sake, whom he chose,
21 he shortened the days. And then if any man shall
say unto you, Lo, here is the Christ; or, Lo, there;
22 believe ¹*it* not: for there shall arise false Christs and
false prophets, and shall shew signs and wonders, that
23 they may lead astray, if possible, the elect. But take

¹ Or, him.

prophetic past tense.) Various causes did combine to shorten the siege of Jerusalem, so that the Christians in the neighboring place of refuge were not so much exposed. These causes were: (1) Herod Agrippa had begun to fortify the walls of Jerusalem against any attack, but was stopped by orders from Claudius about 42 or 43. (2) The Jews, being divided into factions, had totally neglected any preparations against the siege. (3) The magazines of corn and provision were just burned before the arrival of Titus. (4) Titus arrived suddenly, and the Jews voluntarily abandoned parts of the fortification. (5) Titus himself confessed that he owed his victory to God, who took the fortifications of the Jews. (6) It was not the original intention to storm the place, but events at Rome made it necessary that Titus should hasten back, and he therefore adopted this method of shortening the siege.—But the strong language of the verse and the prophecy of Daniel (chap. 12 : 1), which is here alluded to, point to a providential interposition in the great days of tribulation which are to come in *the last times*. The shortening of the days will be the hastening of the Lord's coming.

Ver. 21. **And then.** Sufficiently indefinite to favor any or all of the interpretations of the passage. During the subsequent period, is exact enough.—**If any man shall say to you**, etc. This indicates that the disciples *then* expected that the second Advent would immediately follow; and was first of all a caution against impostors. But while such did arise in the first century, the details of the following verses point to something further.—**Believe it** (or, 'him') **not.** This phrase furnishes no argument against the visible personal coming of Christ, which seems to be taken for granted throughout.

Ver. 22. **False Christs.** While this may refer to the impostors of the first century, it now points to 'Antichrist,' or the many 'antichrists' (1 John 2 : 18), constantly arising.—**False prophets.** Such arose among the Jews, but have arisen ever since.—**Shew great signs and wonders**; in appearance probably, but this cannot be insisted upon. See 2 Thess. 2: 9-12.—**That they may** (the tendency and purpose) **lead astray, if possible,** implying that it is not, **the elect.** Others will be deceived, led astray from our Lord, the real Messiah and true Prophet. It indicates that a period will come, when the 'deceivableness of unrighteousness' shall be augmented.

Ver. 23. **But take ye heed.** This is the third time this warning

12

ye heed: behold, I have told you all things beforehand.

24 But in those days, after that tribulation, the sun

word occurs in the discourse.—**Told you all things** (peculiar to Mark) **beforehand.** A warning which can scarcely have been exhausted in the first century.

Vers. 24–27. THE SIGNS OF THE COMING OF THE SON OF MAN.—Parallel passages: Matt. 24: 29–31; Luke 21: 25–28. From this point, the reference is to the second coming of Christ, the fulfilment of all these things (ver. 4), in the widest sense. This paragraph seems to refer almost exclusively to the Second Advent; see below.

Ver. 24. **But.** Here almost equivalent to 'nevertheless;' although I have foretold you all things, yet the subsequent tribulations may still astonish you.—**After that tribulation.** The length of the interval is not definitely indicated. Comp. Matt. 24: 29, 30, where a number of details are added; Luke 21: 25, 26, where the language is quite different. This is to be referred, not to the tribulation attending the destruction of Jerusalem, but to the period of trial which belongs to the 'last times,' for the following reasons: 1. In Luke 21: 24, the period of Jewish dispersion and the fulfilling of 'the times of the Gentiles' is put before this prediction, while the expression in Mark 13: 24, also permits the supposition of a long interval. 2. The reference to the destruction of Jerusalem is attended with the greatest difficulties. It takes all the expressions of vers. 24–27 in a figurative sense, but the figure exceeds any reality that occurred in those days. The interval between the horrors of the siege and the actual destruction itself was too short to allow of any events worthy of such a figurative representation as we find here. 3. To refer it to a merely *providential* coming of Christ in judging and purifying nominal Christendom, is not at all in keeping with the specific character of the representation.—**The sun shall be darkened.** A reference to the events attending the destruction of Jerusalem seems impossible. So long as the prophecy is not yet fulfilled, its exact meaning cannot be insisted upon. Two views: (1.) Visible phenomena in the heavens at the visible appearance of Christ; in which sense the rest of the verse needs little explanation, except to determine the difference between 'the stars' and 'the powers of the heavens.' The former may mean meteors and the latter the host of stars, or better, the former the stars in general, the latter the greater heavenly bodies that affect the earth (the solar system). This view suggests also the possibility of actual changes in the physical universe to prepare for 'the new heavens and the new earth.'—(2.) Spiritual events to occur at the same time. The following is the most plausible interpretation of this character: 'The sun shall be darkened,' *i. e.*, the knowledge of Christ, the Sun of the Church and the world shall be obscured; **the moon shall not give her light;** the reflected light of science, which derives its excellence

25 shall be darkened, the moon shall not give her light, and the stars shall be falling from heaven, and the
26 powers that are in the heavens shall be shaken. And then shall they see the Son of man coming in clouds
27 with great power and glory. And then shall he send forth the angels, and shall gather together his elect from the four winds, from the uttermost part of the earth to the uttermost part of heaven.

only from Christ, the true Sun, shall cease to guide (or it may refer to heresy and unbelief in the Church, for that leaves her merely a scientific or temporal organization); **the stars shall be falling from heaven** (a vivid form, peculiar to Mark); the leaders and teachers of the Church shall become apostates: **the powers that are in the heavens** (the greater heavenly bodies) **shall be shaken**; the influences which rule human society shall be disturbed. Others refer the whole to the fall of heathenism with its worship of Nature (sun, moon, and stars), but this is less probable, since terrifying occurrences seem to be meant (see Luke 21: 25, 26).

Ver. 26. **And then.** So Luke; Matthew being less definite. All three Evangelists give the thought of this verse with precisely the same details, and yet each varies from the other two in words. A striking proof of independence.—**Shall they see the Son of man coming.** (Matthew speaks of the visible 'sign of the Son of Man.') This coming is evidently that referred to in 1 Thess. 4: 16, at the first resurrection (Rev. 20: 5, 6); a comparison with Rev. 19: 11 sqq., suggests that this Advent precedes the millennium, but upon that point there has been much dispute. Certainly nothing is said here of the general judgment, but only of the gathering of Christ's people (ver. 27). Mark alone has: **in clouds**; Matthew: 'on the clouds of heaven,' Luke: 'in a cloud.'—**With great power and glory.** Manifested in the establishment of His kingdom on the earth. Some prefer to regard this coming as the beginning of a series of judgments, covering the period symbolically set forth in the term 'thousand years' in Rev. 20: 5, 6; but with the exception of the final judgment, all these are represented as occurring before this coming of the Lord. The safest opinion is, that a Personal coming of Christ is here meant, to take place after the times of the Gentiles are fulfilled (Luke 21: 24), and to be preceded by great catastrophes.

Ver. 27. **Send forth the angels, and shall gather together his elect**, the individual believers, over against the organizations which contain or conceal them. A gathering, either of living and raised believers into one place, or of the saints hitherto scattered among the nations into one organization. It is implied that before that time no one organization will include all true believers. A lesson against sectarian bigotry wherever found.—**From the uttermost**

28 Now from the fig tree learn her parable: when her branch is now become tender, and putteth forth its
29 leaves, ye know that the summer is nigh; even so ye also, when ye see these things coming to pass, know ye
30 that ¹ he is nigh, *even* at the doors. Verily I say unto

¹ Or, *it.*

part of the earth, etc. Probably an allusion to the apparent junction of earth and sky at the visible horizon, but in any case it refers to the whole world. Matthew gives a different form, and inserts 'with a trumpet of great sound.'

Vers. 28–37. THE CLOSING WARNING.—Parallel passages: Matt. 24: 32–51; Luke 21: 29–36. In this paragraph, vers. 28–31 are almost word for word the same with Matthew. In Luke 21: 29–33, the form is different, but the thought precisely identical. In the latter part the three accounts, while preserving the same general tone, differ in details. Matthew (vers. 37–41) refers to the days of Noah, as illustrating the suddenness of the Lord's coming, and then records the exhortation to watchfulness in connection with the figure of a thief breaking in, then of a lord who surprises his servants. Luke is almost literal in his account of the warning, while Mark introduces a regular parable, which bears some resemblance to the figure in Matthew's account, but makes the 'porter' the chief person. This accords with the repetition of the phrase, 'take heed.' Watchful honesty on the part of the steward is the prominent feature in the figure recorded by Matthew; honest watchfulness on the part of the porter, in the parable recorded by Mark. Possibly ver. 34 contains an allusion to the parable of the talents (Matt. 25: 14–30).

Ver. 28. **Now from the fig tree learn her** (lit., 'the') **parable,** namely, what follows.—**Putteth forth its leaves.** The blossoms precede the leaves, and when the leaves come, the fruit season is near. The cursing of the barren fig tree may be in mind even here. Alford: 'As that, in its judicial unfruitfulness, emblematized the Jewish people, so here the putting forth of the fig tree from its state of winter dryness, symbolizes the future reviviscence of that race.'

Ver. 29. **Even so ye also.** Addressed to the disciples, as representing all Christians. It does not mean that they should live to see what He had predicted; two of the four certainly died before the destruction of Jerusalem.—**These things,** *i. e.*, the signs mentioned, culminating in those predicted in ver. 27.—**Know that he is nigh.** Christ Himself, since they had asked of His coming (Matt. 24: 3). The marginal rendering (so A. V.) is equally grammatical, but less probable.

Ver. 30. **This generation.** Explanations. 1. 'Generation' in the literal sense, the reference being to the destruction of Jerusalem. 2. 'Generation' in the sense of 'race,' meaning that the Jewish people shall remain until the fulfilment of all these things, and that one of

you, This generation shall not pass away, until all
31 these things be accomplished. Heaven and earth shall
32 pass away: but my words shall not pass away. But
of that day or that hour knoweth no one, not even the
angels in heaven, neither the Son, but the Father.
33 Take ye heed, watch [1] and pray: for ye know not when

[1] Some ancient authorities omit *and pray.*

the signs of the final fulfilment will be a sudden greening of that withered race. The former is the simpler view, but does not agree so well with ver. 32. The latter, while striking, presses 'generation' into an unusual sense. If the former be accepted, then the double reference of the prophecy is necessarily excluded here.—**Until all these things,** including apparently both the signs and the coming.—**Be accomplished,** literally, 'become.' The idea of actual occurrence is the prominent one, not that of fulfilment.

Ver. 31. **Heaven and earth shall pass away.** Not merely a strong asseveration (sooner shall heaven and earth pass away), but also a plain declaration that they shall pass away. Comp. Ps. 102: 26; Is. 51: 6. The time is not indicated.—**But my words shall not pass away.** Scoffers imply: Heaven and earth cannot pass away (comp. 2 Pet. 3: 34), but Christ's words are losing their force. 'Of this we wait the proof.' 'Not pass away' means more than 'not remain unfulfilled;' the words of Christ will abide as true in the hearts of all His people who look for and haste unto His coming. It is implied that some time will elapse.

Ver. 32. **But of that day and hour knoweth no one, not even the angels in heaven.** 'The angels' are here distinguished from **the Son.** (So in Matthew, according to the more probable reading.) It is plainly affirmed that Christ did not know the day and hour of His future coming. The explanations, that Christ did not know this 'officially,' or the sense: did not choose to tell the disciples, are make-shifts. This seems to be a *voluntary self-humiliation* in knowledge, a part of Christ's emptying of Himself (Phil. 2: 8). Christ could, of course, not lay aside, in the incarnation, the metaphysical attributes of His Divine nature, such as eternity, but He could, by an act of His will, limit His attributes of power and His knowledge and refrain from their use as far as it was necessary for His humiliation. His voluntarily not knowing, or 'sacred unwillingness to know,' the *day* of judgment during the days of His flesh, is a warning against chronological curiosity and mathematical calculation in the exposition of Scripture prophecy.

Ver. 33. **Watch,** or, 'be awake;' not the word usually thus translated. The words 'and pray' are omitted by some ancient authorities. —**For ye know not when the time is.** Because of this uncertainty, be awake. Not, be always expecting what will come unexpect-

34 the time is. *It is* as *when* a man, sojourning in another country, having left his house, and given authority to his ¹servants, to each one his work, commanded also 35 the porter to watch. Watch therefore: for ye know not when the lord of the house cometh, whether at even, or at midnight, or at cock-crowing, or in the 36 morning; lest coming suddenly he find you sleeping. 37 And what I say unto you I say unto all, Watch.

14:1 Now after two days was *the feast of* the passover and the unleavened bread: and the chief priests and the scribes sought how they might take him with sub-

¹ Gr. *bond-servants.*

edly, nor be seeking to know what cannot be known, but be always in the state of readiness, because of the uncertainty.

Ver. 34. **It is as when a man.** The whole matter of watchfulness is as in the following parable.—**Sojourning in another country.** More accurate than the A. V.—**Having left his house, and given authority** (*i. e.*, the delegated power necessary for their duty) **to his servants, to each one his work** (the authority being joined with duty), **commanded also the porter** (as it were at the door, just as he went away) **to watch.** This injunction is the main point of the parable.

Ver. 35. **Watch therefore.** 'Ye' is to be omitted, since 'watch' is the emphatic word.—**Whether at even,** etc. With that graphic detail which characterizes this Gospel, four watches of the night (closing at 9, 12, 3, and 6 o'clock) are mentioned. The coming, unexpected and sudden, will be at night.

Ver. 36. **Coming suddenly** (as He will come) **he find you sleeping** (which was a neglect of His express command). The special duty of the Apostles, as representing the ministry, is doubtless referred to.

Ver. 37. **I say unto all, watch.** Though the Apostles and the ministry are watchmen and porters, yet all believers are to be incessantly watchful and for the same reasons. The time of our Lord's coming, whether at our death or in His personal appearing, is uncertain; therefore we should always be ready. Faithfulness to Him bids us not only work but watch. Matthew (chap. 25) gives an account of the parables which followed, but the most important part of the discourse is doubtless what is contained in all three narratives, namely, the coming of the Lord and our duty to be watchful.

CHAP. XIV: 1, 2. THE PLOT OF THE CHIEF PRIESTS AND SCRIBES.—Parallel passages: Matt. 26: 1-5; Luke 22: 1, 2. Luke agrees very closely with Mark; but Matthew

2 tilty, and kill him: for they said, Not during the feast, lest haply there shall be a tumult of the people.

3 And while he was in Bethany in the house of Simon the leper, as he sat at meat, there came a woman hav-

inserts another prediction made by our Lord respecting His death. The time is given, probably because this was the evening when Judas went to the rulers (see vers. 10, 11).

Ver. 1. **After two days.** Probably on Tuesday evening, after the denunciation of the scribes, etc. Possibly, however, on Wednesday. —**The feast of the passover and the unleavened bread.** The passover meal was the beginning of the feast of unleavened bread, which lasted for seven days.—**And the chief priests and the scribes.** Matthew tells us that they gathered 'unto the court of the high-priest, who was called Caiaphas.' Probably a formal assembly of the Sanhedrin.—**With subtilty.** On account of the impression made by our Lord upon the people, which still continued (Luke 21: 38).

Ver. 2. **Not during the feast,** *i. e.*, the passover week, during which the multitudes (sometimes reckoned at three millions on such occasions) remained at Jerusalem.—**Lest haply there shall be a tumult.** The form indicates expectation that this would certainly result. Most of Christ's followers were Galileans, and the Galileans were all considered bold and quarrelsome. This feast was often the occasion of insurrection, according to Josephus. They could not take Him when they would (John 10: 39), yet must take Him at a time when they purposed not, but which He had predicted (Matt. 26: 2). But the taking and killing took place between the evenings of Thursday and Friday, which made up the first passover day. Even in the greatest humiliation His power and truth still shine forth.

Vers. 3-9. THE ANOINTING AT BETHANY.—Parallel passages: Matt. 26: 6-13; John 12: 1-8. Matthew and Mark place the anointing at Bethany between the counsel of the chief priests and the treacherous proposal of Judas. John places it just after the arrival at Bethany, 'six days before the Passover,' the entry to Jerusalem taking place 'in the next day.' The latter seems to be the correct date.

1. While the marks of time in the several accounts do not decide which is the more exact, John 12: 9 speaks of something as following, which must have occurred previous to the public entry to Jerusalem, while Matthew 26: 14, and Mark 14: 10, do not necessarily imply that the proposal of Judas immediately followed the supper at Bethany.

2. According to John, the occasion was a supper made for Jesus, not an accidental eating there. Such an entertainment was more likely to have been given on the triumphat progress to Jerusalem than while Christ was so occupied in His public ministry in the temple. There would scarcely have been time for such a supper on Tuesday evening, as He went to the Mount of Olives at night (Luke 21: 37), and then delivered a long discourse. Wednesday evening is too late, for the proposal of Judas

ing ¹an alabaster cruse of ointment of ²spikenard very costly; *and* she brake the cruse, and poured it over

¹ Or, *a flask.*
² Gr. *pistic nard*, pistic being perhaps a local name. Others take it to mean *genuine*; others, *liquid.* Am. Com. read *pure nard*, with marg.—Or, *liquid nard.*

followed, and the words of Mark, 'and he sought how he might conveniently deliver him unto them' (similarly Matthew), suggest a longer interval than from late on Wednesday night to Thursday night.

3. No valid reason can be assigned for John's displacing it, while a displacement by Matthew and Mark can be accounted for. (*a*) In history the recapitulation of events is more natural than the anticipation; (*b*) The prophecy of the speedy death would suggest the anointing for the burial; (*c*) Judas had murmured (John 12: 4), and the rebuke no doubt had its effect in ripening his treachery, which is mentioned at this point by Matthew and Mark. Although neither of them speak of Judas as the objecter, they cannot have been ignorant of the connection between the two events, which probably led them to group them together.

Ver. 3. **While he was in Bethany.** Indefinite, as in Matthew's account. On Saturday evening, see note above.—**In the house of Simon the leper.** Probably already healed by Jesus, since otherwise he would have been unclean. He must not be confounded with the Pharisee called Simon, at whose house in Galilee a similar anointing had taken place long before (Luke 7: 36–70). The two occurrences are clearly distinguished in many ways. One tradition makes this Simon the father of Lazarus; another the husband of Martha, who served on this occasion. Both families may have occupied the same house; or Simon may have been the owner, and Lazarus his tenant.—**A woman.** Mary, the sister of Lazarus (comp. Luke 10: 38–42; John 11); not the woman (in Luke 7), 'a sinner.' The latter person is generally, but without reason, identified with Mary Magdalene, and the three women confounded.—**Having an alabaster cruse.** Alabaster cruses were considered by the ancients the best receptacle for valuable ointments or fragrant oils. The vessels usually had a long neck and were sealed at the top. The margin of the Revised Version takes the word rendered 'alabaster cruse' as equivalent to 'flask,' irrespective of the material.—**Ointment.** John: 'a pound,' etc.—**Spikenard,** Gr. 'pistic nard.' 'Nard' means an oriental gum, but the Greek word 'pistic' is akin to the word meaning 'faithful,' and probably refers to the purity of the precious gum. But others understand it as meaning 'drinkable,' *i. e.*, liquid; some think that the adjective refers to the place from which it came.—**Very costly.** See ver. 5; comp. John 12: 5.—**She brake the cruse.** Crushing the neck of the cruse with the hand. Mark alone gives this detail.—**Poured it over his head.** The quantity of ointment permitted her to anoint His feet also (John 12: 3). The Oriental custom of reclining

4 his head. But there were some that had indignation among themselves, *saying*, To what purpose hath this 5 waste of the ointment been made? For this ointment might have been sold for above three hundred ¹pence, and given to the poor. And they murmured against 6 her. But Jesus said, Let her alone; why trouble ye

¹ (Am. Com., *shillings*.) The word in the Greek denotes a coin worth about eight pence half penny.

at table made the latter easier than the former. The expression used hints that from the head it flowed over the whole body. It was also usual to wash the feet of honored guests with water, but the anointing of the feet would indicate the highest honor. Mary may have intended only to show this honor, but this action symbolized Christ's Messiahship, and had a deeper significance, as our Lord points out (vers. 8, 9).

Ver. 4. **There were some.** Matthew: 'His disciples;' John: 'one of His disciples, Judas,' etc. The best authorities omit the words, 'and said.' Judas alone spoke out; the feeling was general, though no doubt instigated by him. Mark distinguishes 'some' in a company of which the disciples formed a part; John mentions the author of the objection, and gives his motives. If John and Judas were reclining at this table in the same relative positions as at the Last Supper, John would probably have heard nothing but the remark of Judas.—**To what purpose hath this waste**, etc. Simon the Pharisee, in the similar case, objected to the character of the woman; here the value of the ointment is thought, as Judas suggested, to have been squandered by this act of Mary. Sacrifices, made out of love to Christ, seem wasteful to the world, and even to the Church when under the influence of a mercantile spirit.

Ver. 5. **Sold for above three hundred pence.** About £9 or $45, a large sum in those days. Pliny says that a pound of this ointment cost more than four hundred *denarii*.—**Given to the poor.** This suggestion, put forward by Judas, was with him a mere pretext (see John 12: 6); the other disciples may have honestly felt it. Judas may have hoped to get the money in his possession, but not necessarily to make off with it; his intention was scarcely ripe enough for such a scheme. Those who hold trust funds, even for benevolent purposes, are often as unscrupulous in adding to them as in increasing their private store.—**And they murmured against her.** Peculiar to Mark. The original seems to indicate a harsh address to Mary, though there was probably also a general murmur against her.

Ver. 6. **Let her alone** (so John, but addressed in the singular to Judas).—**Why trouble ye her?** The chief concern is for the

7 her? she hath wrought a good work on me. For ye have the poor always with you, and whensoever ye will ye can do them good: but me ye have not always. 8 She hath done what she could: she hath anointed my 9 body aforehand for the burying. And verily I say unto you, Wheresoever the gospel shall be preached

affectionate Mary. Her noble act of love had been misjudged, and remarks made which would disquiet or confuse her conscience. First of all our Lord defends and encourages her. The impulses of genuine love to Christ, or His people, are often thus checked, even by real Christians, who for the time being speak the cold and selfish language of the world.—**A good work.** Christ measured the moral quality of the act by the motive, the disciples by its seeming utility. This utilitarian age presents many temptations to follow the lead of Judas.

Ver. 7. **For ye have the poor always with you, and whensoever ye will ye can do them good** (peculiar to Mark): **but me ye have not always.** His speedy death is foretold; but the main point is, that this opportunity could never return; while the care of the poor would be a daily 'duty to humanity down to the end of time.' The act was justified by the special occasion. It ought not to be cited to defend expensive modes of worship at the cost of neglecting the poor. Such special occasions may, however, recur in our lives. This verse suggests that no reorganization of society will ever banish poverty from the earth. There is but one way of doing this, namely, by Christ's people recognizing the poor as 'with them' and under the impulse of love like that of Mary, making the care of them the usual expression of that love.

Ver. 8. **Hath done what she could.** Lit., 'what she had she did.' Peculiar to Mark. High praise! What she did was a costly work in itself, and yet is judged by the same standard as the act of the poor widow (chap. 12: 44), on whom a similar commendation is bestowed.—**She hath anointed my body aforehand.** These words most plainly indicate that Mary, even if she did not understand the full significance of her act of love, in some sense anticipated His speedy death.—**Burying.** The Greek word refers to the whole preparation for the tomb. If she was conscious of the meaning of her own act, then her love discerned what the disciples could not perceive; if she was not, then the Lord gives to acts of love a significance beyond the intention. The latter view seems the more probable one, if the earlier date be accepted, though the language used in John 12: 7, suggests that she had a presentiment of an impending crisis, after which anointing would be unnecessary or impossible.

Ver. 9. **And verily,** etc. A solemn preface.—**The gospel.** The tidings of salvation, with special reference to Christ's death, just alluded to.—**Throughout** (literally 'into') **the whole world.** This

throughout the whole world, that also which this woman hath done shall be spoken of for a memorial of her.

10 And Judas Iscariot, [1] he that was one of the twelve, went away unto the chief priests, that he might deliver
11 him unto them. And they, when they heard it, were glad, and promised to give him money. And he

[1] Gr. *the one of the twelve.*

graphic touch pictures the future work of evangelization; the gospel going out into the whole world.—**That also which this woman hath done** (lit., 'did') **shall be spoken of for a memorial of her.** Fulfilled to the letter. John, before he tells of this, speaks of Mary as well known on this account (John 11: 2). It is right to record and remember the good deeds of those who love Christ, but when the desire to be put on record enters, the ointment is spoiled. This is the only case where such a promise is made; therefore the incident has a weighty lesson and holds up a noble example. Alford suggests, that this prophecy points to a *written* record: that it shows the Gospels cannot have been made up from some original document now lost; since Luke omits this incident, and such a document would have contained it; Luke could not have seen the Gospels of Matthew and Mark, or he would have inserted this to aid in fulfilling the prophecy.

Vers. 10, 11. The Agreement of Judas with the Chief Priests.—Parallel passages: Matt. 20: 14–16; Luke 22: 3–6. Both of the other accounts are fuller than that of Mark.

Ver. 10. **And Judas Iscariot, he that was one of the twelve,** lit., '*the* one of the Twelve,' pointing to a well-known one.—**Chief priests.** Luke adds: 'and captains.' The latter were the guardians of the temple and its treasures. This probably took place while the Sanhedrin was assembled (vers. 1, 2); but Judas may have made the offer to both, in the hope of getting a better reward.—**That** (in order that) **he might deliver him unto them.** The definite purpose of Judas is brought out more fully here than by Matthew. The delivery to them involved all the rest of our Lord's sufferings.

Ver. 11. **When they heard it.** Hearing the proposal. This is peculiar to Mark.—**Promised.** The money was propably not paid until the night of the betrayal. The amount was 'thirty pieces of silver' (Matthew).—**And he sought how he might conveniently deliver him unto them.** The word is that frequently rendered 'betray.' He was to discover the best time and place to avoid 'tumult' (ver. 2). But he was not merely to tell where they could take Him, but himself to be the active agent in taking Him and transferring Him into the hands of His enemies (see vers. 47–50, 57). So that 'betray' is the real meaning.

The principal motive of Judas, as is inferred from the strong ex-

sought how he might conveniently deliver him *unto them.*

12 And on the first day of unleavened bread, when they sacrificed the passover, his disciples say unto him, Where wilt thou that we go and make ready that thou

pression of John (12: 6), was *avarice.* Other views: that he was undecided whether he would betray his Master, and wished to see if the chief priests would offer a sufficient inducement; that he felt it his duty to deliver Jesus up; that he tried an experiment, to see if our Lord would save Himself by a miracle, or establish a temporal kingdom. None of these theories agree with the strong language used by our Lord in ver. 21, and John 17: 12, or with the positive statement of Luke, that before the interview with the chief priests, 'Satan entered into' him. The character of Judas laid him open to this Satanic influence, and nothing could do this more effectually than love of gain. Temporal ambition doubtless had a place in his heart; but even this was a part of his avarice: for, being treasurer of the Twelve, he might hope to be treasurer of the kingdom. His practical talent must have been marked, to secure this position for him, and the scene at Bethany shows that he had influence among his associates. Whatever was known to our Lord, whatever the purpose of God, the motive of Judas at the time when the Twelve were chosen, was probably the same as that of the others. The rest were neither well instructed nor highly spiritual, and in outward appearance Judas was probably equal to any of them. All were more or less self-seeking; but over him the love and spirit of Christ had no such influence as over the others. As the Lord drew near to Jerusalem, ever telling of His death, Judas could not fail to manifest his real spirit. This was done at the supper in Bethany. The reproof then administered had its effect (hence the order of Matthew and Mark). The triumphal entry of the next day may have encouraged his false hopes; but the subsequent occurrences only disappointed him the more. Seeing the enmity of the rulers, hearing the denunciations upon the class, who as rich and honored filled the stations to which his desires pointed, convinced from the final prediction (Matt. 26: 2) that our Lord would be put to death, the hour had come when his sordid soul was ready to listen to the suggestions of Satan; 'then entered Satan into Judas, surnamed Iscariot.' The same expression is used by John (13: 27), at the critical moment when Judas left the Passover feast. His remorse is readily explained. Even that was Satanic.

Vers. 12-16. THE PREPARATION FOR THE PASSOVER.—Parallel passages: Matt. 26: 17-19; Luke 22: 7-13. It is generally agreed that the Lord's Supper was instituted on Thursday evening, the crucifixion taking place on Friday. But from the second century until now, it has been disputed, whether this Thursday was the fourteenth day of the month Nisan, or the thirteenth. The former view places the institution at the

13 mayest eat the passover? And he sendeth two of his disciples, and sayeth unto them, Go into the city, and there shall meet you a man bearing a pitcher of water:

regular time of eating the passover (Exod. 12: 6, 8; Lev. 23: 5); the other places Christ's death at that date, when the paschal lamb should be slain, the Lord's Supper taking place a day earlier than the passover feast. Learned men differ; but practically the question is not of vital moment. The earlier date distinguishes the Lord's Supper from the Jewish passover; but so do the accounts, whichever date be adopted. I. In favor of the fourteenth day it is urged: 1. The first three Gospels plainly give the impression that the feast took place at the regular time. This is especially true of ver. 12: 'when they sacrificed the passover.' As they prepared the passover in a strange house (vers. 13–16), any anticipation of the regular time would have been noted; but Luke 22: 14 says, 'when the hour was come.' 2. Christ came to fulfil the law, and would not have deviated from its requirements in this solemn hour. 3. As the lamb was to be slain in the temple, this would not have been permitted on the day before. These reasons seem to be conclusive. II. In favor of the thirteenth day it is urged: 1. That it was fitting Christ should die at the very time the paschal lamb was slain. 2. That an execution would not take place upon a feast-day, which would be the case on the other theory. Neither of these reasons is of much weight. 3. Certain passages in the Gospel of John indicate that the Lord's Supper was instituted before the regular time of the passover meal. John 13: 1: 'Before the feast of the passover;' but this does not necessarily mean the day before. John 13: 27: 'What thou doest, do quickly,' compared with ver. 29. The references to purchases for the feast seems opposed to the view that the regular time had come; but 'quickly' would not be appropriate if a whole day intervened. John 18: 28: the fear of defilement was because they had not yet eaten the passover; but this might refer to the continued celebration, and the defilement would have ceased in the evening in time for the passover meal, if that evening were the regular time. John twice (19: 14–31) speaks of that Friday as a 'preparation;' but this probably means the day before the sabbath, rather than before a feast-day. It may be added, as against this view, that the chief priests were present at the crucifixion; but if it were the time when the paschal lambs were slain, this could scarcely be the case.

Ver. 12. **On the first day of unleavened bread.** The 14th of Nisan, when the leaven was removed. In the evening of this day (after the 15th had begun) the passover was eaten. (See above.)—**His disciples.** It is probable that they came with the intention of inquiring on this point, and their thought was answered by the command mentioned in Luke 22: 8, to which they responded: **Where wilt thou,** etc. As strangers they must join some household in the city. (See on ver. 14.)

Ver. 13. **Two of his disciples.** Luke gives their names: 'Peter and John.'—**Go into the city,** *i. e.*, Jerusalem.—**A man bearing a pitcher of water.** This was the sign by which they should know him. The vessel was earthen, but the fact has no necessary significance. This mode of directing the disciples would prevent Judas from knowing

14 follow him; and wheresoever he shall enter in, say to the goodman of the house, The ¹Master saith, Where is my guest-chamber, where I shall eat the passover 15 with my disciples? And he will himself shew you a large upper room furnished *and* ready: and there 16 make ready for us. And the disciples went forth, and came into the city, and found as he had said unto them: and they made ready the passover.

17 And when it was evening he cometh with the

¹ Or, *Teacher*.

the place in time to betray our Lord at the passover meal. Our Lord here shows superhuman knowledge; for even if he had previously arranged with the master of the house, of which there is no evidence, this meeting could not have been preconcerted.

Ver. 14. **To the goodman of the house**, or, 'master of the house.' Evidently not the man they followed.—**The Master saith**. This would indicate that the householder knew something of Jesus and His disciples, recognizing Him as at least a noted 'Teacher'.—**My guest-chamber**. 'The word used properly denotes a place where a traveller unloads his beast, or halts for the night; then an inn or place of public entertainment; then a hired room, as here' (Alexander). The correct reading 'my,' is suggestive. Our Lord lays claim to it, even though it were to be hired. This message seems stranger to us than it would to the man, even if he had little knowledge of Jesus. The visitors at Jerusalem joined some household in the city at the passover meal. Each householder provided a lamb on the tenth day of Nisan, and on the fourteenth, between three and six o'clock in the afternoon, presented it in the temple, slaying it himself, while the priests received the blood in silver basins to be emptied at the foot of the altar.¹ This took the place of the sprinkling of blood on the doorposts. The fat of the lamb was burned on the altar by the priest; but the animal itself, with its skin bound about it, was carried home to be used at the feast. The man to whom they applied would be expected to make such preparations in any case, and to have a room where those who celebrated with him should gather.—**Where I shall eat the passover**. Such a place might be hired for such a purpose, probably was in this case.

Ver. 15. **Upper room**. On the second floor. Some think it was the 'Alijah,' or the room on the housetop, but this seems less likely.—**Furnished**, *i. e.*, with tables and couches.—**Ready**, *i. e.*, by the householder, who provided the lamb, etc. See on ver. 14.—**Make ready**. The further preparations necessary for the passover.

Vers. 17-21. The Passover Celebration; Announcement that One Should Betray Him.—Parallel passages: Matt. 26: 20-25; comp. Luke 22: 14-18, 21-23; John

18 twelve. And as they ¹sat and were eating, Jesus said, Verily I say unto you, One of you shall betray me,

¹ Gr. *reclined.*

13: 1-30. The four Evangelists are entirely independent in their accounts of the Last Passover. Luke (17: 15-18) records the expression of our Lord's desire to eat the passover with them; and this seems to be the first recorded incident. The washing of the disciples' feet is mentioned by John only (13: 4-12), and this preceded the announcement of the betrayer (John 13: 21-30) here narrated. The strife as to who should be greatest, mentioned by Luke only (22: 21-30), seems to have been the immediate occasion of the washing of the disciples' feet; hence the probable order was: (1) the expression of desire; (2) this strife; (3) the washing of the disciples' feet; (4) the announcement that one should betray Him, mentioned by all four Evangelists.—The passover celebration. The following account of the ancient mode of celebration is from Godet (*Luke*): 'First step: After prayer, the father of the house sent round a cup full of wine (according to others, each one had his cup), with this invocation: "Blessed be Thou, O Lord our God, King of the world, who hast created the fruit of the vine!" Next there were passed from one to another the bitter herbs (a sort of salad), which recalled to mind the sufferings of the Egyptian bondage. These were eaten after being dipped in a reddish sweet sauce (*charoseth*), made of almonds, nuts, figs, and other fruits, commemorating, it is said, by its color the hard labor of brick-making imposed on the Israelites, and, by its taste, the divine alleviations which Jehovah mingles with the miseries of His people. Second step: The father circulates a second cup, and then explains, probably in a more or less fixed liturgical form, the meaning of the feast, and of the rites by which it is distinguished. Third step: The father takes two unleavened loaves (cakes), breaks one of them, and places the pieces of it on the other. Then uttering a thanksgiving, he takes one of the pieces, dips it in the sauce, and eats it, taking with it a piece of the paschal lamb, along with bitter herbs. Each one follows his example. This is the feast, properly so called. The lamb forms the principal dish. The conversation is free. It closes with the distribution of a third cup, called the *cup of blessing* because it was accompanied with the giving of thanks by the father of the house. Fourth step: the father distributes a fourth cup; then the *Hallel* (Ps. 113-118) is sung. Sometimes the father added a fifth cup, which was accompanied with the singing of the great *Hallel* (Ps. 120-127, according to others, 135-137).'

Ver. 17. **And when it was evening.** Luke: 'And when the hour was come.' All the impressions indicate that it was the usual time of celebration.

Ver. 18. **As they sat,** (Greek, 'reclined'). The passover was originally eaten standing; but this was altered by the Jews when they came to the land of promise and rest. **Were eating.** The passover feast was in progress.—**One of you shall betray me, even he that eateth with me.** The first clause is word for word the same in the accounts of Matthew, Mark, and John; the last clause, so graphic, and so full of grief, is peculiar to Mark. This indefinite announcement would give Judas an opportunity of repentance. But it produced no effect, except to startle and sadden them all.

19 *even* he that eateth with me. They began to be sorrow-
20 ful, and to say unto him one by one, Is it I? And
he said unto them, *It is* one of the twelve, he that
21 dippeth with me in the dish. For the Son of man
goeth, even as it is written of him: but woe unto that
man through whom the Son of man is betrayed! good
were it ¹ for that man if he had not been born.
22 And as they were eating, he took ² bread, and when
he had blessed, he brake it, and gave to them, and

¹ Gr. *for him if that man.*   ² Or, *a loaf.*

Ver. 19. **Is it I, Lord?** Comp. the fuller details in John 13: 18–30. The Greek form of this question implies a denial; hence the hypocrisy of Judas in asking the question by himself, after the others. Yet every Christian may ask such a question at the Lord's table.

Ver. 20. **He that dippeth with me in the dish.** One near Him. There were probably a number of dishes, or bowls, distributed along the table, containing the broth called *charoseth*, prepared of dates, figs, etc., which was used at the Supper, representing (see above) the Egyptian bricks or clay. Even this statement may not have definitely pointed out Judas to the others. There is a pathetic tenderness in the language (comp. Ps. 41: 9, quoted in John 13: 18).

Ver. 21. **For the Son of man goeth, even as it is written of him.** Luke: 'As it hath been determined.' This prophecy implied the purpose.—**But.** God's purposes include our freedom (comp. Acts 2: 23)—**Woe unto that man.** Stier: 'The most affecting and melting *lamentation of love*, which feels the woe as much as holiness requires or will admit.' Our Lord seems to forget His own woes in pity for this man.—**Good were it for that man,** etc. (Comp. the exact form in the margin.) A proverbial expression for the most terrible destiny, forbidding the thought of any deliverance however remote. The question of Judas (Matthew) and the reply of our Lord are omitted here.

Vers. 22–26. THE INSTITUTION OF THE LORD'S SUPPER.—Parallel passages: Matt. 26: 26–29; Luke 22: 19, 20; comp. 1 Cor. 11: 23–25; John 6: 51 sq. Mark's account resembles closely that of Matthew. The account of Luke makes it clear that the usual celebration of the passover went on, and that during its progress the Lord's Supper was instituted. Some have thought that the latter followed, entirely separated from the Jewish rite. But this is incorrect. At the same time, the formal acts of the Lord's Supper were in themselves probably distinguished from the Jewish forms. So that it is not necessary to show exact correspondence between the two. The Jewish passover was transformed; the new festival was linked with, but distinct from, the old one. It is probable, though not certain, that Judas withdrew before the Lord's Supper was instituted.

23 said, Take ye: this is my body. And he took a cup, and when he had given thanks, he gave to them:

Ver. 22. **As they were eating.** During the paschal feast, hence this was probably not the usual breaking of the passover cakes — **Took bread.** The unleavened cakes, used on these occasions, easily broken. — **And when he had blessed.** As was the custom. Luke and Paul say: 'gave thanks,' which is the same thing. All the accounts, including that of Paul (in 1 Cor. 11: 23, 24), agree in mentioning the distinct acts of taking, giving thanks (or blessing), breaking, and giving. The same acts occurred in the same order in the two miracles of feeding the multitudes, which are rightly regarded as pointing to the Lord's Supper. The word 'Eucharist' ('thanksgiving') is a common name of the Lord's Supper, as a feast of thanksgiving. Our Lord probably did not Himself partake.—**Take ye**: the best authorities omit: 'eat.'—**This is my body.** The meaning of this clause has been discussed for centuries. In the original, 'bread' is masculine; but 'this' is neuter, and hence means not this bread, but rather bread used in this service. The main question is, Did our Lord mean, This represents my body, or, This is (literally) my body? The former is the view of most Protestants; the latter, that of the Romanists and (in modified form) of the Lutherans. There are four leading theories of our Lord's presence in this sacrament: two of them based on the figurative sense of the words of the institution, and two on the literal sense. The Zwinglian view accepts a symbolical presence of Christ in the ordinance; the Calvinistic, a spiritual real presence; the Lutheran, a bodily presence in, with, and under the unchanged elements (consubstantiation); the Roman Catholic, a bodily presence, the bread and wine becoming the real body and blood of Christ (transubstantiation). It will be seen at once that the last two views are not actually literal. The Roman Catholic theory makes the sacrament a sacrifice, and in so doing exalts it above the word of God, at the same time exalting the priest above the people. The Zwinglian view is often held in too bald a form, making of the ordinance only a memorial service, and leading to a low estimate of its significance. Certainly the bread is to be received in memory of Christ's death. But as bread is for nourishment, we are reminded that Christ nourishes our spiritual life (compare John 6). So in the passover, the lamb, though a sin-offering, was not consumed on the altar, but eaten by the household of the offerer. We should be grateful that the blessing does not depend upon the correctness of our theory, important as that may be in its place, but upon our child-like faith in receiving the sacrament. This is a permanent ordinance of the Christian Church, pointing to Christ's death in the past, to His life in the present, to His coming in the future; of which it is a Christian duty to partake, and a sin to partake unworthily, since it is a communion of believers as members of the same body of Christ (1 Cor. 10: 16, 17).

Ver. 23. **And he took a cup.** Luke and Paul: 'after supper.'

24 and they all drank of it. And he said unto them, This is my blood of ¹the ²covenant, which is shed for

¹ Or, *the testament.* ² Some ancient authorities insert *new.*

Although the institution may have been independent of the regular mode of celebrating the passover, the giving of thanks mentioned here, taken in connection with 1 Cor. 10: 16 ('the cup of blessing'), indicates that this was a cup of thanksgiving, hence probably the *third* cup of the passover feast.—**And they all drank of it.** This Mark substitutes for the command: 'Drink ye all of it.' In each case 'all' is significant in view of the Romanist usage, which denies the cup to the laity.

Ver. 24. **For this is my blood of the covenant.** ('Testament' is an improbable meaning here, as in most cases.) The wine, poured-out, is a symbol of the blood of Christ shed for us. Both here and in Matthew the word 'new' is omitted by the best authorities, though it occurs in the accounts of Luke and Paul. It was still the same covenant. Hence as the old covenant forbade the drinking of blood, it could not be commanded here in a literal sense. As Moses (Exod. 24: 8) sprinkled blood upon the people and said, 'Behold the blood of the covenant,' our Lord points directly to the shedding of His blood on the cross as 'the blood of the covenant.' He thus comforted His disciples by explaining His death to them, and we can find no blessing in it apart from this explanation.—**Which is shed** (or, 'being shed') **for many** (Luke: 'for you'; Matthew adds: 'unto remission of sins'). Our Lord here declares, with reference to His own death, that it was an actual dying for others. 'Shed' means 'poured out.' The figure is taken from the pouring out of the juice from the grape, and this represents the shedding of Christ's blood, when 'bruised for our iniquities' (Isa. 53: 5). These words told the disciples the purpose of His death. They needed such instruction just then. But it tells all, that Christ's death is the ground of our pardon. While the 'bread' points more to Christ's life in us, and the 'wine' to Christ's death for us, the two are inseparable; for the bread was broken to signify His death also, and the wine is drunk to signify our partaking of His life also. The Lord's Supper is therefore a feast of the living union of believers with a crucified yet living Saviour, and with each other. It signifies and seals these truths. The central fact is the atoning death of Christ, which we commemorate; but the present blessing is the assurance conveyed by visible signs, that this Saviour is ours, and nourishes us with His life unto life eternal. 'Not discerning the Lord's body' (1 Cor. 11: 29), is not having that hearty faith which understands, appreciates, and appropriates the main truth set forth in the sacrament. Godet well remarks, 'We know already what we have to do to celebrate a true communion. We may leave to God the secret of what He gives us in a right communion.' The word 'many' seems to hint at the communion of believers with one another.

25 many. Verily I say unto you, I ¹will no more drink of the fruit of the vine, until that day when I drink it new in the kingdom of God.

26 And when they had sung a hymn, they went out unto the mount of Olives.

27 And Jesus saith unto them, All ye shall be ²offended: for it is written, I will smite the shepherd, and the

¹ *shall* (Am. Com.).   ² Gr. *caused to stumble.*

Ver. 25. **I will no more**, etc. 'Shall' is preferable to 'will,' since this is a prediction of a fact, not a declaration of a purpose. He is done with earthly rites, and at this sad moment points them to a future reunion at the Marriage Supper of the Lamb. The ordinance now receives its prophetic meaning (comp. 1 Cor. 11: 26 'till He come'), directing believers to the perfect fruition of that future fellowship, through the foretaste which this sacrament is designed to give. It is a tame interpretation which finds here only a declaration that the Jewish passover is superseded by the Lord's Supper.—**Drink it new**, on some peculiar and exalted festal occasion.—**The kingdom of God.** Not to be weakened into 'in the Christian dispensation.' It points to the victory of the Church, not to its conflicts; and the continued celebration of the Lord's Supper is an expression of assured victory on the part of His militant Church.—After the institution of the Lord's Supper there occurred the touching interview with the eleven disciples, recorded by John (from chap. 13: 31 to 17: 26).

Ver. 26. **And when they had sung a hymn** (Ps. 115–118), **they went out unto the mount of Olives**, to Gethsemane (ver. 32). The place of eating the passover was probably kept concealed, to give time for that closing interview, appropriately called, 'the Holy of Holies.'

Vers. 27–31. THE WAY TO GETHSEMANE.—Parallel passage: Matt. 26: 31–35; comp. Luke 22: 31–34; John 13: 36–38. This conversation seems to have taken place on the way across the brook Kidron to Gethsemane. Luke inserts a similar prediction, in connection with the incident about the two swords, which must have taken place before the departure. John, too, places the prediction before the farewell discourse (chaps. 14–17, the *whole* of which must have been delivered in the room. If there was but one intimation of Peter's denial, it was at the point where it is placed by Luke. The order is: After the singing of the hymn, the prediction about Peter, then the incident about the swords (in Luke), next John 14, then the rising to go (John 14: 31), then the remainder of the discourse and the prayer (John 15–17), then the actual going out. Matthew and Mark, however, connect the prediction of Peter's denial with another important prophecy, not mentioned by Luke and John, and with difficulty fitted into their narratives. They indicate that the prediction about Peter was occasioned by something else, and record a less presumptuous answer from him. It is probable that our Lord gave *two* intimations on this point, the first mentioned by Luke and John (as

28 sheep shall be scattered abroad. Howbeit, after I am
29 raised up, I will go before you into Galilee. But Peter said unto him, Although all shall be ¹offended, yet
30 will not I. And Jesus saith unto him, Verily I say unto thee, that thou to-day, *even* this night, before the

¹ Gr. *caused to stumble.*

above), the second by Matthew and Mark, uttered on the way out to Gethsemane. We then have, what would scarcely be lacking, a conversation on the way. The phrase 'this night' favors this view. The account of Mark agrees closely with that of Matthew.

Ver. 27. **All ye.** Not without a contrast to Judas who had gone.—**Shall be offended**; 'caused to stumble,' 'fall away.' The words 'because of me this night' should be omitted.—**For it is written** (Zech. 13 : 7). Our Lord, knowing what would come, knew also that it was designed to fulfil this prophecy.—**I will smite the shepherd**, etc. In the prophecy: 'Smite,' a command. This change suggests that the coming sufferings were not only at the hands of men, but in some proper sense inflicted by God Himself; God smote Him instead of His people (comp. Is. 53 : 4–10). 'The shepherd' is Christ, and in the original prophecy meant the Messiah (comp. Zech. 11 : 7–14; 12 : 10).—**And the sheep**; the Apostles, but with a wider reference also to the Jewish people.—**Scattered abroad.** This occurred both in the case of the disciples, and of the Jews, after they had rejected the smitten Shepherd.

Ver. 28. **Howbeit**; stronger than 'but' (Matthew); 'notwithstanding' this scattering, you will be gathered again in Galilee.—**After I am raised up.** The Resurrection is again announced.—**I will go before you.** The figure of a shepherd is continued. Comp. the remaining words of Zech. 13 : 7 : 'And I will turn my hand upon the little ones.—**Into Galilee.** In Galilee He collected His disciples: Matt. 28 : 16; John 21; 1 Cor. 15 : 6. This gathering was the pastoral work after the Resurrection; hence the other interviews in Jerusalem are not referred to.

Ver. 29. **Although all**, etc. The utterance of affection, yet of self-confidence and arrogance, since 'all' refers to the other disciples. Hence he was allowed to fall lower than the rest. This reply differs from that given by Luke and John. Its tone points to a previous declaration respecting his want of fidelity.

Ver. 30. **That thou**; emphatic, 'even thou.' The detailed form of this saying, together with Mark's relation to Peter, suggests that this is the exact form in which it was uttered. Peter afterwards (ver. 72), and doubtless always, called to mind this saying.—**To-day.** During the twenty-four hours, beginning at sundown.—**This night.** The prediction becomes more specific.—**Before the cock crow twice.** Before the usual time of the second cock-crowing, about

31 cock crow twice, shalt deny me thrice. But he spake exceeding vehemently, If I must die with thee, I will not deny thee. And in like manner also said they all.
32 And they come unto ¹a place which was named

¹ Gr. *an enclosed piece of ground.*

three o'clock in the morning. This was usually called 'cock-crowing' (chap. 13: 35). Our Lord meant the actual cock-crowing to be a warning for Peter (ver. 72). It is said that the inhabitants of Jerusalem kept no fowls because they scratched up unclean worms. But this is not certain, and such a prohibition would not affect the Roman residents.—**Deny me thrice.** Deny knowing me (Luke 22: 34), a denial of any relation to Christ, virtually a denial of faith in Him, as the Son of God; in contrast with the previous confession (chap. 8: 29).

Ver. 31. **He spake exceeding vehemently.** This might be paraphrased: 'he went on repeating superaboundantly.' The correct reading emphasizes the intensity of the denial.—**I must die with thee.** In Luke and John, something like this precedes the prediction of the denial; in Matthew and Mark, it occurs at this point. This favors the view that two different occasions are referred to.—**And in like manner also**, etc. The ardent spokesman influenced the rest. Their asseverations were probably not so strong, but were as inconsiderate. So 'all' left Him (ver. 50), but Peter alone denied Him. These protestations occupied some time, probably continuing until they entered Gethsemane.

Vers. 32-42. THE AGONY IN GETHSEMANE.—Parallel passages: Matt. 26: 36-46; Luke 22: 39-46. The latter account has the most marked peculiarities. This conflict in Gethsemane took place after the serenity of the Last Supper, and before the sublime submission in the palace and judgment-hall. It therefore seems to be a *specific* agony of itself: the sorrow and grief was not about the future merely, but in and of that hour, and yet not to be accounted for by the merely human influences which would then affect Him. Upon Him there rested a sense of the world's sin, which He was bearing, probably conjoined with the fiercest assaults of Satan. Otherwise, in this hour Jesus seems to fall below the heroism of martyrs in His own cause. The language of His prayers shows that His sorrow was either sent *directly from God*, or, purposely permitted by God. The agony was a bearing of the weight of our sins, in loneliness, in anguish of soul threatening to crush His body, yet borne triumphantly, because in submission to His Father's will. Three times our Lord appeals to that will, as purposing His anguish; that purpose of God in regard to the loveliest, best of men, can be reconciled with justice and goodness in God, only on the view that the sufferings were vicarious; our Lord suffered anguish of soul for sin, that it might never rest on us. To deny this is, in effect, not only to charge our Lord with undue weakness, but to charge God with needless cruelty.

Ver. 32. **Unto a place named Gethsemane.** Luke (22: 39)

Gethsemane: and he saith unto his disciples, Sit ye
33 here, while I pray. And he taketh with him Peter
and James and John, and began to be greatly amazed,
34 and sore troubled. And he saith unto them, My soul
is exceeding sorrowful even unto death: abide ye here,

says in general 'to the Mount of Olives' though hinting at a customary place; John (17: 1-2) tells us that was a 'garden' beyond the brook Kidron, known to Judas, 'for Jesus ofttimes resorted thither with His disciples.' 'Place' means 'a piece of land,' 'field' (see John 4: 5; Acts 1: 18, etc.), 'Gethsemane' means 'oil-press.' It was probably an enclosed olive-yard, containing a press and garden tower, perhaps a dwelling-house. It was at the western foot of the Mount of Olives beyond the Kidron ('black brook'), so called from its dark waters, which were still more darkened by the blood from the foot of the altar in the temple (see note on ver. 17). The spot now pointed out as Gethsemane lies on the right of the path to the Mount of Olives. The wall has been restored. Eight olive trees remain, all of them very old (each one has paid a special tax since A. D. 636), but scarcely of the time of our Lord, since Titus during the siege of Jerusalem, had all the trees of the district cut down. Dr. Thomson (*The Land and the Book*) thinks the garden was in a more secluded place further on, to the left of the path.—The name has been connected with the bruising of our Lord for our sins.—**His disciples.** Eight of them, as appears from what follows.

Ver. 33. **Sit ye here.** They would form an outer watch to warn of the danger which they must have felt was impending.—**While I pray.** Our Lord speaks of the coming struggle as prayer. So Abraham (Gen. 22: 5), when he, almost on the same spot, was going to the greatest trial of his faith.—**He taketh unto him.** Toward a more secluded spot; not into a house.—**Peter and James and John.** These three had seen His glory (chap. 9: 2-8); they were now chosen to witness His anguish. Though they could not help Him, their presence seems to have been a comfort to the Man of sorrows.—**To be greatly amazed, and sore troubled.** The first expression is stronger than that used by Matthew, the second is the same in both Gospels. The former word refers to the effect of the woe that falls upon Him; the latter to the feeling that He was forsaken, driven into solitude by the weight of His trouble.

Ver. 34. **My soul.** 'It is the human soul, the seat of the affections and passions, which is troubled with the anguish of the body; and it is distinguished from the *spirit*, the higher spiritual being.' (Alford.) Soul and body interacted in Him as in us.—**Even unto death.** His body would have given way under the sorrow of His human soul, had not angelic ministration sustained Him (Luke 22: 43).—**Abide ye here, and watch.** Matthew: 'Watch with me.' He would have

35 and watch. And he went forward a little, and fell on the ground, and prayed that, if it were possible, the
36 hour might pass away from him. And he said, Abba, Father, all things are possible unto thee; remove this cup from me: howbeit not what I will, but what thou
37 wilt. And he cometh, and findeth them sleeping, and

friends near Him, but does not say: *Pray* with me; in this conflict He must be alone. His command was not merely to keep awake out of sympathy with Him, but to be on their guard against coming dangers. Even then He showed care for them.

Ver. 35. **And he went forward a little.** 'About a stone's cast' (Luke 22: 41), since that seems to refer to this second withdrawal. Into the Holy of Holies He goes alone. Luke, a physician, gives more vivid statements.—**Fell on the ground.** Luke: 'kneeled down.' Kneeling and prostration were scarcely distinguished in the East. —**If it were possible, the hour might pass away from him.** The 'hour' representing the specific conflict of that hour in the garden. See above. 'Our Lord endured precisely the same kind of suffering which any mere man would experience in the same situation, but without sin of His own. He therefore shrank from death, and sunk beneath the sense of God's wrath, no less really than we do. But, besides this unavoidable participation in the sufferings of the race whose nature He assumed, His sufferings even in the garden were vicarious: He not only suffered with, but for, men.' (J. A. Alexander.)

Ver. 36. **Abba, Father.** Mark gives, not only the substance of the prayer (ver. 35), but some of the words of our Lord. 'Abba' is the word for 'Father' in the dialect of that time and country. In explanation Mark adds the Greek word. But before this Gospel was written, 'Abba, Father,' came into general use as an address to God (Rom. 8: 15; Gal. 4: 6), probably from our Lord's use of the former word.—**All things are possible unto thee.** Peculiar to Mark, and doubtless a part of the very form used.—**Remove this cup from me.** This refers to His sufferings, including those of that hour (comp. chap. 10: 38). The prayer was not prompted by fear of death alone. God answered the prayer by giving Him strength to drink it. The removal of the suffering was not 'possible.' The sorrows were necessary, not for Him, but for us.—**Howbeit not what I will.** The form differs from that of Matthew, and might be paraphrased: 'But, *the great question is,* not what I will, but what thou wilt.' In this real struggle, *His will* was still fixed in its obedience to that of His Father. As the God-man, He foreknew all the bitterness of the cup, and His human will desired relief; but that will was overruled by the Divine purpose, which coincided with His Father's will, and led to submission.

Ver. 38. **Findeth them sleeping.** In a drowsy, dozing con-

saith unto Peter, Simon, sleepest thou? couldest thou
38 not watch one hour? ¹ Watch and pray, that ye enter
not into temptation: the spirit indeed is willing, but
39 the flesh is weak. And again he went away, and
40 prayed, saying the same words. And again he came,
and found them sleeping, for their eyes were very

¹ Or, *Watch ye, and pray that ye enter not.*

dition, as the result of excessive sorrow (Luke 22: 45), probably not in a sound sleep (comp. ver. 40).—**Unto Peter.** Who had been so boastful in his expressions of allegiance (vers. 29, 31).—**Sleepest thou?** Disappointment, rather than displeasure, is indicated.

Ver. 38. **Watch and pray.** However much he wished them to watch with Him (ver. 34), even during His own soul-struggle He cares for them. They needed always to be on their guard, and just now a special danger was impending. This danger was a spiritual one, though occasioned by the earthly one; hence the *purpose* of both watching and praying is: **that ye enter not into temptation.** (The margin of the Rev. Vers., less correctly, joins the clause with 'pray' only.) They would be tempted, as we all are; but watchfulness and prayer would guard against the temptation. Occasions *test* our faith: they become temptations, only when we are not 'kept by the power of God.'—**The spirit indeed is willing,** etc. The words 'spirit' and 'flesh' are used in the Epistles in a technical sense, traces of which are found here. They are never used as exact equivalents of 'soul' and 'body,' but rather with the thought of the Holy Spirit influencing our 'spirit,' and of depravity manifesting itself in our 'flesh.' The best explanation here is: The human spirit (when acted upon by the Holy Spirit) is willing to do the present duty; but the flesh, which is weak (and weakened through sin), hinders and often produces failure. There is probably also an application to our Lord. In Him, though weighed down by sorrow, so that the flesh almost gave way to death in its weakness ('even unto death'), the willingness of the spirit triumphed. There is a constant conflict in believers between the 'spirit' and the depraved nature ('flesh'); in the case of the disciples its actings were through the weary body.

Ver. 39. **And prayed, saying the same words.** The form of the second prayer, given in Matt. 26: 42, indicates more resignation: 'O my Father, If this cannot pass away, except I drink it, thy will be done.'

Ver. 40. **For their eyes were very heavy.** Perhaps their sleep was lighter than on the first return. Drowsiness, not deep sleep, is meant.—**And they wist not,** etc. Comp. Peter's remark on the Mount of Transfiguration (chap. 9: 6). They could make no reply, either from a sense of their failure, or more probably from physical stupor.

41 heavy; and they wist not what to answer him. And he cometh the third time, and saith unto them, Sleep on now, and take your rest: it is enough; the hour is come; behold, the Son of man is betrayed into the
42 hands of sinners. Arise, let us be going: behold, he that betrayeth me is at hand.

Ver. 41. **The third time.** The third prayer, mentioned in Matt. 26: 44, is of course implied here.—**Sleep on now**, etc. These words are not a question, but a permission. They are bidden to sleep for the little time that remained; nothing remained for them to do. To take the language as ironical, as suggested by Chrysostom, seems unwarranted by the circumstances.—**It is enough.** That is, enough of your watching with me, or seeming to watch with me. Even could you watch, it would no longer avail, **the hour is come.** A number of other interpretations have been given, but they are open to serious objections. It can scarcely mean, it is enough of sleep; and it is very improbable that between that permission and this expression sufficient time intervened to allow them to sleep. Some explain it: the conflict is over; others: he (*i. e.*, the betrayer) is still far off. But the former is contrary to usage, and the latter to the context. The single word in the original is therefore well rendered; 'it is enough,'—**The hour is come.** The hour of darkness (Luke 22: 53), when His enemies should apparently triumph.—**Behold the Son of man is betrayed into the hands of sinners.** The word 'betrayed' is that often rendered 'delivered up,' but the bad sense is apparent here. 'This expression, into the hands of sinners, should be noticed, as an echo of the Redeemer's anguish: it was the contact with *sin*,— and death, the wages of *sin*,—which all through His trial pressed heavily on His soul' (Alford.)

Ver. 42. **Arise; rouse yourselves.**—**Let us be going.** The language betokens haste and anxiety. Even in His submission our Lord seems desirous that the moment of the treachery be hastened. Probably by moving forward, He wished to gather the little band of disciples together, as if to protect them (comp. John 18: 8, 9).—**Behold, he that betrayeth me is at hand**, etc. The continued idea of approach is here indicated. The next verse shows that the hostile band was now in sight. The occurrence suggests these thoughts: Even our Lord had His favorite places (John 18: 2) and companions. —Those who see our Lord's glory must see His suffering.—A man of sorrows, and acquainted with grief, is our great High Priest.—Human sympathy utterly fails to enter into the depths of our Lord's vicarious agony.—If we shrink from trial, we may have His sympathy.— From Him alone can we learn to say, Thy will be done.—Even in Gethsemane He cared for His own, who could not watch with Him.—Trial will come to us; but it will be temptation only when we forget to

43 And straightway, while he yet spake, cometh Judas, one of the twelve, and with him a multitude with swords and staves, from the chief priests and the scribes
44 and the elders. Now he that betrayed him had given them a token, saying, Whomsoever I shall kiss, that is

watch and pray.—Our human spirit at its best is weak: without God's Spirit it is controlled by the 'flesh.'—God often answers prayer, not by removing the cup, but by giving strength to drink it.—What a load sin is, if this was its effect on One who bore it for others!

Vers. 43–50. THE BETRAYAL.—Parallel passages: Matt. 26: 47–56; Luke 22: 47–53; John 18: 3–12. All the Evangelists narrate this occurrence with interesting variety in details, showing their entire independence. It shows the glory and majesty of our Lord even in such an hour; the reference to the fulfilment of the Scriptures (vers. 54–56) confirms the view that the preceding conflict was proposed and permitted by God.

Ver. 43. **Straightway.** Mark's favorite expression; the appearance of Judas and his band was sudden.—**While he yet spake,** *i. e.*, while He was speaking.—**Judas.** He knew the place (John 18: 2), and had, no doubt, represented how easy it would be to take Jesus without provoking a tumult among the people. Thus the rulers, contrary to their plan, put our Lord to death on the feast-day (ver. 2).—**One of the twelve.** A solemn emphasis is thus placed upon the discipleship of Judas. Something similar occurs at every mention of his name.—**A great multitude.** The crowd was heterogeneous: there was a detachment of Roman soldiers (John 18: 3, 12), another from the Jewish temple watch (Luke 22: 52), and a mixed mob of servants of the high priests (ver. 51), a few of the rulers probably (Luke 22: 52), and such others as would gather to see the capture.—**With swords and staves,** or, 'clubs,' the former in the hands of the soldiers, the latter among the mixed crowd. They had lanterns and torches (John 18: 3), though the moon was at the full. Gethsemane was in a deep valley. So great a multitude may have been deemed necessary, either because of our Lord's known power, or to make Pilate and the people think Jesus was a dangerous criminal.—**From the chief priests,** etc. They had organized the armed band to take Him. —**The scribes.** Peculiar to Mark, as in other cases.

Ver. 44. **Had given them a token.** This is brought out more distinctly here than in Matthew. The word 'token' indicates that the Roman soldiers had been instructed to obey this sign.—**Whomsoever I shall kiss.** A token of affection and fidelity (Gen. 29: 11), then as now.—**Take him**; take hold of Him. It is indicated that he thought the capture would be difficult, on account of the resistance of the disciples, or the power of Jesus Himself. Before the kiss was given, the incidents narrated in John 18: 4–9, probably took place, so that most of the multitude knew which was Jesus before the signal was

45 he; take him, and lead him away safely. And when he was come, straightway he came to him, and saith,
46 Rabbi; and ¹kissed him. And they laid hands on
47 him, and took him. But a certain one of them that stood by drew his sword, and smote the ²servant of the
48 high priest, and struck off his ear. And Jesus answered and said unto them, Are ye come out, as against
49 a robber, with swords and staves to seize me? I was daily with you in the temple teaching, and ye took me

¹ Gr. *kissed him much.*   ² Gr. *bond-servant.*

given. But for the Roman soldiers this signal was necessary.—**Lead him away safely.** Either in such a way as to prevent any attempt at rescue, or 'confidently,' without being afraid of Him. The former is more probable.

Ver. 45. **Rabbi.** This was hypocritical reverence. At the passover feast, Judas used the same word, while the disciples said 'Lord' (Matt. 26 : 25, 22).—**Kissed him,** or, 'kissed him much,' as the original implies (so Matt. 26 : 49). 'The sign was the simple kissing; but the performance was more emphatic, a caressing, corresponding with the purpose of Judas to make sure, and with the excitement of his feelings' (Meyer).

Ver. 46. Mark omits our Lord's words to Judas.—**Laid hands,** etc. This does not imply undue violence. He was probably not bound until afterwards (comp. John 18 : 12).

Ver. 47. The stroke of Peter is mentioned most briefly here.—**One of them.** Peter, as was well known (John 18 : 26), but only John gives the name.—**Drew his sword.** According to Luke (22 : 49), the question was first asked, 'Shall we smite with the sword?' Peter did not wait for the answer. They had two swords (Luke 22 : 38); the wearer of the other one was not so rash.—**The servant of the high priest.** Named 'Malchus;' John 18 : 10.—**His ear.** The 'right ear' (Luke and John). Peter was no swordsman, for he missed his blow. In any case carnal weapons used in Christ's cause deprive His opponents of 'ears,' *i. e.,* of willingness to listen to the truth. Christ's grace may restore this willingness, as it healed this ear. The healing is mentioned by Luke (the physician) only. The double effect of Peter's rashness, damage to Malchus and danger to himself, were thus removed.—The rebuke to Peter is omitted here.

Ver. 48. **And Jesus answered,** etc., *i. e.,* to their actions. He was probably bound at this time, but His protest does not imply a desire to resist.—**As against a robber,** not, 'a thief,' against whom no such display of force would be needed.

Ver. 49. **Daily** From day to day, as during the past week.—**In the temple,** the most public place in Jerusalem.—**Teaching.** Not

not: but *this is done* that the scriptures might be fulfilled. And they all left him, and fled.

51 And a certain young man followed with him, having a linen cloth cast about him, over *his* naked *body*: and 52 they lay hold on him; but he left the linen cloth, and fled naked.

unobserved, so that you needed to seek me; nor yet riotous or robbing, as your present conduct implies.—**And ye took me not.** They dared not (chap. 12 : 12); the method now adopted showed the malignity of an evil conscience, and also a deceitful purpose to turn the current against Him.—**But this is done that the scriptures might be fulfilled.** Matthew mentions a previous reference to the Scriptures, while Luke uses another expression, supplementing this: 'but this is your hour, and the power of darkness.' This word of our Lord is therefore His final surrender of Himself to death; a willing offering of Himself for others, in accordance with the purpose of a merciful God. **They all,** (i. e, the disciples) **left him.** All who had joined with Peter in his protestation (ver. 31). This forsaking is connected with the last word of our Lord. He says He submits; their courage fails them. Only after Christ died for men, could men die for Him.—**And fled.** Not absolutely. See vers. 51, 54; Luke 22 : 54; John 18 : 15. When the Eleven forsook the Lord, other disciples, as Nicodemus, and Joseph of Arimathea, took a more decided stand for Him. The Church can never fail; new Christians take the place of the old ones.

Vers. 51, 52. THE YOUNG MAN IN GETHSEMANE.—This account is peculiar to Mark.

Ver. 51. **A certain young man.** Not one of the Apostles, all of whom had fled (ver. 50), but a disciple. He may have been seized because of some expression of sympathy, or simply because of his strange attire.—**Having a linen cloth.** Either a sheet or a nightgarment, the material alone being definitely mentioned.—**Over his naked body.** He had just risen from bed, having probably been asleep in a house near by, possibly on the 'place' itself. Further all is conjecture. It may have been Mark himself; others think it was the owner of the garden; others again that it was a member of the family where the passover had been eaten; others, James the brother of our Lord; others, the apostle John. The first theory would account for the insertion of this incident here, with the name suppressed. A few years later Mark was living with his mother in Jerusalem (Acts 12 : 12), and probably at this time also. If it was any one well-known to the first readers of the Gospel, it was no doubt the Evangelist himself. The words 'the young men' (A. V.) are omitted, according to the best authorities.

Ver. 52. **Naked.** Bengel says: 'Modesty was overcome by fear in this great danger.' The words 'from them' (A. V.) are to be omitted.

53 And they led Jesus away to the high priest: and there come together with him all the chief priests and 54 the elders and the scribes. And Peter had followed him afar off, even within, into the court of the high priest; and he was sitting with the officers, and warm-

Vers. 53–65. THE NIGHT TRIAL BEFORE THE COUNCIL.—Parallel passage: Matt. 26: 57–68; comp. Luke 22: 54, 55, 63–71; John 18: 12–24. This paragraph gives the second trial of our Lord by the Jews; during which the denials of Peter took place. There seem to have been three judicial examinations of our Lord. (1.) An examination before Annas, who, although deposed, was considered the real high-priest by the Jews, while they were obliged to recognize Caiaphas. This is mentioned by John only (John 18: 13, 15, etc.), who followed and at once went into the palace court. It was not formal, no witnesses having been called, but rather an attempt to ensnare our Lord in His own words. (2.) The more formal night examination mentioned in this paragraph. Caiaphas, whom Mark never names, was the son-in-law of Annas, and probably lived in the same palace with him (see below). This would obviate the difficulties arising from the views of the Jews and the authority of the Romans. The guard seems to have remained in the same palace court during both examinations. (3.) In the morning of Friday the final and formal examination before the Sanhedrin (chap. 15: 1; Matt. 27: Luke 22: 66). Matthew and Mark give the details of the *second* examination, Luke of the *third*, John of the *first*. Peter's denials occurred during the period from the first to the close of the second examination. John's account shows this. The other Evangelists treat that subject as a whole, hence Matthew and Mark put it *after*, and Luke *before* the examination. A threefold examination by the secular authorities succeeded on Friday morning. These repeated trials were probably caused by a consciousness that their proceedings were morally unwarranted.

Ver. 53. **To the high-priest.** Matthew: 'Caiaphas the high-priest;' comp. John 18: 24. Josephus says that he was originally called Joseph. John (11: 51; 18: 13) says he was 'high-priest that same year,' and son-in-law of Annas, who had also been high-priest and was still called so (Acts 4: 5). The office was hereditary in the family of Aaron, and held for life; but Antiochus Epiphanes (B. C. 160) sold it to the highest bidders, and the Romans removed the incumbent at pleasure. Caiaphas was appointed by a Roman proconsul, his predecessor having been deposed, and was removed by a Roman emperor about six years after this time. Though of the party most hostile to the Romans, he and his associates raised the cry: 'We have no king but Cæsar' (John 19: 15).—**Come together with him**, *i. e.*, the high-priest. Mark mentions the three orders of the Sanhedrin; **and the scribes** being peculiar to this account. The examination before Annas would allow time for them to come together.

Ver. 54. **Peter had followed him afar off.** Not out of curiosity, yet like a mere spectator. Such following leads to danger, not to victory.—**Even within.** Peculiar to Mark.—**Into the court of the**

55 ing himself in the light *of the fire*. Now the chief priests and the whole council sought witness against
56 Jesus to put him to death; and found it not. For many bare false witness against him, and their witness
57 agreed not together. And there stood up certain, and
58 bare false witness against him, saying, We heard him say, I will destroy this ¹ temple that is made with

¹ Or, *sanctuary*.

high-priest. Not the 'palace,' but the area enclosed by the building (which may not have been a 'palace'). The entrance to this was through the 'porch' (ver. 68). John (18: 15, 16) tells that he himself, as an acquaintance of the high priest, went in, while Peter stood without; the former procured admission for the latter. The first denial occurred about this time (see next paragraph).—**And he was sitting with the officers**, not, 'servants' (A. V.). Those who had been engaged in the capture (see ver. 43). He remained there for some time, from about midnight to cock crowing (three o'clock).—**And warming himself in the light of the fire.** Lit., 'in the light' (comp. Luke 22: 55, 56). The open fire in the court gave light, and Peter was recognized by the light of the fire (ver. 67), comp. also John 18: 15, 16, 18. The fire had been kindled in the courtyard of the house where Annas lived (according to John), and Mark and Luke, who tell of the examination before Caiaphas, refer to Peter's warming himself there. Annas and Caiaphas therefore probably lived in the same house.

Ver. 55. **The whole council.** The Sanhedrin; Joseph of Arimathea and Nicodemus probably being absent (Luke 23: 51), since their opposition would have been in vain (comp. John 7: 50; 9: 22). It was not the first time this body had consulted against Him. See John 7: 45–53; 9: 22; 11: 57; 12: 10.—**Sought witness.** Knowing that true witness could not be had, they actually sought 'false witness' (Matthew). Such a sin is greatest in judges.—**And found it not**, *i. e.*, to answer their purpose.

Ver. 56. **For many bare false witness**; as was natural; but two witnesses to one specific point were required (Numb. 35: 30; Deut. 17: 6; 19: 15).—**Agreed not together**; 'were not equal.' Not necessarily implying contradiction. No two so agreed as to give the evidence necessary for a legal conviction.

Ver. 57. **Certain.** Matthew, more definitely, 'two.'

Ver. 58. **We .... I.** These words are emphatic.—**Temple**, or, 'sanctuary'; the inner sacred enclosure.—**Made with hands .... made without hands.** Probably our Lord had used these expressions, since, as we *now* understand them they express so plainly the correct meaning of the saying mentioned in John 2: 19, etc. An al-

hands, and in three days I will build another made
59 without hands. And not even so did their witness
60 agree together. And the high priest stood up in their midst, and asked Jesus, saying, Answerest thou nothing? what is it which these witness against thee?
61 But he held his peace, and answered nothing. Again the high priest asked him, and saith unto him, Art

lusion to Dan. 2: 34, is possible. The witness was 'false,' since the saying was construed into blasphemy. The witnesses were probably guilty of wilful misinterpretation. The Sanhedrin knew what the true sense of the words was (Matt. 27: 63), and the witnesses were probably fully aware of it. Our Lord's zeal in cleansing the temple (chap. 21: 12-13). should have been an evidence to all that He would not speak slightingly of it. Besides, if they supposed He meant the temple in Jerusalem, they heard His promise of restoring it, which could not imply hostility to the temple itself. The words of our Lord are a prophecy of His death, and yet of His ultimate victory; this, in their blindness and fanaticism they could make a ground for condemnation.

Ver. 59. **Not even so**, etc. Even in regard to the statement just made, their evidence varied.

Ver. 60. **And the high priest stood up in the midst.** With a show of holy horror.—**Answerest thou nothing?** Silence would be a contempt of important testimony.—**What is it which these witness against thee?** Is it true or false? if true, what is its meaning? To make but one question of the high-priest's language does not suit the vehemence natural to the occasion.

Ver. 61. **But he held his peace.** Before Annas He had spoken (John 18: 19-23), but that was not an official hearing. Here under false witness and reproach (as before Herod) He is silent, in patience and confidence of victory. The testimony was false in fact, even if partially true in form. An answer would have involved an explanation, which His opposers either knew already or were too hostile to accept. The silence does not, as early interpreters thought, point to our silence before the judgment seat of God, had He not taken our place and been silent before His judges; for His silence led to their greater judgment and self condemnation. His claim to be the Messiah was the ground of their hostility and also the only ground on which they could demand His death. His silence implied this, and served to bring the whole matter to an issue.—**The high-priest asked him.** Putting Him on oath, according to Matt. 26: 63. Our Lord's silence compels the abandonment of the subterfuge. Yet the deceitfulness remained. They would not believe Him, as He afterwards told them (Luke 22: 67). They merely offered the alternative of a conviction as a blasphemer or an impostor.—**The Son of the Blessed**, *i. e.*, of God, since the Rabbis used a word of this meaning as the ordinary name for

62 thou the Christ, the Son of the Blessed? And Jesus said, I am: and ye shall see the Son of man sitting at the right hand of power, and coming with the clouds 63 of heaven. And the high priest rent his clothes, and 64 saith, What further need have we of witnesses? Ye have heard the blasphemy: what think ye? And they

God. It occurs only here in the New Testament. The action of the high-priest indicates that this implied a distinct question: Do you claim, in claiming to be the Messiah ('the Christ'), to be also 'the Son of God.' Caiaphas probably used it in a sense similar to that we now attach to it. 'He and the Sanhedrin wittingly attached to it the peculiar meaning which, on previous occasions, had been such an offence to them (John 6: 18; 10: 33); and Jesus, fully understanding their object, gave a most emphatic affirmation to their inquiry. Of all the testimonies in favor of the divinity of Christ, this is the most clear and definite' (Gerlach).

Ver. 62. **I am.** (Matthew: 'thou hast said'). Any allusion to the significant name of God: 'I Am' (Ex. 3: 14), is very improbable. To be silent would be construed as an admission that He was not the Messiah.—**And ye shall see.** Mark omits the phrase: 'from henceforth.'—**The Son of man sitting**; as they now sat to judge Him, with a reference to the quiet confidence of His future position in glory. —**At the right hand**, *i. e.*, the place of honor.—**Of power**, *i. e.*, of God, who is Almighty. This expression is used in contrast with His present weakness. The whole alludes to Ps. 110: 1, which He had quoted to them in the last encounter (chap. 12: 36).—**And coming with the clouds of heaven.** 'The sign from heaven' they had demanded (chap. 8: 11). This refers to Christ's final appearing, but may include His coming to judgment on the Jewish people, at the destruction of Jerusalem.

Ver. 63. **And the high-priest rent his clothes**, his uppergarment, not the high-priestly robe, which was worn only in the temple. Rending the clothes was a sign of mourning or of indignation (Acts 14: 14), but in the former sense was forbidden to the high-priest (Lev. 10: 6; 21: 10). Instances of the high-priests using this sign of indignation occur in the first Book of the Maccabees and in Josephus. The Jews found in 2 Kings 18: 37, a precedent for rending the clothes on occasions of real or supposed blasphemy. Such an action, at first natural, became a matter of special regulation, hence more theatrical than real.— **What further need**, etc. They had difficulty in getting witnesses. The true Witness answered; they refused to believe, but found His confession sufficient for their purpose.

Ver. 64. **Ye have heard the blasphemy.** This language implies: (1.) That our Lord, when solemnly adjured, had claimed to be Divine, else it could not be called blasphemy; (2.) That the high-priest, while

65 all condemned him to be ¹ worthy of death. And some began to spit on him, and to cover his face, and buffet him, and to say unto him, Prophesy: and the officers received him with ² blows of their hands.

¹ Gr. *liable to.*   ² Or, *strokes of rods.*

compelling Him to be a witness in His own case, at once declared His testimony to be *false*, else it could not be called blasphemy. Every one who hears of Jesus now must accept either His testimony respecting Himself or the verdict of the high-priest.—**What think ye?** A formal putting of the question to vote. The high-priest assumes that they all agree with him, the verdict being pronounced in hot haste.—**And they all condemned him.** Peculiar to Mark.—**To be worthy of** (Greek, 'liable to,' obnoxious to the punishment of) **death.** This formal condemnation was, as they imagined, according to the law (Lev. 24: 16; comp. Deut. 18: 20). The Sanhedrin was forbidden to investigate any capital crime during the night, and according to the Roman law a sentence pronounced before dawn was not valid. This test vote, however, they considered as settling the question; hence the ill-treatment which followed (ver. 65). They were scrupulous in holding another meeting in day-light, and there passing the final sentence (chap. 15: 1; Luke 22: 7). Yet even this was illegal, for a sentence of death could not be pronounced on the day of the investigation. All the examinations took place within one Jewish day, beginning in the evening.

Ver. 65. **And some began to spit on him.** Others than the 'officers,' spoken of below. The context (ver. 64) points to members of the Sanhedrin as engaged in this cruelty (comp. Acts 7: 54, 57; 22: 2). At all events they permitted it. It was an expression of the greatest contempt. Our Lord was treated as one excommunicated, though the final sentence had not been passed.—**And to cover his face, and to buffet him,** etc. His face was covered, and after each blow, He was asked who gave it. The lower officials probably continued this scoffing amusement for some time. The Roman soldiers were apt in the same kind of mockery (chap. 15: 16–19). First, condemned as a blasphemer, He was treated as an outlaw. Luke (22: 65) adds: 'Many other things spake they against Him, reviling Him.'—**The officers.** Probably those who had been by the fire (ver. 54); comp. John 18: 22.—**Received him with blows of their hands.** The correct reading is thus rendered, describing the conduct of the officers when they received Jesus again as their prisoner. The marginal reading is, however, a probable one; possibly He was maltreated in both ways. This abuse seems to have taken place, in part, when Jesus was led into the court to be kept there until the morning. The officers were probably those warming themselves by the fire, and just then Peter denied Him for the third time, so that

66 **And as Peter was beneath in the court, there cometh**

our Lord turned and looked on him (Luke 22 : 61). It should be remembered that there is a mocking of our Lord, which cannot strike His human body, though directed against His Person, His office, His mystical body.

Vers. 66–72. PETER'S DENIAL.—Parallel passages: Matt. 26: 69–75; Luke 22: 55–62; John 18: 16–18, 25–27. The account of John shows that these denials of Peter occurred during the period from the examination before Annas to the close of that before Caiaphas. All four Evangelists narrate the main facts. Their candid statements respecting what might seem derogatory to the good name of one of the chief Apostles is a guarantee of honesty and presumptive evidence of truthfulness. (Mark, who probably wrote under Peter's own direction, is very full.) They agree in this namely, that Peter *was recognized on three occasions* during the night; that he was *on all three a denier of his Lord;* but they differ in details. They mention different recognizers, especially in the second and third case, they record different replies and different circumstances. It follows that not one of the four consulted the narrative of the others, or derived his account from the same immediate source. Having four independent, competent witnesses, even if at our distance we cannot arrange all the details, the variations ought not to shake our faith in the entire accuracy of each and all the narratives. The theory of evidence that is most satisfactory accepts three occasions of denial, without counting each answer as a separate denial; the more numerous recognitions may have been nearly simultaneous, and the answers belonging to each occasion, given in well-nigh immediate succession. Peter was in an excited crowd at night, for probably two hours or more. Three single questions and three single answers would scarcely comprise all that occurred, but rather three episodes of suspicion and denial. The variations therefore go to prove not only the *independence*, but also the *truthfulness* of the narratives. Forgers would have made their accounts agree; writers of legends would have shown a common source; but these differences prove that the occurrences took place and were reported by credible independent witnesses. Moreover, every point of the narrative accords not only with Christian experience, but with the character of Peter as sketched in the New Testament, and with our Lord's predictions and warnings to him. This internal evidence of truthfulness indicates that the variations in the accounts are evidences of independence, and not real discrepancies.

Vers. 66–68. *First Denial.* Ver. 66. **And as Peter was beneath.** Below the hall where the trial took place (comp. ver. 54). If this room were open towards the court, as was sometimes the case, then Peter could see something of the trial. John tells (18: 15, 16) how he gained admission. But warming one's self with Christ's enemies has its dangers.—**One of the maids.** The same one mentioned by Matthew and Luke; possibly, but not necessarily the porteress referred to by John. The last Evangelist connects with this denial Peter's standing by the fire in the court, expressly mentioned by Mark and Luke. But two maid-servants may have made a similar charge on this occasion.

67 one of the maids of the high priest; and seeing Peter warming himself, she looked upon him, and saith,
68 Thou also wast with the Nazarene, *even* Jesus. But he denied, saying, I ¹neither know, nor understand what thou sayest: and he went out into the ²porch;
69 ³and the cock crew. And the maid saw him, and began again to say to them that stood by, This is *one* of

¹ Or, *I neither know, nor understand: thou, what sayest thou?*   ² Gr. *forecourt.*
³ Many ancient authorities omit *and the cock crew.*

Ver. 67. **Thou also wast with the Nazarene, even Jesus.** 'Nazarene,' used in contempt. The language is that of contemptuous banter, or light ridicule, not with a view to serious accusation. The maid may have followed him into the court, repeating the banter, which he repelled in the different words recorded by the different Evangelists.

Ver. 68. **But he denied.** Matthew: 'before them all.'—**I neither know,** etc. The marginal rendering is even more graphic. On this first occasion he denies, not only his discipleship and knowledge of Jesus (Luke and John), but even that he understood what she could mean (Matthew and Mark); possibly to two different maids. He practised evasion, which leads to direct lying, often to perjury. Christ's cause is not helped, nor His people defended, by crafty policy. Peter drew his sword in the presence of an armed band, but lied to a bantering maid-servant. In the Bible accounts of the fall of good men, women have usually been the occasion, though not the cause, of the crime.—**Into the porch,** or, 'forecourt,' a different word from that used by Matthew, but referring to the same place. In his embarrassing position, he left the fire, going out to the arched gateway leading from the court to the street: probably no further.—**And the cock crew.** The first or midnight crow. As Peter himself probably informed Mark of this, it was not the cock-crow that brought him to repentance; nor does he conceal his forgetfulness of the signal. The omission of this clause in some authorities was probably due to a confusion of the two cock crowings.

Ver. 69. *Second Denial.*—**And the maid saw him,** etc. This second recognition seems to have been a general one, beginning by the fire (John, who probably stood there, and tells what he himself witnessed), recurring in the porch, where this maid attacked him (Matthew, Mark). If the maid mentioned in ver. 69 was not the porteress, then it is possible she takes up her banter again. Luke tells of a man recognizing him; probably a servant standing in the porch, one of those to whom the maid spoke. At such a time such a charge would awaken further remark.

70 them. But he again denied it. And after a little while again they that stood by said to Peter, Of a truth thou art *one* of them; for thou art a Galilæan. 71 But he began to curse, and to swear, I know not this 72 man of whom ye speak. And straightway the second time the cock crew. And Peter called to mind the word, how that Jesus had said unto him, Before the cock crow twice, thou shalt deny me thrice. ¹And when he thought thereon, he wept.

¹ Or, *And he began to weep.*

Ver. 70. **But he again denied it.** Matthew: 'with an oath,' uttered to this maid. From evasion to perjury, one sin leading to another.

Vers. 70–72. *Third Denial.*

Ver. 70. **And after a little while.** About an hour elapsed (Luke 22: 59).—**Again.** Notice the correct position. Peter probably remained in the porch, as a less conspicuous place.—**They that stood by.** A very general recognition by those in the porch. The second denial had allayed the indignation; but the examination was about concluded, and there was more stir and excitement. The first man who recognized him, was probably the one mentioned by Luke; then the bystanders joined in: **Of a truth thou art one of them; for thou art a Galilæan.** This was the proof; or, if we accept the more literal rendering: 'for thou art also a Galilean,' this is an added reason. They recognized him, and his being a Galilean confirmed them. The last clause (A. V.): 'and thy speech agreeth thereto,' was probably inserted from Matthew; it is omitted by the best authorities.

Ver. 71. **But he began to curse,** or, 'to call down curses on himself,' if what he said was not true.—**And to swear;** to call God to witness that it was true. Probably at this time he was recognized by the kinsmen of Malchus (John 18: 26), who had been in the garden of Gethsemane, and doubtless in the audience room, until our Lord was brought out after the examination, or he would have seen Peter before.

Ver. 72. **And straightway the second time the cock crew.** This was at the second crowing, about three o'clock in the morning. Just then (according to Luke 22: 61), our Lord 'turned and looked on Peter.' We infer that this occurred as He was led out after the examination. Peter was in the porch, not the court. This view accounts for the fact of so many having recognized Peter there, and agrees with the requirements of time.—**And Peter called to mind,** etc. His memory was helped by our Lord's look of reproachful love.—**The word.** Mark repeats the saying of our Lord with the same accuracy

15: 1 And straightway in the morning the chief priests with the elders and scribes, and the whole council, held a consultation, and bound Jesus, and carried him

as in ver. 30.—**And when he thought thereon, he wept.** Continued weeping is implied. The word translated 'thought thereon' means literally, 'casting on;' then casting it over, reflecting on it. The calling to mind was the momentary act of remembrance occasioned by the crowing of the cock, this the serious and continued reflection on the sin. Other interpretations are given: 'rushing forth,' *i. e.*, he threw himself out of the place; 'beginning,' (so marg. Rev. Ver.), 'continuing,' 'covering his head,' etc. The most fanciful view is: '*casting* (his eyes) *on*' (Him), *i. e.*, looking at the Saviour as He passed.

What befell Peter may befall any Christian who relies on his own strength, especially after self-exaltation (vers. 29-31), lack of watchfulness and prayer (vers. 37-40), and presumptuous rushing into danger (vers. 47-54). The account of Peter's repentance also finds its confirmation in the Christian heart. It was occasioned in part by a natural cause (the crowing of a cock), yet even that was a direct sign from the Lord: by a look of compassion and love; by a remembrance of the Lord's words, recalling his past sin of *pride* quite as much as his present denial. All were from Christ, and hence the penitence was genuine. It was sudden as his sin had been; it was secret, sincere, and lasting. 'A small matter (a mean servant) makes us fall when God does not support us; a small matter (the crowing of a cock) raises us again, when His grace makes use of it' (Quesnel).

Chap. XV: 1-5. OUR LORD DELIVERED TO PILATE.—Parallel passages: Matt. 27: 11-14; Luke 22: 66; 23: 1-3; John 18: 28-38. This account is closely related to that of Matthew; but the remorse and suicide of Judas are omitted. The morning meeting of the Sanhedrin is mentioned more particularly by Luke (22: 66-71). They must apply to the Roman governor to have their formal sentence against Jesus executed. Leading Him to the governor, they first attempted to obtain Pilate's consent to the death of Jesus, without formal accusation (John 18: 28-32). Failing in this, they make the political charge (Luke 22: 2). Then comes the question of Pilate (ver. 2). Our Lord acknowledges His Messiahship, but first inquires in what sense Pilate puts the question (John 18: 34). Before His Jewish accusers He was silent (vers. 3-5). Pilate finds no fault in Him, but hearing He is a Galilean, sends Him to Herod (Luke 23: 4-12). This occurred immediately after what is narrated in this paragraph.

Ver. 1. **And straightway in the morning.** Luke: 'as soon as it was day;' comp. John 18: 28. Probably about sunrise, since the twilight is short in that latitude —**The chief priests . . . and the whole council.** This detailed statement (comp. Luke 22: 66) shows that this was a formal meeting of the Sanhedrin, evidently a second one. The mocking spoken of in chap. 14: 65, must have inter-

2 away, and delivered him up to Pilate. And Pilate asked him, Art thou the king of the Jews? And he 3 answering saith unto him, Thou sayest. And the

vened. Luke (22: 66) indicates that this meeting was held in the council-chamber within the temple-area, where alone, according to the Talmud, sentence of death could be pronounced; also that a formal procession conducted Him thither. It is characteristic of Pharisaism to be most formal when most unjust.—**Held a consultation**, etc. Their plan appears to have been: 1. To ask Pilate's consent, without inquiry, to their sentence of death (John 18: 30). 2. If necessary, to make the vague charge that Jesus claimed to be King of the Jews (comp. ver. 2). This was the ground on which they forced Pilate to consent. 3. Another charge mentioned by John (19: 7), that He claimed to be the Son of God, may have been determined on, in case He denied the political character of His Messiahship. But it had no effect, and the other accusation was resumed.—**And bound Jesus**. The bonds put on Him in the garden seem to have been removed some time during the night.—**And carried him away**. Probably in a solemn procession, with a view of influencing both the people and the governor.—**Delivered him up**. The same word often translated 'betrayed.'—**Pilate**. The office held by Pilate was that of Roman 'procurator,' whose chief business it was to collect the revenues, and in certain cases to administer justice. Palestine had been thus governed since the banishment of Archelaus (A. D. 6), and Pilate was the sixth procurator, holding the office for ten years under the Emperor Tiberius (probably from A. D. 27-36). The usual residence of the procurator was in Cæsarea (Acts 23: 33; 25: 1, 4, 6, 13); but during the great festivals he was generally at Jerusalem, to preserve order and to uphold the supremacy of the Roman power, perhaps also to administer justice. Pilate had an unyielding and severe disposition (comp. Luke 13: 1), and his conduct led to repeated revolts among the Jews, which he suppressed by bloody measures. He was therefore hated and at last removed in consequence of the accusations made against his administration by the Jews. He died by his own hand. There are many legends about him, invented by both the early Christians and their opponents.

Ver. 2. **And Pilate asked him.** In 'the judgment hall' (John 18: 28), which the Sanhedrin did not enter for the fear of defilement. —**Art thou the king of the Jews?** They had condemned Him for 'blasphemy;' but they bring a political accusation now, since Pilate would probably not take notice of the religious one (see John 18: 31).—**Thou sayest,** *i. e.*, 'yes.' He first inquires in what sense Pilate puts the question, and then explains the nature of His kingdom (John 18: 34-37). This is implied here. Had Pilate understood it in the political sense, he would not have been so anxious to release Him.

4 chief priests accused him of many things. And Pilate again asked him, saying, Answerest thou nothing? 5 behold how many things they accuse thee of. But Jesus no more answered anything; insomuch that Pilate marvelled.

6 Now at ¹the feast he used to release unto them one 7 prisoner, whom they asked of him. And there was

¹ Or, *a feast.*

Ver. 4. **Behold how many things!** Comp. Luke 23: 5, as a specimen of the testimony, or accusations, they brought. The main charge was true in form, but false in fact: His claim to be a king was not a political offence. So as to the evidence: He had stirred up the people, etc., but not to mutiny or for political purposes. Honest advocates at the bar should avoid the tricks of these murderers of Christ. —**Accuse thee of.** The same word as in ver. 3, according to the best authorities.

Ver. 5. **But Jesus no more answered anything.** An answer would not have convinced them, nor furthered Pilate's wish to release Him.—**Pilate marvelled.** The silence of our Lord continued until just before the final decision (see John 19: 10, 11). Those accused are not often silent, and Pilate had probably found the Jews tried at his bar especially vehement.

Vers. 6-15. PILATE AND THE MULTITUDE; BARABBAS RELEASED, JESUS DELIVERED TO DEATH.—Parallel passages: Matt. 27: 15-26; Luke 23: 18-25, John 18: 39! 19: 16. Mark's account is much briefer than the other three. On the return from Herod, Pilate offers them the choice between Jesus and Barabbas, seeking to release Jesus (Luke 23: 13-17); but the multitude, under the influence of the priests, ask that Barabbas be released (ver. 11). Luke records three successive efforts of Pilate to release our Lord; Matthew three answers of the people. Mark indicates these three attempts in vers. 9, 12, 14. The second and third occurred after the message from Pilate's wife (Matt. 27: 19). Yet, by having put Christ on a level with Barabbas, he had already committed himself, and gave way to avoid a tumult. Matthew alone mentions the significant hand-washing and the awful response of the multitude. Pilate may have hoped that the scourging, which was inflicted after these fruitless attempts to release Jesus, would satisfy the Jews; for, after the crown of thorns had been put upon Christ, Pilate exhibited Him to the multitude (John 19: 1-4, '*Ecce homo*').

Ver. 6. **Now at the feast,** or, 'a feast.' Annually at the passover.—**Used to release,** etc. Expressly mentioned by three Evangelists. When the custom arose is unknown, but it was undoubtedly designed to soften the Roman yoke. A turbulent people always sympathizes with criminals condemned by hated rulers. That they could choose the prisoner was a prominent feature.

Ver. 7. **Barabbas,** 'Bar-abbas,' *i. e.*, 'the son of his father;' al-

one called Barabbas, *lying* bound with them that had made insurrection, men who in the insurrection had 8 committed murder. And the multitude went up and began to ask him *to do* as he was wont to do unto them. 9 And Pilate answered them, saying, Will ye that I re- 10 lease unto you the King of the Jews? For he perceived that for envy the chief priests had delivered 11 him up. But the chief priests stirred up the multi-

though other meanings have been discovered in it. Some minor authorities call him 'Jesus Barabbas,' and many think he was a false Messiah; but this is a mere conjecture.—**With them that had made insurrection**, etc. Peculiar to Mark. Barabbas, doubtless the leader, was one of these insurgents and murderers. John calls him 'a robber.' Probably one of the Zealots, of whom Josephus speaks. His crime was really political.

Ver. 8. **And the multitude went up** (so the best authorities), *i. e.*, before the residence of Pilate, **and began to ask**. This picture of the mob in Jerusalem is true to the life. As the day wore on, the crowd collected, partly to see the trial, partly to call for the usual release of a prisoner, partly to be in a crowd, as is always the case on festival occasions. Pilate proposed to the rulers the choice between Jesus and Barabbas (Matthew, Luke), but the mob had probably already desired the latter as a political prisoner.

Ver. 9. **And Pilate answered them**. His policy was crooked. He ought to have released Jesus, but he would avoid opposing the council. He chose this expedient, probably with the idea that the popularity of Jesus would lead the multitude to call for His release. But he was outwitted, or at least mistaken. To put Jesus, as yet uncondemned, on a level with Barabbas, was a crime; a cowardly shirking of responsibility, and a blunder; for this proposal placed Pilate in the power of the Sanhedrin. Pilate was not 'weak and irresolute,' but baffled in his purpose by superior cunning. Yet his purpose, like his character, was lacking in moral earnestness; the grand defect of the heathen world at that time. Comp. his question, 'What is truth?' (John 18: 38), and his mocking tone throughout; indicated even here by his applying the phrase, **the King of the Jews**, to the prisoner he would release.

Ver. 10. **For envy**; of His popularity. This implies that Pilate had already known something of Jesus; but it shows his injustice, in not protecting Him as innocent. Still Pilate, while not wishing to directly oppose the rulers, really desired to thwart them.

Ver. 11. **The chief priests stirred up the multitude**. Probably while Pilate was receiving the message from his wife. The leaders would say: 'Jesus had been condemned by the orthodox court.

tude, that he should rather release Barabbas unto
12 them. And Pilate again answered and said unto
them, What then shall I do unto him whom ye call
13 the King of the Jews? And they cried out again,
14 Crucify him. And Pilate said unto them, Why,
what evil hath he done? But they cried out exceed-
15 ingly, Crucify him. And Pilate, wishing to content
the multitude, released unto them Barabbas, and delivered Jesus, when he had scourged him, to be crucified.

Barabbas was, on the contrary a champion of freedom; that Pilate wished to overthrow their right of choice, their civil rights, their spiritual authority, to persecute the friend of the people,' etc. The fact that Jesus was a Galilean may also have been used against Him.—**Rather release Barabbas.** Pilate's cunning recoiled on himself. From this point he was committed against Jesus. When questions of justice are entrusted to a mob, the innocent usually suffer.

Ver. 12. **What then shall I do unto him whom ye call,** etc. An effort to escape the consequences of his previous false step by appealing to the people, perhaps also an expression of surprise, mixed with contempt.

Ver. 13. **Again.** They cried out a second time, but the cry was not the same.—**Crucify him.** Pilate did not expect this. Their own law would have punished Jesus by stoning. But Pilate had placed Jesus on a level with Barabbas and they ask the punishment due to him. They put the Innocent One in the place of the guilty. Thus the details of prophecy in regard to the manner of Christ's death were to be fulfilled. Contrast this demand with the 'Hosannas' of the previous Sunday. Popular movements which do not rest on *moral* convictions are as shifting as the sand. The 'voice of the people,' when misguided, may be the voice of Satan; yet God overrules even this for good.

Ver. 14. **What evil hath he done?** Pilate repeated this question three times, joining with it the proposal to chastise Him and let Him go (Luke 23: 22). The only answer is a more excited demand: **they cried out exceedingly.** The mob was now in a dangerous mood (comp. Matthew 27: 24). The persistence of Pilate shows his real desire to release Jesus.

Ver. 15. **Wishing to content the multitude.** The word 'wishing' points to a decision, a determination, neither a hearty desire, nor a mere permission. In Matt. 1: 19 the same word is translated 'was minded.' The multitude felt that Pilate, by his previous proposal, was committed to a decision against Jesus. Hence a governor, representing the proud Roman power, the nation of legal enact-

16 And the soldiers led him away within the court,

ments, was forced to parley with a mob, which at another time he would have crushed with the severest measures. When Christ is to be crucified, no alliance of godless men is impossible, comp. Luke 23 : 12.— **Released unto them Barabbas, and delivered Jesus.** The delivery was to the Roman soldiers who executed the sentence, and yet it was also to the will of the Sanhedrin (comp. Luke 23 : 25). The guilty one was released, and the innocent one entered upon this punishment.—**When he had scourged him.** Scourging usually preceded crucifixion. As Pilate made further attempts to release Jesus (John 19 : 4-15), some have thought that this scourging was not the one which usually preceded crucifixion, but a distinct punishment—others even think that our Lord suffered twice from the lash. Pilate probably ordered the usual scourging, hoping still to release Jesus. He then showed Him (Ecce Homo) to the people, but in vain, as he might have known, for he had (Luke 23 : 16, 22) already twice proposed this punishment. Roman scourging was a fearful punishment. The entire body was bared, the lashes were given without number, thus differing from the Jewish mode. It could not be inflicted upon a Roman citizen (Acts 22 : 25), but was for slaves. In this case it was inflicted by soldiers. So that the whips were thongs with lead or bones attached. The prisoner was usually bound in a stooping posture so that the skin of the back was stretched tightly; as their backs were flayed by the process, they frequently fainted, and sometimes died. The soldiers who afterwards mocked Him, were not likely to be mild in this case. Yet the representative of civil justice proposed this as a milder punishment for One who was innocent. Thus Pilate sacrificed his independent position as a representative of the Roman law, to the fanaticism of the Jewish hierarchy. The State became a tool in the hands of an apostate and bloodthirsty Church. Pilate's conduct is an awful warning to rulers, who to gain popularity pander to religious fanaticism. His political fall was due to the accusation of these very people.

Vers. 16-20. THE MOCKING BY THE ROMAN SOLDIERS.—Parallel passage: Matt. 27 : 27-30. This occurrence must be distinguished from the similar one mentioned in Luke 23 : 11; the details being quite different.

Ver. 16. **And the soldiers.** Those to whom He had been delivered (ver. 15).—**Within the court, which is the Prætorium,** or, 'palace.' The governor's residence. The word *prætorium* was applied first to the general's tent in the Roman camp, then to the residence of the provincial governors, who were usually generals. Pilate, when in Jerusalem, probably lived in the former palace of Herod, 'on the northern brow of Zion, overlooking the enclosure of the temple, and connected with it by a bridge' (J. A. Alexander). But Lange thinks that Herod Antipas would probably have occupied this, and Pilate the castle Antonia.—**The whole band.** The tenth part of a

which is the ¹Prætorium; and they call together the whole ²band. And they clothe him with purple, and plaiting a crown of thorns, they put it on him; and they began to salute him, Hail, King of the Jews! And they smote his head with a reed, and did spit upon him, and bowing their knees worshipped him.

¹ Or, *palace*.   ² Or, *cohort*.

legion, the 'cohort,' numbering from four hundred to six hundred men, then on duty at Pilate's residence. It was probably in the open guard-room of the cohort, but this does not prove that the place was the castle Antonia.

Ver. 17. **And they clothe him with purple.** Matthew says: 'And they stripped Him, and put on Him a scarlet robe.' His clothing was replaced after the scourging, and probably also the robe which Herod had put on Him to mock Him (Luke 23: 11), usually supposed to have been white, marking Him as a *candidate* for royal honors. This robe was removed, and instead they put on Him a scarlet or purple robe, as the sign of His having attained royal honors. It was probably an ordinary military cloak. Both Mark and John speak of it as 'purple;' but imperial or royal purple is more scarlet than blue. Lange: 'The scarlet military cloak no more required to be a real purple, than the crown of thorns required to be a real crown, or the reed a real sceptre; for the whole transaction was an ironical drama, and such a one, too, that the infamous abuse might be readily perceived through the pretended glorification. The staff must be a reed, the symbol of impotence; the crown must injure and pierce the brow; and so, too, must the purple present the symbol of miserable pretended greatness: and this was done by its being an old camp-mantle.'—**A crown of thorns.** This would wound as well as mock Him, though the latter was the chief design. It is difficult to determine what kind of thorns was used. Alford says: 'Hasselquist, a Swedish naturalist, supposes a very common plant, *naba* or *nubka* of the Arabs, with many small and sharp spines; soft, round, and pliant branches; leaves much resembling ivy, of a very deep green, as if designed in mockery of a victor's wreath.'

Ver. 18. **And they began to salute him.** In feigned homage, greeting Him in the usual form: **Hail, King of the Jews!** A symbolical meaning may be found in all this mock-adoration.

Ver. 19. **And they smote his head with a reed**; this had been placed in His hand as a mock sceptre (Matthew).—**And did spit upon him.** The sport of wicked men wounds; if they are rough, it becomes brutality. Yet the Jews had done this (chap. 14: 65); Herod had taught these rude soldiers how to mock, and Pilate invited them to do it.

20 And when they had mocked him, they took off from him the purple, and put on his garments. And they lead him out to crucify him.

Ver. 20. **And when they had mocked him.** After this occurred the presentation to the people, the new accusation on the part of the Jews, the subsequent interview of Pilate and Jesus, the threat of the Jews, the final decision of Pilate, his taunts calling forth the cry: 'We have no king but Cæsar.' (See John 19: 4-15.) But his previous permission of the mockery shows a great lack of moral earnestness. 'The tender mercies of the wicked are cruel.' Though Pilate was neither weak nor irresolute, he exhibited that lack of moral principle which then characterized the heathen world. His position, authority, and convictions, render the course he pursued one which entitled his name to the continued pillory of shame accorded to it in the Apostles' creed.—**And they lead him out.** From the city Executions took place outside of the camp, here outside of the holy city. Num. 15: 35; 1 Kings 21: 13; Acts 7: 56. This may have been the Roman custom also. As Pilate had no lictors, soldiers led our Lord forth; a centurion (ver. 54) as usual headed the company. A herald generally went before the condemned person, but the Evangelists do not mention this.

Vers. 21-32. THE CRUCIFIXION; THE MOCKING.—Parallel passages: Matt. 27: 32-44; Luke 23: 26-43; John 19: 17-27. In Mark's account the chief points are: Simon of Cyrene; Golgotha; the bitter wine; the parting of the garments; the superscription; the two robbers crucified with Jesus; the blasphemies of the foes; the mocking by the robbers. As regards the place of the crucifixion, there is great uncertainty. Tradition has for fifteen centuries pointed out the site of the present 'Church of the Holy Sepulchre' as the actual spot. The arguments in favor of this popular opinion are—the unbroken tradition; the fact that no good case has been made out for any other locality. But tradition has proved an unsafe guide on such points, and it is highly probable that this spot was *inside* the city wall at that time. Nor is it necessary to fix the site, the whole question, however interesting, being of little practical importance. The Apostles and Evangelists barely allude to the place of Christ's birth, death, and resurrection. They fixed their eyes upon the great facts themselves, and worshipped the exalted Saviour in heaven, where He lives forever. Since the age of Constantine, in the fourth century, these localities have been abused in the service of an almost idolatrous superstition, yet not without continued protest from many of the wisest and best men of the Church. (There is a curious tradition that Adam was buried where the second Adam died and rose again.) It is repugnant to sound Christian feeling to believe that a spot so often profaned and disgraced by the most unworthy superstitions, impostures, and quarrels of Christian sects, should be the sacred spot where the Saviour died for the sins of the race. A wrong estimate of these holy places has already led to countless evils: even those who profess to be above such superstitions often spend more of time, trouble, and money in journeyings of sentimental curiosity thither, than they do for the spread of the gospel of the crucified and risen Redeemer. It would, therefore, seem a wise ordering of Providence that the exact locality *cannot* be determined.

21 And they ¹compel one passing by, Simon of Cyrene, coming from the country, the father of Alexander and Rufus, to go *with them,* that he might bear his cross. 22 And they bring him unto the place Golgotha, which

¹ Gr. *impress.*

Even if the traditional site be accepted, it is very unlikely that our Lord passed along the so called 'Via Dolorosa,' whether Pilate lived in the palace of Herod or in the castle Antonia.

Ver. 21. **And they compel,** *i. e.*, 'impress,' **one passing by,** etc. Probably a Jew who had come to attend the Passover, as many of them lived in Cyrene (in African Libya), frequently coming to Jerusalem (comp. Acts 2: 10; 6: 9). Some think he was chosen, because he was an African; others, because he was a slave, as one of this class would be considered fit for such a service; others, because he was a disciple: others still, because, meeting the procession, he showed some sympathy for Jesus. The last is the likeliest supposition. Simon Peter was not there; **Simon of Cyrene** took his place. —**Coming from the country.** Lit., 'from the field.' This statement throws no light on the reason why they impressed him for this service, nor upon the question whether it was the regular feast day or not.—**The father of Alexander and Rufus.** Persons well known to the first readers of this Gospel. As Mark probably wrote in Rome, the 'Rufus' saluted in Rom. 16: 13 may be the person here spoken of. But the name was a common one. This 'Alexander' can scarcely be the man put forward by the Jews at Ephesus (Acts 19: 33), who may or may not be identical with the person mentioned in 1 Tim. 1: 20; 2 Tim. 4: 14.—**That he might bear his cross.** Jesus at first bore His own cross (John 19: 17), as was customary. Tradition says that our Lord sunk to the ground beneath the load, but the more exact expression of Luke ('that he might bear it after Jesus'), shows that the after part of the cross alone, which usually dragged upon the ground, was put upon Simon. Those who bear the cross after Jesus the lightest end. Another incident on the way is mentioned by Luke (23: 27-31).

Ver. 22. **Unto the place Golgotha.** More correctly perhaps, place of Golgotha, answering to **place of a skull,** since Golgotha means 'skull,' and Luke (23: 33) calls the place simply 'skull.' It is very unlikely that it was the place of execution, and that the name arose from the skulls of the criminals lying there. The Jews did not leave bodies unburied, and in their mode of execution (stoning) the skulls would be broken; there is no evidence that the Jews had a special place for public execution; and a rich man like Joseph of Arimathæa would not have a garden near such a spot (John 19: 41). In that case, too, the name would have been, 'the place of skulls.' It is now generally believed that the form of the elevation (scarcely a *hill*) resembled a skull.

23 is, being interpreted, The place of a skull. And they offered him wine mingled with myrrh: but he re- 24 ceived it not. And they crucify him, and part his garments among them, casting lots upon them, what

Ver. 23. **They offered him,** or, 'were giving Him;' it was offered merely, not forced upon Him.—**Wine mingled with myrrh.** The correct reading in Matt. 27: 34 is, 'wine mingled with gall.' It was a stupefying draught, such as was commonly given before execution. The custom was, however, a Jewish rather than a Roman one.—**He received it not.** Matthew: 'When He had tasted it, He would not drink.' He afterwards took the unmixed vinegar wine, when He was about to say, 'It is finished' (comp. John 19: 28–30). He tastes this mixture, to show that He was aware of its purpose, and refuses it. He would drink of the cup His Father had given Him, but not of this. The early martyrs felt justified in thus mitigating their pains; but His vicarious sufferings must be borne to the fullest extent.

Ver. 24. **And they crucify him.** Crucifixion was a terrible punishment. Crosses were of different shapes; but in this case the form was probably that represented by the usual crucifix. Sometimes the victim was fastened to the cross after it had been set up; as often the condemned one was first fastened to the wood, and then the cross erected, and let fall into the hole dug for it, thus causing a fearful shock. A stupefying draught was often given; but our Lord refused to take this. In the perpendicular beam there was a small piece of wood, on which the sufferer rested. This was to prevent his weight from tearing the body from the nails; but it protracted the sufferings. Jesus was nailed to His cross through His hands and feet, as seems to have been usual. The punishment was Roman, not Jewish, but was deemed degrading by both nations. The physical suffering was intense, as physiologists have shown. To all this, in the case of our Lord, we must add the effect of such sufferings upon a soul so sensitive as His, also the effect of ingratitude, loneliness, taunts from His chosen people.—Men may honestly differ in their statements of the doctrine of the Atonement; but that our Lord then and there so suffered for men, that by virtue of His death we may be at peace with God, who hates our sins, is the only view that accounts for the facts. Hence the cross, the instrument of such torture, the sign of such shame, and on that account in itself a hindrance to the gospel among those who saw in it only this, has become the symbol of honor, blessing and redemption. Our forgetfulness of its original significance is an evidence of this change. Even the superstition that bows to it, however to be deprecated, witnesses that *the cross* is the centre of the Christian scheme.—As according to Jewish custom, the bodies must at once be taken down and buried, death was hastened by the *Crucifragium,* the breaking of the legs, to which was sometimes added 'a mer-

25 each should take. **And it was the third hour, and** 26 **they crucified him. And the superscription of his**

cy-stroke,' that is, the piercing of the body. If they were already dead, the latter alone was given, to make the matter sure. The act of crucifixion in the case of our Lord was attended with the prayer: 'Father, forgive them,' etc. (Luke 23: 34), commonly called 'the first Word from the Cross.'—**Part his garments.** The four soldiers (John). The clothes of those crucified were given to the executioners. —**Casting lots.** John tells us why it was necessary to do this (John 19: 23, 24). Gambling in the church has its fit prototype in this gambling by the cross for our Lord's garments.

Ver. 25. **And it was the third hour,** *i. e.*, nine o'clock in the morning. The last examination before the Jewish rulers took place at daybreak; three hours intervened, during which occurred the examinations before Pilate and Herod. A later hour would scarcely give time for all the incidents up to noon, at which time the darkness began. As death on the cross set in slowly, the period could not have been shorter than from nine o'clock to early evening, before sunset (see ver. 42). The accounts of Matthew and Luke accord with that of Mark in regard to the time of the darkness, and thus support the accuracy of this verse. But John (19: 14) says the final effort of Pilate to release Jesus was 'about the sixth hour.' 'The third hour' might mean some time during that watch (*i. e.* between nine and twelve, noon), and 'about the sixth' some time before; but such an explanation is very unsatisfactory. An error in the text of John is possible, owing to the resemblance between the Greek signs for 3 and 6; but this explanation is not supported by any considerable evidence. A third and the most probable solution is, that John uses the Roman mode of reckoning time, from midnight to midnight. In other cases (1: 40; 4: 6) it is not certain that he uses the common Jewish method from sunrise to sunset. The supposition of a mistake on the part of one of the Evangelists is inadmissible. About the events of such a day these two men *could not make a mistake.* With memories so correct about such minute details, they could not possibly forget *precisely when Christ was crucified.* Some good explanation can be given, even if we are not competent to do so. An apparent discrepancy of such long standing is a proof (1) that there was no collusion between the two writers, if the difference originally existed; (2) that those who have held these writings as sacred have been very honest, or such an apparent disagreement would have disappeared long ago.

Ver. 26. **And the superscription,** etc. It was customary for the person to be crucified to carry 'a title,' suspended from his neck, to the place of execution.—**Was written over.** Fastened to the upright beam of the cross. It was written in three languages—Greek, Latin, and Hebrew (John 19: 20. The clause in Luke 23: 38 is to be omitted). John also tells that Pilate, having written 'this title,' re-

accusation was written over, THE KING OF THE JEWS. 27 And with him they crucify two robbers; one on his 29 right hand, and one on his left.¹ And they that passed by railed on him, wagging their heads, and saying, Ha! thou that destroyest the ²temple, and buildest it

¹ Many ancient authorities insert ver. 28 *And the scripture was fulfilled, which saith, And he was reckoned with transgressors.* See Luke xxii. 37. ²Or, *sanctuary*

fused to alter it at the request of the chief priests. The 'accusation' was a sneer at the Jews, but the proper title of our Lord. 'By this inscription, so humbling to the Jews, Pilate took vengeance for the degrading constraint to which they had subjected him by forcing him to execute an innocent man.' (Godet). The three languages were those most important in the history of Christianity.—**The King of the Jews.** The four Evangelists each give a different form. This is a proof of independence, but *not* of inaccuracy. Three forms might have been given in three different languages; while the fourth (most likely that of Mark) is a partial transcription, giving the words common to all four accounts. Matthew and Mark make prominent the fact that this was the one charge against our Lord.

Ver. 27. **And with him they crucify two robbers**; who had been led out with Him (Luke 23: 32). These may have been associates of Barabbas, and hence placed on either side of Jesus, who had taken the punishment due to Barabbas. This proceeding carries out the mockery implied in the title; these two representing the subjects of 'the King of the Jews.' The usual punishment for robbery was crucifixion.

Ver. 28. This verse (a quotation from Is. 53: 12) is omitted by the oldest manuscripts and rejected by the latest critics. In Luke 22: 37, its genuineness is undoubted. Mark rarely quotes prophecies so directly.

Ver. 29. **They that passed by.** People walking about, probably coming that way, for the purpose of seeing the execution. The morbid taste for horrors no doubt existed then, and popular hatred was aroused. Besides, the dignitaries were there (ver. 31)! The elevation seems to have formed a natural stage for the public exposure of the crucified.—**Railed on him**; lit., 'blasphemed.' They reviled, but it was in this case blasphemy.—**Wagging their heads** (comp. Ps. 22: 7), in malignant triumph mingled with contempt.—**Ha!** The Greek word is the one used in the ancient games, as a shout of applause; here it seems to be applied ironically to our Lord. But it might have been an expression of reproach.—**Thou that destroyest the temple**, etc. The people had heard the report of the trial (chap. 14: 58), and, being proud of the temple, naturally made this taunt. Such conduct is not uncommon in a crowd at an execution.—**Save thyself.** If He could rebuild the temple, He could do this. They

30 in three days, save thyself, and come down from the
31 cross. In like manner also the chief priests mocking
him among themselves with the scribes said, He saved
32 others; ¹ himself he cannot save. Let the Christ, the
King of Israel, now come down from the cross, that
we may see and believe. And they that were crucified
with him reproached him.

¹ Or, *can he not save himself?*

little knew how truly He would fulfil the words they quoted. The variations in the language, discoverable in the different accounts, are equally natural; some would say one thing, some another, though the tone was in general the same. Luke says (13 : 35): 'the people stood beholding.' It appears therefore that the derision of the people was by no means so malignant as that of the rulers. But their taunts were especially ungrateful.

Ver. 31. **In like manner also the chief priests**, etc. All classes of the Sanhedrin were represented, probably in large numbers, and their taunt is of a public, national character. Thus the chief ecclesiastical personages acted on the great festival day of their religion. The language is differently reported by the several Evangelists. The mockery was probably continued for some time, and would vary in form.—**He saved others.** This may be ironical, or it is a recognition of His miracles of mercy, to taunt Him with a supposed loss of power just when He needed it most for Himself. His very mercy is used in mockery.—The marginal rendering is even more cutting.

Ver. 32. **Let the Christ, the King of Israel,** etc. Ironical, with a mocking suggestion of still being open to the proof of His Messiahship. But He is the true king of the real Israel.—**That we may see and believe.** Unless there was an *atoning* purpose in Christ's death, it will always seem strange that He did not offer some such miraculous proof of His power. The soldiers repeated this reproach, but of course without this last clause (see Luke 23: 36, 37). Matthew here inserts a citation, made in mockery, from Ps. 22: 8.— **And they that were crucified with him reproached him.** Luke (23: 39-43) alone tells of the penitence of one. Both probably at first reproach Him, but one was afterwards converted, during the three hours they hung side by side. It is not satisfactory to refer 'the robbers' to but one. (At this point occurred the touching incident in John 19: 26, 27.) The robbers were placed beside Him in mockery; but over one of them He displayed His kingly power. How can we deny sin when we listen to the mockery on Golgotha! Christ came to save men by His atoning death, hence He could not come down from the cross. The whole story is full of paradoxes explained only by the fact of a real Atonement made by the Son of God. Jesus

33 And when the sixth hour was come, there was dark-
34 ness over the whole ¹land until the ninth hour. And

¹ Or, *earth.*

Christ, declared righteous, took the place of the guilty, that we who are guilty might be declared righteous.

Vers. 33–41. THE DARKNESS, AND THE DEATH OF JESUS.—Parallel passages: Matt. 27: 45-56; Luke 23: 44-49; John 19: 28-30. The account of Mark resembles that of Matthew, but omits some details given by the latter. These two Evangelists give but one utterance from the cross (ver. 34). The order of the Seven Words (as they are called) is: Before the darkness: 1. The prayer of Christ for His enemies. 2. The promise to the penitent robber. 3. The charge to Mary and John. At the close of the darkness: 4. This cry of distress to His God. Just before His death: 5. The exclamation: 'I thirst.' 6. 'It is finished.' 7. The final commendation of His spirit to God.

Ver. 33. **The sixth hour,** *i. e.,* at noon. The form of the verse, as well as the connection, shows that our Lord had already hung for some time upon the cross (see ver. 25). From midday to three o'clock in the afternoon, usually the brightest part of the day, **there was darkness.** Besides the testimony of the three Evangelists, early Christian writers speak of it and appeal to heathen testimony to support the truth. It could not have been an ordinary eclipse, for the moon was full that day. Although an earthquake followed (Matt. 27: 51), yet even that was no ordinary earthquake, and the obscuration was too entire and too long continued to be the darkness which often precedes an earthquake. It was a miraculous occurrence designed to exhibit the amazement of nature and of the God of nature at the wickedness of the crucifixion of Him who is the light of the world and the sun of righteousness. To deny its supernatural character seems to impair this design. If Jesus of Nazareth is what the Gospels represent Him to be, the needs of humanity ask Him to be, and the faith of the Christian finds Him to be, the supernatural here seems natural.—**Over the whole land.** Possibly only the whole land of Judea; the main point being the fact in Jerusalem. Still it may refer to the whole earth (see margin), *i. e.,* where it was day, especially as the heathen notices of what is generally supposed to be the same event, justify an extension beyond Judea. Heubner: Suidas relates that Dionysius the Areopagite (then a heathen), saw the eclipse in Egypt, and exclaimed: 'Either God is suffering, and the world sympathizes with Him, or else the world is hurrying to destruction.'

Ver. 34. **And at the ninth hour.** During the three hours of darkness, our Lord was silent. He seems not to have become gradually exhausted, for after nearly six hours on the cross, according to three Evangelists, **Jesus cried with a loud voice** (comp. ver. 37). The agony resembles that in Gethsemane, but seems even more intense.—**Eloi.** The opening words of Ps. 22, in the Aramaic dialect then in use. Our Lord probably used the Hebrew form ('Eli') given by Matthew, which more closely resembles the name Elijah. A quotation

at the ninth hour Jesus cried with a loud voice, Eloi, Eloi, lama sabachthani? which is, being interpreted, 35 My God, my God, [1] why hast thou forsaken me? And some of them that stood by, when they heard it, said, 36 Behold, he calleth Elijah. And one ran, and filling a

[1] Or, *why didst thou forsake me?*

from the Old Testament would naturally be made in Hebrew, but the manuscripts give a variety of forms, both here and in Matt. 27: 46. That the whole Psalm was a prophecy of Christ, even if it had another primary reference, is the opinion of the Evangelists at least; and it may be added, of our Lord Himself in His deepest sorrow.—**My God, my God, why hast thou forsaken me?** The marginal rendering is more literal, but the sense of the Hebrew is better conveyed by the usual form. This language cannot be accounted for by physical causes alone, nor be regarded as a meaningless citation of well-known words. Only the burden of sin, borne in the place of others, could create the feeling which thus found expression. There was an experience of sin and death in their inner connection and universal significance for the race, by One who was perfectly pure and holy, a mysterious and indescribable anguish of the *body* and the *soul* in immediate prospect of, and in actual wrestling with, death as the wages of sin and the culmination of all misery of man, of which the Saviour was free, but which He voluntarily assumed from infinite love in behalf of the race. In this anguish He expresses His actual feeling of abandonment. But His spirit still holds fast to God, and thus our hold on God is established. We need not despair, even if God seems to hide His face from us.

Ver. 35. **And some of them that stood by.** Of the Jewish spectators, hardly of the soldiers, who would know little or nothing of Elijah.—**Calleth Elijah.** There was such a resemblance between the Hebrew word 'Eli' and the name of Elijah, as to suggest this sarcastic remark. Elijah was expected to appear before the Messiah came, and this one, who claimed to be the Messiah, was now calling for His forerunner to come. A real misapprehension is very improbable. Even this profoundest expression of atoning love was mocked at.

Ver. 36. **And one ran.** This was occasioned by our Lord's cry, 'I thirst' (John 19: 28), but all occurred in quick succession.—**And filling a sponge.** It would be impossible to use a cup.—**Vinegar.** The sour wine (without the 'myrrh') used by the soldiers, and placed there in a vessel for their refreshment. The soldiers had offered Him drink (Luke 23: 36) much earlier, so that this was probably not one of them.—**A reed.** 'Hyssop,' according to John. This was to reach it to Him. The head of one crucified would be about two feet above that of one standing on the ground.—**Gave him to drink.** He drank (John 19: 30), and this reception of refreshment from one who

sponge full of vinegar, put it on a reed, and gave him to drink, saying, Let be; let us see whether Elijah 37 cometh to take him down. And Jesus uttered a loud 38 voice, and gave up the ghost. And the veil of the

still mocked is a token that His love vanquishes the world's hate.—**Saying, Let be,** etc. In Matthew's account, these words are addressed *to* the man who gave the vinegar, here spoken *by* him to the others. A sign of accuracy; such a conversation is natural; the one addressed by the crowd flinging back their own words. 'Let be' means 'let this suffice,' until we see Elijah coming. The man may have had the passing earnest thought that Elijah might come. But to keep on good terms with the excited jeering rabble, he assumes the same tone with them.—**To take him down.** Matthew: 'to save Him. The two Evangelists give two distinct parts of the same conversation.

Ver. 37. **And Jesus uttered a loud voice.** The last words were those recorded in Luke 23: 46: 'Father, into thy hands,' etc., immediately preceded by the triumphant cry, 'It is finished' (John 19: 30). The latter cry is probably meant here, since the 'loud voice' (Luke 23: 46) seems to refer to a previous cry (but see margin there). 'His soul has recovered full serenity. Not long ago He was struggling with the Divine sovereignty and holiness. Now the darkness is gone; He has recovered His light, His Father's face. It is the first effect of the completion of redemption, the glorious prelude of the resurrection' (Godet).—**Gave up the ghost**; the literal sense here is, 'breathed out,' expired. 'A beautiful substitute for *died*, which all the Evangelists appear to have avoided' (J. A. Alexander). The interval between the agonized cry, 'My God,' etc., and the actual death in triumph and confidence, was very brief. The physical cause of His death has been thought by many to have been rupture of the heart. There was no gradual weakening, but a sudden death. Furthermore, this view accounts for the statement of John 19: 34: 'there came out blood and water,' rupture of the heart being followed by an effusion of blood into the pericardium, resulting in a separation of its solid and liquid parts. These parts would be termed 'blood and water,' in ordinary language. But far more important than this is the fact that the accounts represent our Lord's death as in great measure a voluntary surrender of life. His Father accepted the offering, which His own justice had required (Rom. 3: 25, 26). The expression of human want ('I thirst'), seems to have been uttered to show that one of our race was suffering there, and at the same time to obtain the physical support needed to proclaim the victory won by that One of our race for us. After the victory came the spirit's rest in the Eternal Father. More than victory is rest in God.

Ver. 38. **The veil of the temple,** etc. The veil before the Holy

¹temple was rent in twain from the top to the bottom. 39 And when the centurion, which stood by over against him, saw that he ²so gave up the ghost, he said, Truly 40 this man was ³the Son of God. And there were also

¹ Or, *sanctuary.*
² Many ancient authorities read *so cried out, and gave up the ghost.*
³ Or, *a son of God.*

of Holies, separating it from the Holy Place. This may have been a result of the convulsion mentioned in the next clause, but the accounts do not indicate this. Supernatural agency is more than probable, in view of the significance of the occurrence. This took place toward the time of the evening sacrifice. Even if at first known only to the priests, it would still be made known to Christians, since 'a great company of the priests' were afterwards converted (Acts 6:7). It was 'a sign of the removal of the typical atonement, through the completion of the real atonement, which insures us a free access to God: Heb. 6:19; 9:6; 10:19.'

Ver. 39. **The centurion.** Mark here and in vers. 44, 45, gives the Latin term; Matthew and Luke, the Greek.—**Stood by over against him,** *i. e.*, in front of Him, 'watching' (Matthew) Him.—**Saw that he so gave up the ghost.** The peculiar cry is mainly referred to, hence this was very early inserted, and is retained in the A. V. (see margin above). Mark alone gives prominence to this point, and it is characteristic of his Gospel. 'The Lion of Judah is, even in His departing, a dying lion' (Lange).—**Truly this man was the son of God,** or, 'a son of God.' The heathen officer may have used these words in the heathen sense: hero or demi-god; but this is not probable. For he had heard this accusation, must have known something of Jewish opinion; heathen became Christians through the preaching of the cross, why not through the sight of the dying Redeemer? Such a conversion would be thus indicated. Nor is it certain that this phrase meant demi-god. It might be the germ of a Christian confession, without being expressed in the full form, *the* Son of God. Comp. the statement of Luke (23:47), which does not oppose this view. Only the centurion thus spoke, but as the soldiers 'feared,' some decided spiritual effect may have been produced on them also.

Ver. 40. This verse and the following one agree in substance with Matt. 27:55, 56; but the order is different, and the other variations throw much light on the questions which have arisen as to the persons mentioned.—**And there were also women.** Luke (23:40) speaks of 'all His acquaintance' before these women. John was certainly present, probably some of the other disciples.—**Beholding from afar.** At one time a few ventured near the cross (John 19:25-27), but not 'many.'—**Among whom were both Mary Magdalene.** Mentioned first here and in Luke 8:2 (among those who

women beholding from afar: among whom *were* both Mary Magdalene, and Mary the mother of James the 41 ¹less and of Joses, and Salome; who, when he was in Galilee, followed him, and ministered unto him; and many other women which came up with him unto Jerusalem.

¹ Gr. *little.*

ministered to Him). Comp. chap. 16: 1, 9; Matt. 28: 2; John 20: 1, 11–18. There is no evidence that she was the sinful woman who anointed our Lord's feet in the house of Simon the Pharisee (Luke 7: 37). Many confuse her with another Mary, the sister of Lazarus (who anointed our Lord in Bethany, chap. 14: 6–13, etc.).—**Mary the mother of James the less**; Greek, 'little.' Undoubtedly the wife of Alpheus (John 19: 25), hence 'James the little' is the Apostle 'James the son of Alpheus' (chap. 3: 18; Matt. 10: 3). She was *not* the sister of our Lord's mother (see chap. 6: 3; John 19: 25); but **Salome**, 'the mother of the sons of Zebedee' (Matt. 27: 56), probably was. An additional reason for this view, and also against the opinion that James the son of Alpheus, here spoken of, is identical with 'James the Lord's brother' (Gal. 1: 19), is to be found in the expression here used: 'James the little.' This may refer either to his age or his stature, probably the latter; but in any case it is used to distinguish him. James the son of Zebedee had been put to death many years before this Gospel was written (Acts 12: 2), and the readers of this Gospel would need this term only to distinguish this person from James the Just, the brother of our Lord, who was well known throughout the early church, and the author of the General Epistle of James.—**Joses.** Against the view that this too was one of the Lord's brothers (Matt. 13: 55; Mark 6: 3), is the fact that his name occurs here twice (vers. 40, 47) to distinguish this Mary, when, according to the theory we oppose, two other brothers (Judas and Simon), who are thus assumed to be Apostles, are not mentioned. Mary, the mother of our Lord, had probably been conducted away by John before this time (see Matt. 27: 56; John 19: 27).

Ver. 41. **Who, when he was in Galilee,** etc. This refers, probably, more particularly to the three just named. Comp. on these ministering women, Luke 8: 2.—**And many other women,** etc. All had come up from Galilee, and it is not necessary to distinguish the two groups very exactly; the three are named, doubtless, because of what follows in ver. 47 and chap. 16: 1. These pious women, who, with the courage of heroes, witnessed the dying moments of their Lord and Master, and sat over against the lonely sepulchre (Matt. 26: 61), are the shining examples of female constancy and devotion to Christ which we now can witness every day in all the churches, and which will never cease.

42 And when even was now come, because it was the
43 Preparation, that is, the day before the sabbath, there came Joseph of Arimathæa, a councillor of honourable estate, who also himself was looking for the kingdom of God; and he boldly went in unto Pilate, and asked
44 for the body of Jesus. And Pilate marvelled if he

Vers. 42-47. THE BURIAL OF JESUS.—Parallel passages: Matt. 27: 57-61; Luke 23: 50-56; John 19: 38-42. Mark's account contains some minor incidents passed over by the other Evangelists. On the events which occurred immediately before the request of Joseph (the piercing of His side, in consequence of the scruples of the Jews, which required burial that evening), see John 19: 31-37. This early death was unusual (comp. Pilate's surprise, ver. 44), but thus the Scripture was fulfilled (John 19: 36-37). The burial, as an important fact, proving the reality of the death of Jesus, is mentioned by all four Evangelists.

Ver. 42. **And when even was now come.** The first evening before sundown, at which time the bodies must be removed (Deut. 21: 23). Our Lord's death took place at three in the afternoon.—**Because it was the Preparation,** etc. The first day of the passover (Friday) was in one sense a Sabbath, hence this designation is more definite. It has also been supposed that the word 'Preparation' was the solemn designation in use among the Christians to distinguish the Friday of the crucifixion (Meyer).—**The day before the sabbath,** *i. e.,* Friday. Joseph and the Jews (John 19: 31) desired 'that the bodies should not remain upon the cross on the Sabbath.' The Sabbath of the festival week was, as usual in such cases, a 'high day' (John 19: 31).

Ver. 43. **There came.** Probably, to the company of women standing on Golgotha (ver. 41). His going to Pilate is mentioned afterwards.—**Joseph of Arimathæa.** Either Ramah in Benjamin (Josh. 18: 25, comp. Matt. 2: 18) or Ramah (Ramathaim) in Ephraim, the birth-place of Samuel (1 Sam. 1: 19). The form favors the latter view; the addition of Luke: 'a city of the Jews,' the former. One Joseph takes care of Jesus in His infancy, another provides for His burial.—**A councillor of honourable estate.** He was a member of the Sanhedrin, of high character, who had not consented to the murder (Luke 23: 50-51).—**Who also himself was,** etc. He expected the Messiah, and had been a secret disciple of Jesus (John 19: 38).—**And he boldly went in,** etc. He had probably seen the breaking of the legs of the other two, was aware of the request of the Jews that the bodies should be taken down. If he would pay this tribute of respect to one whom he had followed in secret, he must quickly and publicly take this step, this was therefore the decisive act which marked the change from a secret to an open discipleship.

Ver. 44. **And Pilate marvelled.** Not at the request, but: **if he were already dead.** This shows there was something unusual

were already dead : and calling unto him the centurion, he asked him whether he ¹had been any while dead. 45 And when he learned it of the centurion, he granted 46 the corpse to Joseph. And he bought a linen cloth, and taking him down, wound him in the linen cloth, and laid him in a tomb which had been hewn out of a rock; and he rolled a stone against the door of the

¹ Many ancient authorities read *were already dead.*

in this case of crucifixion. Pilate had already given orders to have the legs of the crucified broken and the bodies taken down. The first part of the order had been carried out, but our Lord was already dead. The two other bodies were probably taken down at once, but Joseph, appearing at Golgotha (as Matthew and Mark state) made known to the soldiers his purpose; hence they left the body of Jesus on the cross, perhaps going with Joseph to Pilate, in the expectation that his request (as that of a rich and influential man) would be granted. The sudden announcement to Pilate of the rapid death of this Person, in whom he had been so interested that day, amazed him, and led to his inquiry of the centurion.

Ver. 45. **Granted the corpse to Joseph.** Presented it to him. The position of Joseph seems to have occasioned this ready compliance, though Pilate was doubtless glad to hear that Jesus was dead and to have Him buried.

Ver. 46. **And he bought a linen cloth.** It has been argued from this purchase that the day was 'not the first day of unleavened bread, which was one of sabbatical sanctity;' but in Lev. 23 : 7, labor alone was forbidden on that day.—**Taking him down.** Mentioned by all the Evangelists but Matthew.—**Wound him in the linen cloth**; or a winding sheet. This would enclose the spices used in the temporary embalming, which now took place. Nicodemus having brought the spices (John 19 : 39, 40). There was not time enough to embalm on Friday evening, so the costly gifts of Nicodemus were used to preserve the body, the women preparing in the interval what they thought necessary for the further anointing.—**In a tomb.** (In the Revised Version an effort has been made to discriminate between two similar Greek words by the use of 'tomb' and 'sepulchre' for each respectively.) That the tomb belonged to Joseph is implied here, that it was new is omitted by Mark alone. The fact that it was 'new' (comp. Luke 23 : 53; John 19 : 41), seems designed to overcome any suspicion as to the identity of Him who rose. The location was in a 'garden' (John 19 : 41), near the spot of the crucifixion and hence well adapted for the hurried burial.—**Hewn out of a rock**, an artificial excavation, probably prepared at great cost. It seems to have been cut horizontally and not downward—**He rolled a stone.**

47 tomb. And Mary Magdalene and Mary the *mother* of Joses beheld where he was laid.

16: 1 And when the sabbath was past, Mary Magdalene, and Mary the *mother* of James, and Salome, bought

The common method of closing sepulchres.—**Against the door of the tomb.** There was but one entrance.

Ver. 47. **Mary the mother of Joses.** The same person mentioned in ver. 40.—**Beheld,** lit., 'were beholding,' a continued action. Matt. 27: 61: 'sitting over against the sepulchre.'—**Where he was laid.** Luke (23: 55), although mentioning the Galilean women more generally, says: 'and how His body was laid.' Evidently the inspection was with a view to mark the spot, for the future anointing; but affection made these two linger. The original indicates that they came after the burial, entering without hesitation the garden of the rich councillor. The two members of the Sanhedrin (Joseph and Nicodemus; John 19: 38, 39) were still probably there. The company was a singular one, but a type of the Christian congregations collected together by the death of Christ.—Salome was absent. If she were the sister of our Lord's mother, she should go to comfort her mourning sister, who had probably left the scene of the crucifixion under the conduct of John some time before. Their temporary residence would be in the same place (John 19: 27). An incidental hint of accuracy and truthfulness.

Chap. XVI: THE RESURRECTION.—Early on the first day of the week, the women came to the tomb, and found it empty. The Lord had risen. The various accounts are in apparent confusion, setting forth the mingled doubt and joy of that day, as the several sets of the disciples became convinced of the fact. On this fact rests the apostolic preaching, historical Christianity. If it is not a fact, then Christianity is a stream without a fountain, an effect without a cause. The difficulty in harmonizing the narratives satisfactorily in every particular, arises naturally from our want of knowledge of all the details in the precise order of their occurrence. Indeed, minor differences with substantial agreement confirm the main facts far more than a literal agreement would. The Gospel witnesses suggest no suspicion of a previous understanding and mutual dependence.

The New Testament writers refer to *ten* distinct appearances of the Risen Lord; *five* on the day of the Resurrection, and *five* subsequently. The following order is the most probable:

(1.) The appearance to Mary Magdalene (John 20: 14; Mark 16: 9).

(2.) To the other women (Matt. 28: 9). The main difficulty in harmonizing the accounts is just here. (See below.)

(3.) To Peter (Luke 24: 34; 1 Cor. 15: 5).

(4.) To the two disciples on the way to Emmaus, toward evening on Sunday (Mark 16: 12, 13; Luke 24: 13–32).

(5.) To the Apostles (*except* Thomas), on Sunday evening (Mark 16: 14; Luke 24: 36; John 20: 19, 24).—These five occurred on the day of the resurrection.

(6.) To the Apostles *with* Thomas; a week after (John 20: 24–29), in Jerusalem, where they had waited throughout the Passover. That ended on Friday; on Saturday (the Jewish Sabbath) they would not start for Galilee; perhaps they waited over Sunday, because they already regarded it as holy.

(7.) In Galilee, at the Lake of Gennesaret, to seven disciples (John 21), the *third time* to the assembled Apostles (John 21: 14).

(8.) To the multitude of disciples on a mountain in Galilee (Matt. 28: 16–20; comp. Mark 16: 15–18; 1 Cor. 15: 6). Possibly the passage in 1 Cor. refers to still another appearance.

(9.) To James (1 Cor. 15: 7). It is doubtful which James this was, and equally so whether it was in Galilee or Jerusalem.

(10.) The final appearance, closing with the Ascension (Luke 24: 50, 51; Acts 1: 9, 10). Probably referred to in the last clause of 1 Cor. 15: 7. Others make that a distinct appearance, and so reckon (see under 8) *twelve* instead of ten.

Of these appearances this chapter mentions three: That to Mary Magdalene (ver. 9); that to the two disciples (vers. 12, 13), and a third to the Eleven, which may be either (5.) or (6.).

No account is given of the Galilean appearances, although the command to return there is indicated (ver. 7). Mark does not mention the appearance to the other women, in his account of the visit to the tomb; but in combining the narratives it is necessary to arrange the details somewhat as follows: Three women, Mary Magdalene, Mary the mother of James, and Salome two of whom had watched by the sepulchre Friday evening (chap. 27: 61), start for the sepulchre early on Sunday morning (Mark 16; 1; comp. ver. 1), followed by others bearing spices (Luke 24: 1). These three finding the stone rolled away are differently affected: Mary Magdalene starting back to meet the male disciples who are also coming (John 20: 2); the other two remaining, approach nearer, and see one angel sitting upon the stone (vers. 2–7). They go back to meet the other women coming with the spices. While all are absent, Peter and John come, and find the tomb empty (John 20: 3–10). Mary Magdalene returns, sees two angels in the grave (John 20: 12), and turning round sees Jesus, and takes the tidings to the disciples (John 20: 14–18). The other two, surprised by the message of the angel, meet the other women bringing spices; all visit the tomb, and see the two angels standing (Luke 24: 4–7), one of whom was sitting on the right side as they entered (Mark 16: 5). As they go back they meet the Lord (Matt. 28: 9). It will be noticed that all the appearances of the Risen Lord were to disciples. To have revealed Himself to others, would have misled or hardened them, would have interfered with the quiet training of the disciples during the forty days He lingered here. It is idle to suppose that such appearances to His enemies would have increased the weight of testimony to His resurrection. This world beholdeth Him no more (John 14: 19).

Chap. 16: 1–8. The Visit to the Tomb.—Parallel passages: Matt. 28: 1–8; Luke 24: 1 10; comp. John 20: 1–10. The independence of the Evangelist is clearly shown in this paragraph; see above.

Ver. 1. **When the sabbath was past.** After sunset on Satur-

2 spices, that they might come and anoint him. And very early on the first day of the week, they come to
3 the tomb when the sun was risen. And they were saying among themselves, Who shall roll us away the
4 stone from the door of the tomb? and looking up, they see that the stone is rolled back: for it was ex-
5 ceeding great. And entering into the tomb, they saw

day. On the three women, see chap. 15: 40.—**Bought spices.** Luke 23: 56 does not necessarily imply that the preparation of spices took place on Friday, before the beginning of the Sabbath. Even if most of the women began the preparations at that time, these three were not thus engaged. The two Maries sat over against the sepulchre late on Friday (Matthew), and Salome had probably rejoined her sister Mary. The resting on the Sabbath is expressly affirmed by Luke.—**Anoint him.** Nicodemus (John 19: 39–40) had done this in a necessarily hasty manner; see chap. 15: 46.

Ver. 2. **Very early.** In the East this would mean before sunrise, as the other accounts show. The anxious women would go to the tomb as soon as possible.—**When the sun was risen.** This may be taken literally as referring to the time when they reached the tomb, or less exactly, 'when the sun was about to rise.' The accounts vary in form; John saying: 'while it was yet dark;' but in Palestine the twilight is short, and all point to the same time, namely, near daybreak.

Ver. 3. **And they were saying,** etc. This rendering is more striking as well as more exact.—**Who shall roll,** etc? A natural and graphic touch in the narrative. The Lord had removed the difficulty before it was actually encountered.

Ver. 4. **Looking up.** They may have been looking down before, absorbed in their conversation; the tomb was probably above them, cut horizontally in the face of the rock at a slight elevation.—**They see that the stone is rolled back.** Possibly 'rolled up,' as if it had rested in a hollow at the door of the tomb.—**For it was exceeding great.** This does not mean that the greatness of the stone was the reason of their anxiety and questioning, although this was doubtless true, but that its size enabled them to notice the position, even in the early morning. A vivid touch peculiar to Mark. An angel had removed it (Matt. 28: 2).

Ver. 5. **And entering into the tomb.** That it was of great size is evident. This entrance (as suggested above) took place after an interval, during which the three separated, after the angelic message mentioned in Matt. 28: 2-7, the two Maries returning with the other women, and entering the tomb. On the other intervening events, see above.—**A young man.** Mark thus vividly describes an angel. Luke speaks of 'two men,' afterwards referring to them as 'angels' (24:

a young man sitting on the right side, arrayed in a
6 white robe; and they were amazed. And he saith
unto them, Be not amazed: ye seek Jesus, the Nazarene,
which had been crucified: he is risen; he is not here:
7 behold, the place where they laid him! But go, tell
his disciples and Peter, He goeth before you into
Galilee: there shall ye see him, as he said unto you.

23). Mark describes the first impression as the women went in. Luke is more general; but it is not probable that he joins the two angels spoken of separately by Matthew and Mark. For, according to John, Mary Magdalene saw two angels sitting *in* the tomb, and this was probably *before* the entrance of these women.—**Sitting on the right side.** Compare John 20: 12, which refers to a different occasion. Also, Luke 24: 4, which tells of the same occurrence *within* the tomb, but less definitely. Peter and John had already been there and seen *no* angel (John 20: 3-8). The mission of the angels was to comfort and instruct the disciples, not to perplex them and us by the mysterious disappearances, and reappearances which some other explanations suggest.—**White robe.** A supernatural brightness may be implied, as in chap. 9: 3. Comp. Matt. 28: 3; Luke 24: 4.—**And they were amazed.** As was natural, even if there had been a previous appearance of angels.

Ver. 6. **Be not amazed.** (In rendering words indicating astonishment, the Rev. Vers. has preserved the correspondences and variations of the original.)—**Which hath been crucified.** The form used is common in the New Testament, pointing to what *has* happened, but with present results.—**He is risen.** Hilary: 'Through woman death was first introduced into the world: to woman the first announcement was made of the resurrection.' This is probably not identical with the message in Matt. 28: 5-7, given outside the tomb, but a second one (reported by Luke also), which is, however, substantially a repetition of the previous one.

Ver. 7. **But.** Emphatic: instead of lingering here, **go tell**, etc. —**And Peter.** A special token of love to this one who had denied Him, and a recognition of his prominence among his equals.—**He goeth before you into Galilee**; as had been foretold in chap. 14: 28. Comp. Luke 24: 6-7; John 10: 4.—**There shall ye see him.** Still part of the message, and yet indirectly applicable to the hearers also —**As he said unto you.** The command to go into Galilee is found in Matthew's account, and John tells in greatest detail what occurred there, so that both the command and its fulfilment are well established. Luke 24: 49 is not in conflict with this; judging from the context there, that command was given *after* the return from Galilee. The disciples would naturally linger at Jerusalem; hence the first

8 And they went out, and fled from the tomb; for trembling and astonishment had come upon them; and they said nothing to any one; for they were afraid.

9 ¹Now when he was risen early on the first day of the week, he appeared first to Mary Magdalene, from whom

¹ The two oldest Greek manuscripts, and some other authorities, omit from ver. 9 to the end. Some other authorities have a different ending to the Gospel.

command was needed, to bring them to the most fitting place for the appearance to the whole Church (in Galilee where it was safer, and where the new Church would be most separated from the Old Economy).

Ver. 8. **And fled from the tomb.** In a tumult of excitement. **For trembling and astonishment had come upon them.** This was the reason of their fleeing.—**And they said nothing to any one; for they were afraid.** Matthew twice (28: 8–11) speaks of their going to deliver the message, hence some explain this clause: they told no one *by the way.* But Mark's words mean that they did *not,* immediately at least, deliver the message. The 'fear' spoken of by Matthew is made prominent here; joined with the fright from what they had seen was a fear that their reports would be (as they actually were) deemed 'idle talk' by the disciples (Luke 24: 11). In this state of indecision, as they ran back, the Lord meets them (Matt. 28: 9–10), overcomes their fear ('Fear not,' He says), and they go on with the message, now coming from the Lord Himself. The remarkable events of that day produced mingled and indeed confused emotions. To that of fear and indecision, Mark gives prominence. Even these faithful women were full of doubt; a fact that upsets all theories resembling the Jewish falsehood, mentioned by Matthew. Strangest of all, however, would be the sudden ending of the Gospel at this point of indecision. See below.

In the Revised Version, vers. 9–20 of this chapter are separated from the previous part of the Gospel, and the above note added as an honest statement of the facts discovered in the early authorities. The judgment thus indicated amounts to this, that it is doubtful whether this passage formed a part of the Gospel originally, but that the evidence supporting it is too strong to allow it to be rejected. It seems to be *authentic* (*i. e.,* its statements are correct), but it may not be *genuine* (*i. e*, Mark may not have written it). The doubts arise from the following reasons: These verses are not found in the two *oldest* and best manuscripts of the New Testament (the Sinaitic and the Vatican); but in one of them (the Vatican) there is a column left blank between ver. 8 and the words, 'According to Mark,' while in every other instance the next book begins on the next column. In some other manuscripts it is indicated that the passage is doubtful. (2.) In the times of Jerome (d. 419), according to the testimony of some Church Fathers, the passage was wanting in most copies. (3.) The section contains

10 he had cast out seven ¹devils. She went and told them that had been with him, as they mourned and

<small>Gr. *demons.*</small>

no less than twenty words and expressions not found elsewhere in Mark's Gospel, and has a compendious and supplementary character.

But, on the other hand, some of the earliest Fathers recognized it as part of Mark's Gospel. Especially Irenæus († 202), who lived more than two hundred years before Jerome, and was a pupil of Polycarp (the pupil of John), quotes ver. 20, word for word, as the conclusion of the Gospel. The close of ver. 8 is very abrupt in the Greek, and cannot be the proper conclusion of the Gospel. Even those who reject this paragraph think that some other conclusion must have existed, which has been lost. The omission in the early manuscripts (fourth century) can be accounted for. The Fathers state that the Roman Christians were very anxious to obtain Mark's Gospel. An incomplete copy (as Lange suggests) might have got into circulation, which would find favor in the fourth century, because it omitted the unbelief of the Apostles. It is possible that it was written by Mark, but later than the Gospel itself. There are other conjectures, namely, that the last leaf of the original Gospel was early lost; that the section was erased because it was supposed to be inconsistent with the other Gospels. The best writers admit the great antiquity of the section, even if written by another hand than that of Mark. Its statements, therefore, may be regarded as authentic.

CONTENTS of vers. 9-20. Three appearances of our Lord are here mentioned: (1.) To Mary Magdalene; (2.) To the two on the way to Emmaus; (3.) To the eleven (on the same day or a week later). The date of the discourse which is added (vers. 15-18) cannot be determined. The whole chapter emphasizes the slowness of the disciples to believe in the Resurrection, gives the steps by which their disbelief was overcome, tells of the great commission (vers. 15-18), and closes with a brief statement of the Ascension (ver. 19) and the subsequent activity (ver. 20).

Vers. 9-11. THE APPEARANCE TO MARY MAGDALENE.—Parallel passage: John 20: 11-18; comp. Luke 24: 11.

Ver. 9. **On the first day**, etc. Not the same expression as in ver. 2. The emphatic repetition suggests that the readers knew the sacredness of 'the first day' among Christians.—**Appeared first.** See the full account of John (20: 14-17).—**From whom he had cast out seven devils** (Greek, 'demons'). See Luke 8: 2. This fact has not been previously stated in this Gospel, and this is an argument in favor of the genuineness of this section. Here, where Mary Magdalene is mentioned alone, was the most appropriate place for this description. The first manifestation of our Lord's victory over the grave was made to one in whom He had won such a victory over Satan.

Ver. 10. **She went and told.** Comp. John 20: 18. Emphasis seems to rest on the word 'she;' she was the first to tell them, the others probably returning later, after they had seen the Lord on the way (Matt. 28: 9).—**Them that had been with him.** An unusual expression for 'disciples,' probably including the whole com-

11 wept. And they, when they heard that he was alive, and had been seen of her, disbelieved.
12 And after these things he was manifested in another form unto two of them, as they walked, on their way
13 into the country. And they went away and told it unto the rest: neither believed they them.

pany of His followers.—**As they mourned and wept.** A natural touch, showing how little they anticipated His resurrection.

Ver. 11. **Had been seen of her.** Another expression peculiar to this section. But 'new facts, new words.'—**Disbelieved.** A different form from 'believed not' (ver. 12). Comp. Luke 24: 11. Their disbelief has been overruled for good; it furnishes abundant proof that they did not *invent* the story of the Resurrection.

Vers. 12, 13. THE APPEARANCE TO TWO DISCIPLES.—Parallel passage: Luke 24: 13-35. The latter Evangelist gives a detailed account. There can be little doubt that this appearance is here referred to.

Ver. 12. **After these things.** This expression, peculiar to this section, marks definitely a *second* appearance, after the 'first' (ver. 9). The appearance to Peter is not mentioned; the author is emphasizing the unbelief of the Eleven, so that he chooses a revelation to two, not of their number.—**Was manifested** (a different word from that used in ver. 9), etc. See Luke 24: 13-35, where this manifestation is narrated with richness of detail.—**In another form,** so that they did not recognize Him. Luke says: 'their eyes were holden.' But there was some actual difference in the bodily appearance of our Lord. —**Two of them,** of the disciples in the wider sense (vers. 10, 11).— **As they walked,** to Emmaus. The manifestation took place at the close of the walk; but this is the language of brevity. Had the account been more explicit, a captious criticism would have asserted that this verse was copied from Luke.

Ver. 13. **They.** Emphatic, giving prominence to these successive messages.—**The rest,** *i. e.,* of 'them that had been with Him' (ver. 10).—**Neither believed they them.** Despite the repeated testimony. Luke (24: 34) tells how these two met the company who told them: 'The Lord is risen indeed, and hath appeared to Simon.' But he speaks immediately after of their terror at His appearance (24: 37); their state of mind was not one of decided belief. The same impression is conveyed by Matt. 28: 17; John 20: 20. A conflict of doubt and belief would be very natural, or even a division of opinion, some doubting and some believing. Even if all believed that the Lord had appeared to Simon, some might, for various reasons, still doubt the message of the two disciples. This apparent discrepancy with Luke may have encouraged the copyists to omit the passage, if they found any authority for doing so.

14 And afterward he was manifested unto the eleven themselves as they sat at meat; and he upbraided them with their unbelief and hardness of heart, because they believed not them which had seen him after
15 he was risen. And he said unto them, Go ye into all the world, and preach the gospel to the whole crea-
16 tion. He that believeth and is baptized shall be saved:

Vers. 14–18. THE APPEARANCE TO THE ELEVEN.—This was in all probability the last manifestation on the day of the Resurrection, which is fully detailed by Luke (24: 36, etc.) and John (20: 19-23). The discourse here given sums up the more important points of the revelations made on various occasions up to the time of the Ascension.—Vers. 16–18 are peculiar to this Gospel, and quite characteristic. They may have been uttered on the mountain in Galilee, or, more likely still, just before the Ascension, men ioned immediately afterwards (ver. 19).

Ver. 14. **Afterward.** 'Later,' not, 'last,' though the word may bear such a meaning.—**Sat at meat.** In strict accordance with Luke 24: 41–43, though. evidently written independently.—**Upbraided them with their unbelief.** He instructed, as well as upbraided them; but the matter is here described from one point of view. This unbelief was respecting the fact of His resurrection.—**Hardness of heart.** They seem to have remained that day in an intellectual and moral stupor.—**Because**, etc. The specific reproach was that in the face of sufficient evidence they doubted a glorious fact, which He, whom they loved, had predicted again and again.

Ver. 15. **And he said unto them.** There is no reference to the appearances in Galilee; and it is difficult to fix the date and place. The most probable view is that which identifies this command with that given in Matt. 28: 18–20; but here the style is brief, energetic, as usual in Mark's narrative.—**Preach the gospel**, proclaim the glad tidings; not simply give instruction in Christian morality, but announce the facts they had been so slow to believe, that Jesus who had been crucified is risen, is the living Saviour for lost men.—**To the whole creation.** To men chiefly, as the subjects of salvation; but probably not without a reference to the whole moral universe. Comp. Col. 1: 15, 23; Rom. 8: 19–23. The duty to evangelize the whole world, so plainly stated here, is even strengthened by this view of the passage. The ground for this command is the fact s ated by our Lord (Matt. 28: 18): 'All authority hath been given unto me in heaven and on earth.' Evidently the duty rests, in an important sense, on all Christians, and was so understood in the early Church (Acts 8: 1, 4).

Ver. 16. **He that believeth and is baptized shall be saved; but he that disbelieveth shall be condemned.** The obvious lessons of this verse are pressing and practical. (1) The belief is belief in Jesus of Nazareth, crucified and risen again, as *an*

17 but he that disbelieveth shall be condemned. And these signs shall follow them that believe: in my

all-sufficient Personal Saviour. It is belief of the gospel (ver. 15), because the gospel presents Christ. (2) Baptism is generally, but not absolutely, necessary to salvation. It is not said, He that believeth not *and is not baptized* will be condemned. The first trophy of the crucified Lord was the unbaptized, yet believing, robber. Many martyrs had no opportunity of baptism. Multitudes of unbaptized children die in infancy, and the Society of Friends reject water-baptism. Yet the other clause shows the general necessity. Baptism cannot be deemed indifferent in view of this command. None are condemned simply because not baptized, but positive unbelief is the one certain ground of condemnation, whether the person be baptized or not baptized. (3) Nothing can be proved from this passage as to the *order* in which faith and baptism must always come. In Matt. 28: 19, 20, it is altogether different. (4) The form of the original is peculiar, and points to a future and permanent division of mankind into 'saved' and 'condemned.' (5) The condemnation for the sin of unbelief implies a previous offer of the gospel. The preceding verse points to a proclamation of the offer to every one, without exception, and the sin of unbelief has its spring in something independent of any such offer. Blessedness is impossible for those who when they know of Christ do not trust Him. (6) The word 'condemned' implies just what our Lord has expressed again and again in awful language (chap. 9: 43-49; Matt. 24: 51; 25: 30-46).

Ver. 17. **And these signs shall follow them that believe.** This promise is to be taken literally; but is it to be limited to the Apostolic times, or is it to be extended to all Christians? In favor of the limitation may be urged: the reference to the *founding* of the Church, which runs through the whole passage; the cessation of the necessity for such 'signs' as proofs of the truth, and the cessation of such miraculous gifts as a fact in the history of the Church. Yet it is highly probable that the promise is more general. Alford: 'Should occasion arise for its fulfilment, there can be no doubt that it will be made good in our own or any other time. But we must remember that "signs" are not needed where Christianity is *professed*, nor by missionaries who are backed by the influence of powerful Christian nations.' Fanatical and superstitious use of the promise is due to a failure to understand the nature of these things as 'signs.'—**In my name.** This presents the power by which all the succeeding miracles should be wrought.—**Shall they cast out devils** (Greek, 'demons'). It is characteristic of Mark to emphasize this form of miraculous power. —**They shall speak with new tongues.** See Acts 2: 4; 10: 46; 1 Cor. 13 and 14. This was literally fulfilled. A symbolical meaning, such as new forms of spiritual truth, is unnecessary. As the whole was written after the manifestation of the gifts of tongues in the Apos-

name shall they cast out ¹devils; they shall speak
18 with ²new tongues; they shall take up serpents, and
if they drink any deadly thing, it shall in no wise
hurt them; they shall lay hands on the sick, and they
shall recover.
19 So then the Lord Jesus, after he had spoken unto
them, was received up into heaven, and sat down at
20 the right hand of God. And they went forth, and
preached everywhere, the Lord working with them,

¹ Gr. *demons*.   ² Some ancient authorities omit *new*.

tolic times, this clause is no proof of a later origin of the section. These 'tongues' were the most striking signs for the first success of the gospel; hence we might expect to find such a promise.

Ver. 18. **They shall take up serpents.** See Acts 28: 3-5, where this promise was fulfilled in the case of Paul. We, therefore, retain the simple meaning: they shall take up serpents without injury, as a 'sign.' As the word translated 'take up' has a variety of secondary meanings, some explain it here, 'drive forth,' 'destroy,' but the other is the more obvious sense. Still untenable is the fanciful symbolical interpretation which finds an allusion to the brazen serpent in the wilderness (John 3: 14).—**And if they drink any deadly thing.** While literal fulfilments of this promise are not recorded in the New Testament, such may have occurred.—**And they shall recover.** Instances abound in the Acts of the Apostles.

Vers. 19, 20. THE CONCLUSION.—The nearest parallel is found in Luke 24: 51; Acts 1: 2, 9. The entire Book of the Acts is an expansion of ver. 20.

Ver. 19. **So then.** This phrase, not found elsewhere in this Gospel, introduces the conclusion.—**The Lord.** A term of the highest reverence in this case.—**Jesus** is inserted on good authority.—**After he had spoken unto them.** Both the time and place of the discourse are indefinite, and the fuller account of the Ascension is not contradicted by anything here stated.—**Was received up into heaven.** See Luke 24: 51; Acts 1: 9. The original suggests also the idea of being taken back again.—**And sat down at the right hand of God,** in the place of honor and power. The Ascension is the natural completion of the Resurrection. After such a glorious triumph over death and hell, Christ could not die again, but only return to His former glory, and take possession of His throne and kingdom, at the right hand of God the Father Almighty.

Ver. 20. **And they went forth.** Not out of the room (ver. 14), but out into the world (ver. 15), to preach everywhere. It is equally plain that the writer cannot mean to say that our Lord

and confirming the word by the signs that followed. Amen.

ascended from that room —**Everywhere**. The gospel was diffused very rapidly, and at the date of Mark's Gospel the use of this general term was perfectly justifiable.—**The Lord working**, etc. The fulfilment of the promise in vers. 17, 18, is here stated. This close corresponds admirably with the character of the whole. The wonder-working Son of God is represented as continuing to work through His Apostles. The emphasis hitherto given to His miracles is preserved in this brief sketch of their activity, and that, too, in closer connection with Him as the Glorified Redeemer, still working the same wonders. J. A. Alexander: 'If the original conclusion of this book is lost, its place has been wonderfully well supplied.'—**Amen**. This word is better supported here than at the close of the other Gospels, but even here is of doubtful authority.

www.ingramcontent.com/pod-product-compliance
Lightning Source LLC
Chambersburg PA
CBHW021410230426
43666CB00006B/703